This book recovers the lost history of Spanish socialism during the turbulent years of the civil war (1936–1939). Just as the energy of the socialist movement had sustained the pre-war Second Republic as an experiment in reform, so too it underwrote the Republican war effort in the crucial years of the conflict which would determine Spain's long-term future. Leading Socialist Party (PSOE) cadres formed the bedrock of the government, while thousands of Party and union militants helped bear the tremendous weight of the war effort. The role of the PSOE in the construction of Republican political unity during the civil war was pivotal. Yet, paradoxically, previous accounts of wartime Republican politics have virtually written the PSOE out of the script by concentrating exclusively on the fierce ideological dispute between anarchists and communists. But the key issues of revolution and state power marked all the forces in Republican Spain, none more so than the socialist movement. As the traditional party of the working class and the only mass party in Spain as late as 1931, PSOE militants were to be found on both sides of the revolutionary/reformist divide which split fatally the Republican forces during the civil war. The PSOE's disintegration was a function of that of the Republic itself; but the reverse was no less true. The book investigates the responses of organised socialism to the complex issues raised by the conflict, as it charts the PSOE's devastating experience of political power and desperate crisis in a war it could not win.

Socialism and war

Socialism and war

THE SPANISH SOCIALIST PARTY IN POWER AND CRISIS 1936 – 1939

HELEN GRAHAM

Lecturer in the Department of Spanish,
Portuguese and Latin American Studies,
University of Southampton

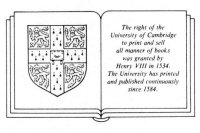

The right of the
University of Cambridge
to print and sell
all manner of books
was granted by
Henry VIII in 1534.
The University has printed
and published continuously
since 1584.

CAMBRIDGE UNIVERSITY PRESS

Cambridge
New York   Port Chester
Melbourne   Sydney

Published by the Press Syndicate of the University of Cambridge
The Pitt Building, Trumpington Street, Cambridge CB2 1RP
40 West 20th Street, New York, NY 10011, USA
10 Stamford Road, Oakleigh, Melbourne 3166, Australia

First published 1991

Printed in Great Britain by
The Bath Press, Avon

British Library cataloguing in publication data
Graham, Helen *1959–*
  Socialism and war: the Spanish socialist party in power
  and crisis, 1936–1939.
  1. Spanish Civil War
  1. Title
  946.081

Library of Congress cataloguing in publication data
Graham, Helen, 1959–
  Socialism and war: the Spanish Socialist Party in power and
crisis, 1936–1939   Helen Graham.
      p.   cm.
  Includes bibliographical references and index.
  ISBN 0–521–39257–8
  1. P.S.O.E. (Political party) – History.   2. Socialism – Spain –
History.   3. Spain – History – Civil War, 1936–1939.   1. Title.
JN8395.P15G73   1991
324.1′7′094609043 – dc20   90–43911   CIP

ISBN 0 521 39257 8

Contents

Acknowledgements   ix
List of abbreviations   xi
Introduction   1

PART I   THE STRUGGLE FOR CONTROL OF
         THE PSOE'S NATIONAL
         ORGANISATION
         1934–1936

    1   Internal divisions in the Spanish socialist
         movement 1934–1936   15
    2   The break-up of socialist unity and the
         coming of the civil war   34

PART II THE SOCIALIST LEFT IN POWER
         1936–1937

    3   The appointment of the Largo Caballero
         government   53
    4   Political realignments inside the socialist
         movement   69
    5   The socialist left: crisis and collapse   86

PART III THE BATTLE IN THE PARTY
         1937–1938

    6   Ramón Lamoneda confronts the PSOE
         left   107
    7   The purge of the party left and the
         growing crisis in the reformist camp   126
    8   The atomisation of reformist socialism   150

PART IV THE DISPUTE IN THE UGT

9   The battle for control of the union and
     the eclipse of the socialist left 1937–1938   167
10   The *caballerista* old guard: entrenchment
     and resurgence   198

PART V SOCIALIST – COMMUNIST
          RUPTURE

11   The Casado coup and the end of the war   223

Appendices
1 Wartime executive committees   245
2 *Dramatis personae*   249
3 Organisational structure PSOE/UGT   255

Notes   257
Bibliography   302
Index   321

Acknowledgements

This book is based on my doctoral research which was carried out in Oxford and Spain during the 1980s. In the course of researching and writing I contracted debts of gratitude to friends and colleagues in Britain and Spain who are too numerous to mention here individually. But their help was highly valued and is well remembered. At Oxford my doctoral supervisor, Raymond Carr, offered support and constructive criticism and Frances Lannon was generous with her time and effort, especially at the crucial stage of writing-up. Additional research for this book was carried out in Spain in the spring and summer of 1989 and I would like to acknowledge the financial assistance of the British Academy whose funding facilitated a problem-free sabbatical term. I was also greatly assisted by awards from the Advanced Studies Committee and Arts Faculty of the University of Southampton. In my search for the jacket photographs I had advice and help from Sheelagh Ellwood, from Dave Morgan (International Brigade Archive, Marx Memorial Library), from the staff of the Archivo General de la Administración, Alcalá de Henares, Madrid, and from Manuel Cerdá (Publications Department, Diputació Provincial de Valencia). Mike Richards produced the index with speed and efficiency. A number of friends provided invaluable help with proof reading, but the hero of labour is incontestably Penny Green. Above all here, I want to thank Paul Preston for years of unfailing support and encouragement as a friend and teacher.

Finally, as an academic study, what follows is often highly critical of the protagonists. I would like therefore to dedicate it to the men and women of the Spanish labour movement who fought for three years against overwhelming odds to defend the Republican cause. As historians we still have much to learn about the dynamics of victory and defeat. But nothing diminishes the magnitude of their example.

Abbreviations

ASM	Agrupación Socialista Madrileña – the Madrid section of the PSOE.
CEDA	Confederación Española de Derechas Autónomas – the largest political grouping of the parliamentary right under the Republic.
CGTU	Confederación General de Trabajo Unitaria – the communist trade union organisation which rejoined the UGT in December 1935.
CNT	Confederación Nacional del Trabajo – anarcho–syndicalist trade union.
Esquerra	Catalan nationalist equivalent of the Republican Left.
FAI	Federación Anarquista Ibérica – the purist insurrectionary vanguard of the anarchist movement.
FIJL	Federación Ibérica de Juventudes Libertarias – anarchist youth federation.
FJS	Federación de Juventudes Socialistas – PSOE youth movement which amalgamated with its communist counterpart in April 1936 to form the JSU.
FNTT	Federación Nacional de Trabajadores de la Tierra – landworkers' section of the UGT.
Generalitat	the Catalan government.
GOSR	Grupos de la Oposición Sindical Revolucionaria – communist trade union groups inside the UGT.
GSS	Grupos Sindicales Socialistas – socialist trade union groups inside the UGT.
Izquierda Republicana – centre-left republican party.	
JAP	Juventudes de Acción Popular – CEDA youth movement.
JSU	Juventudes Socialistas Unificadas – the joint

	socialist–communist youth movement controlled by the PCE.
PCE	Partido Comunista de España – the mainstream/Moscow-oriented Communist Party.
PNV	Partido Nacional Vasco – the Basque Nationalist Party.
POUM	Partido Obrero de Unificación Marxista – a dissident revolutionary communist party, created in December 1935 by the fusion of the left communists of the *Bloc Obrer i Camperol* and the *Izquierda Comunista*.
PSOE	Partido Socialista Obrero Español – the Spanish Socialist Party.
PSUC	Partido Socialista Unificado de Cataluña – founded in July 1936 by the amalgamation of socialists and communists in Cataluña, it was effectively the Catalan Communist Party.
SIM	Servicio de Investigación Militar – the Republican counter-intelligence service during the war.
UGT	Unión General de Trabajadores – the socialist-led trade union organisation.
UJC	Unión de Juventudes Comunistas – the communist youth movement prior to the April 1936 unification.
Unión Republicana	– centre-right republican party.

Introduction

> Men [and women] make their own history, but they do not
> make it as they please; they do not make it under circumstances
> chosen by themselves, but under circumstances directly
> encountered, given and transmitted from the past.
>
> K. MARX
> *The Eighteenth Brumaire of Louis Bonaparte*

If one turns aside from the devastating human tragedy and wasted
potential consequent upon the Republic's military defeat in 1939, to
examine the political cost of that defeat to the component organisations of the Republican side, then none was worse affected than the
Spanish socialist movement, comprising the party (PSOE) and
union (UGT). After half a century's existence, the party which had
sustained the Republic from its birth in 1931, was all but annihilated
by the experience of the civil war. The PSOE would only be restored
to its leadership position in Spain's political life in the 1970s. But the
Socialist Party which emerged then, although claiming historical
continuity, bore little resemblance to its predecessor. It was a new
party for a new Spain.[1] The defeat of the Republic in April 1939 had
precipitated the final crisis of the 'historic' PSOE. But while the
PSOE's disintegration was a function of the Republic's own, the
reverse was no less true, as this study seeks to show.

Born in the last quarter of the nineteenth century (PSOE 1879,
UGT 1888), the Spanish Socialist Party was an archetypical social
democratic party, defined by its commitment to gradualist political
change. In this it was sustained by the belief that the PSOE was
ultimately destined to inherit the state.[2] In control of the government, the party would then implement social and economic reform
from within. At the same time, the Spanish Socialists' radical discourse, dating from their experience as an 'outsider' party under the
Restoration Monarchy (1874–1923), for a long time prevented the
PSOE's hegemonic position as *the* party of the Spanish working class
from being successfully challenged on the left. In particular, the
PSOE's combination of reformist praxis and revolutionary discourse
was an important factor impeding the development of the Spanish
Communist Party (PCE) as a serious rival. This state of affairs was
to last until the civil war.

Inside the socialist movement, the union's relationship to the
party observed, in theory at least, the classic social democratic

schema. Although much larger than the PSOE, the UGT was autonomous only in the labour sphere. Where political action was concerned, it was held to be subordinate to the programme and directives of the party. This relationship worked as long as there existed a common political culture between the two wings of the movement. Historically this was based on the fundamental illegitimacy of the Spanish state which excluded the Socialists from power. But the coming of the Second Republic in 1931 would alter perceptions of the state in socialist ranks, fracturing the traditional relationship between the party and union organisation.

The birth of the Second Republic in 1931 was perceived as heralding the PSOE's 'historic' moment. The Republic brought for the first time in Spain a genuine if very imperfect pluralist parliamentary democracy – and thus resumed the minimum, if not necessarily sufficient, requirements for enacting a programme of social and economic reform, and above all fundamental land reform. Such a scenario seemed to guarantee a major political future for the PSOE. Progressive republicanism needed the PSOE as much, indeed more, than the PSOE needed the Republic. This was not only because the Socialists' commitment to parliamentary reform was clear, but most crucially because socialist support alone could ensure a reasonable chance of success for the reforming enterprise. The PSOE was the most powerful parliamentary force on the left in Spain. (The Spanish Communist Party was tiny and thus of marginal importance, while the powerful anarchist movement opposed all parliamentary activity.) Of all the groups operating in parliament only the Socialists had a coherent national organisation. This was the legacy of the UGT's collaboration with Primo de Rivera's dictatorship in the 1920s. But it must also be remembered that the PSOE's status as the only mass political party in 1931 depended on its being backed by the formidable strength of its labour movement.

The future looked promising. But, in fact, the reality of the socialist experience in the 1930s was to lead not to the fulfilment of the party's perceived political destiny but to organisational disintegration and eclipse. The Republic's social and economic reform foundered in the face of powerful and entrenched conservative opposition between 1931 and 1936. The bitter experience of this effectively split the socialist movement down the middle – the bone of contention being the advisability and efficacy of socialists bolstering the weak forces of progressive republicanism in government. By spring 1936 the lines inside the socialist movement had been drawn between the left socialists, who opposed collaboration in government, and the parliamentary socialists who saw it as the best and only viable means of achieving reform. To explain the ensuing internecine strife which was to cost both the Republic and the socialists themselves so dear, one must look to the organisational rivalry between the two wings of the movement: parliamentary socialists and trade unionists. This consistent line of fracture within Spanish socialism had already manifested itself in the 1920s in the conflicting reactions towards Primo de Rivera's military dictatorship.[3] But the significance of the Second Republic increased the gravity and impact of the division. As the first real parliamentary democracy, it reversed the traditional balance of authority, promoting the protagonism and strength of the parliamentary party over that of the traditional 'senior partner', the union. It also meant the end of the shared political culture based on the illegitimacy of the state, thus initiating an internal battle between the two wings for control of the PSOE's maximum leadership body: the national executive committee.

The left socialists' position can be explained by the fact that their leaders were mainly prominent trades unionists whose power depended on their recognising and responding to the mood of the UGT membership. The most salient feature of this membership in the 1930s was the process of acute radicalisation undergone by its most numerically important sector – the Socialist Landworkers' Federation (FNTT). From 1930 onwards it experienced a massive influx of landless labourers from Spain's impoverished rural south. The landless labourers were the incarnation of Spain's backwardness, their plight epitomising the need for the structural reform of her agriculture. The landless flooded in to the FNTT in the hope of government-led agrarian reform. But when this was stymied by conservative obstruction in parliament and the localities then the landless took direct action, for example by seizing estates in the south-west in March 1936. As the socialist left's real political 'muscle' derived from its role as the mediator of such demands, which it channelled into national politics, it responded to the FNTT's radicalisation by mouthing an increasingly revolutionary rhetoric.

The PSOE left's leaders blocked the parliamentary socialists' road to collaboration in government, arguing that either the republicans would enact reform or there would be a revolution which would bring the PSOE control of the state. But the socialist left were indulging in mere revolutionary posturing. Its leaders remained bound by the weight of their union responsibilities. Ultimately they were bureaucrats who were not prepared to risk the whole of the UGT – carefully constructed over the past four and a half decades –

in one revolutionary throw of the dice. The socialist left said it wanted to 'bolshevise' the PSOE, turning it into a revolutionary cadre party. But, in reality, it did nothing. It did not reorganise the socialist sections nor train or arm a militia. The party left had no blueprint for seizing power – as was to become painfully obvious when the military backlash occurred in the shape of the 17–18 July coup in 1936.

The left socialists' strategic bankruptcy thus worsened an already tense situation. They were inciting the right – which had most of the fire power – but had not the least idea how to meet its draconian response. Yet still they refused to allow the parliamentary socialists to enter the government, while the moderates would not collaborate without the support of the left. This stalemate was to prove fatal to the Republic. For the Socialists were the only group capable of taking direct action against conspiratorial officers in order to defuse the coup already being planned in the provincial garrisons by spring 1936, in the wake of the centre-left victory at the polls the previous February. The military rising against Republican reforms in July 1936 erupted thus into the middle of the Socialists' own private war.

The experience of civil war (1936–9) was to prove consummately disastrous for the PSOE. In the course of the war the Spanish socialist movement suffered a total eclipse. The most spectacular symptoms of socialist decline were the loss of the Socialist Youth (FJS) to the Spanish Communist Party (PCE) at the beginning of the war and the extent of PCE conquests in the UGT – achieved in the course of a bitter power struggle in the union. Such a dramatic decline in itself poses major questions, but the response assumes added importance in view of the lasting impact of the experience on the PSOE. Indeed, so profound was it, and so great the resulting antipathy towards the PCE, that the socialist leadership in exile, by persistently rejecting any suggestion of socialist–communist collaboration, consigned itself for decades to the margins of the democratic opposition to the Franco regime (1939–75).

On initiating this investigation, the available answers regarding socialist eclipse all seemed acutely unsatisfactory. The bitter mythology of exiled socialism, inscribed in the intensely subjective memoirs and correspondence of civil war veterans laid the sole responsibility for the socialist débâcle at the door of the Comintern and the PCE. Nor did scholarly works escape this simplism. Most notably, for all its bibliographical wealth, a similar conspiracy theory confines Burnett Bolloten's pioneering work within an interpretative vacuum which seriously impairs its usefulness.[4]

For a long time, however, the consequences of the civil war – exile and dictatorship – ruled out a more wide-ranging investigation of PSOE decline. In Spain the archives and newspaper libraries were closed, while the PSOE's own party archive – lodged in Moscow – was equally inaccessible. Sharing the fate of so many militants, it too endured a lengthy exile, returning to Spain only with the end of the Franco regime. The Moscow Historical Archive contains a vast amount on the PSOE during the Republican period and the civil war. It is this material – executive minutes, reports, circulars and, above all, a voluminous correspondence – which has furnished the documentary foundation of the following study. While both personal memoirs and party press proved extremely useful, the Moscow archive provides the key to reconstructing the wartime history of the Spanish socialist movement, as well as offering crucial insights into the balance of power inside the Republican camp. Most importantly, by offering a perspective on the PSOE across the entire Republican experience of reform, reaction, revolution and war, the Moscow archive illuminates the complex interaction of factors which provoked the socialist crisis, thus allowing us to travel beyond the sterile simplism of earlier conspiracy theories.

That the growth of the PCE was inextricably bound up with socialist eclipse is certainly demonstrated by the study which follows. What is challenged, however, is the assumption that the PCE was the primary cause of socialist decline. This received wisdom has been sustained – in Bolloten particularly – by a careful choice of chronology. He examines the war period (1936–9) in isolation. Once a wider perspective is taken, however, it is evident that PCE growth was partly a symptom of a pre-existing crisis *inside* the Spanish socialist movement.

By locating the origins of wartime eclipse in this internally generated conflict under the Republic (1934–6), this study highlights the essential continuity in the PSOE's history across the military rising. This continuity has in the past been obscured by a tendency to view the eruption of civil war as an absolute cut-off point. Partly this periodisation derived from a methodological problem, namely the fragmentation and inaccessibility of civil war sources for the PSOE. Nevertheless, implicit in the idea of the military rising as a watershed was the assumption that it qualitatively transformed the internal life of the socialist movement – as if the fact of civil war and the extreme circumstances it produced somehow galvanised the Socialists, creating unity out of division and harmony out of bitter internecine antagonism. But neither military coup nor popular revolution nor full-scale civil war wiped the slate clean. The real effect of the war was rather to exacerbate the old pre-war conflicts inside the socialist movement. A major contributory factor in the intensification of this internal war was the emergence of the PCE as a serious rival to the PSOE, competing for members, political influence and ultimately for control of the Republican war effort.

PCE ascendancy was partly the consequence of international political circumstances beyond the Socialists' control. The civil war brought the Spanish Socialists state power. Ironically though, they 'inherited' too late. Once the military coup had escalated into full-scale war, the locus of control shifted beyond Spain. Victory and defeat came rapidly to depend on political choices made outside her frontiers. In concrete terms this well-known internationalisation of the conflict meant that the fate of both sides ultimately depended on foreign intervention (including Non-Intervention) and the political realities which underlay it. Fascist and Nazi intervention on Franco's side combined with the non-interventionist stance of the Western democracies meant the slow strangulation of the Republic. This in turn made Soviet aid to the latter essential to any attempt at survival. It was the Republic's dependence on Soviet arms, imposed by Non-Intervention, which established the preconditions for PCE expansion. But the political repercussions of Soviet intervention had devastating domestic consequences which would eventually wreck the Spanish socialist movement, destroying Republican political unity in the process.

But although the PSOE was in a very real sense handicapped by a series of external factors, this was far from the whole story. From the very beginning of the war the strength of the PCE's appeal lay in its superior discipline and organisation. Superior, that is, compared to the factional disarray of Spanish socialism. The emphasis which this study places on organisational rivalry inside the socialist movement is certainly confirmed by developments during the war. In the course of 1937 the internal socialist conflict emerged very clearly as a power struggle whose goal was control of the PSOE's national organisation. Moreover, the supposed ideological division inside the socialist leadership was itself brought into serious question by wartime developments. For the military coup, by precipitating a grass roots revolution in the Republican zone, provided a kind of litmus test of the socialist left's self-proclaimed revolutionary faith. In September 1936 it assumed control of the Republican government. But instead of furthering the social and economic radicalism released by the military rising, the socialist left chose to curtail it. Throughout its period in office (September 1936–May 1937), the socialist left allied itself with non-proletarian political forces and adopted policies which facilitated the restoration of the bourgeois Republic. For all its past radical posturing, the left socialists in government appropriated wholesale the collaborationary, or Popular Frontist strategy of their reformist opponents.

For the reformists, the PSOE left's volte-face was sufficient proof that a genuine ideological division had never existed in the socialist movement. Their conviction that the left's opposition had always been motivated by a mixture of opportunism and ambition strengthened the PSOE reformists' determination to eradicate the left and its destructive impact from the socialist organisation. It was the reformists' decision to purge the left from both the party and union movement which determined the course of the Socialists' internal conflict during the war.

The lines along which the socialist movement divided during the war also cast light on the nature of the socialist division under the pre-war Republic. In particular, they reinforce the view that the real strength of the socialist left between 1934 and 1936 lay in its role as a political mediator. It channelled the demands of the radicalised landless labourers of Spain's rural south into the national political arena. During the war, the reformists' attempt to destroy the socialist left's power base ultimately failed because it could always count on the support of the most powerful union in the UGT – namely the agrarian labourers federation (FNTT). Even after the reformists had ousted the left socialists from control of the UGT's national executive (October 1937), they were able to entrench themselves in the FNTT. In the PSOE too, the enduring support for the left came overwhelmingly from its southern federations and from socialist deputies who represented constituencies in the rural south.

But as this study demonstrates, the private civil war being waged inside the ranks of Spanish socialism was not the only power struggle to undermine the stability of the Republican war effort. Even more damaging in its effects was the explosive rivalry between the PSOE and the PCE which erupted during the war. This can be defined as, at root, a struggle between two ideologically similar parties for the predominant position on the left. It is argued here that while the circumstances of the civil war determined its particularly acute form, socialist–communist organisational rivalry was inherent in the nature of the Popular Front alliance itself.

In Spain, the Popular Front was the name given to the electoral coalition of middle-class and proletarian political parties which won the February 1936 elections on a reformist ticket. Before July 1936 its central axis had been the republican–socialist alliance. But, as Spanish republicanism disintegrated under the impact of military coup and popular revolution, the imperatives of Republican defence

– and especially the Soviet arms factor – determined the reconstruction of the Popular Front around a socialist–communist axis. The viability of the Republican war effort thus came to depend on the creation of a successful working relationship between the Socialist and Communist Parties. Not only was this never realised, but a savagely destructive conflict developed between their respective cadres. The origins of this conflict can be traced back directly to the objectives of Popular Front as envisaged by the Comintern.

The Comintern's adoption of Popular Frontism in 1935 had been motivated by a desire to contain the threat which fascist advance in Europe posed to the Soviet Union. It was envisaged that this objective would be achieved in two ways. Firstly, by building bridges to the bourgeoisie, creating, wherever possible, defensive alliances between proletarian parties and those of the progressive liberal middle classes. But secondly – under a banner which proclaimed strength in unity – the Comintern also sought the fusion of Socialist and Communist Parties in a single class party. In Spain particularly, where before 1936 the Communist Party was a tiny party eking out an existence on the margins of political life, the Socialists viewed this as a crude attempt to gain access to its rank and file. However, the civil war radically altered the political equation. Not only did it create the basis for the expansion of the PCE, by allowing it to assume the mantle of Spanish republicanism, but the imperatives of Republican defence also made it impossible for the PSOE publicly to repudiate the idea of proletarian unity. As the war progressed, spurred by their conquest of the Socialist Youth, the Catalan socialists and Catalan UGT, as well as several of the union's constituent national industrial federations, communist cadres put increasing pressure on their socialist counterparts to unite at the local and provincial level in order to force recognition of the *de facto* existence of the 'partido único' (single party) from the PSOE leadership.

The realisation that the PCE was out to absorb the socialist base, combined with the evidence of the Communists' aggressive proselytising techniques, provoked growing outrage among socialist cadres. The PSOE's reformist leadership attempted to control this reaction, primarily because they realised that open war between socialists and communists would destroy the Republican war effort. However, the disaffected socialist left, ejected from its power base in the UGT by the combined efforts of their reformist socialist opponents and pro-communist trade union leaders, was by 1938 rapidly re-establishing a political platform by channelling the growing discontent of the socialist grass roots. By this point, internal socialist conflict was inextricably caught up in the hostilities between socialist and communist cadres. When these tensions eventually erupted, their explosive force utterly wrecked the Popular Front. Once it collapsed, the end of Republican resistance was inevitable.

Ultimately the collapse of the Popular Front at national level would have been determined by its failure internationally, that is, by the non-realisation of the Soviet Union's cherished objective of collective security. But here it is argued that the effect of the Munich agreement of September 1938 between the democracies and the dictators (and the beginnings of the withdrawal of Soviet aid from the Republic) had such a dramatic and immediate effect in Spain precisely because the constant political infighting between the PSOE and the PCE – the parties on which the Republican defence rested – had already eroded the Popular Front alliance from within. Yet the failure of socialist–communist relations was itself determined by the very contradictions of Popular Front as applied to 1930s Spain. Tactically and ideologically it undermined the PSOE–PCE alliance. Tactically, because the aggressive sectarianism which was the stuff of daily interchange had a cumulatively erosive effect. Ideologically, too, Popular Frontism was flawed. Or, more accurately, because Popular Front was a strategy applied efficiently and uniformly in Republican Spain, it was the maximum reflector of the acute political contradictions born of Spain's social and economic disparity. The policy thrust of the PCE's 'historic compromise' *circa* 1936 was geared more towards the liberal centre than towards social democracy. In the Spanish case, this was particularly inappropriate – and especially once the civil war was underway – because the degree of social and economic polarisation in evidence, combined with the historic weakness of the liberal middle class in Spain, made the PCE's defence of the political centre untenable.

The limited social stratification of 1930s Spain – the product of decades of economic retardation – had led to the formation of blocs which were confronting each other in the civil war. To be sure, in exceptional, economically developed and industrialised areas like Cataluña, the PCE (or PSUC), could defend the interests of the commercial and industrial bourgeoisie. But, by and large, Spain was not Cataluña. It was a rural economy where the monolithic structure of backwardness obtained – the landed faced the landless. And here, during the war, the PCE was often to be found defending landed interest against the rights of the socialist and anarchist collectives. By charting the history of this daily strife between socialists, anarchists and communists, we gain a clear picture of how the Popular Front was undermined. The PCE sought to placate the political centre – which the eruption of civil war itself had annihilated –

instead of pursuing more radical policies which could have secured genuinely popular support for the Popular Front.

But, however serious the disunity in their ranks, the final responsibility for the defeat of the Republic in 1939 undoubtedly lies other than with the Spanish Loyalists. Ultimately the outcome of the civil war was decided not in Spain but in the cabinets and chancelleries of Europe. Whilst it is not the business of the historian to deal in counterfactual hypotheses, it seems unlikely that even perfect political unity on the Republican side could have reversed the outcome of the war. The crippling material impediments endured by the Republicans would have remained. Non-intervention was not a product of loyalist disunity – although to an extent the reverse was true. A united Republic would still have lacked what their Nationalist opponents possessed in abundance – political and material support from Europe. In the end Franco did not have to conquer the Republic militarily. Isolated in the world, without a land frontier to its name, lacerated by bombs, it collapsed inward under an intolerable weight of hunger and sheer hopelessness – burying for ever the reforming ideal it had enshrined. And when the defeat occurred, one of the main political casualties was Spanish socialism. The movement whose strength had once sustained the Republic's hopes of reform lay shattered amid the wreckage of battle.

The account which follows focuses mainly on the civil war period (1936–9). However, the first section (comprising chapters 1 and 2), deals with the socialist movement under the Republic (1931–6). Within this section the opening chapter provides both a thematic and a chronological introduction to the study as a whole. The theme of Spanish socialism in the civil war obviously has a potential for exploration so vast as to be unmanageable within a single study. The structure of this account has thus been determined by its central purpose: to explain the origins of socialist eclipse. Thus I have focused not on the grass roots revolution behind the Republican lines, but rather on the political consequences of its containment. The central narrative and interpretation is built around what I understand as the central tension within Republican ranks – once a socialist-led cabinet had overseen the reconstruction of the Republican state and redefined its war effort in non-revolutionary terms. This tension was the growing rivalry between the PSOE and the PCE for political influence, members and ultimately for control of the Republican state at war. The peripheral treatment of the anarcho-syndicalist organisation (CNT) here I would argue accurately reflects its political status within the Republic once the short-lived revolutionary phase of the war had ended. The CNT's vast mobilising capacity, which made it a vital component of the Republican war effort throughout, was never channelled in such a way as to give the anarchists political leverage. One reason for this was the internal rift in the CNT. The seeds of this internal crisis were already present before the war. By 1936 its traditional anti-parliamentarianism had come up against the massive popular support for the Popular Front initiative which sought a parliamentary route to social and economic reform. This produced a line of fracture inside the CNT which during the war emerged as the conflict between the purist anarchists and the *políticos* who argued that the CNT had to enter the parliamentary arena or risk political eclipse. The failure to consolidate the revolution politically in the early months of the war reflected this division as well as exacerbating it. The reconstruction of the Republican state around a socialist–communist axis of Popular Front began the process whereby the CNT was progressively distanced from the centres of state power. Moreover, the outcome of the internal dispute in the socialist movement also contributed to the CNT's marginalisation. Both the political choices made by the left wing of the PSOE and its eventual crisis and collapse condemned the CNT to isolation on the peripheries of Republican politics. In geographical terms, I focus mainly on the centre-south of the Republican war zone, (i.e. Madrid, the Levante provinces and the Republican south). Valencia in particular features prominently. As the seat of the central government until October 1937, which was also a focal point of the internal dispute in the socialist movement, it was for a long period the centre both of Republican politics and partisan conflict. Cataluña is not dealt with in any great detail here. Socialist organisation in the region had always been tenuous. Thus the loss which the PSUC's formation signified reflected a historic weakness rather than a contemporary crisis. This study touches upon the tensions between the Generalitat (Catalan government) and the central Republican state, but it does not incorporate an analysis of wartime politics in Cataluña. Involving as it would a detailed investigation of relations between the CNT, Esquerra and PSUC, which were specific to the Catalan political spectrum, this clearly constitutes the starting point for a quite separate investigation.

PART I
The Struggle for Control of the PSOE's
National Organisation 1934–1936

1 Internal divisions in the Spanish socialist movement 1934–1936

The history of the Spanish Socialist Party (PSOE) during the civil war cannot be understood in isolation. The events of 1936–9 need to be placed in the context of a pre-existing internal struggle to control the party organisation. This battle set the party left – known as the left socialists or *Caballeristas* – against the reformist wing. The wartime behaviour of the opposing factions – and especially that of the reformists, who came to control the PSOE's national executive – needs to be analysed as a response to political developments during the period of the Second Republic (1931–6) and most especially between 1934 and 1936.

The history of the enduring and ultimately fatal division in the PSOE is one which long predated the Second Republic. Reduced to its essence, the growing division within the Spanish socialist movement concerned the validity, both in terms of principles and practical benefits, of collaboration with bourgeois political forces. The issue surfaced in a major way in the conflicting reactions to Primo de Rivera's dictatorship in the 1920s and began to have a real impact on the socialist organisation towards the end of the decade – with the crisis of the monarchy.[1] With the arrival of the Second Republic in 1931, and with it the first genuinely representative elections, the polemic emerged from the realms of political principle to become a matter of pressing practical concern. The division was to become truly destructive as a result of the Socialists' experience of government between 1931 and 1933.[2] In this period of republican–socialist coalition, the PSOE's immense will to carry out reform was matched only by the enormity of the need for a programme of social and economic modernisation. This will to reform initially united the entire party. However, the intransigence of the clerical-conservative right – determined to protect the privileges of oligarchy and to preserve the pre-republican social and economic status quo, both by means of filibuster in parliament (the Cortes), and by obstructing new legislation at a local level – provoked two very different reactions within the PSOE.

15

For many on the party left, the experience of government was entirely negative. This attitude often reflected their close links with the socialist-led trades union federation, the UGT. Its general secretary, the PSOE veteran and leader of the party left, Francisco Largo Caballero, as labour minister in the republican–socialist coalition, had been the target of particularly violent conservative attack. 1931–3 was taken as proof that meaningful reform was impossible within a bourgeois democracy. The PSOE left proclaimed that the party had to prepare to seize political power in order to implement a fully socialist programme and pressed successfully for an end to socialist participation in coalition government. Yet even after the PSOE had freed itself from its commitments to the republicans in 1933, the praxis of the socialist left remained inveterately reformist. This political caution derived from the make-up of the socialist left leadership. They were, in the main, trade union leaders whose conservative values reflected their desire to protect the size and strength of a labour organisation constructed over many decades. The enormous inconsistency between the rhetoric and the political practice of the party leftists was to be seized upon later by their antagonists, the moderate parliamentary socialists.[3]

The reformists in the PSOE reacted to the conservative intransigence of 1931–3 in quite the opposite way. They simply became more determined to ensure the enactment of thoroughgoing reform. Initial failure only convinced them of the absolute necessity of persevering with the republican–socialist pact, in order to maximise their chances of electoral success and therefore of maintaining access to the apparatus of the state.

The socialist who epitomised this intense commitment to reform was Indalecio Prieto. He defended a collaborationist tactic on the basis of his assessment of the balance of class forces in Spain in the 1930s.[4] Prieto believed that the weakness of the republican parties – reflecting that of the middle classes in Spain – made it necessary for the Socialists to take on the historic task of the bourgeois democratic revolution. The modernisation of Spain would be accomplished by means of a programme of social and economic reforms which, whilst not integrally socialist, would be immensely radical in the context of Spain's economic backwardness.[5] Thus, in a sense, Prieto's critics on the left were correct to charge him with 'thinking as a republican'. However, the logical concomitant of such a criticism would have been the elaboration of an alternative revolutionary tactic to that of collaboration. But the socialist left made no attempt to provide such an option – beyond mouthing a hollow revolutionary rhetoric. This became doubly damaging in the circumstances. It antagonised the political right when the left had no strategy for meeting its catastrophism. Moreover, it also deepened the division in the PSOE by alienating the parliamentary wing which was aware, as early as 1934, that the left's maximalism amounted to nothing more than empty posturing. The crucial event in alerting the reformists to this was the October 1934 Asturian revolution.

The events of October 1934 were triggered by the entry into the Madrid government of three members of the mass clerical-conservative grouping (CEDA) which had emerged as the PSOE's mirror image and its chief antagonist on the right. The CEDA claimed the three most sensitive ministries – labour, justice and agriculture. For both the Spanish left and progressive republicanism this signified the disfigurement of the Republic and a negation of its reforming *raison d'être*. The general strike which had been planned by the socialist organisation to meet such an eventuality failed almost everywhere – most notoriously in the *caballerista* stronghold of Madrid. Only in the northern coalmining region of Asturias, with its long history of working-class militancy, did resistance flourish. Against a sombre European backdrop of fascist advance, the Asturian Commune was born. For fourteen days the miners held out against twenty-six thousand troops of the Foreign Legion and Army of Africa in the name of a revolutionary social and economic order. But their resistance was eventually broken and a widespread and violent repression ensued.[6]

The significance of the rising and the assumption of responsibility for it formed the substance of heated political debate, both within the PSOE itself and between socialists and communists. Most crucially, the Asturian rising revealed the bankruptcy of the socialist left to the rest of the party. The *Caballeristas* were totally unprepared to lead the revolution they had supposedly been organising for the best part of a year. That the left had certainly seen itself as planning a revolution is well documented.[7] A joint PSOE–UGT committee had been appointed and funds and arms collected. But when the Asturian revolt broke out it was something quite separate from the national committee's strategy and indeed took both the PSOE and UGT leaderships quite by surprise.[8] Insofar as the revolt of the Asturian miners had a 'general staff', it was the socialists, anarchists and communists organised together at the provincial level who led it, not the national leadership of the socialist left.

The Asturian episode raised the fundamental problem of the socialist left's real nature as against its own revolutionary perceptions of itself. In the aftermath of October, the left socialists and most stridently the socialist youth organisation, the Federación de Juventudes Socialistas (FJS), began their campaign to purge the party of the reformists to whom the failure of the October revolution was attributed. But the vitriol of the socialist youth leaders did not deceive the PSOE parliamentarians. They viewed the campaign to 'bolshevise' the party as a cynical device, a smokescreen to obscure the real lesson of October, namely that the left socialist leadership had been tried and found wanting. Nowhere had October been less of an event than in Madrid – where the most vehement bolshevisers were concentrated and where they had controlled the PSOE–UGT revolutionary committee.[9]

It was, however, significant that the Socialist Youth (FJS) should have taken the lead in 1934 in the campaign against the reformists. Impatient and angry at their gradualism and parliamentary faith, the radicalised socialist youth leaders had identified with the party left because Largo Caballero's revolutionary rhetoric seemingly endorsed their own chosen course.[10] This identification with the PSOE left's camp, however, proved but a transitional stage in the radicalisation the youth organisation was undergoing. For FJS protagonism in the October drive to 'bolshevise' the PSOE marked the beginning of the youth leadership's rapid gravitation into the orbit of the Spanish Communist Party. The first joint committees of socialist and communist youth were formed immediately after the events of October 1934. Between then and April 1936, in the course of negotiations undertaken by the FJS leaders and their communist youth counterparts, it was agreed to merge their respective organisations in a single unified youth movement.[11] The attraction exerted over sectors of the socialist left by the Spanish Communist Party would eventually lead during the war to the internal fracturing of the *Caballeristas'* power base, with grave consequences for the PSOE as a whole. A graphic illustration of this dislocation is evident in the political careers of the three co-authors of *Octubre Segunda Etapa*, the so-called bolshevisation blueprint, published by the FJS in 1935. By 1937, two of the three – FJS general secretary, Santiago Carrillo and UGT executive member, Amaro del Rosal would have given their allegiance to the Spanish Communist Party,[12] while the third, FJS president Carlos Hernández Zancajo, became a front-ranking left socialist opponent of the Communist Party during the war.

The bolshevisation campaign may have successfully deflected public attention from the PSOE left's passivity during October 1934, but the miners' defeat reinforced the cautious political praxis of left socialism's trade union leadership. Traumatised by the extent of the repression and fearful for the future of the socialist organisation, Largo Caballero publicly disavowed responsibility for Asturias at his trial. This was entirely a pragmatic exercise of damage limitation. The buildings and property of the Spanish socialist movement were in danger of sequestration and the consequences of the organisation's being denied the right to a legal existence were simply not to be contemplated.[13]

By jettisoning Asturias, the socialist left provided a valuable political opening for the Spanish Communist Party (PCE) which had, hitherto, been forced to operate at the margins of working-class politics in Spain, unable to increase either its size or its influence. The party set about creating its own Asturian legend for the purposes of propaganda and party recruitment. This was to have far-reaching consequences, above all for the PSOE left. The association with heroic, revolutionary Asturias increased the PCE's attractiveness in the eyes of the radicalised FJS leadership. This, in turn, accelerated the process of socialist–communist youth unification which effectively meant that the *Caballeristas* would lose control of the socialist youth federation. Thus, by declaring itself to be 'responsible' for the events of October 1934, the PCE was able to break out of the political ghetto – to which its own sectarianism had largely consigned it – by harnessing the power of Asturias as a powerful symbol of proletarian unity. In the summer of 1935, José Díaz, general secretary of the PCE, trumpeted the party's exhilarated annexation of responsibility: 'In case there should still be any doubt, in the name of the Communist Party I accept full responsibility for the organisation of the Asturian October.'[14]

While the bolshevisers' campaign against the reformists in the PSOE grew apace in 1935, those targeted were outraged by the malicious incongruity of the attack. If the events of October 1934 had exposed the shortcomings of any one group then it was those of the left itself whose political praxis had been revealed as entirely at odds with its rhetoric.[15] The extent to which October clarified matters for the reformists would become apparent years later when, under the extreme pressures generated by the war, the antagonism stemming from October erupted in a string of startling denunciations against the left by leading PSOE figures. At the party's national committee meeting in July 1937, committee member and front-ranking Madrid unionist Rafael Henche made a blistering and very telling attack on Largo: 'I marvel at the degree of personal loyalty which comrade Caballero is able to command. When, in the cold light of day, he has far from measured up to the standards of our party, either before October, during October or after October.'[16] PSOE general secretary Ramón Lamoneda was equally scathing, 'Caballero successfully managed to offload the blame – which was his – for a whole series of disasters which hit the party between 1933 and 1937.'[17] By contrast, the events of October 1934 convinced Indalecio Prieto of the folly and sheer impracticality of revolution as a means of achieving social and economic change in Spain.

Thus Prieto, actively encouraged by his supporters on the PSOE national executive, was soon setting a rapid pace towards an electoral pact with the republicans in an attempt to restore the reforming government coalition of 1931–3. To bolster Prieto in his endeavours, one of his supporters, Juan Simeón Vidarte – who in the absence of the other leaders, who were mainly in jail, was virtually running the PSOE's national executive single-handed – issued an important circular to the party rank and file in March 1935. In it he argued that the Republic had signified considerable progress over the monarchy. He interpreted the October rising as a popular attempt to defend republican legislation against obstruction by the economic oligarchy. Vidarte stressed that as the right would certainly go into the forthcoming elections united, the left must do the same. In short, Vidarte made an intelligent plea for the use of the legal possibilities afforded by the Republic to defend both the socialist movement and the working class in Spain. The 'Vidarte Circular', as it became known, opened up the debate in the PSOE over the possibility of resurrecting the republican–socialist alliance. It constituted an attempt at an official rectification of the anti-collaboration line that the Socialist Party had followed, at the instigation of the party left, since the elections of 1933.[18] In spite of the fact that Largo Caballero himself had approved Vidarte's circular, its reformist provenance was apparently sufficient to provoke the instinctive hostility of the *caballerista* sector. Backed by his supporters on all three executive committees of the socialist movement – party, union and youth – Largo sent a letter of protest to the PSOE executive in May 1935. This signalled the birth of the *caballerista* faction proper. For it was hardly normal practice in the socialist organisation that the youth and trade union leaderships, supported by a minority on the party executive, should have joined forces to protest about the policy line of the party leadership. As the left's campaign against the reformists exacerbated tensions in the PSOE, the internal division was rapidly crystallising as a battle to control the party apparatus.

The centre of contention here was the republican–socialist electoral alliance. As always the *Caballeristas* were sensitive to currents emanating from the rank and file, which, in this case, was moved overwhelmingly to support the projected pact in order to secure an amnesty for the prisoners of October. This pressure from the socialist grass roots effectively obliged the *Caballeristas* to accept Prieto's coalition initiative. But such an acceptance inevitably threatened the left's position in the party. Support for Prieto's option, which really aimed at resurrecting a government alliance, would logically mean support for *prietista* leaders in the party apparatus. To bolster their own authority against the reformist sector Largo Caballero and his supporters sought to attract to themselves the forces of the left. Predominantly, this meant making overtures to the PCE, which they began to do in November 1935.

Simultaneously, on 16 November 1935, the PSOE executive formally agreed to commence negotiations with the republican groups.[19] However, the price of Largo's support was the added stipulation that the electoral pact should be widened to include not only the UGT but also the PCE and its trade union, the CGTU. By taking the PCE with him into the alliance Largo was at once seeking to prevent Prieto outflanking him on the right, while ensuring that the PCE did not do the same on the left.

The left's response to the PSOE's reformist sector reflected the increasing organisational rivalry between the two. The line of fracture inside Spanish socialism dividing parliamentarians and trade unionists was far from new. But with the birth of the Second Republic the rivalry acquired a new virulence, as the traditional balance of authority was reversed and the traditional 'senior partner', the union, had to contend with the growing protagonism and strength of the parliamentary party.

But in drawing close to the PCE for tactical reasons related to the PSOE's internal dynamic, Largo and the socialist left effectively became the instrument whereby a previously marginalised PCE was able to establish itself in the mainstream of left politics in Spain. Moreover this entry did not correspond to any increase in PCE membership nor to any consolidation of the party's relationship with socialists at the grass roots. From November 1935 the socialist left would pursue a policy line whose ostensible objective went far beyond negotiations for a finite electoral coalition, to aim at the organisational unification of the socialist and communist movements. As a first stage in this process, labour unity was achieved in December 1935 when the PCE's trade union (CGTU) was dissolved and its membership entered the UGT. It is inconceivable that either Largo or his closest like-minded supporters envisaged party unification as anything but the PCE's absorption by the PSOE – just as the CGTU had been absorbed into the UGT. Such a process, it was intended, would kill two very important birds with one stone. First, it would restore the lost unity of the socialist family, shattered in 1921 by communist schism. Secondly, it would, so the *Caballeristas* perceived, block the drift towards Prieto, thus preventing too many concessions being made to the liberal bourgeoisie – and Largo for one was still smarting from his political experience between 1931 and 1933.

But Largo's calculations had not taken account of the conflicting interests and priorities within his own support group. As he would discover, to fatal effect, not all the *Caballeristas* in either the Socialist Youth or the UGT shared his own preoccupation with protecting the organisational prerogatives of the socialist movement. This was to become earliest manifest in the FJS.

The fact that the *Caballeristas* were apparently steering towards party unity boosted the enthusiasm of the FJS leadership for rapid organisational unity with the Union of Communist Youth (UJC). It was by no means certain that the pro-Caballero sector in the FJS constituted the majority by 1935–6. But in the youth organisation, as in the PSOE, the left made the most noise. As a result, by early spring 1936, the preparations for unifying the two youth organisations entered their final stages. FJS hostility to Prieto and the reformists had made the youth organisation a useful weapon for the socialist left in its strategic battle inside the PSOE. But the fusion of the FJS and UJC in April 1936 was altogether alien to the intentions of Largo Caballero. Nevertheless, the fact remains that the responsibility for it can be traced directly to the pro-unity line which the *Caballeristas* were apparently pursuing by the end of 1935. Taken overall, the socialist left's policy was effectively helping the PCE – its greatest potential rival as a mass party of the left in Spain – to establish the material basis from which to challenge PSOE predominance. And the PCE was well prepared to seize the opportunity. Since mid 1935 its leaders had been calling for the formation of a 'popular antifascist concentration'.[20] Following the Comintern's new policy of class collaboration, secretary general José Díaz invoked the spirit of Asturias in his speeches. But it no longer symbolised revolution. Instead, in the name of Asturias, the Spanish proletariat was exhorted to recreate its famous unity – but this time for the sake of Popular Front electoralism.[21] Inevitably, the socialist left's overtures to the PCE also deepened the division in the PSOE. Not only was the reformist sector opposed to the unification of the Socialist and Communist Parties, but neither did they want the PCE included in the electoral coalition.

The organisational battle to control the PSOE erupted in earnest in January 1936. The left clashed with the reformists over the elections for party president in a way which prefigured a number of wartime confrontations. The elections had been precipitated when in December 1935 Largo Caballero resigned from the presidency of the PSOE's national executive, along with his three supporters – Pascual Tomás, Wenceslao Carrillo and Enrique de Francisco. The immediate cause of these resignations was the fact that a majority on the PSOE national committee had approved Prieto's proposal that the parliamentary party be subject to the authority of the PSOE's national executive. However, the underlying cause was the growing dispute between Largo and Prieto over the constitution of the electoral pact with the republicans. The PSOE national committee refused to accept the resignations of Largo Caballero's three lieutenants, whilst the executive committee issued a circular recommending Largo's own re-election as party president.[22] Clearly the reformists' primary concern was to contain the divisions in the party and to avoid a *caballerista* mutiny as potentially damaging to the prospects of an electoral understanding with the republicans.

The reformists' appeal for unity and discipline in the party, published in *El Socialista* on 4 January 1936, was geared likewise to keeping the PSOE on an even keel so as not to hinder an electoral accord with the republicans. However, the *Caballeristas* – who were pressing for the election of an entirely new national executive committee in the belief that the level of support for them in the party would ensure that they swept the board – used the issue of the presidential referendum to publicise their hostility to the existing national executive committee. The UGT newspaper *Claridad*, mouthpiece of the socialist left, published the Madrid Socialist group's (ASM) nominations for an entirely new, left-controlled national executive which had been ratified in a general assembly of the Madrid group.[23] As the reformists judged the situation, however, such an irresponsible display of faction and indiscipline required resolute counter-action, not public, vociferous protest – especially not at such a delicate time, with the general elections less than a month away. Prieto and his supporters thus ignored the correspondence from pro-Caballero socialists and bided their time.[24] By the end of January 1936 it was announced in *Claridad* that Largo Caballero had been returned as party president by an overwhelming majority.[25] Largo, however, was never to return to the post, maintaining his previously expressed view that the executive needed to be unanimous, as the 'homogenous organ of an iron leadership'. This unsatisfactory state of affairs would only be resolved when, in May 1936, the PSOE national committee officially recognised the resignations of Largo Caballero's three lieutenants from December 1935 and proceeded to new elections for the vacant posts on the national executive committee.[26]

The series of tactical manoeuvres employed by both sides in January 1936 provided a foretaste of how the internal party dispute was to be waged in the future. In particular, the reformists' strategy of turning PSOE statute against the left could already be discerned in their approach to the voting returns of the January referendum. It was clearly stated by the executive that rank-and-file votes had been computed at face value, without any enquiries as to the 'regulatory status' of the socialist sections concerned, ('sin comprobar el estado reglamentario de las Agrupaciones').[27] By the time of the June 1936 elections to the national executive, however, the reformist returning officers would be wielding the weapon of party statute to exclude a percentage of the left's vote – either because of dues arrears or other statutory transgressions. Such administrative devices would, during the civil war, feature very prominently in the reformist arsenal.

The Popular Front Elections: February 1936

The manoeuvres and counter-manoeuvres in the PSOE during January 1936 took place in a wider political context wherein the major concern on the left was the forthcoming negotiations with the republican groups and the nature of any subsequent electoral agreement. For both reformist socialists and progressive republicans the objective was to restore the reforming impetus of the liberal biennium (1931–3) which had been interrupted by the period of clerical-conservative government between 1933 and 1935.

Pressure from the socialist grass roots for a political amnesty to free the prisoners of October 1934 had been sufficient to win Largo over by the end of 1935 to supporting Prieto's initiative of an electoral pact. But his support did not extend to a re-run of republican–socialist coalition government. While the left reluctantly accepted the inevitability of an electoral agreement with the republicans, it was determined to impose a strict time limit on this. Any permanent coalition would have seriously jeopardised the left's influence inside both the Socialist Party and the UGT. For if the socialist organisation supported long-term coalition with the republicans, then it would have, logically, to support the *Prietistas* whose policy this was.

Although in the event the electoral pact was negotiated between republicans and socialists, the fact that the latter also represented the entire range of political and union forces to their left – with the exception only of the anarcho-syndicalists (CNT) – turned Prieto's preferred initiative of a narrow-based republican–socialist alliance into the Popular Front coalition. Thus the signatories to the pact which would contend the 16 February elections extended from the republicans via the left socialists and the PCE to Angel Pestaña's Partido Sindicalista and the dissident communist POUM.[28]

The Popular Front electoral campaign provides a study in microcosm of the internal dispute in the PSOE.[29] Although they had agreed on the need for such a pact, the left socialists and the reformists were each concerned to ensure that the other emerged with as little leverage as possible within the PSOE parliamentary party, or *minoría* as it was known. The *Caballeristas* felt that the decisions of the national committee of the Popular Front – which was responsible for drawing up the alliance's list of candidates – were being used as a means of limiting left socialist representation. In any case, the PSOE would, as a whole, secure fewer candidates than its voting strength warranted. For one thing, the party would sacrifice posts to republican candidates who were being afforded a number of candidates on the alliance's list which exceeded their voting strength on the basis of the 1933 elections. This was necessary in order to ensure a sufficient majority for them to govern subsequently alone, until such time as Prieto was able to vanquish or circumvent the left's resistance to PSOE re-entry to government. Secondly, the communist candidates also had to be drawn from the PSOE's quota which meant a further reduction in relation to the PSOE's true voting strength.[30] In fact the way the provincial candidate lists had been drawn up reflected a specific national political option – namely that of Prieto and the progressive republicans who sought the institutional route to modernisation via a moderate republican administration. Although both were aiming at the eventual recreation of the republican–socialist axis, in the interim, PSOE votes, having once secured an electoral victory, would thereafter be required to bolster a republican government in the chamber, thereby ensuring the realisation of a programme of social and economic reforms. Given this strategy, it was impossible to apportion candidates on the basis of the grass roots strength of the pact's constituent parts. Nevertheless, the fact that the PSOE representatives on the national committee of the Popular Front, Ramón Lamoneda and Manuel Cordero, were identified with the reformist wing of the PSOE, tended to increase the *Caballeristas'* suspicions of the motives behind its decisions. At the same time, however, the PSOE left preferred to see republicans elected rather than 'republicanoid' (i.e. reformist) socialists. Whilst this particular preference reflected the bolshevisers' concern to achieve a majority within the socialist parliamentary minority, better still from the *Caballeristas'* point of view would have been a higher proportion of communist candidates in lieu of republicans.[31]

After the triumph of the Popular Front in the February 1936 elections, and in an attempt to limit the consequences of the success which this victory signified for the reformists – and for Prieto in particular – Largo Caballero suggested on behalf of the UGT executive that a joint Popular Front inter-party liaison committee should be established.[32] This was to comprise two representatives from each of the groups which had subscribed to the Popular Front pact. The ostensible function of the committee was as an extra-parliamentary pressure group to ensure the enactment of the reformist legislation which had been the *raison d'être* of the electoral coalition. But the left's proposal was instantly vetoed by the PSOE executive. Although it was vice-secretary Vidarte who replied to Largo and the UGT, Prieto's decisive influence is clear.[33] While Prieto was inevitably suspicious of any suggestion emanating from his rival, there was a more substantive issue at stake here. The moderate leader had, from the outset, opposed any widening of the republican–socialist alliance. His hostility to the Popular Front idea insofar as it was a departure from the 1931–3 coalition stemmed from his basic conception of the reform process.[34] This meant legislative reform from above, agreed between liberal republicans and the PSOE. In challenging this model, Largo was not moved only by his personal experience of rightist obstruction during the liberal biennium (1931–3). This had indeed left an indelible impression. But Largo was also articulating the feelings of sectors of the PSOE base. There was a fairly general suspicion among rank-and-file socialists in some areas as to the reasons for the sudden groundswell of republicanism. In many cases the new republicans with whom the socialist cadres had to deal were outright political opportunists. They were often those who, having been members of the liberal or conservative parties under the monarchy, had joined the republicans in 1931 simply to be able to continue functioning in the changed political circumstances.[35] The appeal of a wider alliance to bolster the left is thus understandable. Ironically, Asturias, a *prietista* stronghold, is a good example of an area where socialists saw the Popular Front as more than an electoralist strategy or a parliamentary initiative.[36]

The left's response to the veto was, predictably, to accuse the PSOE executive of bad faith. Largo, in his reply to Vidarte, argued that the combined extra-parliamentary weight of the working-class parties and organisations would significantly have increased the chances of implementing reform inside the legislature.[37] But there was a real bomb contained in Largo's reply. It declared that, as a reprisal for the executive's jettisoning of the committee proposal, the UGT executive was releasing itself in turn from its commitment to the Popular Front electoral pact. This meant that in the municipal elections, scheduled for 12 April 1936, the left socialists were intending to break party discipline, and would seek thereafter to make exclusively workerist electoral alliances with the Communists.[38]

In the event, the municipal elections of 1936 were never held. When the Constituent Cortes met on 3 April 1936 they were postponed indefinitely so that all parliamentary groups could be present to debate President Alcalá Zamora's previous proroguing of the chamber.[39] The Spanish Communist Party, heavily committed to the Comintern's new inter-class strategy of Popular Front and thus to an alliance with the republicans, was thereby spared having to decide whether publicly to side against the *Caballeristas*. The PCE's reformism remained satisfactorily obscure, behind a Bolshevik image which ensured the party's continuing appeal to left socialism's natural constituency among the radicalised working class. Above all, youth unity remained on course. In March 1936, a joint FJS–UJC delegation left for Moscow to negotiate the details of unification with the leaders of the Communist Youth International.[40]

The suspension of the municipal elections thus allowed the PCE to retain a foot in both camps. The party was eager to make a reality of the *Caballeristas'* suggestion of a Popular Front joint committee and Vicente Uribe and José Díaz were nominated as representatives.[41] But, in the event, the initiative was taken no further. The explanation for this has as much to do with the characteristic passivity of the socialist left as it does with the PSOE executive's veto.

The question of a joint committee of Popular Front signatories would only be raised again in July 1936, just before the military rising, and then with entirely negative results. This time the PSOE executive approached the UGT leadership with its own proposal of a joint committee to coordinate defensive action against the likelihood of a military rebellion. But it was confronted by a degree of obstructiveness from the UGT which amounted to a veto. This was justified as a response in kind to the party executive's March snub. It was at this point that relations between the reformists on the PSOE national executive commitee and the party left, with its stronghold in the Madrid socialist group (ASM) and the UGT, would break down completely.

The lines of the organisational dispute in the PSOE were drawn on 8 March 1936 when the left socialists took control of the executive committee of the influential Madrid socialist group.[42] This, in the left's eyes, cancelled out the moral advantage which the Popular Front victory had given the reformists. Thereafter, the ASM was to become the spearhead of the *caballerista* challenge for control of the party organisation – although various prominent reformists were included among its members.[43] Between March and July 1936, the party left increasingly challenged the legitimacy of the 'rump' national executive of *Prietistas*, from which Largo and his supporters had resigned, orchestrating the campaign against reformist initiatives and finally petitioning for an extraordinary party congress to be held in Madrid.[44]

From March 1936 onwards there was serious organisational dislocation in the PSOE. Many socialist sections sympathetic to the left were writing directly to the ASM instead of to the national executive. Some would even urge the ASM to assume the functions of the national body until a full party congress could elect a new, 'representative' executive.[45] However, the immediate objective of the *caballerista* ASM executive was to establish contact with sympathetic groups in order to mobilise them against the initiatives of the *Prietistas*. The gravity of the internal division was also reflected in the fact that those socialist sections which petitioned the national executive to provide speakers for local meetings were told, when the request was for a *Caballerista*, to contact the individual directly.

After the experience of October 1934 and the subsequent bolshevisation campaign of the party left, Indalecio Prieto adopted, on behalf of the reformists, a tactical approach to the internal division which amounted to an attempt to draw the sting of the left by revealing the fatuity of its revolutionary claims. His initial plan was to call a general party congress. As a homage to the heroism of Asturias, it was suggested that this should take place in the north, in Sama de Langreo or Mieres, instead of in Madrid, as was customary.[46] The case for an Asturian congress was laid out by the party executive in a cautious, measured document published on 26 February 1936 in *El Socialista*. It stressed that, whatever the relative merits of the two sides in the dispute, a party congress would resolve the fundamental threat to the PSOE's very structure caused by the indiscipline symptomatic of the conflict. Thus, in the very heartland of October, which was also, ironically, *prietista* territory, the reformists' titular head hoped to debunk the purely verbal maximalism of the socialist left and to defuse what he saw as the threat which it posed to the discipline and strength of the party. The reformists were clearly counting on the left's overriding commitment to party unity, believing that it would be virtually impossible for the *Caballeristas* to set themselves against the resolution of a national congress. Prieto was motivated in all this by the desire to establish an unambiguous line on party policy so as not to waste the opportunity provided by the Popular Front electoral victory.

The socialist left very quickly identified the double danger inherent in the Asturian congress proposal. It saw that the apparently incidental reference to the exclusion of those socialist sections with dues arrears was likely to affect adversely the level of support for the left. For a substantial section of this was to be found among the sections of the socialist landworkers' federation (FNTT), especially in the impoverished rural south. So the congress's geographical location and its likely timing, in early summer, would also militate against the party left.[47] The *caballerista* counter-attack was mounted on two fronts. Characteristically, the minutiae of party statute were ranged against the executive, as the party left queried the validity of holding an ordinary party congress outside the month of October. The ASM was quick to point out the 'sovereignty' of the socialist base in deciding such matters.[48] It also sought to head off the threat of Asturias by proposing to the PSOE executive on 18 March that all the political parties and organisations should jointly organise a mass meeting as a means of paying tribute to Asturias separately from the congress. The congress, the left was insistent, had to be held in Madrid. The ASM wrote in this vein to the PSOE executive on 18 March (1936) and the tone of the letter, as if between equals, is striking.[49] To reinforce its case the ASM also sent out circulars to sympathetic socialist groups to encourage them also to express a preference for the capital.

The response received by the reformists on the PSOE executive from the party sections was, overall, hardly favourable to the suggestion of an Asturian congress and the clear rebellion of pro-Caballero sections was sufficient to force a retreat on the part of the *Prietistas*. Given that their overriding consideration was to prevent any deepening of the internal division, the reformists chose to give way rather than force a confrontation in Asturias. Instead it was agreed that, as a compromise, an ordinary party congress should still be held at the end of June, but in Madrid rather than the north. This solution was, if not without criticism, publicly accepted by the party left by the beginning of April 1936.[50]

By the middle of March 1936 the preparations for unifying the socialist and communist youth organisations were entering their final stages. After the return of the FJS–UJC delegation from Moscow, a joint meeting of the two national youth executives was held. At this, unity was approved on the basis of the integration of Young Communist members into the existing Socialist Youth federations. Once the UJC members had joined a given FJS federation then new elections to the executive body would be held. This arrangement duplicated the basis agreed the previous December for the CGTU's integration into the UGT.[51] The new unified youth organisation was to be known as the United Socialist Youth (Juventudes Socialistas Unificadas, (JSU)).

The terms of the unity pact itself were extremely general. They emphasised basic and uncontroversial political principles – such as the defence of the economic and cultural interests of proletarian youth – and declared the JSU's opposition to fascism, imperialism and capitalism. But the pact scarcely touched upon how the new organisation would function. Its terms did, however, stipulate that the merger was envisaged as providing the nucleus for 'a new mass organisation of the kind outlined at the VI congress of the Communist Youth International'. Unity was to be ratified by the socialist and communist memberships jointly at a national unification congress which would also decide on the precise nature of the relationship between the JSU and the two parent parties, the PSOE and PCE. Until then, however, the unity pact stipulated that the JSU should maintain 'normal' relations with the PSOE.

Once it was clear that youth unity was unavoidable, the socialist youth members closest to Prieto and the PSOE executive, who had consistently opposed the radicals on the FJS executive, took emergency action. They formed the so-called 'Jupiter Sporting Madrileño' (JSM), a sports club 'cover', in order to maintain intact the Juventud Socialista Madrileña (JSM). It was this group, led by JSM president, Enrique Puente, which also formed the 'Motorizada', the PSOE's youth militia during the war.[52] Among the *caballerista* youth leadership, the conditions of the unity agreement provoked little comment. Of those pro-Caballero young socialists who, during the civil war, would violently oppose the JSU and its policies, such as FJS president Carlos Hernández Zancajo, Leoncio Pérez of the Valencian youth federation and FJS/JSU executive committee member, Segundo Serrano Poncela, only the last made public his qualms about the unity agreement at the time it was signed. As a socialist trades union leader, Carlos Hernández was also a zealous guardian of PSOE interest and influence. But, presumably, the unification procedure itself, whereby UJC members were to enrol in the existing FJS federations, combined with the Young Socialists' overwhelming numerical superiority, created a false sense of security. There is no absolute agreement over the relative sizes of the socialist and communist youth organisations at the time of unification. Estimates range from 50,000 for the FJS and 3,000 for the UJC to a total of 40,000 for the newly unified organisation. But the vast superiority of the FJS cannot seriously be contested.[53] Likewise the provision of a joint FJS–UJC committee to oversee the unification process, to arbitrate in cases of disagreement and to organise the unification congress plus agenda, sounded eminently reasonable and scrupulously fair. Hernández was himself appointed to the six-strong national unification committee – along with Carrillo and Federico Melchor. Significantly, however, the clause relating to procedure at the mooted congress was so vague as to be meaningless. It simply stated that democratic procedures would be followed.

Doubts about the consequences of the youth unity pact were first aired publicly when Serrano Poncela, as editor of *Renovación*, the FJS newspaper, published a report on the VI congress of the Communist Youth International (October 1935) in which he was highly critical of its adoption of the new Popular Front line.[54] As the terms of the Spanish pact had been inspired by the policy directives of the VI congress, Serrano was, by implication, criticising the conditions of unity agreed by the FJS. It was not the superficially controversial embellishments of the Spanish pact, such as the reference to the JSU's adherence to the Communist Youth International as a 'sympathiser', which detained Serrano. Rather he concentrated on the JSU's declared commitment to the Comintern's Popular Frontist concept of a 'new style' (i.e. mass) youth movement. This, he insisted, was quite simply incompatible with the essence of a *socialist* youth organisation. As a salutory warning, Serrano cited the cases of the Scandinavian social democratic parties with their choirs and picnics. The influx of a politically uneducated mass membership, such as the Comintern's Popular Front strategy envisaged, would completely destroy the political, class content of the youth movement. It would, in effect, cease to be socialist. But for the PSOE, a politically conscious youth movement was crucial because the socialist youth had always functioned as a training ground for the adult party. It quite literally guaranteed the PSOE's future.

The seeds of future wartime divisions between the Spanish Socialists and Communists were present in Serrano Poncela's critique. The espousal of Popular Front by the Comintern implied the transformation of European communist parties and their youth organisations into mass affairs. Thus the PCE and JSU leaderships would be bound actively to pursue mass recruitment policies which were substantially at odds with the traditional approach of the PSOE and UGT. It was not that Spanish socialists – young or old – were opposed to the Popular Front line *per se*. They understood its rationale for the Soviet Union, as a means of building up allies against the threat of fascist encroachment.[55] But they saw a crucial difference between, on the one hand, collaboration in inter-class alliances of Popular Front for specific, short-term objectives, and, on the other,

permitting the qualitative transformation of the socialist organisations themselves. The absolute clash of political principles and
objectives which would set the PSOE against the PCE and socialists
against communists in the JSU during the war is encapsulated in
Spanish socialist opposition to a policy statement made at the VI
congress of the Communist Youth International. 'The Communist
Youth is *not* the Young Communist Party ('la Juventud Comunista
no es el Partido Comunista de la juventud').[56] For the PSOE and its
youth organisation quite the reverse was true.

Once the unity agreement had been approved by the national
leaderships of the youth organisations in March 1936, a series of
meetings and conferences was organised throughout the country. It
is indisputable that the constant pressure from the base in favour of
unity was an important factor, and one which carried the Socialist
Youth's general secretary, Santiago Carrillo, effortlessly over such
opposition as was voiced by some socialist youth federations.[57] Cases
were also recorded of local unification which pre-empted by a
number of months the national agreement between the FJS and
UJC.[58] The local and provincial meetings culminated on 5 April
1936 in a so-called meeting of national unification in Ventas (Madrid). This was the signal for all the provincial sections. From May to
the outbreak of war in July these were involved in unification
congresses, intended as the preliminary stage before the celebration
of a national congress of unification.[59]

It has generally been assumed that Largo Caballero's silence over
youth unification can be counted as evidence of tacit approval. But
the bases for such an assumption are far from convincing. The fact
that, after the event, Santiago Carrillo paid tribute to Largo as the
progenitor of youth unity can hardly be considered as adequate
evidence.[60] Largo's highly developed sense of the PSOE's organisational prerogatives precluded any favourable response. In 1921 he
had stood opposed to entry to the Third International and thereafter
his tireless response to all the PCE's calls for unity was that it could
be satisfactorily achieved if those who had first broken the unity of
the Spanish working class in 1921 were to rejoin the PSOE. For
Largo, all organisational unity was to be based, *a priori*, on socialist
organisations: the CGTU, the communist trade union, had been
broken up and its members had joined the UGT on an individual
basis. So too young communists should simply rejoin the Socialist
Youth. But the JSU was theoretically independent. Moreover, it
contravened the tacit rule that youth unity should not precede that of
the adult parties. Largo's political outlook is entirely consistent with
the details related by UGT executive member, Amaro del Rosal,

who witnessed Largo's profound distress when Santiago Carrillo came to inform him that the youth unification was an accomplished fact.[61]

Largo's encouraging of youth unity had been part of the socialist left's tactical game in which the radicalism of the Young Socialists functioned as a means of controlling the parliamentary wing of the party, led by Prieto. The convergence of the FJS and the Communist Youth was only of use to Largo as long as it remained a process which fell short of consummation. Once unification was a fact, the Socialist Youth effectively passed out of the left socialist orbit. With full-scale youth unity on course, however, the spring and summer of 1936 was not a propitious moment for criticism which, as Largo well knew, would have redounded to the detriment of the critic. This is the only possible explanation for Largo's failure to voice criticism of the JSU manifesto of 25 March (1936) which declared the organisation's adhesion to the Communist International as a 'sympathiser'.[62]

The unity forged provisionally on the basis of the existing cadres of the FJS, pending the celebration of a national unification congress, would become irreversible with the military rising of 18 July 1936. The outbreak of civil war swept away any possibility of such a congress. But only in 1937 would the exclusion of socialists from leadership posts become sufficiently clear to the old FJS base within the JSU to enable those who had retained their left socialist faith to take up the cause of an independent socialist youth. But by then it would already be too late.

The loss of the youth organisation in the spring of 1936 dealt a serious blow to the *Caballeristas*, weakening their own position *vis-à-vis* the reformist camp in the party, while at the same time handing a considerable advantage to the PCE – the PSOE's major rival as a mass parliamentary party of the left. Ideological antagonism apart, the internal divisions in the PSOE had become more intractable by 1936 because of the reformists' perception of the left's political opportunism. Prieto and his supporters held the *Caballeristas* responsible for sabotaging socialist unity and strength. The crime was a double one because a strong and united socialist party was, they believed, the essential prerequisite of a viable, reforming republican government.

2 The break-up of socialist unity and the coming of the civil war

By the spring of 1936 the political tension in Spain was growing apace. As a result of the February 1936 electoral débâcle, the right had determined to take its struggle against reform beyond the parliamentary arena. The links between the politicians of the clerical and monarchist right and the military conspirators were tightened and in May, faced with the growing threat of military sedition, Prieto attempted to bolster the republican government by taking over as prime minister. It was the elevation of prime minister Manuel Azaña to the presidency of the Republic which gave Prieto the opening he needed to attempt socialist reintegration into government. This had been Prieto's fundamental objective all along since the refloating of the republican–socialist accord in 1935. However, his initiative was checked by both the party left and the UGT. On 6 May the latter again threatened to break up the Popular Front should the PSOE executive permit the entry of socialists into the republican government.[1] Although both the PSOE executive and its national committee were solidly behind Prieto, within the PSOE parliamentary party *caballerista* hostility was clear.[2] The left's majority there – the result of the February 1936 elections – condemned Prieto's proposal of a broad-based Popular Front government to defeat. As a result, on 10 May, when Azaña, sworn in as the new president, charged Prieto with the task of forming a government, the latter refused on the grounds that he could not rely on the support of the *caballerista*-controlled socialist parliamentary party in the Cortes.[3]

Ironically, in one crucial respect, the two wings of the party were basically in agreement over the political role the PSOE was required to fulfil. For both the left and the reformists the PSOE's function was to break the paralysis of government. This had resulted from the panic of the republicans when faced by the evidence of working-class demands for radical social and economic reform. In the weeks and months following the Popular Front electoral victory these had taken the form of direct action, most notably through land seizures. Spontaneous land occupations, 'anticipating' the government's agrarian

34

reforms, occurred in various provinces in March 1936, including Salamanca, Toledo and Madrid. Direct action had thus exposed the Spanish republicans' underlying ambivalence to matters of reform which Prieto had long understood. The weakness of republican groups in Spain had been the *point de départ* for reformist socialist policy since 1931. But whereas this perception had led the reformists consistently to defend socialist collaboration in government as the essential precondition of genuine reform, by 1936 the party left subscribed to a different scenario. Somewhat unrealistically, in view of the evident crisis of Spanish republicanism, the *Caballeristas* were waiting for the republican administration to fulfil the Popular Front programme before pushing for an all-socialist cabinet. Nevertheless Prieto's own behaviour during the May 1936 cabinet crisis also requires careful scrutiny. The significant lack of foresight and down-right passivity which he displayed leads one necessarily to question the soundness of his political judgement. His attempt to secure the premiership was the complement of a two-part strategy whose first premise had been the elevation of Azaña to the presidency. To remove Azaña as prime minister, the strong man of progressive republicanism and the single most important factor of cohesion between the parties of the left, at a moment of such enormous political tension, could only be justified if he could be replaced by someone of equal political capacity. That such a gap could only be filled by Prieto was generally recognised. However, equally well appreciated was the absolute opposition of the PSOE left to his appointment. It is difficult to understand why a politician as astute as Prieto should have behaved as if he were oblivious to the fact that the PSOE bolshevisers would not countenance a repeat of the 1931–3 coalition. They were advocating the formation of a single class party ('partido único') and by April 1936 the ASM was proposing to table a resolution for socialist–communist unification at the next PSOE congress.[4] Thus the hostility of the left did not suddenly spring forth when Prieto put forward his proposal in May. If he was not prepared, as he clearly was not, to forge ahead regardless of the left's position and thus to accept responsibility for the inevitable damage to an already precarious socialist unity, then Prieto should not have backed Azaña's promotion with all the force of his vital and dynamic personality.

Among the reformist socialists who controlled the national executive, Prieto was considered to have made a grave tactical error even to have consulted the left.[5] Azaña had not made Prieto's appointment conditional on the unanimous support of his party and the socialist executive itself urged him to accept the premiership regardless.[6] It argued that he would not be breaking party discipline and, even more importantly, that Largo would not actually use his control of the PSOE parliamentary party against him in the Cortes. Prieto, however, chose to decline the power being offered to the PSOE without resorting to the full range of inner party mechanisms to bolster his case. Most particularly, he did not call upon the PSOE's national committee to mediate between the executive and the parliamentary party. Prieto appears thus to have lacked the courage of his convictions as a statesman.[7] The direct consequence of Prieto's refusal was that the government mandate was granted to the weak and ineffectual republican politician, Santiago Casares Quiroga. He was entirely unequal to the task of countering the growing military conspiracy which threatened the Republic's very existence.[8] Prieto, himself must therefore bear some part of the responsibility for the fatal undermining of the republican government in the spring of 1936. His concern for party unity has been cited as a defence of his behaviour in May. But others have argued that May 1936 was the first sign of Prieto's fatal flaw as a politician – his fear of accepting direct political responsibility because of the risk of failure. This, it has been suggested, is the explanation for his scrupulousness and self-sacrifice, not only in May 1936 but also at crucial moments during the civil war itself.[9]

The thwarting of Prieto's bid to lead a resurrected coalition government of republicans and socialists as a result of *caballerista* opposition was to have a profound effect on the internal struggle in the PSOE. The outcome of the May cabinet crisis led to a change in the tactics of the reformist wing. This change emerged in the course of the meetings of the *prietista*-controlled PSOE national committee held at the end of the month.

During the session of 25 May 1936 the national committee decided to postpone the Madrid party congress from the end of June until October.[10] The key to this tactical revision lay in another of the national committee's resolutions which dealt with the re-establishing of internal party discipline. It was unanimously agreed that the PSOE's executive committee should be given the power to dissolve and reorganise those socialist sections which persisted in their 'indiscipline' by refusing to acknowledge its authority. This resolution meant that the reformists had abandoned the idea of precipitating a direct confrontation with the party left, such as would have occurred at a party congress. Instead, the national committee had laid the foundations for a purge of the party organisation whose objective was the restitution of internal discipline. The recent developments in the youth organisation had served to increase the reformists' sense of urgency and it was intended that this purge should begin immediately. However, as a result of the outbreak of civil war and popular revolution, this concerted attack on *caballerista* nuclei in the party was perforce delayed, in the event, for a whole year.[11] Nevertheless, throughout the second half of 1937 it was to be this resolution on party discipline which served as the chief weapon against any manifestation of what the PSOE executive interpreted as left factionalism.

Such an onslaught against the left could be properly directed only by a strong general staff. Accordingly, the *prietista* 'rump' announced partial elections to fill the vacant seats on the executive committee. The vacancies, which included the presidency itself, were deliberately created when the national committee, in session in May 1936, finally and formally accepted the resignations of Largo Caballero's three supporters which had been submitted in December 1935. The list of replacement candidates drawn up by the national committee consisted entirely of reformists, although these included men whose prestige was considerable throughout the entire party. For example, Ramón González Peña, who stood for the presidency to replace Largo Caballero, was a veteran of Asturias. Luis Jiménez Asúa, the law professor who ran as vice-president to replace the moderate Remigio Cabello who had died in April 1936, was also widely esteemed, both for his defence of Largo Caballero at the latter's trial after the events of October 1934, and because of the assassination attempt he had personally suffered at Falangist hands in March 1936. Ramón Lamoneda, a former *Caballerista* who had moved into the reformist camp and who also occupied a powerful position in the printing union (Artes Gráficas), stood as general secretary – a post previously occupied by the fervent *Caballerista*, Enrique de Francisco. Francisco Cruz Salido stood as administrative secretary to replace the *Caballerista* Pascual Tomás and the list also included Jerónimo Bugeda and Manuel Albar as new ordinary members. One of these two posts had previously been occupied by Wenceslao Carrillo, Largo's lieutenant and a leader of the powerful iron and steel federation. The second post was intended to cover a shortfall in the executive's stipulated complement of eleven which had existed since Antonio Fabra Ribas' resignation in December 1933.[12] While Albar had briefly been a supporter of Largo Caballero, both Cruz Salido and Bugeda were known as reliable, long-serving socialists whose loyalty to the party was uncontested and uncontroversial. Of all the new executive appointments, the most crucial was Ramón Lamoneda's. As Prieto's protégé, it was his task to manoeuvre within the party organisation in order to purge the left. His objective in so doing was to restore party unity as a means of restoring the coherence and therefore the strength of the Spanish socialist movement.[13]

On sending out its list to the party base, the PSOE national committee added a warning to the effect that votes were to be cast only for candidates to replace those who had resigned. Any votes cast for an *entirely* new executive committee would be considered as evidence of blatant indiscipline and therefore counted null and void.[14] However, since the left, and more specifically its visible head, the ASM executive committee, chose to ignore this and to offer the socialist rank and file not only alternative candidates but a list comprising an entirely new executive committee, then a clash was inevitable.[15]

Whilst also presenting an alternative candidacy, the left tried everything within its means to delay the elections until after an extraordinary congress of the PSOE. This they were insistent should take place in the capital as soon as possible – which effectively meant at the end of July 1936.[16] The intricate and seemingly interminable dispute over the congress and its agenda was really a struggle between the reformists and *Caballeristas* respectively to maintain or seize the initiative. The ASM elaborated an extremely ambitious agenda which was sent out to the local socialist sections for consideration and comment. It ran the gamut of the political issues dividing the party: the events of October 1934, socialist–communist unification, socialist participation in government and the election of a new national executive. Most crucially, the left wanted a national congress as a forum in which to elect the new party executive. They very much doubted that a poll conducted among all the local socialist groups would favour their candidates, as the reformists would be controlling the procedure as returning officers.

In the event, the *Caballeristas* found themselves facing a *fait accompli*. At the same time as it was announced that a referendum would be held to decide for or against the left's proposal of an extraordinary party congress, the victory of the national committee's list in the executive elections was announced. The results as published on 1 July in *El Socialista*, the PSOE executive's newspaper, were in stark contrast to those which appeared in the left's mouthpiece, *Claridad*. According to the latter the *Caballeristas* had taken the new executive by a substantial majority.

The acrimonious debate which followed hinged upon the validity of the exclusion of a significant percentage of the vote for the ASM's candidates by the returning officers, the reformist socialists Ramón Lamoneda and Juan Simeón Vidarte.[17] The left demanded to examine the returns and to know on what grounds those of so many sections which had voted for the left's candidates had been declared invalid. The debate raged over dues arrears and the exclusion of socialist youth and UGT votes. Whilst Lamoneda and Vidarte could rightly have pointed out that many union and youth members were not card-carrying members of the PSOE and therefore had no right to vote, the ultimate response of the executive and the returning officers was that the left's manifest indiscipline in promoting an entirely new executive justified such exclusions as they had seen fit to make.[18]

It has been calculated that powerful though the party left was in certain areas, such as the south, the Levante and Madrid itself, in terms of the total number of party militants throughout Spain, it would have been unlikely to have achieved, as a maximum, more than a third of the total party vote. Thus even had the disqualified votes been allowed, this would not have reversed the reformist victory.[19] However, in terms of the real significance of this victory for the internal life of the party, the arithmetic of the defeat was second-ary to the effect which the event had upon the perceptions of the left. The veteran *Caballerista* Justo Martínez Amutio claimed, years later, that the violence against Prieto and González Peña during a political meeting at Ecija (Seville) on 31 May 1936 was a direct result of anger in the south at the massive exclusion of the left's votes.[20] The *Caballeristas* convinced themselves that they had been defrauded and so strong was this conviction that henceforward they held that the PSOE had no legitimate or representative executive beyond the ASM.

It was at the beginning of June 1936 that the reformists first openly accused the ASM of placing itself 'in open rebellion'. This was certainly in part because of its insistence on the celebration of an extraordinary party congress, but even more because of the way in which it was usurping the executive's own functions by correspond-ing with an increasing number of sympathetic socialist groups all over Spain. On 27 May the city of Almería's socialist group, which had been in touch with the executive early in March to repudiate the proposal of an Asturian congress, wrote again, delivering a violent attack on the reformist party leadership. It was not they but the ASM which embodied 'the real feeling of the masses today'. The socialist group from Alcira (Valencia province) also wrote accusing the reformists of exercising a dictatorship in order to gag the 'genu-inely marxist socialist groups' and insisted that it could not be legitimately expelled because the *prietista* rump lacked the necessary moral authority.[21] Coming as this did after a wave of hostile correspondence from the base, the national executive acted swiftly, expelling the Alcira group, as the first of several, from the party. It was this kind of determination which led *Claridad* on 4 July 1936 to declare that the reformists were out to provoke a split in the party by 'expelling the majority'.[22] As usual, the left was equating vociferousness with numbers, although it had no real basis to support its claims.

The new executive's complaints to the ASM had no curbing effect on its factionalism. Indeed in reality, apart from some token expulsions, the May 1936 national committee resolution on internal discipline remained manifestly inoperative. Indeed even a group such as Alcira was able to continue functioning under the protection of the *Caballerista*-controlled provincial socialist federation of Valencia. This is a good illustration of the real problem of dislocation in the PSOE. The mandate to restore the unity of the socialist organisation granted to the PSOE executive in May 1936 would only begin to make an impression when Ramón Lamoneda, as general secretary, felt able to tackle the dissident provincial federations, the most prominent of which was in Valencia. The genesis of the policy of controlling, containing or replacing hostile federations (used by Lamoneda during the war) lies in this serious organisational dislocation of the party in 1936.[23]

The final phase of the party dispute in the pre-war period again displayed the increasing weakness of the party left. For, in the event, it failed in its bid to secure an extraordinary party congress. The results of the referendum in the party proved a great disappointment. The *Caballeristas* were seemingly oblivious of the fact that it would not be sufficient for them to gain a majority of the votes cast, but rather that a favourable result would depend on their gaining an *absolute* majority in terms of the entire party membership. In fact, insufficient votes were cast nationally for the left to have achieved even half of the absolute majority it needed to win. Even in its stronghold, the ASM, the left failed to secure the absolute majority needed to pass the congress resolution.[24] The left may have won a majority of the votes cast, but the silent majority could not be supposed to be supporters of the left, as *Claridad* naively proclaimed.

From mid-1936, it was clear to those on the left of the party that the reformists had determined to turn the party machine against them. The struggle during the war would be of the same nature, supremely a struggle to control the party organisation. From December 1935, when the *Caballeristas* had resigned from the PSOE national executive, the tenuousness of the socialist left's position within the central party organisation had become increasingly evident. Whilst it is virtually impossible to assess quantitatively, it is probable that the noise made by the bolshevisers within the party itself has led to an over-estimation of their numerical weight.[25] The *Caballeristas'* strongholds had of course always been in the union and youth federations rather than in the party itself. But the gravity of the left's situation by 1936 was precisely the result of its growing weakness in these other sectors of the socialist organisation. Developments in the youth federation would end in the eradication of the left's influence therein. The unification timetable agreed at the beginning of April 1936 between the pro-Caballero socialist youth leadership and its communist counterpart would lead within the space of eight months to the effective loss of the socialist youth from the *Caballeristas'* orbit. This would depart as the fervent young bolshevisers of the FJS transferred their allegiance to the PCE – as the party of the revolution, *par excellence* – taking their rank and file with them.

But from the standpoint of July 1936, before such momentous and irrevocable events had occurred, PSOE reformists felt optimistic. The press in general was of the opinion that the outcome of the party referendum augured well for them *vis-à-vis* the ordinary congress scheduled for October 1936. For the reformists, victory at the congress was crucial above all because it would reopen the door to socialist collaboration in government, a door which the party left, according to its rhetoric, wished definitively to close. The argument over the referendum was still raging in the second week of July when the military rose. With the outbreak of civil war, a party congress was entirely out of the question. Nevertheless, the legitimacy of Ramón Lamoneda's purge of the socialist base during the war rested upon the moral conviction that, had the October congress taken place, then the reformist option would have emerged victorious.[26]

The fact that the Lamoneda executive had to postpone the process of purging the party base until 1937 was to be the result of political developments extraneous to the party dispute – namely that, with the eruption of the civil war, at the beginning of September 1936 the socialist left would become the nucleus of a wartime coalition government of the Popular Front. However, this seeming victory for the party left rested on a precarious base. But before considering the left in power and the débâcle which ensued, we need, to understand it, to look back at the internal tensions and contradictions of the *Caballeristas'* power base.

The Erosion of the Socialist Left 1934–1936: An Overview

By the time of the Popular Front elections in February 1936, two parallel developments can be discerned which were to be central to the erosion of the socialist left and thus, ultimately, to the cabinet crisis of May 1937 which saw its exclusion from power. In the first place, the Comintern's policy volte-face, its espousal of inter-class collaboration in the form of Popular Front, signified the beginnings of the realignment which would eventually lead to the wartime collaboration between the PCE and the parliamentary, reformist wing of the PSOE. The basic philosophies of both over the constitution and aim of Popular Front were the same. Prieto's conviction that the need to re-establish the republican–socialist government coalition was paramount came to be echoed by the communist leadership which was similarly seeking the election of a coalition of republicans and moderate socialists, or even of an entirely republican cabinet.[27] Nevertheless, in 1935 it was the socialist left, unaware of the magnitude of the Communists' policy volte-face, which sought closer relations with the PCE. It would take the outbreak of war, and the radical alteration of the political equation which the urgent necessity of Soviet aid supposed, to convince Prieto of the need for a socialist–communist alliance.

Whilst the political attitudes and objectives of parliamentary socialists and communists in Spain were converging by late 1935, left socialist relations with both the anarchists (CNT) and left communist groups were in a state of crisis. Indeed, they had been so ever since 1933. The underlying reason for this enduring failure can be summed up as the general suspicion on the left of the absorptionist intentions of the *Caballeristas*. If we analyse the development of the left socialists' relations with both the anarchists and the leninist left, it becomes clear just how isolated the PSOE left had become by the spring of 1936. This isolation boded particularly ill because, as we have seen, it was soon compounded by the left's tactical defeat at the hands of the PSOE reformists in the elections to the party executive and in the referendum over the extraordinary party congress (July 1936). Moreover, the unification of the socialist and communist youth organisations, far from strengthening the left socialists, would soon be revealed for what it was – the absorption of the entire socialist youth movement by the PCE. Accordingly, the failure of the *Caballeristas* to consolidate an alternative power base on the left as a bulwark against the concerted onslaught of the PCE, JSU and the parliamentary socialists in 1937 was to be crucial to left socialist demise.

Firstly, let us consider the *Caballeristas'* relationship with the non-orthodox communist left. In 1933 the idea of a Workers' Alliance had been conceived by Joaquín Maurín, the leader of the quasi-trotskyist group, the Bloc Obrer i Camperol, (BOC). His aim was to forge a revolutionary instrument which, by transcending the organisational divisions of the Spanish proletariat, could promote and coordinate united, effective working-class action. But it was only after the break-up of the republican–socialist coalition and the subsequent electoral defeat of November 1933 that the *caballerista* leadership began to show an interest in the idea of a Workers' Alliance. However, the PSOE left had an extremely narrow view of its function. From the beginning it was seen as a means of extending the influence and control of the PSOE and the UGT in areas where, traditionally, socialist organisation was relatively weak – such as, for example, in Catalonia. The function of the Alliance was seen as being supremely a bureaucratic one: it was to serve as a liaison committee between *existing* organisations rather than as a real instrument of rank and file unity.[28] Thus the real potential of the alliance for achieving an important measure of political unity and cooperation on the left was wasted.

Throughout 1934 the dead weight of *caballerista* inaction effectively neutralised the initiatives of the BOC and Izquierda Comunista in the Workers' Alliance. After the events of October had given the lie to left socialist claims to vanguardism, as was equally clear to both the reformists in the PSOE and the revolutionaries in the Workers' Alliance, the *Caballeristas* saw the political initiative pass from their hands. The socialist left was severely traumatised by the extent of the political repression which followed October. Fearful of the effect on the base, the PSOE bolshevisers observed, almost passively, as the mainstream Communist Party (PCE) not only assumed the political responsibility and therefore the kudos for October, but also adopted and thence totally transformed the structure, political significance and objective of the Workers' Alliance. Implemented at the local level, they were to become an expression of the PCE's embryonic popular frontism.[29]

In view of the negligible size of the PCE grass roots and thus the inevitable marginality of many of the local bodies, it may seem at first sight surprising that the left socialist leadership was so hostile to the new-style Alliances.[30] But it was with some justification that the *Caballeristas* perceived them as a mechanism whereby the PCE was seeking to appropriate the socialist rank and file. A number of complaints from socialist cadres in 1935 increased the fears of the left socialist leadership in this respect. In April 1935, Sevillian socialists,

fearing for their own control, boycotted a national assembly of
AA.OO. delegates convened by the PCE for 6 April. In Aragón too,
socialists would only permit the formation of AA.OO. in factories
and workplaces where the constituent organisations were already
established, each in their own right.[31] Socialist left fears were fuelled
precisely because of the fervent grass roots support in the socialist
organisation for unity on the left, above all to secure a political
amnesty for the prisoners of October. The Cordoban socialist federation was one which felt obliged to join the AA.OO. because of the
general mood of its rank and file. And it was this sort of pressure from
below which clinched Largo's own support for Popular Front. To
control a trend it is always best to lead it.

Another influence on Largo here was the anti-Prieto sector of the
socialist youth organisation. Radicalised as a result of witnessing the
obstruction of social and economic reforms by a succession of
conservative governments after November 1933, the socialist youth
leaders had grown closer to their communist counterparts. This
convergence was itself hastened by increasing popular support for
unity from Spanish workers. Against an international backdrop of
fascist aggression in Europe and in the face of the repression which
followed the Asturian rising at home, working-class unity was seen
as a general defence measure – so that the fate of the Italian, German
and Austrian proletariats would not become that of the Spanish
working class. By December 1935 the left-controlled provincial
federation of the PSOE in Alicante, echoing Largo's thinking, suggested that instead of forming a Maurin-style Workers' Alliance,
it would be more appropriate to consider reconstructing the
republican–socialist bloc, along the lines of 1931–3.[32] Ironically,
the sea change in Comintern policy meant that under communist
tutelage the Workers' Alliance had themselves become part of a
wider strategy which sought the revival of a republican–socialist
alliance.[33]

The *Caballeristas* alone had possessed sufficient national strength
and influence to ensure the fulfilment of the Workers' Alliance's
original potential. But suspicion of the socialist left's absorptionist
intent meant that potential was never realised. The *Caballeristas'*
hegemonic designs debarred them from acting upon the tremendous
popular enthusiasm for practical proletarian unity. Most crucial of
all here was the left socialists' failure in 1935 to establish a real united
workers' front with the anarchists. For whilst both left socialists and
anarchists were apparently united in their opposition to reformist
socialism – as epitomised by Prieto's strategy of collaboration in
government – it would be more accurate to affirm that the anarchists

opposed the reformist tendencies of Spanish socialism as a whole whilst the *Caballeristas* opposed the reformist wing of the PSOE.

Throughout 1935–6, relations between the left socialists and anarchists were fraught with difficulty. The *caballerista* leadership's dealings with its anarchist counterpart were always characteristically high-handed. Yet the hegemony of the socialist left in the 1930s could not have been achieved except by means of an agreement with the CNT. That this was never realised had much to do with the intense and increasing rivalry between the two union leaderships and their respective rank and files.

Contrary to what has often been suggested, it is not at all clear that the radicalisation of the socialist left occurred in response to anarchist pressure. Indeed, as CNT radicalism increased, so did the *Caballeristas'* tendency to adopt more moderate positions. By 1933 the socialist landworkers' federation (FNTT) had become the giant of the UGT.[34] The radicalisation of the left socialist leadership – as of the FNTT base – occurred precisely at a time when the CNT appeared seriously weak because of various abortive attempts at insurrection and when the organisation was beset by internal divisions which had seen the secession of both the Federación Sindicalista Libertaria and the Sindicatos de Oposición. Equally, the return of the UGT leadership to its traditional reformist positions came as the anarchist organisation emerged once again as a revolutionary force in the spring of 1936.[35] It is noteworthy that not even during its most radical period (i.e. up to mid 1935), did the socialist left make any move towards a reappraisal of anarcho-syndicalism or of its organisation.[36]

Both the causes and the characteristics of socialist radicalisation in the 1930s, after the break-up of the republican–socialist coalition, have been the centre of numerous studies.[37] Whilst opinion remains divided over the relative weight of external factors, such as the growing threat of fascism and the radicalisation of a significant sector of the socialist base, as against 'internal' factors originating in the struggle to control the party, there is fairly general agreement that the evidence points overwhelmingly to the underlying reformism of the socialist left's union leadership and of Largo Caballero in particular – in spite of the period of revolutionary rhetoric and radicalised posturing of 1934–6. Those non-explanations of the socialist left's behaviour centring on Largo's own supposed 'conversion' to revolution as a result of his prison readings of Marx after October 1934 have now been consigned to a well-deserved oblivion. A self-proclaimed revolutionary faith is not the equivalent of a revolutionary praxis. Proof of the latter would have to be sought in the clear transformation of a party's organisational structure, as the nexus linking theory and practice.[38]

The interpretative difficulties facing the historian attempting either a definition of left socialism or a coherent explanation of the behaviour of its supporters are the inevitable product of the fragmentary nature and the inconsistencies of the socialist left itself. Any analysis of *caballerismo*, to be valid, needs to distinguish, first and foremost, between the phenomenon of rank-and-file political radicalisation in the later period of the Second Republic (1934–6), and the quite separate factors that shaped the political behaviour of the left socialist leadership which apparently espoused the radical cause. There remained an insoluble contradiction between the radical aspirations of the *caballerista* power base and the innate conservatism and political caution of the veteran trade union leaders who constituted the nucleus of the left socialist leadership. Their trade union roots entirely determined their political responses. The fundamental objective remained the aggrandisement of the socialist organisation in Spain.[39]

The period of republican–socialist coalition government during which Largo Caballero was labour minister serves as an excellent illustration of the UGT's objectives. Between 1931 and 1933, as previously during its collaboration with the Primo de Rivera dictatorship (1923–30), the trade union leadership saw the possession of a segment of state power as a means of extending, via extensive patronage, the influence and control of the socialist organisation – at the expense, naturally, of the CNT. The implementation of a system of Jurados Mixtos (mixed arbitration committees), in particular, was viewed by the UGT bureaucrats as a way of stealing a march over their anarchist rivals. As in the 1920s, so under the Second Republic the prize was to be the monopoly of the socialist union federation in the field of labour organisation.[40] However, as in the twenties so in the thirties: the dreams of a union monopoly came to nothing, in the latter case as a result of the fragility of the republican–socialist coalition. Given that the ethos of the socialist trade union leadership was always entirely bureaucratically orientated and reformist and in that it also remained acutely aware of anarchist competition, it is hardly surprising that no common ground could be found for political cooperation with the CNT.

By November 1935, the socialist left and even Largo himself had accepted the idea of a Popular Front electoral pact, if not a repeat of coalition government. This left the anarchists isolated once again, the sole defenders of a homogeneous worker front and of the revolutionary action of the proletariat as the only real protection against fascism. The 'revolutionary pact' which the CNT proposed to the UGT leadership was effectively a way of channelling its antiparliamentarianism at a time when the wide appeal of Popular Frontism ruled out a critique of political and parliamentary tactics.[41]

However, throughout the entire period between January 1936 and the May congress of the CNT at Zaragoza, not once did the left socialist leadership take any initiative to reduce the distance between the two organisations, nor indeed was any move made which might have given the CNT reason to believe that Largo Caballero was genuinely interested in an alliance of equals. Heady from the successful reintegration of the communist trade union (CGTU) into the UGT in December 1935, which the *Caballeristas* viewed as healing the schism of 1921, at least at the union level, the socialist leadership arrogantly proclaimed that the CNT might follow the lead of the unified marxist union but, by definition, all unity initiatives had to be socialist in origin.[42] Thus, by denying or ignoring anarchist initiatives without supplying their own, the socialists lost the propitious moment for a union pact, just as previously they had lost the opportunity to form a united workers' front.[43]

Far from adopting more aggressive policies in order to compete, the UGT leadership was fast reverting to its traditional reformist stance. The defensiveness of the socialist left, its refusal to meet the anarchist challenge, to define itself for or against the revolutionary syndical pact and the Popular Front strategy, as logically mutually exclusive policies, provides the clearest indication that, in the last analysis, it was the trade union leadership which dictated the practical policy of the socialist left.[44] Just as its real strength lay in the union, so too its preoccupations were essentially syndical.[45]

The only possible way of making sense of the apparently schizophrenic nature of the socialist left is to employ the distinction posited by recent scholarship. This places the formulators of its revolutionary discourse (intellectuals such as Carlos de Baraibar and Luis Araquistain) on the outside looking in as far as the workings and policies of the UGT are concerned. They had no impact on the daily action of the union and thus their theory was reduced to a mere tactical weapon in the hands of veteran union leaders. Ultimately, this discourse only served to isolate the socialist left from the parties of the Popular Front, while the very real predominance of reformists in the trade union leadership equally precluded any alternative strategy involving the CNT. The socialist union bureaucracy was condemned to isolation and impotence precisely because its overriding concern was to maintain its organisation intact. This precluded the leadership from tapping the vast political potential of the radicalised sectors of the socialist base, the phenomenon defined as *caballer-ismo*.[46] The socialist left's verbal maximalism, its exalted proclamations of the imminence of a new revolutionary order must not be taken as evidence of the genuine assumption of leadership of a radicalised working class. For all the noise generated by the socialist youth and the ASM bolshevisers, the single most important component of *caballerismo* – without which the others combined amount to little – was the FNTT's rural base. In a country like Spain whose economy turned on an agrarian axis, the political power of the large, radicalised membership of the landworkers' federation was potentially very great. Yet Largo and the socialist left leadership never sought to channel it in any way which would have been consistent with their revolutionary rhetoric.

By the spring of 1936, inter-union rivalry was particularly evident in Madrid where the CNT had begun to mobilise in what was traditionally a UGT stronghold. A transformation in trade union practice had occurred in Madrid which effectively saw the eclipse of the UGT's reformism and the triumph of the more direct tactics of confrontation espoused by the CNT. The relatively rapid shift from an arbitration-based unionism to one of massive worker mobilisation was the consequence of the demographic and industrial transformation of the capital in the twentieth century, combined with the effects of the economic crisis of the 1930s.[47] The CNT was particularly strong among the large numbers of unskilled building labourers who, attracted by the boom in the industry, had flocked to Madrid to work on construction sites during the 1920s. Their situation had worsened as the industry, faced with the effects of recession, began to cut back. With no security or bargaining power, confrontational tactics and the general strike were increasingly the only options available to these unskilled workers. Escalating confrontation between capital and labour and the tangibility of class conflict gave the CNT its chance to use agitation techniques to conquer a significant segment of the UGT base. The growing hostility of the socialist leadership reflected its awareness that the strike waves were threatening not only the stability and viability of the Popular Front option, but also its own control over the Madrid rank and file. In April 1936, on the fifth anniversary of the Republic, many individual *ugetistas* joined the general strike declared by the CNT in spite of the outright opposition of both the Socialists and Communists. Neither the ASM nor the UGT executive nor the socialist union federations' administrative committee based in the Madrid Casa del Pueblo was able to prevent the mass indiscipline of the Madrid UGT's rank and file. Nor were these bodies able to prevent it from joining subsequent strikes in the capital. This was the ultimate trauma for the veteran bureaucrats who led the UGT and whose patrimonial conception of the union naturally began with the membership itself.

By the end of May 1936 there was evidence of a serious decline in relations between the two union leaderships. This was largely because the growing rivalry of their respective bases occurred against the background of the tense and polarised political life of the Republic. Under pressure from an increasingly militant CNT, the UGT moved squarely into the Popular Front orbit and even criticised the anarchists for preaching 'rebellion against the state'. The CNT, for its part, via its newspaper, *Solidaridad Obrera*, reverted to the violent criticism of 1931–3. Largo Caballero was the 'old corrupt, collaborationist socialist of years gone by' ('socialista enchufado de antaño) and his contact with the republican minister of labour, who asked his advice about the strikes, together with the proposal to re-establish the Jurados Mixtos, were taken by the CNT as further evidence of his inveterate reformism. On 30 May *Claridad* declared that the affiliates of the two unions had reached the point of violent confrontation. This really made itself felt as a result of the Madrid construction strike which began on 1 June.

The construction strike which dragged on into July 1936, and was still unresolved by the time of the military revolt, caught the socialist left between the reformists' criticisms and the cries of scab and traitor which were being hurled from anarchist quarters. *Claridad*'s call on 11 July for a return to work, 'for the sake of the Popular Front, for the consolidation of [. . .] victory over the bosses' brought a blistering response from the CNT's *Solidaridad Obrera* which retorted that 'the whole of the Spanish working class is astounded by *Claridad*'s counter-revolutionary tack'.[48] With a significant percentage of the UGT base in the capital hostile to the negotiated agreement for a return to work and siding with the CNT, there was a state of open war between both the leaderships and individual members of the respective unions, although, in the main, *ugetistas* did refuse to cross CNT picket lines.[49]

Within the PSOE there was a considerable hardening of attitudes towards the party left. Already held to be morally responsible for the maverick behaviour of the FJS leadership and its unilateral declaration of independence, the *Caballeristas* were now also criticised for losing control of the UGT base in Madrid. Inside the party too, the left found that its grip on the organisation was being successfully loosened. By the end of June 1936 it found itself faced with an anti-*caballerista* coup in the party. As the victory of a wholly reformist national executive at the polls was announced, the left also discovered that it had lost the battle for an extraordinary party congress. These were the first signs that the political tide was turning against the *Caballeristas* as Prieto and his supporters sought to use the machinery of the party against them. By imposing its discipline, the national executive of the PSOE intended re-establishing internal unity in the party as the essential prerequisite of effective socialist collaboration in government.

PART II
The Socialist Left in Power 1936–1937

3 The appointment of the Largo Caballero government

The military coup of 17–18 July 1936 caught the PSOE at a virtual deadlock in its internal dispute. When the rising occurred the party left was still counting the socialist sections' votes for and against celebrating the extraordinary party congress. The split in the national leadership could be felt throughout the entire organisation. The reformists held the PSOE's executive committee and also controlled *El Socialista*, the official party newspaper. Support for them in the party is difficult to quantify, but was considerable. The party left found its strength in the UGT, although the fact that some unions were keener on bolshevisation than others meant that Prieto also had support in the union federations – most notably in the Asturian miners federation (SMA). The party left also controlled the newspaper, *Claridad* as well as the ASM executive. The Madrid group was the single most influential socialist group. Until 1918 it had controlled the national executive and its influence remained because it incorporated virtually all the leading members of the party.[1] But by the spring of 1936, as we have seen, the ASM committee was competing with the PSOE national executive by functioning as a factional leadership. By July, relations between the two wings of the socialist movement were strained to the point of rupture and only an error by UGT executive member, Manuel Lois, would keep open a door for minimal formal dialogue.

Lois, who had remained behind in Spain when the rest of the union executive left to attend the international trade union conference in London in July 1936, twice met with the PSOE executive to discuss the matter of forming a joint Popular Front committee to counter any military rebellion.[2] The socialist–communist youth organisation (JSU), the PCE and the Madrid Casa del Pueblo were also represented at the meetings.[3] When Largo and the others returned on 16 July, Lois was severely reprimanded for having placed the union in an invidious position. His attendance at the meetings was considered as tantamount to a recognition of the legitimacy of the Lamoneda executive. A retraction had been rendered impossible by the publication of a joint document affirming support for the government.

In the event, the UGT executive was divided on whether the union should have further dealings with Lamoneda. Some of Largo's closest supporters, José Diaz Alor (national treasurer of the bakers and confectioners' federation and vice president of the UGT executive), Ricardo Zabalza (general secretary of the UGT heavyweight, the FNTT), Carlos Hernández Zancajo (general secretary of the transport federation) and Mariano Muñoz (hotel and catering federation) were all opposed, whilst both Amaro del Rosal (federation of workers in credit and finance) and the UGT's treasurer, Felipe Pretel (federation of workers in leisure and entertainment), both of whom were communist sympathisers, supported a continued dialogue. Largo Caballero himself also considered it advisable to continue attending in order to make known the UGT's position. As a result, the executive's administrative secretary, Pascual Tomás and Manuel Lois were designated to attend. However, severe difficulties arose subsequently because Tomás and Lois were not prepared to act as fully empowered representatives of their executive.[4] Even though speed was of the essence, at the third meeting on 17 July the *ugetistas* were not prepared, without further consultation with the rest of the union executive, to endorse even very basic resolutions – such as an initiative to establish a network of joint committees throughout Spain to organise a militia, the soliciting of arms from the government and the purging of military commands. It was not that Largo Caballero or any of the others were likely to object to these measures. Rather the whole incident revealed the inflexible, bureaucratic mentality of the union executive. Everything related to the party executive had to be examined in terms of the internal dispute and the struggle to control the party organisation.

The very fact that virtually the entire union executive had chosen to leave Spain to attend an international congress at such a time indicates that the party left underestimated the threat of a military coup.[5] The *Caballeristas'* irritation at Prieto's warnings of the imminence of a coup had much to do with their blind determination to block the reformists' road to government. The insouciance of the left regarding the military conspiracy served only to feed the anger and frustration of Prieto and those associated with the party executive. This further evidence of the left's irresponsibility – the same as had permitted the divisive campaign after October 1934 and subsequently the organisational dislocation of 1936 – merely strengthened the resolve of the reformists to deal decisively with *caballerista* factionalism. The traditional relationship between union leadership and party executive finally broke down.[6] This occurred, however, exactly when republican debility and vacillation as a result of the 17–18 July military coup was forcing the PSOE to prominence. The PSOE was crucial to the effective defence of the Republic. In terms of its own credo or world view, the PSOE was poised to inherit the government, to fulfil its destiny, thus attaining the classical goal of all social democratic parties.[7] The wartime speeches of Spanish socialists reinforce this impression of the war as the means by which the PSOE would come to fulfil its historic mission, inheriting control of the state. However, in 1936, because there were in effect two socialist parties functioning, the question was *which* would inherit? The struggle between the reformists and the left had become one for control of both party *and* state.

Under the impact of the military coup the government structures of the Second Republic completely collapsed. The resignation of the ailing republican prime minister, Santiago Casares Quiroga, on the morrow (18 July) of the coup symbolised the bankruptcy of Spanish republicanism. One explanation of the paralysis and disorganisation of the republican parties when faced with the military rebellion was that many in their ranks were distinctly ambivalent in their attitude to it. The social and economic radicalism of large sectors of the Spanish working class, evident throughout the spring and summer of 1936, was now being forged into a revolution in the heat of popular resistance to the coup. All of this inspired in most Spanish republicans intense fear and alarm. It was widespread republican anxiety which led the new conservative republican premier, Martínez Barrio, vainly to attempt to avert civil war (and the emergent revolution), via telephone negotiations with the leading military rebel, General Mola. But he was not prepared to treat. Martínez Barrio's actions were interpreted by the forces of popular resistance, organised in party and union militias, as nothing less than attempted capitulation and newly armed workers demonstrated against his government in the streets of Madrid. The central dilemma facing President Azaña and the republican political class was that the defence of the Republic – and there was no choice once Mola had refused to negotiate – meant formally sanctioning the distribution of arms to the popular militia. This, of course, meant conferring political power on the representatives of the proletariat. Both Azaña and the bulk of the republican politicians hesitated to 'arm a revolution in order to defeat a counter-revolution'.[8] But in the end there was no choice. On 19 July, chemistry professor José Giral, a member of Izquierda Republicana and a close personal friend of Azaña's, accepted the premiership and with it the arming of the people.

Throughout the brief period of José Giral's republican administration (20 July–31 August 1936), Indalecio Prieto, leader of the
PSOE reformists, was acting as advisor-in-chief to the government,
dividing his time between the presidential palace and the defence
ministry where the enormity of his labour was matched only by that
of his pessimism.[9] His unparalleled personal intelligence network
made him doubly indispensable to Giral. It also goes some way to
explaining – perhaps even justifying – his notorious pessimism. This
was so contagious that various members of the party executive
ceased visiting him in the Madrid naval ministry during September
and October 1936, for fear of the damage it would do to their
morale.[10]

The men of the UGT were, for their part, operating an emergency
information service from their Madrid headquarters in the Calle de
Fuencarral. This was essential to the government given the total
dislocation of the national communications network following the
military rising.[11] It was thus a period of intense activity for both the
union and party executives, the latter supporting Prieto to the hilt.
There was a contest between the left and the reformists in that both
groups realised how close the PSOE was to achieving power. For
Prieto's supporters especially, August 1936 seemed a period of
'waiting in the wings'. Largo himself recalled how whenever he rang
either the defence ministry or the presidential palace it always
seemed to be a member of the PSOE executive who answered.[12] The
reformists, and especially Prieto, envisaged themselves as on the
brink of claiming the government and premiership lost the previous
May in the face of *caballerista* opposition. Ironically, however,
republican prevarication at the time of the coup itself had robbed
Prieto of his chance to lead a moderate reformist coalition of republicans and socialists. The fact of popular revolution made it impossible to return to a government format such as might have been
implemented in February or May 1936. As both Prieto and Azaña
came to realise, it would be impossible to govern against the popular
will.[13] The grass roots revolution which the military rising had
precipitated had itself put more than a bridgeable distance between
the reformist socialists and the government mandate. By September
1936 the extent of agrarian and industrial collectivisation and the
fervour of the militia were such that Prieto was the first to admit that
Spain's political reality made inevitable a government of a more
radical complexion, and that such a government could only be led by
Largo Caballero. This realisation came very hard to the men of the
party. The *caballerista* leadership had not initiated the revolution, nor
did it attempt to harness its force – in spite of the revolutionary

rhetoric of the previous two years. Yet it was to this grass roots revolution that Largo Caballero would owe his eventual government mandate in early September and the socialist left its consequent temporary advantage in the party dispute.

During August 1936, meanwhile, the socialist left was still optimistically preparing itself to 'inherit' the government of Spain. On the 24th of the month, Luis Araquistain wrote to Largo Caballero outlining his strategy for securing control of the government, or rather its nucleus, for the PSOE left.[14] His letter included a cabinet draft which gave the *Caballeristas* five posts: the premiership and the ministries of war, interior, navy or finance and foreign ministry or agriculture. It was suggested the PSOE reformists be allocated the remaining ministries from the latter options plus the trade and industry portfolio, while the PCE might take public works and labour – one of which would ultimately be destined for the CNT. To Izquierda Republicana, Unión Republicana and the Esquerra, Araquistain's list allocated communications, education and justice respectively.[15] In his letter to Largo he stressed the existing republican government's evident incapacity, attributing the liquidation of political prisoners in the Cárcel Modelo to republican incompetence, 'the republican government is dead ... it must be removed as soon as possible.'[16] However, he was equally anxious that it should not be succeeded by a repetition of the republican–socialist coalition, headed this time by Prieto. Araquistain argued that such a resolution of the republican impasse would in fact solve nothing. He observed that, as Giral's right-hand man, Prieto had effectively been in charge of the government since 20 July. But it was now time to move on, to take an important step, as Araquistain presented it, towards the party left's goal of an all-socialist government.

What was needed immediately was a government whose complexion reflected Spain's new revolutionary order and which could thus secure the confidence and support of the masses. Nevertheless, such a government, even if headed by Largo and containing a left socialist nucleus, would have to be heterogeneous in its overall constitution in order to secure President Azaña's support. In his letter, Araquistain insisted on the need to protect the 'revolutionary' character of the war and to secure the conditions for the full realisation of the revolution in the future. Simultaneously, however, he argued that the creation of a conventional army was an essential precondition of victory and stated that he was perfectly happy to bestow the ministries of agriculture, trade and industry and finance on the reformist socialists. Given that the Spanish revolution was defined by its militia and by the collectivisation of agriculture and industry, his comments immediately provoke the question, in what terms did the socialist left define the revolution? The answer is vital, not least because if one removes the references to an always abstract revolution, then Araquistain's proposals to Largo become indistinguishable from Prieto's blueprint of reformist coalition government which was for so long anathema to the left. Since the only way in which Araquistain's proposals differed concretely from Prieto's was in the choice of prime minister, it is hardly surprising that the reformists should have been convinced that the party left's major motivation was sheer political opportunism. Araquistain's letter of 24 August provides significant evidence of the *Caballeristas'* political 'double think' – the outward manifestation of their fundamental theoretical incoherence.

When, on 4 September 1936, Azaña finally called upon Largo Caballero to form a government, a serious blow was dealt to the prestige and authority of the official PSOE executive. Prieto himself may have accepted the step as both necessary and inevitable, indeed he may even have perceived it as advantageous in the long term. For the exercise of power in such a supremely difficult period of the war would be certain to exhaust the left, revealing its political bankruptcy and thus undermining its prestige.[17] Nevertheless, Largo's appointment constituted a significant, if temporary, setback for Lamoneda in his struggle to regain control of the party organisation.

The controversy surrounding Largo's appointment was considerable. Following Araquistain's guidelines, Largo Caballero vetoed Azaña's suggestion that both wings of the PSOE should appoint representatives to an enlarged cabinet over which Giral would continue to preside.[18] Largo demanded both the war ministry and the premiership for himself, confident that the domestic political reality would prove an irresistible argument. Given Prieto's closeness to both Giral and Azaña, he would certainly have been privy to these developments. His own preparedness to accept Largo as premier stemmed from a single practical consideration. Prieto understood that an effective Republican defence required, above all, the full cooperation of the CNT and that Largo Caballero was the only conceivable prime minister who might procure that.[19] In deference to international opinion, it had already been established that the government should not be homogeneously left-wing, but should be a coalition such as Prieto himself might have led in May.[20] However, in contrast to Prieto's extreme diffidence in the spring, Largo Caballero did not even seek the ratification or approval of the PSOE executive, thus contravening both the spirit and the letter of party discipline.[21] The PSOE executive was requested to suggest individuals to fill its allotted number of ministerial posts, as were the other political parties, but it was not asked to underwrite Largo's acceptance of the premiership.[22]

The party executive was well aware that this was not an oversight on the part of the new prime minister. Rather it reflected the left socialists' view that the Lamoneda executive lacked all authority because its triumph in the June elections had been obtained fraudulently. This bypassing of the executive was merely the beginning of the *Caballeristas'* attempt to marginalise it, to deprive it of its functions until, to all intents and purposes, it ceased to exist. Instead of consulting the party's executive committee, Largo Caballero called upon the general secretary of the ASM, Enrique de Francisco, who had occupied the same post on the PSOE national executive of which Largo had been president. The implication was clear: for Largo and the left the June 1936 executive elections were invalid. In the recreation of party history to which the left implicitly subscribed, the resignations of the *caballerista* executive members in December 1935 had, likewise, been obliterated. In September 1936 Largo Caballero was preparing to take over the reins of government, gathering around him the forces of the left, linked both to the ASM and the UGT. He appointed his close collaborator, Rodolfo Llopis, deputy for Alicante and a leader of the teachers' federation (FETE), as presidential under-secretary and another, less well-known supporter, José María Aguirre, became his political-military secretary. Wenceslao Carrillo, UGT executive member and a leader of the iron and steel federation was appointed as under-secretary in the interior ministry.

The party executive's response in September 1936 could not have been other than it was: silence and a tactical withdrawal. Yet Largo's behaviour was inevitably compared, in the collective mind, with Prieto's excessive scrupulousness four months previously. Even with the unanimous support of the party executive, he had refused to accept the premiership for fear of opposition in parliament from the PSOE's *caballerista*-dominated parliamentary party. Whilst it is true that any analysis of Prieto's motives in May 1936 must go further than a reference to his respect for party discipline, nevertheless, Largo's approach in September verged on reformist-baiting. It was the clearest possible statement from the left: it did not recognise the executive's authority and would oppose it at every level with all the force that control of the state permitted. The relationship between premier and socialist executive would only be properly re-established when Negrín took over from Largo in May 1937 and formally sought its permission to assume the government mandate from President Azaña.[23]

The gravity of the situation lay in the fact that the internal socialist division was about to become a major destabilising factor in the political life of the Republic. The party divide was about to become a schism at the heart of a wartime coalition government. Nevertheless, Largo Caballero was still insistent that Prieto should be included in his government as one of the three PSOE executive appointees. Indeed, as he made it the essential precondition of his forming an administration, the reluctant Prieto had little choice but to comply.[24] Once inside the government, however, Prieto kept a low profile, as if he were playing a waiting game. He may have felt that once the socialist left had been burned out by its efforts to contain the popular revolution, then the opportunity to lead the Popular Front government lost in May 1936 would again be his. But here Prieto fell into the trap he had once warned the party left against. As Prieto had himself remarked, the erosion of any one element of the Popular Front inevitably meant damaging the stability of the Front as a whole.[25] Moreover, as the months of Largo's premiership passed, Prieto grew increasingly convinced that the war was virtually unwinnable for the Republic in such a hostile European climate.

The aloofness of Britain and France had dealt a body blow to the Republic's defence capabilities. Non-intervention was working consistently in favour of the Nationalists, whilst aid was ever more difficult to procure for the Republic. In addition, the crisis of the international socialist movement provoked by the Spanish conflict seriously damaged the prestige and credibility of the PSOE itself. Whilst foreign socialist parliamentarians and labour leaders procrastinated, their communist counterparts, under the auspices of the Comintern, were organising material aid for the beleaguered Republic, which could not but redound to the political benefit of the PCE. Faced by such a desperate European conjuncture, Prieto entered a period of profound personal political crisis. The Prieto of the war was a very different figure from the intelligent and dynamic statesman of the Second Republic (1931–6) and one can point to a number of inconsistencies in his behaviour. For example, Prieto's reluctance to join Largo's cabinet in September 1936 was intensified by the fact that he was only being given control of the naval and air forces, rather than of a unified war ministry. Yet, at the beginning of November 1936, when it appeared that Madrid would fall to the besieging Nationalist forces and the Republican government was on the point of departing for the security of Valencia, Prieto rejected Largo's suggestion that he should take control of a unified defence ministry.[26] According to his friend, fellow socialist, Julián Zugaza-goitia, Prieto saw himself in a double bind. If Madrid was lost, he would be blamed. If it was saved, the unions would take the credit. But Madrid did not fall. The moment of crisis passed and Largo retained control of the defence portfolio. Yet the incident clearly revealed Prieto's ambivalence towards the idea of taking direct political control.[27] It was almost as if his tremendous political drive had been eroded by the repeated contemplation of the events of the May 1936 cabinet crisis. It was as if Prieto had become embittered by the realisation that he had not fought nearly hard enough against the PSOE left in order to take control of the cabinet when this might conceivably have averted war – a war which once begun seemed unwinnable for the Republic. For much of the war, at least until his exclusion from the cabinet in April 1938, Prieto the public politician combined an extraordinary mixture of tremendous energy and intense and contagious pessimism. He would regale his colleagues on the PSOE executive with morale-shattering accounts of how victory was beyond the Republic's reach.[28] Prieto's few public speeches were models of optimism and encouragement, but they were so few for fear his improvised 'conviction' might ring hollow.[29] This desperate perception of the Republic's position caused the paralysis of Prieto's political will, and given his importance to the PSOE and to the Republic, the effects of this deep personal crisis would have grave implications for both, as we shall see.

Meanwhile, in September 1936, Largo Caballero was determined to bind all significant political forces in the loyalist zone to govern-ment responsibility – both as a means of reducing the possibility of damaging criticism being made from the freedom of opposition and as the realisation of his ideal of working-class unity. This was conceived, as always, as unity under the tutelage of the historic party of Pablo Iglesias.

From the very beginning the left socialist leader sought to persuade the CNT to join his government. While its cooperation was essential to the war effort, the anarchist trade union was also the greatest potential source of criticism and therefore the greatest threat to his authority. In November 1936, having won over the CNT by offering four ministries – Justice, Public Health, Trade and Industry – Largo would himself force Azaña to accept the anarch-ists' entry to the cabinet under the threat of his own resignation. At no stage, however, was either the PSOE executive or the parliamen-tary party consulted.[30]

The shape of Largo's first cabinet, finalised on the evening of 4 September, reflected to a great extent Araquistain's draft of 24

August.[31] The left held the presidency and the war ministry, Largo himself, and the foreign and interior ministries, Julio Alvarez del Vayo and Angel Galarza respectively. The socialist executive's unanimous vote that Prieto be given the portfolio of a unified war ministry had been disregarded.[32] However, all did not go smoothly for the *Caballeristas*. The ardently fellow-travelling socialist, Julio Alvarez del Vayo, who had attempted to persuade Largo to accept only the war ministry, leaving Giral with the premiership, was appointed as the left's foreign minister. The events surrounding Alvarez del Vayo's appointment provided the socialist left with its first taste of the political pressure which would be applied increasingly and ever more aggressively by the Soviet Union via both its diplomatic representatives and those of the Comintern. It had been intended that Araquistain himself would serve as foreign minister in Largo's cabinet and his name had been included in the list presented by Largo to Azaña at noon on 4 September. It was the president himself who indicated to his prime minister designate that pressure had been brought to bear, whereupon Largo, quick to anger, insisted with characteristic stubbornness that without Araquistain he was not prepared to form a government at all. Araquistain himself persuaded Largo that a compromise solution was worthwhile, that it would be possible to control Alvarez del Vayo between them by a judicious choice of ministry staff. Araquistain would go instead to Paris as ambassador.[33] Indeed it had been his experience there in August 1936, while attempting to persuade Blum to reconsider his commitment to non-intervention, which had convinced Araquistain that Soviet aid would become crucial to the Republican defence.[34] Thus on the afternoon of 4 September Largo returned to the presidential palace to accept the premiership of a modified cabinet and the constitution of the government was published a few hours later. What the *Caballeristas* had underestimated, however, was the difficulty of controlling not only their foreign minister but also of limiting Soviet interference in both the political and the military sphere. Such a containment would come to be virtually impossible given the Republican government's increasing international isolation.[35]

Alvarez del Vayo's appointment destroyed from the outset any semblance of a left socialist nucleus in the cabinet. He posed a threat to the PSOE left not only because of his sympathy for the PCE and its policies, but also because these, by definition, favoured Prieto and the reformist socialists in the short and medium terms. The lack of a coherent, dynamic centre to the government was to become especially debilitating after the reorganisation of the cabinet in November 1936. This made it a vast, unwieldy affair, totalling some eighteen ministers. Left socialist control was from the start much more apparent than real. Largo's occupation of both the premiership and the war ministry was, paradoxically, an indication of *caballerista* weakness rather than strength. Luis Araquistain, who had drafted the original cabinet proposal, was far away in Paris. Alvarez del Vayo owed his political allegiance elsewhere, as the left well knew, and Angel Galarza, an ex-Radical Socialist who had only recently joined the PSOE, would prove to be a far from competent interior minister.[36]

The news of Galarza's ministerial appointment was greeted with considerable dismay by the PSOE executive. As was also the case with General Asensio, Largo's personal choice as under-secretary of war, the PSOE leadership felt that the career of the individual concerned was somewhat dubious and that the accusation of political opportunism might justifiably be levelled.[37] As minister, Galarza was variously accused by the socialist executive of pursuing a policy which was favourable to the CNT–FAI and then one which was 'comunistoide'.[38] What both these descriptions reveal is that Galarza proved unequal to the task of dealing with the vicious political infighting and bitter organisational rivalries which were particularly acute during the early months of the war.[39] The activities of the anarchist fringe and the phenomenon of the 'uncontrollables' were gravely imperilling the stability of the civilian front. Moreover, he was powerless to check communist excesses. By the beginning of 1937 editorials in *El Socialista* accusing Antonio Pretel, the communist civil governor of Murcia, of sectarianism and political persecution were, by implication, a criticism of the inaction of the socialist minister.[40]

The civil governor in question was removed by Largo after representatives of the socialist executive petitioned him directly, bypassing Galarza. Gabriel Morón, socialist civil governor of Almería at the time of the fall of Málaga in February 1937, was also vehement in his criticism of ministerial incompetence and what he saw as negligence in the face of chaos and civil disorder.[41] By the time of the cabinet crisis in May 1937, the socialist executive had made it one of the conditions of its continued support of Largo as prime minister that Galarza be removed from the interior ministry.[42] Indeed Largo was the first to admit Galarza's inadequacy. However, characteristically, the more savagely Galarza was attacked, not only by the reformist socialists, but also by the PCE and the CNT, the more determinedly Largo supported him. For, as with the campaign against Asensio, not only was the prime minister piqued by criticism of his chosen collaborators, but he also knew it to be an oblique attack on his own political position. Largo knew full well that there was no recognisable left socialist presence in the cabinet and he would finally admit as much to Galarza and Alvarez del Vayo.[43]

Galarza's appointment in September 1936 had also put enormous strain on the relationship between the UGT executive and Largo, as its general secretary, and was thus responsible for increasing the prime minister's political isolation still further. Galarza was apparently appointed because of the experience he had acquired as director general of security under the first government of the Republic.[44] Nevertheless, the choice remains a strange one and the fact that Galarza had come only recently to the PSOE from the Radical Socialist Party did not inspire the union leadership with confidence. In their eyes he was condemned by his past membership of an entity which, like the Radical Party, was associated with political opportunism, demagogy and closet conservatism. Galarza's failure to deal with the numerous communist and anarchist assaults on party and union militants and upon the property of the UGT only confirmed the union leaders in their hostility. In turn this resulted in a less than easy relationship between the prime minister and the UGT executive. PCE aggression was facilitated by communist influence in the security forces. In October 1936 the UGT made vociferous protests to Galarza after the homes of union members were searched. The split in the PSOE meant that *caballerista* provincial federations also tended to complain to the UGT executive about the PCE's behaviour rather than to the *party* leadership. Moreover, it was a UGT executive delegation which visited Barcelona to investigate the disappearance of socialist union and party militants in which it was strongly suspected anarchists had been involved. The UGT headquarters had been ransacked by 'uncontrollables' and there were reports of similar problems in Cartagena and Aragon.[45] Indeed, across the board there existed a heightened sense of organisational rivalry between the rank-and-file militants of the respective unions.

At every level, the assumption that the *caballerista* power base constituted a coherent whole has to be challenged. By the time the war erupted, the left's position inside the PSOE was less than secure. Between April and November 1936 its weakness was compounded by the loss of the socialist youth. This process, initiated by the April unity pact, was consummated seven months later when the majority of the FJS leadership went a crucial step further and joined the PCE. This defection, provoked by the manifestations of political division and crisis in the PSOE, in turn accelerated the internal dislocation of the socialist left.

Nevertheless, interpretations of the youth unification which centre upon the simplistic notion that the FJS was somehow 'sold', or nefariously handed over to the PCE are clearly the product of distortions attributable to the post-war partisan or cold war perspectives which spawned them.[46] The developments within the JSU in fact provide a perfect example of the manner in which, at every level, the reality of civil war transformed the political priorities of those in the Republican zone. The practicalities of Republican defence placed the highest premium on efficient and rapid organisation, particularly in the military sphere. Given the PCE's capacity for organisation, at the very moment when the PSOE was caught in the deadlock of internal dispute, the attraction exerted by the Communist Party should accordingly cause little surprise.

The first days of November 1936 were crucial in the defence of Madrid. But so slight did the chances of defending the city seem that it was evacuated, or 'abandoned' as it was widely viewed, by the left-socialist-led Republican government and also by most of the national leaderships of the political parties. The PCE, alone of those left in Madrid, appeared as a dynamic force, and it was this which clinched the party's meteoric rise. Its conduct secured it the support of the professional middle classes, frightened by the social revolution which they had witnessed throughout much of the Republican zone and attracted to the discipline, hierarchy and organisational genius which the PCE displayed in abundance. Moreover, the PCE's role in the defence of Madrid also assured the party of considerable working-class support as the heroic defender of the glowing symbol of antifascist struggle. The contradiction inherent in the Popular Front strategy, that is, in alliance with the bourgeoisie in a situation of civil war which was at its profoundest level a class war, was not immediately apparent to the rank and file.

It was not that the PCE believed in the viability of defending Madrid any more than did the Socialists or the republican parties. However, the conclusions of the Communists' political calculations were different from those of the rest. The PCE set the political prestige to be gained by remaining in the besieged capital above the risk to the organisation in the event of the city's capture. The PCE's national leadership therefore remained in Madrid while other political parties, including the PSOE, merely left delegates behind them.[47] The risk taken by the PCE paid rich dividends.

As far as the young socialist leadership in the JSU was concerned, their perceptions of the PCE's role in the defence of Madrid in November 1936 transformed the profound attraction exercised by the Communists' organisational genius into a firm commitment to the party. It was no mere coincidence that it was at this precise

moment that the Young Socialists' application for party membership was made.[48] The irresistible appeal which the PCE was able to
exert was not, then, the result of ideological considerations – that is,
of its revolutionary orientation as perceived by the Socialist Youth –
nor even of the powerful Bolshevik myth. The overtures of the FJS to
the UJC in 1936 and the actual unification had a specific objective –
the bolshevisation of the PSOE – which within a few months of the
outbreak of the civil war had been entirely superseded in the minds
of the socialist youth leadership by the practical needs of the war.
The PCE's extreme centralisation, its almost military discipline and
its rigid hierarchy, all contrasted very favourably in the eyes of the
FJS leadership with the division and dispute in the PSOE. The
leadership, in short, was attracted by all those features born of the
Bolshevik experience itself, which would so shackle the JSU to the
PCE. Eventually, the sweeping exclusion of the socialist youth
militants from positions of responsibility in the merged organisation,
and the lack of autonomy within it, would cause them to reject the
authority of the JSU national executive and, ultimately, in the last
months of the war, to rebel openly against it.

A further fragmentation of the socialist left was produced by the
intensely pro-communist stance of certain members of the UGT
executive, namely Amaro del Rosal and Felipe Pretel, who were
constantly pressing for the committee to pass a resolution in favour
of the campaign to unite the PSOE and the PCE. In addition, there
was the increasing alienation of the *caballerista* 'old guard' from
Largo and his cabinet.[49] As it transpired, the union leadership, that
supposed bastion of *caballerismo*, was quite unclear about its status in
relation to the left socialist ministers in the cabinet. This was ironic,
given that when Largo omitted to consult the PSOE executive about
accepting the premiership in September, its members were convinced they had been supplanted by the UGT executive. But in fact
neither body had been consulted about the composition of the
cabinet. All that Largo had requested of the UGT was that they
endorse his acceptance of the government mandate.[50]

The matter was discussed in subsequent UGT executive meetings, and although it was the pro-communist Pretel who raised the
issue, it rapidly became clear that even those members of the union
executive who were closest to Largo himself, such as José Díaz Alor
and Carlos Hernández Zancajo, were equally uncertain as to the
exact nature of the relationship between the UGT and the left
socialist ministers.[51] In November 1936, Hernández Zancajo
referred to the need to clarify whether or not the UGT was directly
represented in Largo's government, and, if so, then the executive

should insist that it be properly consulted over the policy decisions of the ministers concerned.[52] It seems unlikely that the question, in the terms in which it was formulated by the UGT's executive members, ever arose in the course of the formation of either of Largo's two governments. For Largo's patriarchal conception of the UGT doubtless extended to its executive committee. It was to himself, as prime minister of the national Republican government, that the left socialist ministers were responsible. Indeed, the comments made by Largo's secretary, Aguirre, in a letter to Araquistain would tend to suggest that there was no specific UGT mandate. 'Caballero called a joint meeting of the national leaderships of the political parties and unions present in government, *at which the UGT was also represented*'.[53] As general secretary of the UGT, Largo doubtless considered his leadership of the cabinet to be sufficient guarantee that government policies would not harm the union's interests.

Clearly then, from September 1936 onwards there was an ever increasing distance between the UGT executive and the prime minister. Within the cabinet, Largo was almost entirely isolated by the beginning of 1937. The aloofness of the reformist ministers associated with the Lamoneda executive – Prieto, Negrín and Anastasio de Gracia – compounded PSOE fragmentation.[54] Indeed the three reformist socialists tended to exercise their ministerial functions in isolation even from each other. Although Anastasio de Gracia had a capable and efficient under-secretary in Ramón Lamoneda, there was a lack of cooperation and solidarity between the three ministers, as the PSOE executive's appointees.[55] This was a direct result of the precarious state of the party leadership during the second half of 1936. Cut off from the support of the socialist movement as a whole – which could only have been channelled through a strong and confident executive – the reformist socialist ministers had little choice but to cope as best they could on an *ad hoc* basis.

To some degree, of course, the PSOE's dislocation was symptomatic of the general political situation in the loyalist zone. There was a serious lack of coordination between individual ministries and between central government and regional and local authorities. This damaged both the organisation of Republican military defence and the political administration of Republican territory. Nevertheless, the enduring fragmentation of the PSOE was the specific consequence of the internal dispute. In subjective terms, the bitter remoteness of the reformists from Largo's government is understandable. Their policies had been appropriated wholesale by an ideologically bankrupt socialist left. The net result, however, was the weakening of the PSOE as a whole, and not just of its left wing. During the first year of the war Prieto adopted a tactic which in essence consisted of waiting upon the political exhaustion of the left. Yet in so doing, he was emulating behaviour which he had severely criticised in the *Caballeristas*. For he was undermining the stability of the Republic in the pursuit of a partisan political vendetta.

4 Political realignments inside the socialist movement

The National Conference of the JSU

Once the Madrid front had been stabilised, the JSU executive, appointed in September 1936, established its headquarters in Valencia, which was to serve as the Republican capital until October 1937. The unified youth executive comprised eight communists and seven socialists and Santiago Carrillo was nominated as its general secretary.[1] From Valencia, this new, overwhelmingly pro-communist leadership undertook to consolidate its control over the unified youth organisation. Instrumental in this was the national youth conference, held in Valencia in mid-January 1937.[2] The conference, replacing the mooted national congress which had been made impossible by the outbreak of war, served by virtue both of its style and its content to crystallise dissident tendencies within the JSU. The conference format shocked and angered many socialists because it flew in the face of the movement's accepted traditions of internal democracy. All policy directives had been pre-arranged, there was little real discussion, and no voting took place. Both the new national committee and the executive committee were elected indirectly. Socialist hackles also rose at the general style of the conference. The PCE, employing what was to become one of its classic propaganda techniques, flooded the conference with telegrams and messages of goodwill, both from the Spanish sections and from international sympathisers. The overall impression created was that the PCE constituted the vital heart of the JSU.[3]

In his speech, 'En marcha hacia la victoria', general secretary Santiago Carrillo emphasised once again the nature of the new organisation as that of a mass youth movement for which the criterion of membership, beyond age, was an exceedingly ill-defined anti-fascism. This, for many socialists, was the unacceptable face of Popular Frontism. Largo Caballero, on more than one occasion, reminded the youth leaders that genuine youth unity had to be achieved on the basis of clearly defined political ideals held in

common, age was not a sufficient single common denominator.[4] The
new political philosophy was underlined by Santiago Carrillo who
used the factor of quantity itself to justify the new strategy:

> Much criticism has been levelled against the drive for members; many
> have been the voices raised against the new line, the line of the Commu-
> nist Youth International. But against all these negative pronouncements
> stand the figures themselves. They tell the real story: it is thanks to the
> new policy that our federation has been able to expand to such an extent,
> to develop its maximum potential.[5]

This was, of course, no justification but anathema in socialist eyes.
Greeted with equal dismay was the final objective of the new line,
which Carrillo went on to describe. This involved the creation of a
national youth alliance, the 'Alianza Juvenil Nacional', as an
umbrella organisation for all the youth organisations in the Republican zone. The ultimate intention, Carrillo stressed, was the creation
of a 'Federación Unica de la Juventud Española' (one united Spanish youth federation) which would extend as far as Catholic youth
organisations in order to achieve 'the unity of the youth of all nations
and all political tendencies'.[6] To more than a few socialists this
sounded suspiciously like a negation of their own *raison de guerre*; a
strategy which aimed at 'opposing' fascism by embracing it. The
inclusion of Catholic youth in this all-encompassing unity was a
cause for particular consternation, since, under the Republic, the
reactionaries of the mass Catholic party, CEDA – the PSOE's great
antagonists – were only outdone by their own youth movement, the
JAP.[7]

As a theoretical counterpoint to the concept of National Alliance,
the JSU leaders also sought in their speeches at the January 1937
youth conference to recast the image of the civil war as exclusively
one of national liberation against a foreign invader. The occupation
of the south, for example, and the reversing of the Republic's agrarian reform were explained not in the context of a military rebellion in
order to protect the economic interests of a national elite, but rather
as the result of the ravages of an invading, *foreign* army: 'We are
fighting to liberate those young people oppressed by the invaders'
yoke in the occupied areas of our *patria*.'[8] The vaguely delineated
'fascists' were seen as the enemies not of land reform but of the
smallholders whom they exploited and condemned to the clutches of
moneylenders.[9] Thus, the social and political reality of the south and
the central importance of collective land reform were being distorted
in order to fit the theoretical requirements of the Popular Front line.

Again, the contrast between the PSOE and the PCE could be

encapsulated in their differing attitudes towards the experience of 'desgaste' (erosion), suffered by the pre-war cadres of the FJS and UJC. Whereas the socialists closed inwards, the youth in this respect paralleling the adult party, the JSU national executive, like the PCE, accepted the appointment to leadership positions of very recent members who formed part of the massive influx after July 1936. The UJC leader Trifón Medrano bitterly criticised socialist sectarianism in his speech on the new structure of the JSU. 'Others, taking sectarianism to its extreme, have, since 19 July (1936), barred the doors of the youth organisation – doors which remain barred today.'[10] The JSU leadership, on the other hand, was prepared for the influx of the 'uneducated' both in the political and in the literal sense. Indeed Carrillo himself stated that the primary function of the new youth organisation was to be educational. Its most 'revolution-ary' and urgent task was to be the provision of a basic '3 R's' education in order to solve the problem of massive illiteracy. This was deemed to be far more important than any 'abstract' concept of revolution. With this in mind, the JSU sections were reminded that they ought to concentrate on those problems and issues which were of direct and practical relevance to Spanish youth, rather than on general party political issues.[11] These directives were designed to bridge the gap between old and new members, but the effect – if not the express intention also – would be to depoliticise the youth movement in Republican Spain.

During the youth conference in January 1937, the PCE's Popular Front line was reinforced by a succession of speeches from the executive members of the JSU. There could have been no clearer demonstration that the PCE was using the youth organisation to spearhead the implementation of Popular Frontism. The JSU leaders' speeches embraced not only youth matters but all aspects of frontist policy. The need to establish a centralised war economy was endorsed: with every utterance a further blow was dealt to the principles of collectivisation and worker control associated with the social revolution in the Republican zone. There was no longer any question of making a revolution or of instituting any kind of socialist experimentation. General secretary Carrillo, JSU executive member Segismundo Alvarez (formerly of the UJC executive) and Ignacio Gallego, JSU conference delegate for Jaén, all, to varying degrees, pointed out that radical social policies would alienate those middle class groups whose support was a condition of the Republic's vic-tory. The most important of these was the landholding peasantry, and the speeches of the JSU executive members provide the clearest indication of the policy decision which the PCE, or rather the

Comintern, had made to sacrifice agrarian reform to the needs of war as it perceived them.[12]

Segismundo Alvarez stressed the importance of creating rural 'shock brigades' as rapidly as possible to champion the cause of peasant smallholders against the collectives. These brigades, made up of young factory, office workers and students who had not yet been mobilised, had been operating in the rural areas of Republican Spain since September 1936.[13] They served to replace agricultural manpower lost through military mobilisation. But there was also a clear political objective. The shock brigades were designed to win over the smallholders to the PCE by a display of practical aid. The brigades publicised government policy and ensured that the small-holders knew their legal rights and were apprised of the availability of funds from the agriculture ministry for 'the subsidising of individual agricultural enterprises'. Alvarez even referred in January to the possibility of brigades being used forcibly to harvest crops on behalf of smallholders when the ownership of land was in dispute between individual smallholders and a collective.[14]

At the same time, however, the JSU leadership was having to fight to smother a sector within its own organisation which was strongly committed to the concepts of collectivisation and worker control:

> We must cleanse the minds of our young members of all the strange ideas they've latched onto. Because there are cases, in Jaén province for example, where our comrades have held meetings, decided to collectivise the land and have been very happy with themselves. But of course, no one opposed to collectivisation at such meetings felt able to voice their objections – for all the noise made by the enthusiasts . . .[15]

The critical current in the JSU, crystallised by the experience of the national youth conference, represented a resurgence of the FJS old guard, spearheaded by those young socialists who, formerly associated with Largo, had not been co-opted by the PCE. The same names occur repeatedly, for example in Carrillo's speeches of March and May 1937.[16] One leading dissident was Carlos Hernández Zancajo, the former FJS president and acting general secretary of the staunchly pro-Caballero urban transport federation. Hernández Zancajo had also co-authored *Octubre Segunda Etapa*, the bolshevisation blueprint published in 1935. Later in 1937 he was to raise the anti-stalinist standard with *Tercera Etapa de Octubre*, in which he arraigned the PCE as a political renegade and identified the socialist left with the struggle to re-establish a youth organisation with a marxist–leninist content. The youth dissidents would have an uphill task, however, not least because the JSU leadership was afforded valuable time to consolidate its administrative hold over the organisation in the months between the national conference in January and Santiago Carrillo's open declaration of JSU allegiance to the PCE in March 1937.[17]

Thus by 1937 the PSOE had lost the greatest single guarantee of its political future. Nor was it just a matter of numbers. The loss had serious qualitative implications. For the Socialists' youth movement had always been a training ground. In losing the FJS, the PSOE had effectively been deprived of a new generation of leaders. Moreover, the united youth organisation, although theoretically autonomous, was, in reality, subordinated to the political directives of the PCE.

It may be that problems would have arisen over the unity agreement even if the war had not occurred. What is certain is that the war created a series of quite exceptional circumstances which resulted in its conditions being bypassed.[18] The reality of the JSU represented a victory for the PCE. *Raison de guerre* could be used to justify the imposition of an ultra-centralised, hierarchical structure on the JSU. This initially acted as a straitjacket on the 'natural majority' within the organisation which was overwhelmingly socialist at the time of the unification. With the emergence of a mass organisation, however, by January 1937 the majority was no longer socialist, but was composed of the new members of the 'broad organisation of a new type'. The criticism which grew up within the JSU in 1937 took as one of its main arguments the betrayal of the unity agreement by the communists. To a certain extent this was valid in that a unification congress was never held and the power of the executive was increased at the expense of that of the provincial leaderships and the rank and file. What the socialist critics nevertheless neglected to take into account was the consequence of the mass influx into the organisation. This would have had the effect of giving the PCE *carte blanche* even if there had existed a measure of internal democracy. For, by January 1937, the PCE was genuinely able to claim that the majority in the JSU was in favour of its wartime policies. JSU total membership at the time of the merger had been in the region of 50,000. By the beginning of 1937, however, the numbers for the JSU in Madrid province alone were being given as 40,000, comprising 270 groups. By March 1937 it was estimated that 250,000 members of the youth organisation had been incorporated into military units of the Republican army and that this corresponded to 70 per cent of the JSU's total membership. So in general terms there is evidence of a successful swamping action.[19]

The imposition of a democratic centralist structure on the JSU had the effect of gagging youth socialist opposition in the organisation. For the dissident 'old' young socialists, the power of the

Bolshevik spell was finally broken. The experience of youth unity provided first-hand experience of the stalinist phenomenon, 'being a communist . . . means *both* a doctrine and a set of tactics'.[20] But an understanding of what the Popular Front line meant for the 'party of the revolution' had come too late. Democratic centralism removed their right to a critical voice. Those socialist dissidents who were beginning to formulate criticism in the first months of 1937, established a line which closely resembled that of the dissident communists, united in the war as the POUM. Just as surely as the *Poumistas* were vilified as the arch enemies of proletarian unity, so the left socialist dissidents in the JSU were accused of irresponsible sectarianism. Indeed the fate of both groups was determined by a single stalinist imperative. The flooding of a politically conscious youth movement with lumpenproletarian elements was a perfect means of neutralising inconvenient ideological inflexibility. The swamping of the Socialist Youth's 'old guard', like the purge of the anti-stalinist POUM in the Republican zone, was clearly linked to the destruction of the Bolshevik old guard in the Moscow trials. Nothing was to stand in the way of the Popular Front as the crux of the Soviet Union's defence-oriented foreign policy. By the end of the civil war, many Spanish socialists, surveying the political wreckage not just of the Republic but of the Spanish socialist movement in particular, would come to realise not only that the PSOE had lost its youth movement to another party at the beginning of the war, but also that the political potential of a generation of class-conscious youth had been neutralised by the stalinist bureaucracy of the PCE.[21]

By the end of February 1937, Largo Caballero's isolation in the government was giving his political and military secretary, José María Aguirre, great cause for concern.[22] This isolation was manifest in cabinet sessions where republicans, communists and reformist socialists, as representatives of the political parties of the Popular Front, acted increasingly in concert. As a result, the CNT's political ambitions were also on the increase, as their certainty grew that sooner or later Largo and the UGT would have to come to an agreement with them. The emergence of the Popular Front bloc in the cabinet and the resulting isolation of the socialist left also convinced the CNT that in any future discussions for a pact they would be negotiating from a position of superior strength.[23]

The Genesis of the PSOE–PCE Joint Committees

The cabinet alliance of reformist socialists and communists outlined above emerged from and was consolidated by the PSOE–PCE joint committee initiative first mooted at the end of 1936. The wartime collaboration between the PSOE executive and the PCE dates from 26 December 1936 when Lamoneda contacted the politburo to propose that a joint action committee be formed.[24] Publicly, the PSOE's general secretary argued that practical collaboration between both the socialist and communist leaderships and their respective rank and files in order to maximise the efficiency of the war effort was an essential precondition of Republican victory. Privately, however, Lamoneda was seeking an alliance to reinforce the PSOE executive in its battle against the party left. As a result of Lamoneda's proposal, an initial meeting was held on 5 January 1937. After this the Lamoneda executive published its first circular to the PSOE base since its election. This was dispatched on 6 January and appeared the following day in *El Socialista*. On the face of things it was a document singularly lacking in controversy. It reminded members that the national executive was now located in Valencia and stated that, as a result of the exceptional circumstances of the war, conversations had been initiated with the PCE with a view to coordinating practical action. Equally the executive reminded its sections that all grass roots initiatives of fusion or cooperation with the communist base were, however well-intentioned, to cease until such time as a national agreement was reached between the two parties.

For the Lamoneda executive, this circular constituted the first stage of its recovery strategy. The strategy had a dual objective. It was designed to end the period of executive eclipse by re-establishing the committee's control over the socialist rank and file throughout the loyalist zone. Secondly, it was to end the period of 'confusionismo', that is the *caballerista*-inspired, uncontrolled fusion of socialist and communist sections, union groups and party press.[25] These had occurred in the immediate aftermath of the military coup in areas where the party left was strong, and predominantly in Madrid and the Levante provinces. By making its own approach to the PCE at a national level, the Lamoneda executive was thereby hoping to reassert its authority over the party, to secure control over the socialist rank and file in order to stop it from trickling into the PCE in *caballerista* areas. This initiative extended to the socialist union groups in the UGT. The challenge posed by the PCE to socialist dominance in the UGT was clearly perceived by the PSOE.[26] The executive's newspaper, *El Socialista*, repeatedly directed all socialists to join their appropriate union group and to activate them in order to raise the PSOE's profile.[27] All mergers between socialist and communist union groups were naturally forbidden, although joint committees were to be established between the respective union fractions throughout the Republican zone, in accordance with Lamoneda's new policy.[28] By tightening its links with the PSOE union fractions and by attempting to consolidate their strength, the Lamoneda executive had a dual objective. Not only was the PCE to be kept at bay in the UGT, but the *Caballeristas'* monopoly of control in the union federation was also to be challenged. The PSOE executive's determination to reclaim a power base in the UGT is implied in many of *El Socialista*'s spring 1937 editorials. For example, it was the clear message behind the slogan, 'The labour movement needs its political engine as much as the Socialist Party needs its union base.'[29]

By initiating his own carefully controlled approach to the PCE based on the practical needs of the war effort, Lamoneda was hoping to isolate the *Caballeristas* and to impose party discipline on the socialist rank and file, in accordance with the mandate to restore internal party unity granted to his executive at the May 1936 national committee meeting. 'Unity of action' with the PCE was thus to be instrumental both in securing internal discipline in the party and in re-establishing the authority of the national executive.

The leading *Caballeristas*, who were themselves far from happy with the rash of grass roots unity initiatives which threatened their own control over the socialist rank and file, were immediately aware of the Lamoneda executive's intentions. This was apparent from a letter which the party left published in *Claridad* on 6 January 1937. The text – unexceptional in itself as a call to working-class unity, both of parties and unions, in the face of fascist aggression – took on a specific significance in the context of the internal dispute. The left was well able to interpret the message behind the national executive's circular: namely that it was not prepared to capitulate before Largo and the ASM. The experience of the first six months of the war had given the PSOE left very good reason to suppose that the Lamoneda executive – barely elected when the military rose – had in fact conceded defeat before the ascendancy of the left socialists in government. Such had been the executive's passivity when based in Madrid that it had given the impression of being defunct.

Clearly the fact that the party left had been called upon to form a government instead of Indalecio Prieto damaged the socialist executive's prestige and authority and put it at a disadvantage in the context of the party dispute. Its silence had not gone unnoticed: the left referred to the 'ejecutiva silenciosa'. Largo's appointment as prime minister exacerbated the pessimism of the reformist leader. The Prieto of legendary energies withdrew into his ministerial responsibilities. Lamoneda's explanation of this period of extreme passivity as entirely the result of Prieto's influence may seem somewhat simplistic. However, testimonies abound that during this period the executive committee was entirely Prieto's creature.[30] Lamoneda had been hand-picked to wage Prieto's war against the left within the party organisation. Moreover, it is undeniable that the executive's recovery began, as Lamoneda indicated, after the move to Valencia when the ties with Prieto were loosened as a result of his heavy ministerial commitments.

The *Caballeristas*' response to the PSOE executive's circular took the form of the *Claridad* letter of 6 January 1937. Signed by all their leading lights – from political commissars to provincial federation and union leaders to left socialist deputies – it constituted a veritable marshalling of the troops.[31] However, the text revealed the *Caballeristas*' weakness now that a war was being fought. They could not, in such circumstances, openly declare themselves to be opposed to the principle of unity with the PCE. They had been caught out and effectively gagged by a powerful abstraction – that unity equalled strength – and at the beginning of 1937 that was an argument which carried enormous weight with grass roots socialists everywhere. The difficulties for the left were compounded by the fact that the party executive was now taking up the line of unity of action. In a somewhat veiled fashion, however, the left did effectively declare itself to be opposed to the unification of the socialist and communist parties during the war. It declared that all *loyal* fusion – an adjective used with increasing frequency by both left and reformist socialist leaders when referring to the PCE's ever more aggressive methods of proselytism – would naturally have to be in accordance with the 'democratic norms' by which the PSOE had always been governed. By this the *Caballeristas* were in effect saying no unification without the approval of a full party congress. Since they were already well aware of the PSOE executive's view that such congresses were not feasible during the war, this was tantamount to declaring that there could be no unification between the Socialists and Communists until the war was over.

The *Caballeristas*' control of considerable sections of the PSOE base, however, was an important factor in the PCE's calculations. The Lamoneda executive saw itself obliged to accede to the PCE's request that the UGT, as representative of a significant body of socialist opinion, be represented at the unity of action discussions between the parties.[32]

The reason for the delay between the formation of the PSOE–PCE Comité Nacional de Enlace (national joint committee), and the final

agreement in April 1937 to establish a network of joint party committees at a provincial and local level throughout the loyalist zone,
was given by both parties as the blocking action mounted by the
UGT representatives. The latter consistently sought to procure an
agreement which would limit the national committee's activities to
drafting the basis of a plan for national social and economic reconstruction in the post-war period.[33] The PCE went as far as accusing
the UGT of sabotaging the initiative while it went casting around in
search of an alternative alliance with the CNT.[34] However, violent
clashes between anarchist and socialist trade union militants were
severely handicapping initiatives in that direction.[35] The Lamoneda
executive was also clear that the UGT leadership was attempting to
come to some sort of agreement with the CNT. This only confirmed
its belief that the left's new-found hostility to the PCE was motivated
by the most blatant opportunism.[36] Thus it would be without UGT
approval or involvement that the two joint committee circulars of 15
and 24 April 1937 were published. These established the principle of
a national network of joint committees and laid the procedural
ground rules. Decisions were to be based on unanimous agreement.
There would be no system of voting.

Not only was the UGT left behind by the PSOE–PCE agreement
at national level, as embodied in the 15 April circular, but also by
several provincial declarations announcing the formation of joint
committees which pre-empted the national declaration itself. Joint
committees were announced first in Madrid and Albacete on 10 and
31 March respectively and then in Valencia, Córdoba, Jaén, Granada and Alicante.[37] At this stage both the *Caballeristas* and the
reformists were to some extent caught up by the wave of popular
enthusiasm for unity, so the creation of the joint committees at the
base was the work of communists and socialists right across the party
spectrum.

For the time being then, the *Caballeristas* were at a considerable
disadvantage. As always, the socialist leadership's reluctance over
unity stemmed from a desire to protect its organisations. But the
pressure to unite the PSOE and the PCE in the war period was much
greater than ever before. The situation was much more difficult for
the Socialists to deal with because the argument being wielded
publicly by the PCE in its propaganda was such a convincing one
with a wide popular appeal.[38] In the context of 1930s Europe, with
the onslaught of fascism abroad, and indeed at home, it was very
difficult for any Spanish socialist to make a case publicly against
unity. But for both wings of the PSOE, the conviction remained
uppermost that the PCE's enthusiasm for unity was motivated

primarily by its need to acquire a mass base and its recognition that the PSOE controlled such masses.[39] And indeed by late March 1937 an awareness of PCE sectarianism and post-hunting was beginning to damage relations between socialist and communist cadres in Madrid – one of the first places where a joint party committee had been formed.[40]

The PCE was also contacting Largo Caballero's civil governors in an attempt to secure their support for the fusion of the Socialist and Communist parties. The left socialists knew of these attempts because sympathetic civil governors had reported back. Doubts were thus cast on the loyalty of those civil governors who did not make mention of any such approaches – as in the cases of Alicante and Murcia.[41] Largo himself had had his fingers well and truly burned over the disastrous youth unification. Albeit at tremendous cost, the lesson had been learned. When the Soviet ambassador Marcel Rosenberg insinuated that Largo ought to use his influence to bring about the unification of the two parties, the response was an immensely shrewd one. Largo pointed out that although he was prime minister, within the PSOE's structure he was nothing more than an ordinary party member. If Rosenberg had proposals to make concerning unification, then he ought to address himself to the national executive committee.[42] The *Caballeristas* were also aware that the PCE, via its local and provincial committees, was pressurising local socialist organisations to turn the joint party committees into a pro-unification exercise. The communists in Albacete were trying to force the preparation of a joint provincial congress with the intention of pushing through a unity agreement while a propitious political atmosphere existed.[43] Equally, the communist union groups operating inside the UGT's industrial federations, the so-called Grupos de la Oposición Sindical Revolucionaria (GOSR), were bringing ever-increasing pressure to bear on their socialist counterparts, (Grupos Sindicales Socialistas (GSS)), in individual factories and workplaces to merge as a preliminary step to full union and party unification. In fact, under the terms of the communist trade union's (CGTU) reincorporation into the UGT in December 1935, the GOSR ought to have been dissolved.[44] But this simply never occurred. It was mounting evidence of this kind of coercive pressure which fuelled the socialist left's hostility to the Communists during the first year of the civil war. In general, relations between the GSS and GOSR deteriorated as the tensions between socialists and communists in the UGT's industrial federations increased. In Alicante, for example, where the composition of the teachers' federation (FETE) reflected the communist predominance in the union nationally, the GSS was bitterly opposed to the GOSR, mirroring the split in the provincial federation as a whole. Largo Caballero was personally outraged at what he saw as the PCE's no-holds-barred exploitation of the exceptional circumstances of the war, and the premium which this put on proletarian unity, in order to absorb the socialist party and union base wholesale. Indeed, it was Largo's absolute opposition to the 'partido único' (single class party) and, above all, his determination to exclude the PCE from the hierarchy of the UGT which lay at the root of the Communist Party's subsequent campaign against him as prime minister.

The Lamoneda executive itself also had a very difficult task on its hands in attempting to contain and control the socialist base's relations with the PCE by imposing the joint committees and via these its own authority. Reformist anger, directed against the *Caballeristas*, was constantly mounting. It had been the left's 'indiscipline' or 'irresponsibility', as the Lamoneda executive viewed it, that had set the irrevocable precedent of unity in the youth movement. This had robbed the PSOE leadership of all choice in the matter of its relations with the PCE during the war. For Lamoneda and the other members of the national executive, arriving in Valencia in November 1936 after the evacuation of Madrid had been a massive shock. They had been confronted by the spectacle of the socialist grass roots engaging in uncontrolled and unauthorised unity initiatives with the PCE. The ensuing confusion, which was seen as a threat to the very existence of the PSOE, had jolted Lamoneda into action, hence the approach to the PCE and the January circular to the party rank and file. Equally, the reformists' anger had strengthened their resolve to purge the left, whose previous policies were held to be the root cause of the severe organisational dislocation in the PSOE.[45]

But the smooth course of the Lamoneda executive's joint committee policy was to be very short lived. Within a month of the initial agreement, the May 1937 cabinet crisis – which provoked Largo's ejection from government – and the subsequent PCE campaign against him, would result in many local and several provincial joint committees being suspended by the socialist members – as would be the case in Madrid, Valencia and Alicante. The joint committee in Ciudad Real was only renewed again in January 1938, to be re-suspended the following April as a result of Indalecio Prieto's resignation from the government. Indeed by July 1937 it would be clear that the fragility of the joint committees and their frequent suspensions were directly linked to the socialist base's negative daily experience of unity of action. The national crises – Largo's departure from government, the PCE's press campaign against him, Prieto's resignation, accounts of PCE aggression directed at socialist militants at the front – to list only the most obvious examples, functioned as triggers for the socialist base's growing hostility to the PCE.

By July 1937 the Lamoneda executive would be reflecting, to a certain extent, the mood of the party rank and file. A gradual shift in emphasis was apparent regarding the function of the joint committees. The socialist executive began to stress their value as arbitration committees where complaints could be settled amicably and compromise solutions devised. In short, the committees were to act as a kind of safety valve. Equally it would be made clear by the PSOE executive that the policy of maintaining the committees had to be followed by the party base. That Lamoneda had made a fundamental error of judgement in demanding this would become clear during the discussion on unity at the July 1937 PSOE national committee meeting in Valencia.[46]

Lamoneda still had it uppermost in his mind that socialist protests against the joint committees and the frequent suspensions of these by the PSOE's representatives were not solely the result of the fragility of socialist–communist relations at the local and provincial level. Lamoneda accepted that tensions and disputes between socialists and communists did result from rivalries over civil and military appointments and from the PCE's very high profile and aggressive recruitment policy.[47] Nevertheless, he suspected the party left of seeking demagogically to exploit the growing differences between the PCE and PSOE rank and files with the aim of isolating the PSOE executive from its own grass roots, thereby regaining control of the party. The fact that the crisis of the joint committees was particularly acute in Valencia province, which was controlled until late July 1937 by a *caballerista* federal executive, only confirmed Lamoneda in his views. And it is certainly true that by the middle of 1937 the socialist left lobby was attempting to use grass roots hostility to the PCE to oblige Lamoneda to grant them representation on the PSOE's national executive.[48] Lamoneda's repeated references to the days when the same sort of sectarian aggression was *caballerista*-inspired and directed against fellow socialists also reveal his cynical view of the PSOE left. Specifically mentioned by the general secretary was the infamous incident which had occurred at the height of the pre-war internal dispute at Ecija (Seville) on 31 May 1936. There, for the second time in the space of a week, Prieto and Ramón González Peña had been prevented from addressing a meeting which was violently disrupted by pro-Caballero members of the JSU.[49] This sort of behaviour, still remembered vividly by the reformists, removed from the left socialists, *a priori*, the right to complain about communist harassment or to criticise the policy of the party executive.

For exactly the same reasons Lamoneda refused to condone, much less support, socialist dissidence in the JSU. Ironically, the PCE's Popular Front volte-face and its effects on the political perspective of the socialist youth leadership had resulted in a remarkable improve-ment in the relations between the PSOE's reformist executive and the one-time radicals of the FJS.[50] In the early stages of the war it seemed almost as if the reformist socialists believed that the reality of youth unification had turned out to be a small price to pay for ensuring the removal of the FJS from the *caballerista* orbit. Moreover, because the 'visible head' of socialist dissidence in the JSU was *caballerista*, Lamoneda feared that, once again, the youth organis-ation was being manipulated by the party left to create difficulties for the PSOE reformists. But this time it was, inexcusably, in the middle of a war in which the Republic's very survival depended on the unity and strength of the socialist movement. Moreover, it was clearly Lamoneda's own conviction that since members of the CNT had also been responsible for the assassination of socialists in a number of incidents, then the socialist left's targeting of the PCE was largely motivated by an opportunistic desire to continue opposing the PSOE executive.[51] In reality, however, the *Caballeristas'* hostility to the PCE had another more obvious source. Keenly aware of the fact that the PCE coveted the socialist base, the left's hostility in the war period sprang from its appalled discovery that aggressive PCE proselytism, coupled with socialist fragmentation, was causing a serious erosion of the PSOE rank and file.

It was the issue of socialist–communist unification which revealed the internal fragmentation of the *caballerista* power base in the UGT. The personal allegiance to Largo Caballero of *ugetista* leaders such as Carlos Hernández Zancajo (general secretary of the urban transport federation), was strengthened by the fact that they too were battling against the PCE in order to retain control of their own union hierarchies. In contrast, those like Amaro del Rosal, who had been attracted by Largo's apparent enthusiasm for unity with the Com-munist Party, withdrew their support once his underlying hostility to the PCE became overt.

However, there were PSOE reformists who had serious reserva-tions about Lamoneda's exclusive interpretation of rank-and-file discontent. The sort of incidents they related provide the raw material for an analysis of what happens when a stalinist communist party sets out to turn itself from a cadre to a mass party as rapidly as possible. Rafael Henche, for example, as president of Madrid's provincial socialist federation and a national leader of the bakers and confectioners' union, (Artes Blancas), was perfectly placed to observe PCE techniques in action. He identified a major part of the problem when he referred to 'old' and 'new' communists to illustrate the severe conflicts being provoked by the PCE's aggressive sectarianism, evident in its single-minded determination to capture as many positions as possible in the union leaderships at both local and provincial level. The PCE had been particularly active in the Madrid unions, which led to very violent scenes at meetings in the Casa del Pueblo.[52] Henche also referred more generally to the constant stream of complaints about PCE provocation received by the war ministry's office in Madrid. Although there were some more sinister incidents involving the political assassination of socialists, in the majority of cases it was not a matter of spectacular violence or persecution, but rather of a hundred petty tyrannies. Often it was the case that the former lackeys of the rich and powerful, the minions of the local political bosses (*caciques*) who had flourished before the Republic – in general opportunists from a variety of dubious political backgrounds – surfaced again during the war as card-carrying members of the PCE. Party membership having afforded them some degree of power, they would then proceed to make life intolerable for their socialist subordinates.[53] The climate of tension thus produced was revealed in Antonio Llaneza's comments at the PSOE national committee meeting in July 1937: '. . . the PCE is persecuting socialist militants like any vulgar *cacique*. Those who were to the right of Sánchez Román are today swelling the ranks of the P.C. In Asturias the socialist and communist rank and files are in head-on collision – a situation which, apart from the 1925 split, is unprecedented.'[54] By 1938, brigades of the Servicio de Investigación Militar (SIM), supposedly a counter-espionage service, were also known to have carried off PSOE documentation which included the minutes of party meetings.[55] By July 1937, expressing doubts about the wisdom of Lamoneda's determination to enforce the joint committees as a test of the socialist base's party discipline, Henche argued, prophetically, that it would be impossible to impose such a policy for long.[56] However well-intentioned the ultimate objective, it was tantamount to playing into the hands of the left socialists – the very thing Lamoneda himself was so committed to avoiding.

The impact of the civil war had thus precipitated a series of realignments in the socialist movement. These had already been implicit, however, in political developments before the war. By April 1937, the PSOE executive had sealed a formal alliance with the PCE. This initiative was the logical outcome of the common commitment of both groups to the Popular Front – a commitment evident since the spring of 1936. But practical cooperation between the PSOE and the PCE became absolutely essential after July. The severe erosion suffered by the centrist republican groups had made a viable Republican war effort entirely dependent on Popular Front unity.

Ramón Lamoneda also saw the joint committee agreement as a useful weapon against the socialist left. The *Caballeristas*, for their part, still aspired to control the PSOE. But the reformists' determination to neutralise the party left had been redoubled because they saw the *Caballeristas* as the sole authors of the organisational havoc which had fragmented the PSOE and delivered up the socialist youth to the PCE.

The rapidity with which the youth organisation had been subjected to communist party discipline was mainly the result of the political loyalties of its leaders. In the JSU the PCE found both the spearhead of its Popular Front strategy and a fertile area for mass recruitment to the party. But the growing evidence of PCE control in the JSU crystallised a dissident socialist current in the organisation by the spring of 1937. Its leaders were old guard socialists who had not been co-opted by the Communist Party. As the isolation of the left socialists increased, they drew closer to the youth dissidents whose violent hostility to the Communist Party they shared. The *Caballeristas* – both young and old – were reacting, if belatedly, to the PCE's determined drive to absorb the socialist rank and file.

Faced with the PSOE left's startling about-turn – from intense pro-communism to vitriolic and public criticism of the PCE in little over six months – Lamoneda saw opportunism as the only possible explanation for such extreme political inconsistency. Aware of the *Caballeristas'* designs on the party leadership, the PSOE executive took the view that they had alighted on anti-communism as an increasingly popular platform which would facilitate the mobilisation of grass roots support against Lamoneda's policies.

In much the same way, the reformists viewed the left socialists' overtures to the CNT in the first quarter of 1937 as an opportunistic manoeuvre designed to sabotage the joint party committee strategy – then under discussion – precisely because it posed a threat to the political pre-eminence of the *Caballeristas*. An examination of the relations between the socialist left and the CNT, however, reveals that Lamoneda and his party colleagues had little real cause for concern. Ironically, not even the concerted attack of the Popular Front bloc of reformist socialists, communists and republicans would be sufficient to overcome the traditional enmities between the two great trade union organisations.

5 The socialist left: crisis and collapse

UGT–CNT Relations: The Failure of Unity

Relations between the two union federations during the civil war were characterised by the same sort of difficulties, arising both from organisational rivalries and ideological differences, which had marked, and indeed marred, their relations in the pre-war period. The history of Spanish anarchism during the war years is the history of massive internal crisis and debilitation provoked by the gradual abandoning of anarchism's central tenet – namely its rejection of parliamentary politics. Inside the anarchist movement, and particularly within the FAI, an enormous gulf developed between the purists and *políticos* such as Horacio Prieto, Juan Peiró, Juan López and Cardona Rosell. The latter evolved towards a positive acceptance of creating a political party within the CNT, which would thus enable the organisation to share in state power.[1] 'It is thus our view that, in contrast to our previous separatist tradition, it is now the duty of all anarchists to accept functions in as many state institutions and bodies as need be to ensure the consolidation of the new political order.'[2] The supporters of Horacio Prieto and the *políticos* were concentrated in the national committee of the CNT and in the regional federations of the CNT for the North, Asturias and the Levante. The leadership of the purist opposition was concentrated above all in Cataluña. In the Peninsular Committee of the FAI, in its Catalan federation, in the Catalan federation of the CNT and in the anarchist youth federation (FIJL) in Cataluña.

However, in respect of the relationship between the CNT and the leadership of the UGT, far more important than this ideological crisis as a conditioning factor, were the tensions which derived from organisational rivalries. If anything, the ascendancy of the *políticos* should have reduced the political distance between the CNT and the UGT. Nevertheless, organisational tensions were ever present. In the early stages of the war, when the power of the committees was at its peak, there were numerous incidents between *ugetistas* and *cenetistas* in various areas of the loyalist zone, some of which escalated into serious and violent confrontations. This was particularly the case in Barcelona, Valencia and Málaga where internecine union warfare caused the deaths of labour leaders and militants in both urban and rural areas. There were disputes over collectivisation and rivalries between collectives in the Levante and Aragón. In Barcelona the situation became so severe that the UGT's national executive sent a delegation to investigate both the disappearance of socialist party and union members and the circumstances which had led to the ransacking of the UGT headquarters in the city.[3] It is in this context of considerable tension at the grass roots that one must view the emergence of the first national non-aggression pact of the war period between the unions, signed in November 1936.[4] Undoubtedly Largo felt the need for some kind of agreement at union level to consolidate his strategy of bringing the anarchists into the government sphere, to involve them, indeed literally to compromise them, in policy decisions. This was especially important in that the central government had transferred to Valencia which was considered alien territory where the anarchists were strong.[5] Yet relations between the two union leaderships remained difficult despite the pact. Continued clashes between *ugetistas* and *cenetistas* and what the Largo leadership claimed was an extremely lax membership policy on the part of the CNT did not facilitate *rapprochement*.[6]

By March 1937, however, the growing political crisis in the cabinet and Largo's isolation therein brought the UGT seriously to consider the possibility of an inter-union alliance. The fall of the strategic port of Málaga to the Nationalists early in February increased the tension in the cabinet where more vocal opposition to Largo's control of the war effort was beginning to be expressed. The opposition to Largo focused first on his under-secretary of war, General Asensio, against whom the PCE launched a vitriolic campaign accusing him of both incompetence and treachery. As relations deteriorated rapidly between the prime minister and the Communists, Largo was forced to turn towards the CNT in search of much-needed support. Although, in reality, the CNT was no keener on Asensio than was the PCE. The CNT, for its part, had revived its proposals for an Alianza Obrera Revolucionaria at the beginning of 1937, adducing the growing closeness of the PSOE and the PCE and the joint party committees as proof of the urgent need for such an alliance.[7]

As always, however, the UGT leadership's conception was a negative, defensive one. It was interested in a pact because of the protection it could offer against the growing hostility of the 'political bloc' of socialists, communists and republicans. The libertarians' evident confidence that the UGT's left socialist leadership would ultimately have no choice but to come to an understanding with the CNT – if for no other reason than out of a sense of self-preservation – did nothing to lessen the *Caballeristas'* resistance. The UGT executive's reluctance to take an active part in the negotiations between the PSOE and the PCE – which led to the formation of the joint party committees without the approval or participation of the UGT – had been cited by the communist and socialist party leaderships as proof that the UGT executive was deliberately delaying the proceedings while it sought to reach an agreement with the CNT.[8] But, ironically, not even the concerted onslaught of the PSOE and PCE was sufficient to enable the UGT and CNT to bridge their considerable differences in order to sign a political pact with teeth – such as the libertarians envisaged in the Alianza Obrera Revolucionaria.[9] There would be no formal agreement signed between the UGT and CNT until July 1937, by which time, as we will see, the socialist left had been consigned to the political wilderness and it was too late to exploit the defensive potential of an inter-union pact.

The PSOE executive's conviction that there neither existed nor ever had existed an ideological division between itself and the *caballerista* leadership was considerably reinforced by its observation of Largo's policy decisions between September 1936 and May 1937.[10] Undoubtedly the prime minister's innate pragmatism had been substantially reinforced by the series of grave militia defeats in the south during August 1936, and, most specifically, by the bloody massacre at Badajoz in the middle of that month. The pressing need to halt the rebel advance made the militarisation of the militia and the building of a regular, hierarchical army, if a 'popular' one, almost inevitable. Accordingly, Largo's policy options were, across the board, those of the reformist socialists. Indeed, in 1939, Largo would defend the PSOE's relations with the JSU during the war, adducing as the benefits so derived the fact that its militants had acted as a brake on anarchist strength and had also contributed to the consolidation of central state power and the building of a regular army.[11] During the war Largo's foreign policy – based as it was on the need to convince the French, and therefore the British government, actively to support the Republic – also attested to his desire to reconstruct and maintain the bourgeois democratic structure of the Republic, like any reformist socialist. Likewise, the innate conservatism of the trade union bureaucrat was manifest in his determination to rebuild the central state power, to nationalise and centralise the control of industry and to limit the extent of collectivisation by decree.

Largo's correspondence all reflects his reformism and his defence of the Popular Front option. In his letter to the British trade union leader, Ben Tillett, in August 1936, he emphasised that the Socialists were fighting for the victory of democracy but that it was not their objective to establish a socialist society. In an interview with the journalist Charles Reichmann he insisted that the constititution of a purely socialist government had never been the order of the day.[12] However, most significant in the Spanish context was an exchange of letters with the veteran anarchist, Federico Urales, in February 1937.[13] The essential condition of victory, Largo stressed, was discipline on both the military and civilian fronts. The only command which had to be obeyed was that of the national government. Like prime minister Juan Negrín after him, Largo was also striving to achieve for the central government supreme control of political, economic and military affairs throughout the Republican zone. And for Largo this meant using the UGT's national industrial federations as the main instrument for implementing nationalisation.[14] And like Negrín too, he was prepared to confront opposition from the regions in the pursuit of this objective.

On 1 February 1937, in his speech to the Cortes, Largo emphatically set his face against the legacy of the revolution, declaring, 'enough of revolutionary experimentation' ('ya se ha ensayado bastante'). Yet the collectivisation initiatives, especially in that area of the south still controlled by the Republic, were as much socialist-inspired and run as they were anarchist.[15] Largo's unequivocally and unalterably reformist leadership between September 1936 and May 1937, was responsible for severely undermining the projects of the socialist landworkers federation (FNTT), for the thoroughgoing consolidation of agrarian collectivisation in the civil war. Unlike the FNTT – which during the period of the Second Republic had constituted the militant nucleus of *caballerismo* as a phenomenon of mass radicalisation – Largo never seriously took issue with the communist agriculture minister, Vicente Uribe, whose agrarian policies harmed socialist collectives as much as anarchist ones. Throughout some fifteen hundred pages of Largo's political memoirs, there is scant reference to the issue of land reform and none to the FNTT's battle to preserve its collectives.[16]

The growing struggle between Largo and the PCE in the later part of 1936 and the early months of 1937, was largely a result of the considerable and increasing pressure being exerted upon the prime minister to bring about the unification of the Socialist and Communist Parties. Popular Frontism itself, in its extra-parliamentary dimension, had created an unprecedented opportunity for communist parties in general to compete on an equal basis with other, better established working-class parties and organisations which were numerically stronger. The PCE's campaign for a united front from below in the period immediately preceding the frontist about-turn, had certainly facilitated the party's advance by reversing the usual balance of political power as based on size and parliamentary and union influence. However, with the military rising, revolution and civil war, so extreme was the situation created in Spain that the PCE saw its chance to press forward immediately, using the considerable rank-and-file enthusiasm for working-class unity in order to achieve the amalgamation of the PSOE and the PCE in a single class party. The resolution in favour of the *partido único* was passed at the PCE's central committee plenum in Valencia in March 1937. Both the PCE and its Comintern advisers were of the opinion that such was the 'climate of unity' in 1936 that neither the bureaucratic preoccupations nor the organisational jealousies of the socialist leadership would be able to withstand their push for unification. Accordingly, both Vittorio Codovila (Medina), the Comintern's representative in Spain, and Marcel Rosenberg, the Soviet ambassador, employed their best efforts – the latter always assiduously accompanied by Alvarez del Vayo in the somewhat superfluous capacity of interpreter.[17] But this was all to no avail. Neither Stalin's letters nor his personal entreaty that the class parties be unified served to move Largo.[18]

The crisis of Largo's government was latent both in the cabinet and in the streets by the beginning of February 1937. On the fourteenth, just after the fall of Málaga, a demonstration organised by the UGT's provincial secretariat in Valencia in support of the prime minister was neutralised by a PCE-inspired swamping action which shifted the emphasis to that of a general display of support for the government's war effort.[19] The Communists were intensifying their attack on Asensio, Largo's under-secretary of war, as the first stage in the isolation of the prime minister.[20] Although it is also the case that the CNT, UGT, Prieto and the left republicans were all equally critical of Asensio during the war.[21] As a result of this pressure, by the end of February 1937 Largo had performed a kind of judgement of Solomon. Having angrily ejected Rosenberg from his office and berated del Vayo for lending himself to the machinations of the Soviet ambassador, the prime minister replaced Asensio with Carlos de Baraibar.[22]

In Valencia relations between socialists and communists were extremely difficult. There had been a very rapid distancing since 18 July 1936. As PCE pressure on Largo increased this was inevitable, given that the Valencian federation was the organisational bulwark of the socialist left. One immediate casualty of the deterioration in relations was the province's 'unity' newspaper, *Verdad*, which, from the outbreak of the war until the beginning of February 1937, had been produced jointly by socialist and communist editorial staff. The break was provoked by tensions between the UGT and PCE in Valencia. Relations between the two had been worsening ever since the PCE had created the Federación Provincial Campesina (Provincial Peasants' Federation) in October 1936.[23] The socialist land-workers' federation (FNTT), particularly, saw this as evidence of the Communists' blatant political opportunism and it accused the PCE of deliberately feeding the fears of small independent farmers over the extent of future collectivisation for its own political profit. As a result of these tensions, by the beginning of February 1937 separate socialist and communist provincial newspapers were being published – respectively *Adelante* and *Frente Rojo*.[24]

The fragmentation of the left socialist representation in the cabinet highlighted Largo's political isolation. Del Vayo's estrangement from both wings of the PSOE was total. He was also publicly subjected to Prieto's verbal abuse during a mid-February 1937 cabinet session when the latter launched an attack on him for his pro-Soviet ministerial policy. The result of this was a 'stage' resignation which Alvarez del Vayo subsequently withdrew.[25] The series of interviews Largo conducted at the end of the month with the various groups represented in the government reflected the tensions which had surfaced after the fall of Málaga.[26] Largo's tactic consisted of confronting his ministers and especially the PCE's representatives, Jesus Hernández and Vicente Uribe, with the question of their confidence in him and of their willingness to continue supporting him fully. Protestations of absolute loyalty were made across the board on 26 February. However, in a cabinet session the following day, Giral of Izquierda Republicana criticised Largo for publishing a statement on the political situation without consulting the cabinet.[27] His criticism was taken up by the communist ministers and so there began the gradual process of undermining the president's authority. By the time of the May cabinet crisis it became clear that the PCE and the republican parties had, in their joint opposition to Largo, been working consciously in tandem. It was José Giral who informed President Azaña of the PCE's views.[28] Moreover, when the PSOE executive members, Jerónimo Bugeda and Juan Simeón Vidarte went to the PCE's central committee headquarters during the crisis they came upon a meeting between the communist and republican representatives already in progress.[29]

Largo, although a wily and tenacious fighter was badly handicapped by his limited political vision.[30] He was all the more vulnerable, given that his closest collaborators were either physically
absent, such as Araquistain, or fully occupied by other war tasks. In
the government sphere, Carlos de Baraibar, as Asensio's replacement, constituted Largo's only support. On 4 March, after a particularly tense cabinet session, made worse by the knowledge that the
Non-Intervention committee was certain to approve the mooted
control plan for Spain which provided for the evacuation of all
foreign volunteers, Largo suggested to Azaña that he be given leave
to dissolve the cabinet and to form an entirely new one.[31] Given the
president's considerable, if dissembled, antipathy towards Largo, he
was naturally not prepared to sanction the formation of a more
homogeneously *caballerista* cabinet. He suggested to Largo that his
own position in the cabinet was not sufficiently strong that he should
seek to pre-empt a crisis which had not yet been forced upon him.[32]

The cabinet reorganisation which Largo sketched out in his interviews with various government members at the end of February was
to form the basis of the anti-syndicalist campaign launched against
the socialist left by the reformist socialists and the PCE jointly. They
accused the left of seeking a union government which implied subor-
dinating the political parties – who represented the 'national will' –
to the 'sectarian' interests of the union memberships.[33] However, if
we examine the *Caballeristas'* proposals it is clear that, while they
contained a specific logic which their opponents may have felt to be
politically threatening, it was not that of union government. This, as
far as the socialist left was concerned, never existed – except as a
propaganda device manipulated by their opponents.

The four UGT posts outlined in the socialist left's February
cabinet draft did not present any real 'syndical' innovation.[34]
Indeed, Largo himself had always made it clear to the CNT that
union government was not a possibility.[35] Largo, while retaining the
premiership, would also assume control of a unified defence ministry. Luis Araquistain was to be installed as foreign minister, as had
been originally intended in September 1936, and Galarza was to be
moved to the treasury, with de Baraibar moving up a rung from
under-secretary to interior minister. The CNT did have four portfolios in the proposed cabinet which, nominally at least, put them on
an equal footing with the *Caballeristas*. However, in that trade and
industry had been split into two portfolios and the CNT's other posts
were justice and public health, it would be fair to say that the
anarchists had really been given three cabinet posts, including one of
marginal political importance. Whilst they had trade and industry,

the finance portfolio remained beyond their control and with it any scope for radical reform. Clearly it was important for the *Caballeristas* to cultivate the CNT as a crucial support in what would be a hostile cabinet – in spite of the left socialist nucleus of premiership, war, interior and finance. But, just as in Largo's May 1937 cabinet draft, so too in the March version, the socialist left denied the CNT the increase in ministerial influence which it was seeking. The *Caballeristas* were not prepared to increase the CNT's political power, even though this was the necessary precondition for fending off the hostile bloc of Popular Front parties. It is also noteworthy that there was no attempt to modify the PCE's two existing posts in the March draft. Largo was not concerned to remove the agriculture portfolio from Uribe in spite of the FNTT's bitter opposition to his policies. Nor, in the May 1937 cabinet crisis were they ideological factors which led to Largo switching the agriculture ministry to the PSOE reformists.

The reduction of the reformist socialist representation from three to two in the cabinet proposed in February, and particularly the relegation of Prieto to Public Works, was a direct reflection of developments in the party dispute.[36] Indeed, the real object of the cabinet reorganisation was to give the left socialists the control which had eluded them in September 1936. The so-called 'UGT ministers' were hardly that at all: they were simply Largo Caballero's unconditional supporters. However, the fact that the left socialists' stronghold lay in the UGT gave their opponents the opening they needed in order to press home the advantage of the 'anti-union' campaign which had been gestating since the traumatic experience of popular revolution and trade union pre-eminence consequent upon the military rising. Since both the Left Republicans (I.R.) and Republican Union (U.R.) had ministers and the Basques and the Catalans retained their representatives in central government in the same capacity as before, as ministers without portfolio, it was clearly the reformist wing of the PSOE itself which would have suffered most as a result of the proposed government reorganisation.[37]

As regards finance minister, Juan Negrín, there is no doubt that his proposed exclusion from the cabinet was a result of Largo's personal antipathy. The prime minister's puritanism meant that Negrín's lifestyle was a constant source of irritation. Indeed, Largo's first reaction to Negrín's designation by the PSOE executive in September 1936 had been to refuse the nomination. It was the socialist executive's insistence that Largo should accept all three of its nominations or it would make none at all which obliged the prime minister to concede. Also, Largo doubtless realised that the price of

Prieto's acceptance of a portfolio – on which Largo was insistent – was the inclusion of Negrín in the cabinet – on which Prieto was equally insistent.[38] Nevertheless, Largo's moral reservations remained.

Negrín himself had not wanted to accept the ministerial appointment in 1936.[39] He considered the Largo government to be a grave error. For him it signified the victory of October 1934 and as such damaged the Republic's reputation abroad. And for Negrín it was always the international dimension, the reaction of foreign powers to the war in Spain, which constituted the crucial determinant of its outcome.[40] However, like the disciplinarian he was, Negrín realised the choice was not his to make in September 1936. His party had called upon him, or more particularly still, he had been singled out by Prieto. The PSOE executive's first choice for the finance portfolio had been either Lamoneda or Alejandro Otero, the Granadan socialist, former deputy to the Cortes and professor of medicine, but Prieto's opinion had carried the day.[41] Those accounts which attribute Largo's subsequent attempt to exclude Negrín to political considerations, namely that Negrín was, from the moment of his appointment, an undesirable who had conspired with the PCE and the Comintern, have been constructed with the prejudice of hindsight and are as crude as they are inaccurate. To explain Largo's dislike of Negrín in September 1936 by referring, as do many writers, to the usual array of charges brought later against Negrín as prime minister, is a logical absurdity.[42]

By April 1937 the tensions within the cabinet, which remained unchanged because of Azaña's opposition, were becoming increasingly apparent. At government level, Largo's hostility towards the PCE intensified as a result of the manner in which the party opposed him, articulating its discontent through the manipulation of public opinion. The campaign against Asensio was a case in point. The PCE had launched a virulent propaganda campaign, after preparing the ground with months of insinuation and rumour. The party then orchestrated demonstrations, claiming thereafter that its political line had received the ultimate legitimation, bestowed by the popular will.

The May 1937 Cabinet Crisis

Largo Caballero's appointment as prime minister in September 1936 had reflected the ascendancy of the popular revolution over the moderate programme of government reforms championed in the pre-war period by Prieto and the reformist socialists. As premier,

Largo himself initiated policies which limited the extent of the revolution, facilitating the reconstruction of the power of the central state. The reformist socialists' objective remained, nevertheless, to reclaim control of the Republican government. In this they found ready allies in the PCE and the republicans, both equally concerned to re-establish Republican normality. By spring 1937 Largo had successfully contained the revolutionary threat. His continued control of the cabinet was therefore an anachronism. Not only this, but in the eyes of the Popular Front politicians Largo's radical image was also alienating France and Britain as the Republic's potential supporters abroad. The Popular Frontists all identified the international dimension of the war as crucial to a Republican victory. So pragmatism also dictated Largo's removal in order to create an image of the war effort which was suitable for export.

The opportunity which parliamentary socialists, communists and republicans had long been waiting for to initiate a full-blown cabinet crisis – in the hope that it would force Largo and the socialist left out of power – presented itself in the shape of the notorious Barcelona May Days. Between the 3rd and 7th of the month anarchists and their supporters – who on this occasion included the dissident communist POUM – clashed with the PSUC-influenced security forces of the Generalitat on the streets of the city.[43] The violence of the explosion reflected the massive build-up of political tension which had occurred during the preceding months between the two great rival forces represented in the Catalan government – namely the CNT and the PSUC (the Communist Party of Cataluña).[44] The political principles at stake in the battle have been well documented. The Catalan security forces, as the representatives of state power, sought to break the political will of the anarchist organisation in order to consolidate the bourgeois democratic counter-revolution on the civilian front.[45] The clash between the PSUC and the CNT was, however, as much a manifestation of a bitter organisational rivalry as it was a struggle over political principles. Fought in the streets and across the barricades the battle was primarily about political control within the Generalitat.

The left liberal Catalan nationalist party (Esquerra) which held the notional political centre, whilst inclining clearly towards the PSUC in political sympathies, called upon Largo Caballero to send in reinforcements to allow the Generalitat to end the disturbances. These had begun when, on 3 May, a group of assault guards whose immediate commander, police commissioner Rodríguez Salas, was a PSUC member, attempted to seize control of the Barcelona telephone exchange, a CNT stronghold. The ensuing street warfare between anarchists and communists constituted a serious threat to Republican order. Largo Caballero, however, hesitated to act. The Catalan crisis had serious implications for the latent power struggle in his own cabinet. Providing troops for Generalitat president, Luis Companys, would mean strengthening the PSUC. This would inevitably be construed by the anarchists as an act of overt hostility towards themselves. In terms of the national political balance, by sending troops into Cataluña Largo would be alienating the CNT which, for all the distance separating it from the socialist left, constituted in practical terms his only possible source of support against the alliance of socialists, communists and republicans in the Valencia cabinet. In the event, the gravity of the situation obliged Largo to dispatch troops and also to assume control of public order in Cataluña. The Catalan crisis was finally resolved, but at the expense of the region's autonomy which effectively ceased to exist. And in October 1937 Largo's successor as prime minister would follow this policy through to its logical conclusion by moving the central Republican government from Valencia to Barcelona.

The political repercussions of the Barcelona May Days would, however, reach far beyond Cataluña to spark the cabinet crisis which excluded Largo and the socialist left from the Republican government. On 7 May, the left republican minister without portfolio, José Giral, visited Azaña to inform him that the republicans, socialists and communists were agreed upon the need to solve the long-standing latent crisis in the cabinet.[46] This was a virtual declaration that they intended to precipitate the crisis. On the thirteenth of the month, in the middle of a stormy cabinet session in which Largo refused to countenance communist demands for the dissolution of the POUM, the two PCE ministers, Jesús Hernández and Vicente Uribe, resigned, thus initiating the proceedings. Largo's bid to stave off the crisis by pressing on with the cabinet meeting in their absence was thwarted by Indalecio Prieto who indicated that the prime minister was constitutionally bound to inform the president that the ministerial coalition had broken down.[47]

Between 13 and 17 May, when the crisis was finally resolved, there occurred a battle of political wills between Largo Caballero and the hostile coalition of reformist socialists, communists and republicans.[48] The Republican president, Azaña, found himself in a particularly difficult position. On the one hand the considerable personal as well as political antipathy which he bore Largo meant he welcomed the prospect of his prime minister's resignation. However, he was determined that Largo's exclusion from power should be seen to be the declared preference of the other proletarian representatives in the cabinet – namely the PCE and the PSOE – rather than the result of the president's personal prerogative.[49] Shrewdly Azaña realised that, otherwise, not only would Largo's credibility emerge intact but, in the eyes of Spanish workers, his personal political prestige might even be increased.

While the president dissembled in his interviews with his prime minister, Largo, for his part, sought desperately to postpone the cabinet crisis. His first plan was to leave immediately for Extremadura. There he would personally direct a military offensive whose objective was to cut the Nationalists' lines of communication with the south whence they received steady reinforcements of Italian and Moroccan troops.[50] The success of the operation would, of course, significantly have bolstered Largo's position, effectively scuppering the cabinet coalition's attempts to oust him from power. For this reason both the PCE and the reformist socialists moved in a pincer action to scotch Largo's initiative. On the military front, the PCE and its Soviet advisers blocked the transfer of troops and equipment – especially aircraft – without which the southern offensive could not be launched. The PSOE, for its part, moved in to cut Largo off on the political front. On 14 May, Juan Negrín and Anastasio de Gracia, as two of the three PSOE executive appointees to Largo's cabinet, visited the prime minister to announce their resignations.[51] Thus, as a result of the decision of the reformist socialist executive committee, selected in the controversial elections of June 1936, Largo's fate was virtually sealed.

Having consulted the various parties and organisations represented in government, Azaña recalled Largo on the 15th and requested that he form a new government. The provisional list of ministers duly presented to the president on the 16th, however, only confirmed Largo's totally unrealistic view of the balance of political power held by the left. In the draft cabinet placed before Azaña, Largo was to assume control of a unified defence ministry incorporating air and naval forces and controlling four separate subsecretariats (land army, navy, airforce, armaments and munitions). His rival, Prieto, was thereby being relegated to one of the two other ministerial portfolios, finance/agriculture and trade/industry, which constituted the PSOE's entire allocation. Largo's socialist supporters would also be in control of both the foreign and interior ministries, as originally intended in the February/March 1937 cabinet draft. The PCE retained two ministerial portfolios; education and labour, as did the CNT with justice and health. The rest of the cabinet draft was uncontroversial. Izquierda Republicana was allocated two ministries and Unión Republicana one, while the Basque and Catalan representatives remained as ministers without portfolio.[52]

Unsurprisingly the draft proved entirely unacceptable to the reformist socialists, communists and republicans. There was unanimity over the need for Largo to relinquish control of the defence ministry. The PSOE executive was naturally keen for this to pass in its entirety into Prieto's hands, as they had hoped in September 1936. Both the PSOE and the PCE demanded Galarza's removal from the interior ministry.[53] Technically, however, the reformists were able to draw a fine line between their position and that of the PCE by insisting that although they would, in the last resort, have acquiesced in Largo's retaining the defence ministry, the re-incorporation of the communists into the cabinet was an absolute necessity.[54] Given that the PCE was loth to leave Largo with even the premiership and that the latter would in any case countenance nothing less than both portfolios, all these fine distinctions become rather academic and one suspects that both reformist socialists and Communists realised as much at the time.[55] The crisis could only be solved by Largo's exclusion from the government.

While the relegation of the PSOE executive's appointees had been on the agenda since August 1936 and came as no surprise, given the intensity of the internal party conflict, far more staggering was the slight meted out to the CNT. As the organisation's spokesman indicated, it had suffered a double indignity. For not only had the CNT's representation been reduced by a third without consultation – and was thus less than the UGT's – but, as a result, it was on a par with the PCE which had provoked the cabinet crisis.[56] Nor was the concentration in PSOE hands of finance, agriculture and trade and industry acceptable to the CNT. Indeed, that Largo should have allowed such a concentration speaks volumes about his reformism. If the prime minister had purposely set out to alienate his only remaining source of support in the cabinet he could not have succeeded more absolutely. This was dangerous precisely because the political parties were acting in unison. In fact, Largo's behaviour was entirely in the tradition of *caballerista* high-handedness in its dealings with the anarchist organisation. The left socialists' treatment of the CNT does point up the fanciful nature of the PCE's accusation that Largo was, from March 1937 onwards, intent on imposing a union government. It is true that Prieto corroborated this version but one does not have to search too far to discover his motive in so doing. The socialist left's manifest determination slowly but surely to erode the authority of the PSOE executive and to assume its functions are sufficient to explain Prieto's eagerness to join in the PCE's anti-union campaign. This provided a justification for attacking the socialist left, which posed a threat to the reformists, not because it sought to supplant the PSOE as a political party but because it sought control of the party structure itself.

Whilst Largo's most solid supporters were to be found on the executive committee of the UGT, it is worth bearing in mind that there was still no unanimity of opinion therein. This was partly, though not entirely, the result of the presence of the pro-communist members Amaro del Rosal and Felipe Pretel. Del Rosal's support for the PSOE/PCE line in respect of Galarza's dismissal was criticised by Largo's unconditional supporters on the UGT executive, Pascual Tomás, José Díaz Alor and Ricardo Zabalza.[57] And, on 15 May, Hernández Zancajo was in fighting mood regarding the need to defend Largo's position to the hilt, seizing rapidly on the fact that Amaro del Rosal's written communiqué to the executive supported Largo as prime minister but omitted any reference to the war portfolio.[58]

There was, however, another source of division on the UGT executive which re-emerged during the May crisis. This concerned the UGT's relationship with Largo's cabinet. It came as no surprise to the rest of the executive that Amaro del Rosal, consistent with his pro-communist stance, should seek to deny outright that the UGT, as a trade union, was directly represented in the cabinet as such. But this issue split even the old-guard leadership. The unhappy experience with Galarza, over whom the UGT leaders had sought in vain to exercise some influence, led Pascual Tomás to seek a more formal understanding with Largo so that any UGT cabinet appointees would in future be answerable to the union federation's national committee for their actions.[59] Díaz Alor, former national treasurer of the bakers and confectioners union and one of Largo's closest allies on the UGT executive, insisted, however, that Largo's personal control of the cabinet was a sufficient guarantee. This was Largo's own view. Aware that it was important not to give the Popular Front bloc ammunition for its anti-union campaign, Largo argued that, once the cabinet had been formed, then the UGT executive could bargain with him over the precise conditions of its support. In the short term, however, *the important point was that the Socialists should consolidate their hold over the cabinet.*[60]

By 17 May the situation had reached an impasse. The cabinet crisis looked no nearer a solution. Largo, backed by the old guard on the UGT executive and pragmatically out of a sense of self-preservation by the CNT, argued stubbornly that national interest

dictated the indivisibility of the premiership and the defence portfolio. For the sake of political decorum, Azaña made a final attempt
at mediation. But, to his considerable relief, the division in the
loyalist ranks was manifestly unbridgeable. Isolated with his few
faithful supporters, amidst the wreckage of the shattered and fragmented ranks of left socialism, Largo had no alternative but to
abandon the government. Immediately Azaña called upon Prieto's
political intimate, the reformist socialist and ex-minister of finance,
Juan Negrín, charging him with the formation of a new government.
When Azaña requested the PSOE executive to nominate a new
prime minister, he was fully expecting Prieto's name to be for-
warded. Indeed the socialist executive voted unanimously for
him but Prieto himself adamantly refused to allow his name to
be proposed, implying that his skills would be more usefully
employed behind the scenes.[61] Nevertheless with Negrín as prime
minister, the PSOE executive was now firmly in the driving seat.
The waiting tactic had yielded its fruit. The process of purging the
Caballeristas' strongholds in the socialist organisation could begin
in earnest.

Largo Caballero's resignation from the Republican government
on 17 May 1937 is usually recorded as symbolising the death of the
popular revolution. Even more crudely, the collapse of Largo's
government has been viewed purely as the result of the machinations
of the PCE and its allies on the PSOE's national executive.[62] But in
order fully to appreciate the underlying reasons for a political failure
which heralded the beginning of the end for the party left, a much
wider perspective is essential.

The eclipse of the socialist left and the resignation of Largo
Caballero in particular, far from being sudden, were, as we have
seen, the culmination of a lengthy government crisis. In its turn,
this crisis sprang from the basic ideological and organisational
incoherence of the *caballerista* power base. The origins of the cabinet
crisis of May 1937 can be traced back clearly to 1934. It was, in
part, the culmination of a process of erosion initiated by the abortive Asturian revolution of October 1934. As a result of that
débâcle, there were those in the socialist party hierarchy who had
begun seriously to question the revolutionary credentials of the
caballerista leadership. In the aftermath of October the PSOE left,
with its supporters inside both the socialist youth federation and
the UGT, declared itself to be in favour of the bolshevisation of the
socialist organisation, the objectives of which were the expulsion of
the moderates and eventual unification with the PCE in a single
class party. In spite of this statement of intent, the PSOE

reformists' impression of the political charlatanism of the *Caballeristas* grew considerably over the period 1934–6. During that time there was nothing in the practice of the socialist left, nothing concretely achieved, which bore out in the slightest its strident revolutionary rhetoric. In spite of the party left's much vaunted commitment to the bolshevisation of the socialist organisation, pressure from its grass roots had, by November 1935, caused Largo Caballero to accept a re-run of Prieto's strategy of republican–socialist electoral alliance in the shape of the Popular Front pact. 1935–6 also saw the development in earnest of the internal struggle between *Caballeristas* and reformists for control of the PSOE's organisation. In order to bolster their own position in the party, the left socialists drew closer to the PCE, whose Bolshevik legacy apparently conferred on it the seal of revolutionary authenticity. In fact, the logic of the Comintern's espousal of Popular Frontism in 1935 had imposed a radical policy shift on the PCE. As a result, by 1936 the Spanish Communist Party's policy line meant it was moving closer to Prieto's reformists rather than to the PSOE left. The net result of all this was doubly disastrous for the *caballerista* wing. Firstly, it lost control of the Socialist Youth whose radicalised leaders switched their allegiance to the PCE, perceived as the party of the revolution *par excellence*. Weakened by this development, the PSOE left then had to contend with the increased hostility of their reformist colleagues who laid the blame for the loss of the Socialist Youth squarely at the door of the party left's own revolutionary rhetoric. By the summer of 1936, this hostility had crystallised as Prieto's strategy to purge the left from the PSOE hierarchy. Increasingly isolated in the party, as we have seen, the PSOE left were soon faced with a new alliance of reformist socialists and communists, united by the common objectives enshrined in the Popular Front. Only an alliance to the left with the CNT could have shored up the *Caballeristas*. But this too had failed to materialise during the period 1935–6. The failure was, once again, largely the result of left socialist inertia, if not downright reluctance. The CNT remained ideologically alien and organisationally a threat.

If the period 1934–6 seems to indicate that the ingrained reformism of the UGT leaders always prevailed in their dealings with the CNT, the experience of the first year of the war puts the matter beyond all doubt. It is worth stressing the very real distance which remained between the UGT and the CNT in the weeks following the army coup. Union hegemony in government was not a possibility either then or later. From the war's outbreak the differences between the two organisations would, in concrete terms as opposed to rhetoric, certainly not grow less. Both organisations were on the receiving end of a concerted political attack as the parties – socialist, communist and republican – fought to re-establish their pre-eminence. Yet in many ways – and not least as organisations competing for members and political power – the UGT and CNT remained bitter rivals. In spite of the solid basis for at least a defensive pact between the two, the great union alliance which the political parties apparently feared so much was never realised. The *caballerista* leadership remained passive and isolated; ideologically bankrupt, yet still suspicious of the anarchist organisation. In the end it failed to opt for either the union strategy of 'alianza obrera revolucionaria', proposed by the CNT leadership, or the political strategy of the Socialist and Communist Parties. The resulting political isolation provides the key to the débâcle of May 1937.

Largo Caballero's appointment as prime minister was a necessary consequence of revolutionary turmoil and state disintegration. But, as we have seen, the exercise of power exposed the left's ideological bankruptcy and the incoherence of its power base. The disintegration of left socialism made Largo increasingly vulnerable to the hostility of PSOE reformists, communists and republicans. This hostility was soon translated into a direct attack. It is in such a context that the May 1937 cabinet crisis must be set. Largo Caballero was not destroyed by the cunning or voracity of the PCE. If any group can be said to have forced his resignation, then it was the reformist wing of the PSOE which withdrew its confidence in the prime minister by removing its cabinet appointees. But, in the last analysis, Largo's 'fall' has about it an inexorable logic. It was the inevitable result of his failure to consolidate an alternative power base on the left as a crucial support against the collective onslaught of republicans, reformists and communists. But this failure too was inherent in the nature of the socialist left. The *Caballeristas* were superfluous: there was no political space for them to occupy between the Popular Front as defended by the PCE and the PSOE reformists (and in reality by Largo himself), and the revolution identified with the anarchists. In this sense, the reformist socialists were correct in the substance of their accusation that, ideologically, the *Caballeristas* could not be differentiated from the rest of the party. As Lamoneda commented, 'We must ensure mutual tolerance (*convivencia*) in the PSOE – especially given that [the left] has never demonstrated in a convincing way any doctrinal or tactical difference [from the rest of the party] which would justify its behaviour . . .'[63] The contradictions – and consequent passivity – of the socialist left are at the root of its failure to take real control of the party, or even the government, in spite of appearances to the contrary. These same contradictions would ultimately be responsible for the eventual defeat of the party left at the hands of the parliamentary socialists who controlled the PSOE's national executive.

PART III
The Battle in the Party 1937–1938

6   Ramón Lamoneda confronts the PSOE left

The battle inside the PSOE for control of its organisational structures was waged on behalf of the reformist wing largely by one man, Ramón Lamoneda. Although as general secretary he had been in control of the PSOE's national executive since the summer of 1936, it was with the appointment of Juan Negrín as Republican premier in May 1937 that Lamoneda came to real political prominence. The PSOE's general secretary was to become the crucial link whereby the PSOE hierarchy came to be identified with the Negrín government at whose centre was a reflection of the parliamentary reformism and inter-class alliance championed for so long by Indalecio Prieto.

As the socialist leaders of state and party respectively, Negrín and Lamoneda had similarly severe views on discipline. Both tended towards the authoritarian, which, while a certain concentration of power was essential in a wartime situation, would in the future tend to alienate their fellow socialists. Lamoneda's extremely rational and pragmatic approach, above all to the increasingly thorny issue of relations between the socialist and communist grass roots, would lead his critics to accuse him of being cold, callous and impervious to the hardships of the socialist rank and file.[1] Luis Araquistain remarked that he would have made an excellent proof-corrector, so meticulous was his mind. But as general secretary he was a disaster beause he simply could not empathise with the socialist rank and file, angered by the behaviour of certain sectors of the PCE.[2]

Gabriel Morón, the veteran Andalusian socialist trade union leader who until 1937 had been closely identified with Prieto, argues convincingly that Lamoneda's dynamism during the civil war appears so all-consuming, even dictatorial, because like Negrín, he was confronted by the passivity and timidity of other leading socialists, which only increased as the war progressed. For Negrín:

> . . . with his own party, [he] felt as if he was communing with the Void. He faced either glacial indifference or extreme timidity, which, for his

passionate temperament, appeared to be an invitation to accept defeat nobly. All Negrín's faults, his increasingly erratic political decisions, can be traced back to this dearth of support, which was the direct result of the Socialist Party's internal crisis.

And so it was equally with Lamoneda:

> ... who, for all his faults, in spite of all the criticisms one might make, was the only one of all the PSOE's leaders who still felt it his duty to ensure that the [national] executive continued to function. Thus he assumed personal control of a set of functions which ought to have been the collective responsibility of the entire committee – but which could no longer be so because most of its members had already abdicated that responsibility.[3]

Lamoneda had bypassed the option of ministerial office himself, although he did play an important supporting role as ministerial under-secretary during Anastasio de Gracia's occupation of the trade and industry and labour portfolios in Largo's two cabinets. In the main, however, Lamoneda chose to devote his efforts to the PSOE itself – forging internal unity and consolidating the party organisation so that it would be capable of assuming control of the state and providing the administrative cadres which would be crucial after the war.

Lamoneda was not as far to the right of the PSOE as was Negrín. However, both their vision of Spain's post-war needs and their appreciation of what was essential to achieve victory for the Republic in the war were identical. Victory required the dismantling of the revolutionary order of the early months, otherwise the result would be the alienation both of other capitalist countries and the Republic's own bourgeoisie – whereupon defeat would be a certainty.[4] The PSOE executive as a whole would become closely identified with Negrín's economic policies, a link which was personified by executive member, Jerónimo Bugeda, who, as under-secretary in the finance ministry after May 1937, was Negrín's immediate subordinate. Both Lamoneda and Negrín stressed the importance of technical expertise in economic planning. Implicit was a criticism of the left during the Second Republic. It had adopted an ethical stance and certain objectives but no strategies had been developed in order to *realise* those objectives.[5] Equally, both Negrín and Lamoneda realised that, even if the Republic won, international benevolence would be required for survival. Economic autarky was not a possibility because of the deficit in the balance of trade, the acute need for raw materials and the effects of the war on Spanish industry. After the war the unions would be involved in a battle for production in the fields and factories which would be as great and vital as the one being fought during the war itself.[6]

Ramón was also a man of the party whose internalisation of the Iglesian ethic had been as absolute as that of any other reformist. All his speeches, public declarations and interventions at executive and national committee meetings throughout the war reveal not only a keen intelligence but also his intense commitment to the PSOE. There is certainly nothing which would substantiate the wild accusations of Lamoneda's crypto-communism, made in the bitter and desperate climate of the immediate post-war period. The entire Iglesian canon – austerity, sacrifice, discipline, as expressed by the national and provincial leaderships of the PSOE – whether they were *caballerista* or reformist – are reflected and consolidated in the speeches of the party's general secretary.[7] Lamoneda would constantly and vehemently stress the main party line: the 'silence of the Socialist Party'. The only distinguishable voice was to be that of the government whose discipline was all-embracing. This reflects the PSOE leadership's close identification with the state. Party political propaganda was superfluous because the PSOE *saw itself as the state*. This was a far from apolitical line, of course, as it was clearly aimed at curbing the activities of political rivals, and especially the PCE.

The May 1937 cabinet crisis, by forcing the socialist left out of office, triggered a new stage in the battle between the *Caballeristas* and the Lamoneda executive for control of the PSOE. The left's attention was once again focused on the party apparatus. Between July 1936 and May 1937 it had sought to bypass the national executive committee, to block all its overtures towards the PCE, appropriating its functions so that it would eventually atrophy – in the left's view a fitting end to an entity of fraudulent origins. After May 1937, the struggle centred on the party's national committee, of which the executive formed the centre. Controversy raged over the legitimacy of the existing executive authorities and also over their allegedly inquorate and unrepresentative nature. The socialist left's bid for a greater share of power within the party was also being reflected at this time in the parallel struggle unfolding in the union.[8]

On 18 May, *caballerista* representatives from a number of provincial socialist federations held the first of several meetings in the headquarters of the PSOE's Valencian federation. A stronghold of the left from before the war, the Valencian socialist executive had become the focus of *caballerista* opposition to Lamoneda's national executive with the transfer of Largo's government to the provincial capital in November 1936. The Valencia meetings, which continued throughout June and into early July, signalled the revival of the organisational battle in the party.[9] It had been triggered by the May cabinet crisis, for the left was keen to force a public debate over this in the party. The call to the provincial federations' representatives to meet went out from Albacete – where left socialist, Justo Martínez Amutio, was civil governor – on the very day of Negrín's appointment as premier.[10] The party left held the Lamoneda executive responsible for its ejection from power and was infuriated by the fact that the PSOE leadership had not severed relations with the PCE in spite of the latter's vitriolic public criticism of Largo. The aim of the Valencia meetings was to mobilise the left's supporters in the party to force the reorganisation of the PSOE's national leadership.[11] Using the familiar pre-war argument that the Lamoneda executive was unrepresentative of rank-and-file opinion, the *Caballeristas* made a variety of suggestions to the general secretary all of which were designed to break the monopoly established by the reformists in June 1936, thereby regaining a foothold for the left in the national organs of the party.

First, the left's representatives demanded posts on the existing national executive. These posts were to be made available to the left by forcing the resignations of the executive's 'absentee' members.[12] By this the *Caballeristas* were referring mainly to vice-president Luis Jiménez de Asúa and Fernando de los Ríos who were serving as the Republic's ambassadors in Prague and Washington respectively. But the party left had its sights set on an even greater share of the executive posts. Without naming particular individuals, the left implied that ministerial or governmental responsibility should, on the practical grounds of the amount of work involved, automatically preclude those concerned from occupying posts on the PSOE's national executive. This would clearly have affected Prieto, as defence minister, Vidarte as under-secretary to Julián Zugazagoitia, the socialist interior minister, and Jerónimo Bugeda as Negrín's subordinate in the finance ministry. The fact that these suggestions coincided with the left's own exclusion from government did nothing to lessen the impression of their opportunism and Lamoneda dismissed them out of hand.

The left's second plan was even more ambitious, and indeed unrealistic, given the intransigence of Lamoneda and his colleagues. Whilst it underwent several modifications in the course of June and early July, in essence the party left's objective was fundamentally to restructure the PSOE's national committee. Instead of regional representatives it was to be composed of provincial delegates. This was technically permissible under article 29 of the party statutes, but it would have made the national committee an unwieldy body of some sixty members. The existing committee, with an original membership of thirteen, had been reduced to nine as a result of deaths and disappearances consequent upon the July military rebellion. Adolfo Carretero (Andalucía Occidental) was missing, Antonio Quintana and Adrían Fernández (substitute) (Old Castile), shot and missing respectively, Enrique Botana and Juan Tizón (substitute) (Galicia) also shot and missing respectively, Eliseo del Caz and Teodoro Fominaya (substitute) (Morocco) likewise. There was no representative for Cataluña. Rafael Vidiella had resigned in May 1936 and developments in the region since the beginning of the war meant the PSOE was no longer operating there. While Lamoneda stressed only the practical disadvantages of reorganising the national committee, he was clearly aware that the left was seeking to break the monopoly of control enjoyed by the reformists on the existing committee of regional delegates. Moreover, it is worth noting that consistency was not a *caballerista* virtue. At the September 1933 PSOE national committee meeting (by which time the switch from provincial to regional representation was almost complete, as a consequence of the party's growth), *it was Largo Caballero himself* who reproved Murcia for its desire to retain its provincial representative on the national committee. He insisted that all the provinces had to abide by the new structure.[13] In spite of numerous meetings between the *Caballeristas* and Lamoneda's executive the left had made no real progress in their demands by the time Lamoneda convened the PSOE's national committee – in its existing form – on 17 July 1937.

The left's internal offensive in the party was taking place against the background of a mounting military crisis in the north. Bilbao had fallen in the middle of June and, in an attempt to take the pressure off the northern front, Negrín and Prieto turned their attention to Madrid. Thus, as the representatives of the Socialist Party in government were fighting desperately to stop the military rot, the *Caballeristas'* most vital concern seemed to be the pursuit of the political vendetta in the party. This provoked considerable anger among the reformists and only hardened their resolve to deal ruthlessly with the opposition. The very fact that *caballerista* representatives had gathered in Valencia was perceived as an act of gross irresponsibility, for it meant diverting energy and manpower from the main task of the war effort. As preparations went ahead for the PSOE national committee meeting in Valencia, the first week of July 1937 also saw the beginnning of the battle of Brunete, intended to raise the siege of the capital. This it did not come even close to achieving, although by stretching and diverting nationalist resources, the battle did retard the northern offensive and thus the fall of Santander until 26 August.

As Republicans clashed with Nationalists at Brunete, the *Caballeristas* prepared a detailed written petition for presentation to the first session of the PSOE's national committee. In spite of its complexity, length and the bureaucratic language in which it was couched, the petition, which stressed the erosive effect of the war on the existing national committee's membership, merely repeated the left's demand for access to a new one based on provincial representatives.[14] The left cast doubt on the status of two of the regional delegates on the existing committee, claiming that both Francisco Azorín (Andalucía) and Narciso Vázquez (Extremadura), had had their credentials challenged by the socialist organisations to which they belonged. However, while this was true, it is equally doubtful that the party rank and file as a whole was particularly interested in the details of a dispute whose significance remained obscure and which must have appeared an irresponsible and unaffordable diversion in wartime.[15]

The PSOE National Commmittee Meeting: 17–21 July 1937

Faced with a renewed challenge from the party left, Lamoneda and his colleagues on the PSOE executive determined to use the national committee meeting to tighten reformist control of the party leadership. All the executive's members agreed upon the need to stamp firmly upon the left whose activities, if unchecked, would lead to the disintegration of the PSOE. Moreover, the socialist executive was convinced that the party left, stung by its exclusion from power, was motivated primarily by political opportunism. PSOE executive member, Jerónimo Bugeda observed that the charges of 'absenteeism' being levelled at the party leadership by the *Caballeristas* could equally well be brought against the left socialist executive of the UGT. As this was not occurring then the left's campaign against the party leadership appeared singularly self-interested. The Lamoneda executive felt itself to be under virtual siege in Valencia where the left was mobilising against it on several fronts. In addition to the meetings of *Caballeristas* from the provincial socialist federations, the party left attempted to mobilise young socialist opposition in the JSU.

Originally, the socialist youth's old guard – whose leadership was based in Valencia – had proposed the creation within the JSU of socialist nuclei named after the FJS founder, Tomás Meabe.[16] But after the May cabinet crisis these proposals underwent a symbolic transformation. The groups were to be christened after Largo Caballero instead.[17] Worse still, they were to be created inside the PSOE rather than the JSU – which was prepared to expel them – and membership was to be granted to 'sympathisers' of any age. Lamoneda was also worried by the emergence in Valencia of a new publishing venture, the 'editorial Tomás Meabe'. Subsidised by leading members of the socialist left, it was soon producing a range of factional material, including Carlos Hernández Zancajo's *Tercera etapa de Octubre* and various articles by young socialist dissidents on the reality of JSU unity.

It is in such a context that one must set the events of the PSOE national committee meeting whose first formal session met on 19 July. Present at it were the members of the socialist executive, apart from Prieto and Fernando de los Ríos, the Republic's ambassador in Washington. Prieto had asked to be excused because of heavy work commitments connected with the Brunete offensive. Seven out of the thirteen regional representatives were also present.[18] Justo Martínez Amutio, the Valencian executive member and Levante appointee to the national committee, attempted to put the *Caballeristas'* petition before the assembly, whereupon the validity of his own credentials as Levante representative were immediately challenged. This was clearly a tactical manoeuvre. In brief, however, the reformists objected because Amutio's appointment to the national committee had only been ratified by two out of the five Levante provinces – Valencia and Castellón, but not Albacete, Alicante or Murcia. In what was clearly a pre-arranged strategy, Lamoneda, Ramón González Peña and Rafael Henche attacked the left's petition on every count. Using the left's own preferred weapon, party statute, they quoted article 34 to remind the *Caballeristas* that the only body before which a national committee was responsible was a general party congress – impracticable until after the war because such a large percentage of the socialist rank and file had been mobilised. Having been subjected to a barrage of personal criticism, and faced with a unanimous national committee vote to throw out the left's petition, Amutio had no option but to withdraw from the meeting.[19] The bid to break the reformists' hold over the party leadership had failed definitively. By deliberately maintaining a reduced representation on the PSOE national committee, Lamoneda successfully excluded the party left.

The national committee meeting of July 1937 was clearly a watershed in the internal life of the PSOE. The resounding tactical victory for the reformists allowed them to tighten their grip on the party organisation. It was the end of an interim period which had opened with the June 1936 election of the Lamoneda executive. Since then it had been forced to battle hard to survive against the ambitions of the party left. The July 1937 national committee had been, as Ramón Lamoneda himself admitted, the acid test of his executive's authority.[20]

The national committee was crucial in more than one sense, however. Not only does the stenographic record provide us with the clearest possible exposition of the reformists' case against the party left. In addition, the minutes constitute the most lucid statement of the party leadership's overall political position, whilst certain of the arguments developed during the discussion provide important insights into the differences within the reformist camp itself. It was these differences, grown to be as bitter and absolute as the divisions between the reformists and the left, which would totally destroy any hope of unity in the PSOE by August 1938 – ironically, the month in which the party's fiftieth anniversary celebrations were held.[21]

The most vexed domestic questions discussed at the meeting – apart from the initial controversy over the *Caballeristas'* demands – were socialist–communist relations, dealt with in the report on unification, and the state of the socialist youth inside the JSU. Both topics were, of course, closely bound up with the issue of the socialist left.

The PSOE reformists were aware that the complex problems they were having to debate during the sessions had been compounded by the actions of the party left since October 1934. This had the effect of intensifying the desire for revenge felt by the PSOE reformists towards the left. Not only were the left socialists the authors of the massive organisational dislocation within the PSOE itself. In addition, the left was blamed for having created a political climate which made it very difficult for the PSOE executive to deal adequately with the PCE's aggressive pro-unity propaganda and tactics. To add insult to injury, the reformists saw the *Caballeristas'* burgeoning anti-communism as the major factor fuelling socialist–communist tension at the grass roots in the already difficult circumstances of civil war. Moreover, the PSOE left was blamed both for the loss of the socialist youth movement to the PCE and for the massive upheaval in the UGT, where socialist control was being seriously threatened by the PCE's inroads into a number of industrial federations. Nevertheless, all these issues were also beginning to provoke tensions *inside* the reformist camp by the middle of 1937.

It was at the national committee that the final disaffection of the veteran socialist and union leader, Anastasio de Gracia, occurred. The de Gracia affair in fact contains, in microcosm, many of the contradictions and conflicts which wrought such havoc in the socialist movement during the 1930s. Anastasio de Gracia had been, until January 1936, both president of the UGT and an ordinary member of the party executive. However, in that month he finally resigned from the presidency of the union after a long-standing disagreement with the *Caballeristas* which centred on the apparently leftward trend of the national executive under Largo and also, unsurprisingly, on the latter's tactical *rapprochement* to the PCE.[22] De Gracia's desire to withdraw from the national leadership of the union predated, by some considerable time, his resignation. He had felt bound to remain until such time as the UGT was back on an even keel after the October 1934 events when he had been the only member of the leadership not jailed.

After withdrawing from the union leadership, de Gracia naturally gravitated more and more into the political orbit of the reformists. He was nominated by the party as one of its three ministers and appointed to the trade and industry portfolio in Largo's first government. With the November 1936 cabinet reshuffle he became labour minister. He remained in that post until the cabinet crisis of May 1937. It was his resignation, along with that of Juan Negrín, which prevented the postponement of the cabinet crisis after the initial communist walk-out, and was thus crucial in precipitating the fall of the socialist left. This indicates very clearly de Gracia's identification with the men of the party, indeed his under-secretary in both ministries was Ramón Lamoneda.[23]

But just as the issue of socialist–communist relations had provoked the estrangement from his union colleagues, so it caused the same to occur within the party executive. By 1937, de Gracia was disturbed by the extent of PCE inroads into the socialist movement. The JSU was completely dominated by the PCE and the Catalan socialists had vanished without trace in the PSUC, which had become, quite simply, the Communist Party of Cataluña. At the July 1937 national committee meeting, de Gracia alone opposed Lamoneda's view that they should accept the JSU as a *fait accompli* and work within the unified organisation to rebuild its socialist content.[24] Lamoneda argued cogently that by breaking up the JSU the PSOE executive would be playing into the hands of the party left, while also exposing itself to the worst ravages of PCE propaganda which would be bound to portray the Socialists as the saboteurs of unity and the enemies of the Spanish working class. Furthermore, opposing youth unity would have made an utter nonsense of the PSOE's joint committee strategy. In response, de Gracia remarked that, however reasonable Lamoneda's arguments, the PCE would simply never allow the PSOE to work within the JSU in any way which might threaten its own hegemony. Lamoneda had been encouraged when, in response to his criticisms over the way the JSU was functioning, the youth leadership had elected two socialist representatives – Martín Cantal and Alfonso Rodríguez – to the JSU national executive in order to fill the vacancies created in February 1937 by the deaths in an accident of the communists, Trifón Medrano and Luis Cuesta.[25] But this concession meant very little in real terms. By 1937, the communists on the JSU executive outnumbered the socialists four to one. At the JSU national committee meeting of 15–16 May 1937, which coincided with the expulsion of the socialist left from government, the pro-unity lobby had won a complete victory. In his address to the meeting, Santiago Carrillo was vehemently critical of the *Caballeristas* in the youth organisation.[26]

The exchange between Lamoneda and de Gracia encapsulates the Socialists' dilemma. Lamoneda's logic was impeccable, but de Gracia's intuition was right. In July 1937, the PSOE national committee resolved, following Lamoneda's recommendation, to establish a youth secretariat to organise young socialists throughout the Republican zone. But this remained a dead letter virtually until 1938. Moreover, the reformists' low-profile approach to the JSU would not only result in the atomisation of the Socialist Youth inside the JSU. Ironically, it would also eventually stimulate the very reaction that the whole of the PSOE executive's wartime policy had been designed to avoid: namely the recouping of control of the Socialist Youth in 1938 by a resurgent socialist left which had, meanwhile, raised the banner of implacable anti-stalinism.

In July 1937, de Gracia was not only certain that the fusion of the PSOE and the PCE in a single class party would destroy the 'Iglesian tradition', but he was also convinced that his executive colleagues were seriously considering such a unification. By all accounts a rather simple soul, one might view de Gracia as a victim of the PSOE's 'verbal unitarism'.[27] In other words, he had not appreciated the tactical game which the Lamoneda executive was playing, nor understood its rationale. He had simply taken the pro-unity propaganda at face value.[28]

De Gracia finally resigned from the party executive on 21 July 1937 in protest against a speech by his executive colleague, Jerónimo Bugeda, implying that all those who did not support unification were traitors.[29] Neither Bugeda's assurances that he had not been referring to Anastasio de Gracia personally, nor the efforts of the party president, Ramón González Peña, to persuade him that, in a wartime situation, the executive needed all its members, nor calls to party discipline could move him. Lamoneda was particularly anxious to keep the PSOE executive membership static – at least until the end of the war. The resignation of any member would force new elections, and these would give the party left an opportunity to reopen the pre-war 'struggle of tendencies'. But none of these considerations made any impression on de Gracia. He simply ceased attending executive meetings.[30] But the national executive, in order to avoid interim elections, would only formally accept his resignation in September 1938, at the time of the appointment of new members to the committee.

De Gracia's reaction demonstrates just how unenviable and difficult a task faced Ramón Lamoneda. As leader of the party which formed the backbone of the Republican state at war, he had to do his utmost to assure the conditions of victory. That meant presenting a united front with the PCE – however great the tensions between the socialist and communist bases and however serious the level of disaffection among veteran socialist leaders like de Gracia. Nevertheless, as general secretary of the PSOE, Lamoneda was also bound to protect the separate identity of the socialist organisation. In this context, pro-unity propaganda, in the form of speeches and newspaper editorials, was a means of squaring the proverbial circle. Lamoneda is often presented as the prime mover of unity, that is organisational unification, between the PSOE and the PCE. However, in all his major speeches, even as early as mid 1937, an essential and consistent dichotomy in his attitude is evident. Admittedly, he catered somewhat demagogically – if in eloquent and moving language – for both the PCE and the JSU's strident demands for unification. However, Lamoneda was in reality arguing, as did PSOE president Ramón González Peña in all his speeches, for a cautious approach involving a long period of practical joint action which might at any time be halted if there was evidence of a discrepancy of tactics or signs of sectarian antagonism at the base. Above all, Lamoneda stressed, 'We must calm this desire for immediate organisational unity. Because the essential precondition of a single proletariat party in Spain is that socialists and communists should share a common political philosophy and practice.'[31]

The unity issue had created a serious political crisis to which there was no easy solution for the PSOE. In terms of Iglesian mythology, the war was supposed to offer the fulfilment of the party's 'historic destiny' – the inheritance of state power. But the conditions in which it was being fought had changed the political equation, creating an increasingly powerful PCE able to compete with the PSOE for control of the government. One of the most outstanding symptoms of this organisational battle was the increasing insistence in PSOE propaganda on its own history:

> from the summit of half a century's irreproachable conduct, history surveys us. While taking account of present circumstances, we must respond today in a way which befits our past history, if we wish to be faithful followers of those worthy men who bequeathed us a Party rich in moral and political principles.[32]

History and tradition were not only instruments of political legitimation here. They were being wielded desperately to assert the PSOE's moral superiority in a battle in which it had few material advantages.[33] Instructive is an image used by Gabriel Morón. He likened the party to an old patrician whose values are no longer those of the world. He is a noble anachronism, powerless to stop the dissipation of his inheritance.[34] Always implicit is a negative comparison of the PCE. If the PSOE is patrician, the PCE is a party of political *parvenus* of dubious morality. The PSOE's enduring self-image as the party of moral austerity *par excellence* is an interesting one. It dates back to the party's earliest days, but if examined critically in the context of the civil war, it is clear that many socialist leaders stressed this aspect out of a psychological need to compensate for the undeniable fact that the PSOE was losing the organisational battle to the PCE.

The Socialists' problems in this respect were to some extent compounded by the fact that they operated a more restrictive admissions policy. Initially there was a virtual freeze on membership. Then in March 1937, the UGT executive recommended that those who had been recruited after 18 July 1936 should be debarred from standing for office.[35] Although this policy was reversed by the González Peña executive when it took control of the UGT in October 1937, it was a far from uncontentious decision.[36] Left socialists were vehemently opposed to a more liberal membership policy for both ideological and security reasons.[37] In particular, FNTT delegates sought totally to exclude the influence of those who had joined after 18 July 1936 in an attempt to defend collectivist ideas – and indeed the collectives themselves – from the hostility of conservative factions many of which were grouped in the PCE's provincial peasant federations.[38]

A connected issue, which was another bone of contention, concerned the PCE's approach to propaganda. The PCE was a young party in search of a base. To this end, its recruiting style and propaganda techniques were aggressive and highly visible. From the start of the conflict Spanish socialists manifested their disdain for these, but they were also tremendously disconcerted by their effectiveness, as the following extract from the correspondence of the provincial socialist executive in Almería clearly reveals:

> The [Socialist] Party, somewhat startled by communist methods – so given to excessive publicity and dramatic gestures, to vulgar and ornate ritual, to rhetoric, to cultivating people's vanity and ambition – has become even more sparing in its public declarations, which were always austere and dignified. But what we disdain, in terms of the methods employed, we cannot ignore in terms of the effects produced. The people here are uneducated and impressionable. Until very recently they were in thrall to a religious mysticism – which, for all that it was distorted and damaging, met a certain spiritual need in them. Communist propaganda, full of puerile, rhetorical flourishes, peppered with clichés and accompanied by impressive gestures, has filled the void left in these simple people – and principally in the young, male and female alike. The Socialist Party has resolved to take part in each and every initiative, to be present wherever and whenever any sort of meeting or gathering is held – however ridiculous these appear to us to be. The Party will make its voice heard, will keep itself apprised of all the 'popular movements' which are organised. Thus will it attempt to keep a check on all public demonstrations in order not to be taken unawares. We will attempt to counteract communist propaganda by creating our own socialist *mystique* [sic] – which aims to build a civic ethic and to make of men conscious and equal human beings.[39]

The degeneration of relations between the PCE and the PSOE was, of course, attributable to far more wide-ranging factors than party ethos and the quality of propaganda. However, this issue does provide a useful insight into the perceptions of the Spanish socialist movement during the civil war.

The commitment of a rapidly expanding Communist Party to Popular Frontist and pro-unity policies had thus precipitated an intense organisational crisis throughout the Spanish socialist movement. This exacerbated existing internal tensions. Whereas the Lamoneda executive sought to maintain a working political alliance with the PCE, the *Caballeristas* were violently opposed to this. At one level, they were hostile to the PCE because the party had, while professing its commitment to proletarian unity, savagely attacked leading socialists in the press. But more fundamentally the *Caballeristas* opposed the PCE's Popular Frontism because they saw in it a Trojan horse tactic designed to absorb the socialist rank and file. In the left's view, Lamoneda and his party colleagues were, moreover, conniving at this by collaborating in the joint party strategy.

Having failed to breach the reformists' defences at the July 1937 PSOE national committee meeting, the *Caballeristas* opted to publi-

cise the division in the party by convening a series of provincial
socialist congresses throughout the loyalist zone for 15 August.[40]
The major objective was to mobilise rank-and-file support for a
national party congress which Lamoneda would be unable to ignore.
The left's agenda for the mooted national congress confirmed all the
reformists' worst fears.[41] It ran the gamut of the issues dividing
socialists – the reorganisation of the party leadership, the unity of the
marxist parties, relations with the JSU, an analysis of responsibility
for the May 1937 cabinet crisis, PSOE policy towards the trade
unions, Popular Front and unity of action between the anti-fascist
forces. The *Caballeristas* clearly intended publicly challenging the
whole basis of the Lamoneda executive's wartime strategy of joint
action with the PCE. The agenda was a powder keg waiting to be
ignited. But public discussion of it would have done far more than
challenge Lamoneda's authority – it would have torn the socialist
movement asunder. This, in turn, would inevitably have meant the
destruction of Popular Front unity on which the Republican war
effort depended. Lamoneda could not allow this. Accordingly, his
action against the left was swift.

On 25 July, Lamoneda wrote to inform the executive of the
Valencian provincial federation that it was to be removed from office
forthwith for overt factionalism. The following day, both the federation's headquarters and those of *Adelante*, the socialist party press in
the province, were seized by members of the Republican security
forces and *carabineros*. They were acting on the instructions of the
interior minister, the reformist socialist Julián Zugazagoitia, and on
behalf of the PSOE's president, the Asturian miners' leader, Ramón
González Peña, who had petitioned the PSOE-led government for
control of both party and press.[42] The left's anger was intensified by
its awareness of one particularly ironic aspect of the situation. The
reformists, they felt, were only too ready to mobilise the public
security forces against the party left, but they could not offer either it
or the socialist rank and file any protection against PCE
sectarianism.[43]

As an interim measure which would become a permanent
arrangement, the PSOE executive installed the reformist-controlled
socialist group from Valencia (capital) as a caretaker provincial
executive. The city group was headed by Manuel Molina Conejero
who was also the civil governor of Valencia province. By striking at
the Valencian federation and prohibiting its provincial congress,
Lamoneda had successfully quashed the *Caballeristas'* rebellion at
source. A circular from the Valencian reformists was dispatched on
28 July.[44] On 7 August, *El Socialista* also published a warning from

the reformist caretakers in Valencia against any 'factional gatherings' of Valencian socialist groups. The left's attempts to mobilise support in the province by publishing its version of the ejection of the Valencian executive were stillborn.

The ripples of discontent at Lamoneda's actions were not, however, limited to the socialist organisation in Valencia. Beyond the Levante, support for the PSOE left remained in evidence in those southern provincial federations which were still functioning as such – namely Córdoba (Pozoblanco), Jaén (Linares), Granada (Baza) and Almería.[45] But this support was by no means unanimous anywhere. All the provincial organisations contained factions which were hostile to the *Caballeristas*. It is, moreover, difficult to be absolutely certain about the origins of the various allegiances and divisions at the provincial level, either before or during the civil war. Given the generally low level of theoretical debate in the PSOE, it seems highly unlikely that the left–reformist split within individual socialist groups and provincial federations would have been determined solely by ideological differences either before or during the war. But the national debate between the PSOE reformists and the party left did provide a useful channel into which existing political ambitions and tensions could be directed. The opposition to Azorín, the national committee representative for Andalucía, is a case where local political rivalries from the pre-war period seem to have determined to a considerable degree attitudes to the reformist/*caballerista* split nationally.[46] Moreover, during the civil war itself, one must always be acutely aware of chronology when defining support for either the Lamoneda executive or the *Caballeristas*. By early 1937 the *caballerista* camp had split into pro- and anti-communists, with the former featuring as the most vocal supporters of Lamoneda's unity of action strategy. The attempted socialist–communist unification in Jaén in August 1937, discussed below, was the work of pro-communist left socialists on the provincial executive. This internal split in the socialist left's ranks clearly reflects the political contradiction at the heart of its power base. Equally, by 1938 the growing anti-communism of the socialist rank and file in the centre–south zone would bring many socialists previously identified with Lamoneda to define themselves as *Caballeristas* purely because Largo had become the personification of opposition to the PCE's drive to absorb the PSOE.

Lamoneda spent the early part of August attempting to block the other provincial congresses inspired by the party left. This led him into conflict with supporters of Caballero in the Cordoban federation, and relations between it and the national executive became

strained.[47] Cordoban executive member Miguel Ranchal accused
Lamoneda of deliberately ostracising Cordoban socialists.[48] In spite
of all his efforts, however, Lamoneda was unable to enforce a blanket
ban on provincial congresses in the party. The Badajoz federation
went ahead with its August extraordinary provincial congress, held
at Castuera.[49] The congress report reveals clear evidence of the left–
reformist split and of considerable hostility to the PCE:

> The spectacle presented by certain socialists at the last national com-
> mittee meeting of the UGT must not, in our view, recur. Deliberately or
> otherwise, it facilitates the task of those elements which seek to neutralise
> socialist influence in the trade union federations.[50]

There were also overt references to the fractional work of the communist sections (GOSR) in the industrial unions. While these ought
to have been dissolved back in December 1935, in fact the communist union sections had continued to function. In a clear political
slight to the PCE, the Badajoz congress agreed to 'look favourably on
the efforts and objectives of the FNTT's collectives and agrarian
organisations in Jaén province'. Moreover, the joint PSOE–PCE
committees in the province were to be suspended until the PCE had
publicly retracted its criticism of 'men of our Party'.

But Largo Caballero's anti-communist supporters were not the
only source of Lamoneda's problems in August. A serious crisis also
erupted in the Jaén federation in the middle of the month as a result
of the excessive enthusiasm of the pro-communist left socialists on
the provincial executive. On 16 August the unification of the Socialist and Communist Parties in Jaén was announced.[51] As is well
known, the Lamoneda executive acted swiftly to annul the unification, although, in contrast to the head-on attack against the Valencian dissidents, in this case there was no substitution of the provincial leadership *en masse*. Instead, the existing leadership was
supplemented by new members from reliable reformist-oriented
socialist groups in the province.[52] But the whole episode increased
Lamoneda's distrust of the pro-communist left socialists who had
become his most vocal supporters. As general secretary of the PSOE,
he had to maintain a difficult balance between the pro- and anti-
communist tendencies in the party. In August 1937 Lamoneda
wrote to Ranchal about rumours of fusions between socialist and
communist groups in Jaén province. Conversely, by 1938 pro-
communist members of the Cordoban federation were requesting
national executive support against Ranchal – which Lamoneda
refused.[53] The methods Lamoneda employed to maintain a balance

between pro- and anti-communist elements in the PSOE federations unfortunately alienated a good many socialists of every hue in the provincial federations who resented what they saw as his strong-arm tactics. At the Jaén congress in November 1937, for example, there was much criticism of the fact that Jerónimo Bugeda, representing the national executive, had arrived accompanied by several *carabineros*.[54] Lamoneda was seemingly prepared to enforce party discipline with a reminder that he would remove, *a la valenciana*, local leaderships which refused to accept the national executive's discipline.

The bitter organisational rivalry being fought out between the PSOE and the PCE was creating new tensions in the socialist movement, as well as exacerbating existing pre-war divisions. The situation in the Madrid socialist federation is particularly instructive here. In the capital the PCE was strong. As a result, the PSOE's Madrid federation was desperate to secure a socialist civil governor for the province – both to counteract the PCE's increasing influence and to defuse the tension and violence developing apace between socialists and communists in the capital. At the time of the *caballerista* provincial delegates' meetings in Valencia, the Madrid socialists – who were represented at the dissident meetings by the left socialist Carlos Rubiera – bargained their support for Lamoneda against a promise of national executive intercession with the socialist interior minister, Zugazagoitia, over the matter of Madrid's civil governor. 'The socialist federation of Madrid province considered it vital for the political health of the PSOE in the province that a civil governor should be appointed and that he should be a socialist as the two previous ones had been. The provisional nature of Madrid's civilian administration had to be brought to an end once and for all.'[55] The Madrid federal executive – much reduced by the effects of the war – had only three serving members; the president, Henche, secretary, Rubiera and vice-secretary, Cuevas. Lamoneda was its vice-president, but he and other members were fully engaged elsewhere. Rafael Henche and Carlos Rubiera represented the two sides of the PSOE dispute. The latter had signed the January 1937 *caballerista* manifesto and his experience as Galarza's under-secretary in the interior ministry had alerted him to the PCE's increasing political influence.[56] But the Madrid federation's president was Rafael Henche. While he was not uncritical of Lamoneda, nor entirely without sympathy for the socialist left's case against the PCE's proselytism and political methods, Henche was unreservedly hostile to Largo Caballero. He considered Largo's behaviour to have long been grossly irresponsible and the man himself to have been almost

the single cause of the party's misfortune and disunity since October
1934.

Henche's estimation of Largo Caballero was implicit in a letter
sent on behalf of the Madrid socialist executive to *El Socialista* in June
1937. In it Henche declared that the PCE's education minister, Jesús
Hernández, should receive a public reprimand from the PSOE for
his infamous personal attack on Largo Caballero.[57] Henche argued
that it was the duty of every socialist to defend his or her comrades
against outrageous and scurrilous accusations. But, he added, it was
also the organisation's right to call all socialists to account for their
behaviour. Here Henche was outlining diplomatically what he declared much more bluntly during the sessions of the July 1937
national committee meeting: that it was long overdue for the PSOE
to call Largo Caballero to account for his conduct since October
1934.

As the general secretary of Artes Blancas, the bakers and confectioners' federation, Henche was also soon to be at the centre of the
battle in the trade union federation.[58] The suspension of Artes
Blancas from the UGT because of Henche's public criticism of
Largo's prima donna behaviour during the May 1937 crisis brought
the massive division in the union federation to the surface. It also set
the precedent for the spate of suspensions and expulsions of industrial federations by Largo's executive which in turn hastened the
direct intervention of the reformist socialists and thus the removal of
the *Caballeristas* from the UGT's national executive.

The ascendancy of the reformist socialists in the party organisation during the war can be traced directly to the national committee
meeting of July 1937. Its outcome determined the balance of power
in the PSOE until the end of the war. The socialist left had sought to
use party statute to re-establish its presence on the party's national
executive committee. That the *Caballeristas* failed in their endeavours
was largely the result of Ramón Lamoneda's careful managing of
proceedings at the national committee meeting. He turned it against
an excluded left, using the forum instead to strengthen the position of
his executive, whose authority had been in doubt ever since its
election in June 1936. As the maximum authority of the party
between congresses, the national committee endorsed Lamoneda's
policy of joint action with the PCE and backed a purge against the
pockets of *caballerista* support in the provincial and local party
organisations. Indeed, the effective implementation of Lamoneda's
joint action strategy demanded that the party left be forced to accept
national executive discipline.

The reformist victory in July 1937 was, however, far from perfect.

Left socialist opportunism aside, increasing organisational rivalry between socialists and communists was a very real problem. The fate of the socialist youth movement provided a salutory warning, while there were disturbing reports of PCE advances in the hierarchies of several of the UGT's industrial federations. The PSOE executive had to confront the problem of how to block further inroads into the socialist rank and file. Its difficulties were compounded by the unique circumstances of the civil war. The political isolation of the Republic in the international arena made Soviet aid indispensable to the Loyalists. On these grounds alone the PSOE could not afford to be seen publicly opposing the socialist–communist unity option favoured by Stalin and the Comintern. On the practical front too, the efficiency of the Republican war effort depended on co-operation between socialists and communists on a daily basis. These were the factors which determined Lamoneda's wartime strategy. But even in July 1937 his policies were beginning to provoke tensions inside the reformist camp itself, as some socialists – fearing the further erosion of their rank and file – questioned the soundness of joint action in the long term. Such reservations would grow steadily throughout the next year, as tensions increased between the PSOE and the PCE.

7 The purge of the party left and the growing crisis in the reformist camp

Largo Caballero is ousted from the Leadership of the Socialist Parliamentary Party

By the end of July 1937 the PSOE executive had seized control of the socialist left's major stronghold in the party, the Valencian provincial federation. Reinforced by the national committee's vote of confidence, the reformists were determined to clear the left out of its last strongholds and thus to homogenise the organisational hierarchy of the party. Lamoneda's words to the PSOE's national committee had been prophetic and a clear warning of the executive's intentions:

> We are convinced that we will have to take dramatic steps which will perhaps be difficult for us. Were we not prepared so to do, to act resolutely against indiscipline, then the life of this executive would end here in this national committee meeting. The executive cherishes the hope that our comrades will see the error of their ways – or at least hopes that those who do not will constitute such a tiny group, with so slight an influence among the party membership – that the cure for internal disorder will take rapid effect.[1]

The first target was the PSOE's parliamentary party, controlled by the left socialists with Largo Caballero as president, Enrique de Francisco as vice-president and Rodolfo Llopis as secretary. The possibility of *caballerista* opposition here was something the PSOE executive was not prepared to risk, as it was tantamount to treasonous obstruction of the Republican government at war.[2]

Accordingly, on 29 September at the first of four meetings of the PSOE's parliamentary group which preceded the 1 October session of the Cortes, a group of reformist socialists including Vidarte, Zugazagoitia and Molina Conejero, the new president of the Valencian provincial federation, presented a motion calling for the removal of the parliamentary group's executive committee.[3] In the presence of both Largo Caballero and Indalecio Prieto, they proposed that:

126

today it is more vital than ever that the leadership of the PSOE should be united in thought and action, and [...] in order the better to ensure that the activities of the parliamentary party are informed by the policy directives of the Party, it would not only be fitting but is also essential that the leadership of the parliamentary party and the PSOE executive should adhere to the same policy line, and where at all possible, *that they should be composed of the same people.*[4]

Ostensibly, the case against the left-controlled committee of the minority was that it had failed signally to perform its duties, not once calling a meeting of the group during the war. Largo Caballero, who as president was chairing the meeting, replied accurately that the non-functioning of the parliamentary group was merely one symptom of a more generally abnormal constitutional situation provoked by the war itself. If the Cortes itself was not functioning, then meetings of the socialist parliamentary party were superfluous. In this Largo was echoed by his lieutenant, Rodolfo Llopis. Largo was not particularly concerned, however, to defend the group's committee against a charge which he knew and bluntly declared to be a red herring: 'There is no point in our wasting each other's time. Frankly, you have come here with the express intention of throwing us off the executive of the parliamentary party – quite simply that.' Of course, that Largo Caballero was right in this respect must be set against the fact that both the party and the left were equally arming themselves with regulatory pretexts in order to defeat the opposition. The UGT executive, of which Largo Caballero was general secretary, was, at the very same moment, expelling industrial federations ostensibly for dues arrears, but in reality as part of its campaign against the increasing strength of the anti-*caballerista* factions in the union.[5]

There was a great deal of plain speaking on both sides, but the spleen venting came especially from the left in the course of the parliamentary party's first meeting. This doubtless reflected its own awareness of imminent defeat. The PSOE's parliamentary party itself had been badly affected as a result of the military rising. Out of a total of ninety-nine deputies dating from the February 1936 Popular Front elections and among which a clear majority had been Caballero's supporters, some twenty-seven were either dead or listed as missing since 18 July. Although this figure includes both Margarita Nelken and Francisco Montiel, socialist deputies for Badajoz and Murcia respectively, who had both defected to the PCE since February 1936, it is significant that nineteen of the lost deputies were from constituencies in the rural south.[6] Of the remaining members, fifty-nine were present at the meeting of 29 September.

Compared to the pre-war situation, the tables had been turned on the left and by a slim margin of some five votes the reformist socialists were now in the majority. When the reformists' proposal was eventually put to the vote, the *Caballeristas* lost by 24 votes to 32. Although, true to form, Largo, Llopis and de Francisco abstained, their decision either way could not have altered the final outcome in favour of the reformists.

Apart from the proposers, the votes in favour of the reformists' motion included those of Negrín, Prieto, Lamoneda, González Peña and Anastasio de Gracia. The votes against were those of Aurelio Almagro, Luis Araquistain, Cresenciano Bilbao, Eduardo Blanco, Juan Campos Villagrán, Wenceslao Carrillo, Manuel Castro Molina, Enrique Cerezo, Emiliano Díaz Castro, Isidro Escandell, Alberto Fernández Ballesteros, Angel Galarza, Ginés Ganga Tremiño, Salvador García Muñoz, Melchor Guerrero, Carlos Hernández Zancajo, Alejandro Peris, Gabriel Pradal, Luis Romero Solano, Carlos Rubiera, José Sosa Hormigo, Pascual Tomás, Miguel Villalta and Ricardo Zabalza. Out of a total of twenty-four deputies, nineteen, or 83 per cent, came from the south – and in the vast majority they were deputies for either Andalucian or Extremaduran constituencies. This further reinforces the point that the bedrock of support for the *Caballeristas* remained the agrarian south.[7]

The new committee elected on 30 September was constituted as follows: Ramón González Peña was elected as president with thirty-six votes, José Prat as vice-president with thirty-five, and Ramón Lamoneda took the secretaryship with thirty-six votes. The homogenisation of the PSOE's national leadership was, as a result, almost complete. Ramón González Peña had been elected as president of the PSOE in June 1936, and he was now president of the parliamentary minority. Ramón Lamoneda now held both the general secretaryship of the party and the equivalent in the parliamentary group. It only remained for González Peña to take over as president of the UGT for the seal to be set on the reformists' successful conquest of the entire hierarchy of the socialist movement.

The *Caballeristas* withdrew after the sessions of 29 September. Largo's warning that they would rejoin battle at a later date in a different arena, if somewhat melodramatic, foreshadowed the imminent confrontation inside the UGT. Yet this was, in truth, a battle already lost – the *Caballeristas* were locked in the UGT executive as into a last redoubt. In his memoirs, Azaña states that it was Negrín's intention to hold off the opening of the Cortes until Largo had ceased to be general secretary of the UGT in order to defuse the potential impact of any inflammatory speech he might make during its ses-

sion. Negrín, in scheduling the Cortes for 1 October 1937, informed
Azaña that the union's national committee was about to relieve the
entire Largo executive of its duties.[8] More representative of the
reality of the situation than Largo Caballero's bluster was the total
absence of the socialist left from the Cortes after the opening session
of 1 October. The left had been banished from the party, the socialist
minority, the permanent deputation of the Cortes, and Llopis had
resigned as the secretary of the House (*Cámara*), to be replaced by
Lamoneda. The socialist left had been excluded from virtually every
aspect of the national political leadership of Republican Spain.

After the left had lost control of the Valencian federation, the
centre of socialist dissidence, such as it existed, returned to the
ASM. By the beginning of August 1937 the left's 'old guard' was
filtering back into the life of the ASM.[9] The reformists saw this as the
socialist left returning in force to take up the cudgels from where it
had left off in September 1936 when, called to government office, the
ASM's administrative affairs had been entrusted to a provisional
committee.[10] By the beginning of September, the ASM committee
was already at loggerheads with the Lamoneda executive over its
strident and public criticism of the PCE. The ASM published a
particularly inflammatory circular in which it blamed the PCE for
destroying antifascist unity. It portrayed the communists as political
renegades, out to absorb the socialist organisation and, to boot, in
thrall to a supranational authority. (The Comintern was accused
of destroying 'the Spanishness of both the JSU and the PSUC'
('desespañolización de las juventudes y del P. S. de Cataluña').[11] In
response to this broadside from the *Caballeristas*, the PSOE leadership replied via the editorial of *El Socialista*, attacking the left for its
irresponsibility and lack of party discipline.[12] The executive's criticism also bore the marks of Prieto and Lamoneda's conviction that,
at root, the left's disgruntlement could be reduced to a single factor,
annoyance at having been excluded from power. The post-May
rumpus was simply 'a rebellion of the unemployed' ('una subleva-
ción de cesantes').[13]

But although Largo Caballero had regular meetings with the
other left stalwarts of the ASM,[14] in general the centre of heated
battle had switched from the party to the union. This was to be in
every sense Largo Caballero's last battle, if not the last one his
supporters would fight on his behalf. He took the defeat of his UGT
executive extremely personally and the deep sense of failure and
pessimism certainly had a great deal to do with his sudden withdrawal from public life. All the signs of an imminent withdrawal
were in evidence at the separate meeting convened by the left

socialist deputies after their defeat in the parliamentary party on the eve of the Cortes session of 1 October.[15] In the presence of an almost silent Largo, his supporters debated the advantages and disadvantages of splitting the PSOE's parliamentary party and identifying themselves with the UGT executive over the May 1937 cabinet crisis. But Largo himself seemed already to have conceded defeat. 'Do we give in or not? It seems to me that we've already done so.' The discussion at these meetings was immensely revealing of the socialist left's inertia, born of strategic as well as ideological bankruptcy. Cresenciano Bilbao encapsulated its failure when he commented that the party left had wasted its opportunities. The overwhelming impression which emerges from the proceedings is of the left's conservatism and timidity. In the last analysis, it was frightened of the consequences of launching an all-out attack on the Lamoneda executive in the Cortes. As a result, nothing concrete emerged from the meetings. But, typically, neither did the left draw the logical conclusion that it was time to end their war of attrition against the PSOE leadership. Largo himself may have been on the point of opting out of the battle, but the prospects for a reconciliation remained, as ever, non-existent. As Galarza expressed it rather cynically, '... go and ask the party executive for what? An end to the strife? They wouldn't concede it and, anyway, it would be of no use to us.'[16]

Largo would, of course, eventually make his long-awaited speech. But when it came, on 17 October, it was a decided anti-climax. The Teatro Pardiñas in Madrid was packed to capacity. On the platform with Largo sat Araquistain, de Baraibar, Carlos Hernández Zancajo and Enrique de Francisco and the speech was transmitted to a number of other auditoriums which were also full. It was true that it was heavily censored, but this could not have affected the basic tenor of the speech. It came across as a catalogue of personal grievances rather than a lofty or weighty indictment of a political line.[17] Although Largo's isolation after the Pardiñas speech was in part the result of the reformists' determination to clamp down on the left's public dissidence, his withdrawal from public life was also self-willed. Largo seemed to have decided for himself that his personal war with the PSOE was over. From late October 1937, resident in Barcelona as the central government and political parties were based there, Largo devoted most of his time to conspicuously low-key pursuits, such as his duties as a councillor of the Fundación Cesáro de Cerro at the meetings of the Banco de España. His followers had effectively lost their figurehead. Luis Araquistain and Llopis did their best to bring Largo out of his self-imposed internal

exile, but without success.[18] Why this withdrawal occurred must
remain a matter of conjecture. But it seems a reasonable supposition
that, bereft of any coherent alternative strategy, Largo was simply
not prepared to go down in party history as the leader responsible for
tearing the PSOE asunder in the middle of a civil war.

The Lamoneda executive, for its part, was certainly concerned
both to encourage Largo's silence and also to curtail any public
manifestation of internal party division by his supporters. On 14
January 1938 the socialist parliamentary group censured Largo for
complaining directly to Negrín about the restrictions imposed on his
movements. The reformists argued that both discretion and party
discipline ought to have dictated that Largo first approach the
executive of the PSOE's parliamentary group, instead of publicising
the matter by going directly to the prime minister.[19] Araquistain,
Llopis and a third *Caballerista* of long standing, Ginés Ganga, were
also censured for their behaviour.[20] The latter had written to a
number of socialist groups referring to the 'persecution' of Largo by
the Negrín government.[21] The reformists, now in the dominant
position, were determined to maintain their advantage – even at the
risk of over-reaction. In reformist eyes, the very existence of the left
threatened the viability of joint action between the PSOE and the
PCE. But, however justified the resentment which the *Caballeristas*
inspired in the rest of the party, the fact remained that the problematic nature of relations between socialists and communists was *not* an
invention of the party left.

The abiding dilemma for the socialist leadership in the war
stemmed from the incontrovertible fact that both national and
international factors committed them to collaboration with the PCE.
The isolationism of Britain and France and non-intervention gave
the PSOE no choice. Spanish socialists had, moreover, to deal with a
rapidly expanding Communist Party from a position of distinct
inferiority. The PSOE itself experienced enormous frustration at the
crisis of the international socialist movement – of both its political
and labour wings – which crystallised over the Spanish conflict. The
contribution of international socialism, at anything other than the
level of the isolated individual, consisted in numerous declarations of
moral solidarity and little else. By comparison, it was manifestly
obvious that the Comintern was providing support of quite a different order. This inevitably did nothing to enhance either the prestige
or the moral authority of the PSOE. It was in this context that
Spanish socialism had to compete with the PCE and confront the
massive problems on the home front. In public the PSOE never
ceased alternating moderate, reasoned argument with impassioned

plea – how the Spanish Republic's war effort should be seen by Britain and France as self-defence against international fascist aggression. However, in the relative privacy of national and executive committee meetings, the anger at what was perceived as an attitude of political and moral betrayal by the Western democracies and their labour movements was made very plain.[22] Even publicly Indalecio Prieto declared that it was hard for the PSOE to appear as either credible, authoritative or dynamic, as compared to the PCE, when the International to which it belonged was doing nothing for the Spanish Republic.[23] And throughout 1938 *El Socialista* editorials would become increasingly vitriolic about the passivity of the two socialist Internationals.

It was Indalecio Prieto's vivid understanding of the impossibility of the international situation which led him, in sheer desperation in the spring of 1937, to propose to the party executive that it seriously consider accepting unification with the PCE.[24] Such a proposal naturally met with consternation all round and was pursued no further. According to Manuel Cordero, it was he and Lamoneda who took it upon themselves to dissuade Prieto from persisting in his proposal.[25] The comments of executive member, Manuel Albar, reflect the general bewilderment:

> I don't know if the others are mad or if I am. First of all, we have Caballero, who, of all the PSOE and UGT leaders, most opposed the Party's mooted membership of the Third International, and then, suddenly, he proposes to the ASM (which, moreover, accepts), that a resolution supporting the unification of the Socialist and Communist Parties be presented before party congress. And now we have Prieto, who of all of us was the most committed to an alliance with the republicans ... and now he's suggesting exactly the same thing as Caballero. Honestly, I don't know what to think, or what will become of our Party.'[26]

But Prieto's about-turn did not signify an ideological conversion. It was a piece of *realpolitik* deriving from his appreciation of the crucialness of Soviet military aid. For entirely the same motives, Prieto, as always keeping a low profile in the internal life of the PSOE, backed Ramón Lamoneda's negotiation of the PSOE–PCE common action pact in August 1937.[27] Prieto, in his ministerial capacity, had also been extremely close to Rosenberg, the first Soviet ambassador in Spain. Their relationship was a consequence of the frequent consultations necessary between the two after the transfer of the Bank of Spain's gold reserves to the Soviet Union in late 1936. This was an operation of which Prieto had been fully aware. The only effect of his subsequent denials, therefore, was to make him appear ridiculous and dishonest to his party colleagues.[28] Prieto's closeness to Rosenberg further contributed to his conviction that the price of victory in the war was the fusion of the Socialist and Communist Parties. As Araquistain commented ironically: 'Rosenberg is constantly closeted with Prieto, who is more "bolshevised" than us.'[29] But the fact that Prieto, in the course of a PSOE executive meeting in Valencia in April 1937, could have proposed the organisational unification of the PSOE and the PCE – albeit in the light of a desperate international climate – is an indication of the extent of his personal political crisis which had been growing since the events of May 1936. Vidarte's conviction was that Prieto was prepared for anything to win the war, even self-destruction. But the parties would never be united because the majority of the PSOE executive would never agree to it.[30]

The Prieto of the war years was worlds away from the statesman of the Second Republic whose energy and political intelligence were legendary. While one must be clear about the terrifying enormity of the problems confronting the loyalists in their desperate bid to keep the war effort going, an appreciation of the 'other' Prieto's failures and his personal political crisis during the war is essential to our understanding of the erosion of the PSOE. It seemed as if his political will had been corroded by the disappointment and frustration of his defeat at the hands of the party left in May 1936. As an awareness of the magnitude of his error grew – that he had not fought nearly hard enough against Largo then, when it might still have been possible to defuse the military time bomb – so bitterness sapped his energy and distorted his political sensibilities. Given Prieto's stature and importance to the PSOE and the Republic, the effects of his deep personal crisis had disastrous consequences for both in the long term. For Prieto the war consisted of a long series of refusals to act. Once he had perceived that even *his* efforts and will would be reduced to nought as a consequence of the hostile international conjuncture, there is evidence of a clear desire, especially after April 1938, to avoid sharing any part of the responsibility for what he saw as inevitable Republican defeat.

After May 1937 Negrín, as prime minister, was subjected to the same overwhelming negativity from Prieto as the socialist executive had experienced during the early months of the war. The impression given by Vidarte, socialist executive member and Prieto's political intimate of long standing, is one of intense crisis, brought on mainly by an increasing sense of his own powerlessness in the naval and air ministry. Vidarte refers to certain failures of judgement and most

notoriously to Prieto's misplaced confidence in Aranda, the military
commander in Asturias who successfully played a double game
against the Republic which lost it Oviedo. These failures, understandable in themselves, caused an intensification of Prieto's infamous pessimism, which, together with the sudden outbursts of anger
and frustration at whichever of his party colleagues happened to be
closest, finally destroyed the myth of Prieto's infallibility among the
executive.[31] His greatest trauma was undoubtedly caused by the war
in the north.[32] Prieto's constant sense of his powerless to aid his own
patria chica (birthplace/home territory) and the subsequent fall of
Bilbao and Asturias were responsible for a sea change in his behaviour. The acute shortages plaguing the Republican defence and in
particular the lack of air support, exasperated Prieto. In March 1937
when the nationalist bombardment of Bilbao was imminent, his
failure to secure adequate protection for the north resulted in lengthy
attempts to disown personal responsibility for the débâcle. There
occurred a frantic exchange of telegrams between Prieto, Largo
Caballero and Irujo, the Basque minister without portfolio, over
who was responsible for the provision of air support for the north.[33]
Neither Largo nor Prieto was interested in claiming jurisdiction
because both realised the opprobrium attendant on what would be
the almost certain failure of provision.

The opposition came from the central General Staff and their
Soviet advisers who were prioritising the Madrid front and refusing
point-blank to dispatch aircraft to the north. By 1 April, Irujo was
pleading with a desperate and frustrated Prieto. The latter, whose
replies adduced technical difficulties and the opposition of General
Douglas, the head of the Soviet air forces in Spain, seemed mainly
concerned to absolve himself in the face of the probable collapse of
the northern front.[34] Indeed Prieto even attempted to resign over the
loss of Bilbao, as he would later over the loss of Gijón in October
1937. But on neither occasion was this accepted by the government
and Prieto did not persist.[35] It also seems plausible that the sudden
willingness to countenance socialist–communist unification at this
juncture was inextricably bound up with his realisation of the
Republic's absolute dependence on Soviet aid. Impulsive as ever,
Prieto's decision was an instant one. If the price of Republican
victory was the loss of socialist identity, then so be it, because with
defeat everything would be lost.[36]

Prieto's self-distancing from the PSOE was evident in his attempt
to resign from the national executive in October 1937. He argued
that his ministerial obligations were preventing him from attending
its meetings. But Lamoneda declined to accept.[37] A number of

Prieto's close colleagues were also critical of his political dishonesty. Lamoneda commented bitterly in private that 'it would never occur to any of Prieto's colleagues to point to his [close relationship with Rosenberg] as evidence of his having sold out for Russian gold.'[38] Yet this was precisely the sort of crude accusation he levelled so unfairly against fellow-socialists. Particularly irritating were Prieto's ever more vocal protests over his personal 'victimisation' and the widespread 'communist domination' of the political life of the Republic. Veteran socialist Gabriel Morón argued that Prieto's own tolerant policy in the early stages of the war, where the Soviet Union and its advisers were concerned, rendered downright hypocritical his subsequent strident criticism of Negrín's manner of proceeding. As a minister, Prieto had never been particularly rigorous over the political affiliations of those appointed and certainly operated no policy of discriminating in favour of socialists, not even those from his own camp. In Largo's cabinet, he picked a republican as his under-secretary.[39] According to Gabriel Morón, Prieto's own impressionistic recruitment policy – whereby he appointed widely from among friends and contacts – was a major contributory factor to the PCE's ascendancy in the SIM, the Republic's counter-intelligence service which the defence minister himself created.[40] As interim director-general of security in June 1937 and the socialist interior minister's right-hand man, Morón was well placed to observe. He suggests that in the early days Prieto had allowed the PCE its head because its men were organised and efficient.[41] This rings true, especially in view of Prieto's attitude to his ministerial portfolio. He tended to see it as a personal appointment rather than a post he was occupying as a leading representative of the PSOE. This occasioned some tensions inside the party executive which felt that Prieto's increasing inattentiveness to any notion of collective responsibility was seriously undermining its own authority.

Like Lamoneda, Morón too attributed Prieto's intense anti-communism to despair, resentment and a sense of personal failure:

> The case which Indalecio Prieto presents, for all his celebrated intelligence, rings hollow. He overplays the role of victim – giving free rein to his anti-communism, which is how he vents his personal despair. He had the opportunity [...] *not* to let himself be 'taken unawares'.... It was incumbent upon him, as upon no other, to ensure that he was not 'caught out' by developments.

Likewise, both Lamoneda and Morón saw his sudden hostility to Negrín as springing from the same source. 'Because whatever Prieto may say, as eloquent and persuasive as he undoubtedly is, the bitterness of the current dispute [between Prieto and Negrín] is personal in origin.'[42] The very stridency of Prieto's anti-communism, which would achieve legendary dimensions by the immediate post-war period, suggests perhaps an uneasy conscience, and almost certainly an awareness of his own previous mistakes.

Prieto and the Socialist Executive: 1938

After the expulsion of the left socialists from their stronghold in the PSOE's provincial federation in Valencia, there occurred a lull in the internal battle in the party. Or, rather, the epicentre of the dispute between the reformists and the party left shifted from the PSOE to the UGT. In the battle in the union federation, an alliance between reformist socialists and those with communist sympathies (unitarists), confronted the *caballerista* old guard. The resulting conflict is dealt with in detail in a subsequent chapter, suffice it to say here that the final outcome was the exclusion, by 1 October 1937, of Largo Caballero and his supporters from their last power base, the national executive committee of the UGT.[43]

Between autumn 1937 and the summer of 1938 the Republic's military situation was deteriorating steadily and there seemed little prospect of improvement in what was, overall, a bleak international horizon. The northern front finally collapsed in October 1937. In an attempt to divert Franco from an all-out attack on Madrid in December, the Republicans launched the Teruel offensive. With the advantage of surprise on their side, they were successful to the extent that the Nationalist assault on Madrid was postponed and Republican troops took control of Teruel in mid-December. But the Nationalists rushed reinforcements from the Madrid zone and, yet again, their material superiority proved decisive. By the middle of February 1938, Teruel was Nationalist once more. March brought the launching of Franco's offensive in Aragón. On 15 April, Catalonia was severed from the central zone of the Republic when the Nationalists reached the Mediterranean at Viñaroz.

In the midst of this military crisis, on 6 April 1938, Prieto ceased to be defence minister in Negrín's cabinet. Behind that simple statement of fact there has always lain a fierce and bitter controversy. This was to continue long after the end of the war and much of it was the product of Prieto's own voluminous output on the subject. It genuinely seems to be the case that the more he and others wrote, the more the original issue was distorted until eventually, in the partisan excesses of the Cold War, all connection with the context of 1938 was lost. A good illustration of the distortion wrought by a Cold War perspective is to be found in the fervent defence of Prieto by as unlikely a champion as Julián Gorkín of the POUM executive. He is on record as unremittingly hostile to Prieto as 'the Republic's number one political wheeler dealer'.[44] However, in *España, primer ensayo de democracia popular*, published in Buenos Aires in 1961 by the CIA-funded 'Asociación Argentina por la Libertad de la Cultura', his virulent anti-communism, or rather anti-stalinism, has triumphed over his memory. Gorkín states that Prieto was even 'forced to consent' to the liquidation of the *Caballeristas* in the PSOE.[45] Gorkín's case is a perfect example of the kind of process which was operating on much of the historical testimony of those on the anti-stalinist and non-communist left. Such was the virulence of the left dissidents' post-war anti-communism that the enormous ideological divisions which had previously existed between them and Prieto as late as 1938 were simply forgotten.

The origins of the political crisis of April 1938 lay in the fact that the unpromising military situation after the Nationalist recapture of Teruel and the subsequent collapse of the Aragón front undermined Prieto's position as defence minister. A succession of defeats could threaten the position of any war minister. Moreover, as Negrín was quick to point out, by 1938 the immense gravity of the Republic's military situation rendered Prieto's level of pessimism unacceptable in a defence minister. This in itself indicates that the relationship between Prieto and Negrín was no longer what the former envisaged it to be. Negrín had well outgrown the role of political protégé. He was no longer prepared, if indeed he ever had been, to act as the instrument via which Prieto could indulge his passion for governing invisibly and, more to the point, without assuming the responsibility for so doing. By April 1938, a clash of personalities and political perspectives was evident. Negrín placed enormous value on morale as a weapon of resistance. Accordingly, he tried to maintain a total compartmentalisation of cabinet and ministerial responsibilities to prevent the circulation of 'negative' or 'pessimistic' information in order to sustain individual and collective morale.[46] Whilst the Republic's military reverses weighed heavily on Prieto, Negrín, convinced that the international political dimension would determine the Republic's fate, sought to exploit an apparent opening on the international horizon. Hitler's occupation of Austria in mid-March and the subsequent reopening of the French frontier by Blum had given Negrín cause for hope. Faced by the evidence of Nazi Germany's aggressive expansionism, Britain and France might yet be persuaded to abandon appeasement as deeply damaging to their own interests.

By the spring of 1938, the communists were eager to get rid of Prieto, and the reason given publicly was certainly genuine. The PCE and their advisers were seriously worried by his 'defeatism'. They feared that his closeness to Azaña and the republican camp, where the desire for a compromise peace with Franco was growing apace, might mean his involvement in clandestine negotiations for a mediated settlement.[47] In this sense, the PCE's clash with Prieto, in late 1937 and 1938, over communist influence in the army and his attempts to curtail it, reflected a real fear that any reduction of their strength in the armed forces threatened to undermine Republican resistance. Indeed, contrary to the conventional wisdom, the PCE was far from confident about even Negrín's commitment to resistance.[48] This is extremely clear from PCE reports for 1938, which grow less certain about Negrín as the year progresses.

By 1938, the PCE was increasingly strident in defence of the Popular Front. This revealed their fear that, as the other loyalist forces, especially the republicans and the middle-class strata, deserted the strategy as one which no longer served their best interests, the PCE was becoming increasingly isolated. Inevitably, they saw the end of Republican resistance and a mediated, non-military resolution of the conflict as very real and frightening possibilities.[49] This was to lead them to attempt a certain remodelling of the Popular Front strategy in order to try to reconquer mass support for it.

The first indications of an impending crisis were apparent from at least the beginning of March 1938 when a violent propaganda campaign was unleashed by the PCE against Prieto and his recently initiated 'política de silencio'. This was the collective name for a series of measures and directives designed to curb party political propaganda in the army and particularly to reduce the influence of the PCE in the political commissariat.[50] Prieto himself constantly threatened resignation because of the campaign against him. When, on 27 February, Dolores Ibárruri publicly criticised Prieto's policy in a meeting organised by the PSUC in Barcelona, the defence minister wrote to Negrín on 1 March offering to resign.[51] Then, on 29 March, a cabinet meeting was held to review the collapse occurring on the Aragón front. This meeting came in the wake of a massive demonstration in Barcelona, organised by the PCE and supported by the CNT, which was designed to manifest popular opposition to all mediated settlements, but particularly to reject the one recently proposed by Labonne, the French ambassador in Barcelona.[52] In such a context, Prieto's consummate pessimism as defence minister, displayed during the cabinet meeting of 29 March, stunned even those most sympathetic to him.[53] A few days prior to this cabinet session proper, the socialist ministers had also met with the PSOE executive, whereupon the differences between Negrín and Prieto over communist aggression, especially in the army, broke the surface. There were also incipient tensions between Negrín and other socialists close to Prieto, such as Julián Zugazagoitia, over what was seen as the prime minister's misguided willingness to sacrifice the fate of the socialist rank and file on the altar of victory in the war.[54]

But as in May 1936 and on several occasions thereafter, Prieto hesitated. He chose not to put himself at the head of mounting socialist disquiet. Admittedly, the PSOE executive was in a very awkward position, caught between Negrín and Prieto, and socialist opinion was divided.[55] But Prieto had political backing from some socialists and the CNT leadership as well.[56] Yet the most active initiative he took was to insist repeatedly to Negrín that if the latter considered it necessary then he would be happy to be removed from the defence ministry.[57] When this happened, however, it was to be quite a different story. In the published account of the crisis Negrín draws a revealing distinction between his separation of Prieto from the defence portfolio and the latter's *own* decision to abandon the cabinet – which he subsequently imputed to pressure from the premier.[58] In response, Prieto declared, tellingly, that it would have been quite impossible for him to have accepted a lesser ministry, given the status of his previous office.[59]

On 6 April 1938 *El Socialista* carried an extremely skeletal report of the cabinet reshuffle which left Prieto out of the government. Negrín, as prime minister, would henceforth also take personal control of the defence ministry, while being replaced in the treasury by his lieutenant Francisco Méndez Aspe, formerly Negrín's subordinate in the finance ministry. The other socialist ministers, making a total of four, were, Paulino Gómez Sáez, originally a protégé of Prieto's, in the interior ministry, Ramón González Peña as minister of justice and Alvarez del Vayo returned to the cabinet as foreign minister, replacing the former incumbent, the republican José Giral, who remained in the cabinet but without a portfolio.

The internal political balance of the cabinet, 4 socialists, 5 republicans including Jaime Ayguadé (Esquerra), 1 communist, 1 member of the CNT and Irujo for the Basque Nationalists, signalled a return to an integrated government of all loyalist elements, with an increase in socialist and republican representation.[60] Apart from Negrín himself, however, there had been a complete change in the socialist personnel. Not only had Prieto gone, but so had Julián Zugazagoitia. A close collaborator of the ex-minister of defence,

Zugazagoitia had been appointed interior minister by Negrín in May 1937 at Prieto's express request.[61] But Zugazagoitia also came to enjoy the confidence of Negrín, who used him as a go-between cum conciliator during the April 1938 cabinet crisis in a vain attempt to reach a compromise with Prieto and thus keep him in the cabinet.

Rather than a gesture of solidarity with Prieto, Zugazagoitia's departure from the cabinet was in fact the result of long-endured feelings of alienation induced by an acquaintance with the realities of his office as interior minister. Having accepted the post reluctantly, at Prieto's behest, Zugazagoitia had never felt at ease in it. No sooner had he been confirmed in the post than he had to deal with the explosion of political violence against the POUM. Above all, the scandalous disappearance of the party's leader, Andreu Nin, an incident in which communist security forces nominally under Zugazagoitia's control were involved, was a shock from which he never recovered.[62] His replacement in the interior ministry in April 1938, Paulino Gómez, a fellow Basque, had collaborated closely with Zugazagoitia, and came specifically recommended to Negrín by the outgoing minister.[63] For all that Zugazagoitia had jettisoned his ministerial responsibilities, he remained in Negrín's service in the subsecretariat of defence.

The return of the two trade union organisations to the cabinet was an extremely important development, in terms both of its political symbolism and also for the practical needs of the war effort. The CNT representative was Segundo Blanco – Negrín's personal choice from a list of three names (Horacio Prieto, García Oliver and Blanco) presented by the CNT.[64] The UGT was represented by its president, Ramón González Peña, the reformist leader of the Asturian miners' union, who was also president of the Socialist Party. His presence set the seal on the reformists' exclusion of the *Caballeristas* from their last stronghold, the national executive of the union federation. For the reformists this had been a crucial victory, not least because they had viewed the Largo executive's half-hearted support of Negrín since the May 1937 cabinet crisis as virtual treason, given the increasingly straitened circumstances in which his government was forced to function. The election of the new reformist-dominated UGT executive on 1 October 1937 had paved the way for the UGT-inspired practical action pact of March 1938 between itself and the CNT, which directly preceded and was instrumental in the unions' return to government.[65] This pact between the unions – which is discussed in greater detail below – meant victory for the parties and the state over the power and independence of the unions. In the CNT by that point, the political trend (*políticos*) identified with the organisation's former general secretary Horacio Prieto, was in the ascendant. Viewed with hostility by the radical anarchists, the *políticos* were prepared to accommodate the libertarian organisation's doctrine and practice to the political structure of the Republican state. In the UGT, any resistance to the 'depoliticisation' of the unions' role had already been quashed by the socialist union's new reformist-led national executive.[66]

The removal of the communist education minister Jesús Hernández in April 1938 corroborates Negrín's declaration that he sought to retain Prieto in the cabinet in another post. Clearly the removal of the minister who had, under a pseudonym, published savage criticisms of the defence minister's policies was a prerequisite of Prieto's retention.[67] The Comintern was also in favour of at least reducing, if not entirely removing, the communist presence from the loyalist cabinet in yet another attempt to establish a dialogue with the Western democracies. But the PCE's lower profile at cabinet level from April 1938 by no means constituted a commensurate decline in its effective political power and Hernández himself was soon after appointed as chief of political commissars for the Army group of the centre–south zone.

The reshuffle also signified the consolidation in the cabinet of those opposed to capitulation. Whereas Giral had shared Azaña's desire for a mediated settlement, Alvarez del Vayo, who replaced him as foreign minister, was, unsurprisingly, an unconditional supporter of resistance. Indeed, the very resolution of the crisis was a victory for the resistance camp. Since he was now wedded to the idea of a compromise peace, Azaña had procrastinated throughout its course, seeking an opportunity to change the issue on the agenda from a proposed cabinet reshuffle to the feasibility of the Republic pursuing a resistance policy. But the republican groups and their cabinet representatives, while they supported Azaña, were not yet prepared to do so openly and thus risk a breach in the loyalist ranks. In short, then, the resolution of the crisis was also a victory for the policy of Popular Front itself – albeit a tenuous one, given the enormous differences which were now very close to breaking the surface. The fact that the UGT–CNT pact was brought to fruition at this point also provided an important boost for the confidence of the resistance camp. The practical resources, in terms of productive capacity and organisational support, as well as the moral backing of the two great union movements, shored up the Popular Front alliance, providing a vital measure of consolidation at a tense moment when loyalist unity appeared particularly brittle.

Negrín emerged from the April cabinet crisis with his personal authority increased. On 1 May, shored up by the fact that French aid, renewed in March, was continuing to arrive, Negrín sought both to stiffen Republican resistance and to engage the attention of Britain and France by publishing his famous Thirteen Points. These constituted a declaration of the Republic's political position in which the prime minister stressed the need to maintain Spain's political and economic integrity against all foreign penetration. As well as making specific proposals, for example, that all foreign troops be withdrawn, the Thirteen Points emphasised the Spanish Republic's commitment to pluralist, democratic values, such as freedom of speech and religious liberty. Negrín's supreme objective in so doing was to convince Britain and France of their own stake in the survival of the Republic and thus of the necessity of ending non-intervention which was slowly strangling their sister democracy. The absence of any international response to the Thirteen Points was a bitter blow for Negrín. Nothing, it seemed, could budge Britain from its policy of appeasement, whilst in France, Blum's replacement as prime minister by the more cautious republican Daladier led to the frontier being closed once again by the end of May.

At the time of the April 1938 crisis although there was a great deal of comment in the press, Prieto emphasised his continuing total identification with both the government and the socialist executive.[68] Indeed, the nearest approximation to an expression of reservation about Prieto's separation from the defence portfolio came from Lamoneda himself, as PSOE general secretary, and this in spite of Prieto's subsequent accusations of Lamoneda's 'crypto-communism'.[69] The real controversy over the April events was in fact only created several months later as a result of Prieto's infamous speech to the PSOE's national committee in August 1938.[70] However, by the time of the exchange of letters between Negrín and Prieto in 1939, the latter was referring to the 'struggle' to eject him.[71] In terms of startling revelations, Prieto's speech before the PSOE's national committee in August 1938 was a total anti-climax – rather as Largo Caballero's speech of 17 October 1937 had been. Nor does the parallel end there. Both of these veteran socialist leaders delivered petty and vindictive spleen-ventings which amazed their respective audiences, given the fact that the Republic was caught in the middle of a bloody civil war. Prieto surpassed his old rival, leaving stunned the members of the socialist executive and the representatives of the national committee. It was not intimations of high political treason and double-dealing which shocked them but rather evidence of his deep personal crisis and of unsavoury aspects of Prieto's own personality. As Zugazagoitia reported, 'talking informally with friends afterwards, [Prieto] unwittingly offered an apposite criticism of his own speech. "After speaking, I felt the kind of relief one feels after having..." (There followed a verb not normally heard in public.)' Zugazagoitia and Vidarte, both extremely close to Prieto, reported the no less damning comment of Prieto's former right-hand man, PSOE president Ramón González Peña, that the speech was 'small-minded and bitter, like everything he did', 'full of pettiness and resentment like Prieto himself'.[72]

The essence of Prieto's case, both in his speech, in its published form, *Cómo y por qué salí del ministerio de defensa nacional*, and throughout his bitter and nitpicking contribution to the *Epistolario Prieto–Negrín* is that he was thrown out of the defence ministry by Negrín at the behest of the Communist Party. Negrín's own rejection of such a Manichean and exclusive view of the chain of events did not cause Prieto to modify the stridency of his denunciations in the slightest. He was even less mollified by the reminder that he had himself often told the prime minister that he was free to dispose of the defence portfolio as he saw fit and, if so, that he, Prieto, would remain to serve in whatever capacity Negrín judged best.[73]

The prospect of a devastating clash between Negrín and Prieto during the sessions of the August 1938 national committee was more than the socialist collectivity dared to contemplate. In the event, however, this would not occur until the exile period. Only then would the 'time bomb' primed at the PSOE's August meeting explode as the massive battle between Negrín and Prieto which poisoned the party's life for decades.[74] In effect, after having discharged all his rancour before the assembled gathering, Prieto quit the session definitively without waiting even to dispute the crucial policy issues with Negrín – namely the PSOE's political strategy, relations with the PCE, the problem of the youth movement and internal unity in the socialist movement. Yet these were the very issues which Prieto was to claim subsequently lay at the root of his dispute with Negrín and the party leadership.[75] Once again Prieto had run from a fight and ducked his political responsibilities. This is the most favourable judgement one can pass on his withdrawal in August 1938. For if Prieto was not moved by his desire to avoid placing the PSOE and the socialist ministers in a dilemma, then his whole argument has to be seen as a piece of hypocrisy motivated purely by cumulative rancour and hurt pride. Prieto's notorious private war in exile against those of his PSOE colleagues, including most notably Negrín, Lamoneda and González Peña, who went on attempting, for considerably longer than he did, to weather the political storm and to salvage what they could for both the Republi-

can war effort and the socialist movement in Spain, appears extremely hard to justify in the light of his behaviour after the hasty
withdrawal in August 1938.

This withdrawal constituted Prieto's first step in distancing himself from the PSOE's wartime leadership. He clearly saw its attrition
and even destruction as unavoidable given its identification with
inevitable Republican defeat. Prieto's disillusion with Europe was
clear in a speech he made on 9 October 1938 to a gathering of the
Unión Iberoamericana in Barcelona.[76] The Old World was morally
and politically extinct, he declared. Spain would have to look to the
New World for aid in the massive work of economic reconstruction
after the war.[77] Prieto thus proffered his full resignation from the
PSOE's national executive at the August 1938 national committee
meeting in Barcelona. This was, quite naturally, entirely unacceptable to the executive. Prieto, however, engaged in full flight, was
adamant and it fell to Lamoneda to work out a compromise whereby
Prieto would not formally be considered to have resigned, but the
executive would grant him special dispensation from attending
meetings.[78] Thereafter Prieto was as good as his word, consistently
refusing every suggestion by the executive to reinvolve him in the life
of the party. In mid-May 1938, Prieto's rejection of the offer to travel
as Republican ambassador to Mexico was understandable. Azaña
was hoping to procure Negrín's removal and thus wanted Prieto to
step into the breach. This plan was still-born, but Prieto's refusals
became a constant. For example, he refused to represent the PSOE
either at the congress of the French Socialist Party (SFIO) in June
1938, or at that of the Belgian Socialist Party in October 1938.[79] In
the immediate post-war period, Ramón Lamoneda, who had fought
harder than anyone to remobilise Prieto, offered an analysis of his
motives which constitutes a steely judgement upon Prieto's political
career:

> Where [did] Prieto's anti-communism stem from? I think it [formed]
> part of a strategy for exile. As always, acutely sensitive to the political
> climate, Prieto realised that anti-communism was becoming a 'popular'
> platform ... And as Caballero says, quite rightly, Prieto is now falling
> over himself in his eagerness to be first into the fray against Negrín.
> Above all he wants to beat Caballero to the starting line. Cast thus as
> Negrín's adversary, Prieto is secure against the tidal wave of insults from
> the desperate and the embittered. With a degree of cheek which defies
> belief, Prieto strikes the pose of the dissenting spectator. He doesn't seem
> to realise that historical assessments have to take precise account of
> chronology: between 1932 and 1938 many things happened, and in all of
> them Prieto was a protagonist, when not the supreme arbiter of events –

whether by dint of his action or inaction. In the fullness of time, Prieto will be called to account....[80]

The August 1938 national committee meeting was an event whose importance was by no means limited to the controversy surrounding Prieto and the April cabinet crisis. The committee passed votes of confidence in the national executive, in the Negrín government and its Thirteen Points and in the policy of Popular Front. Most importantly, it approved Lamoneda's report which advocated the maintenance of the policy of unity of action with the PCE. All reflected more upon the general secretary's competence and firm control of the proceedings, than upon any real sense of unity within the PSOE. The dominant note was Lamoneda's policy initiative of unity of action with the PCE which he had first presented for approval over a year previously to the July 1937 national committee meeting. The rest of the executive and the regional representatives, some because they were basically in agreement, others because they simply lacked any coherent counter-initiative, fell into line.[81]

Nevertheless, the fact remained that wartime tensions and dilemmas were having an ever more deleterious effect on party unity. This affected even the cohesiveness of that sector which had so far supported the Lamoneda executive and, by extension, the Negrín government. In addition, there is evidence that, at the grass roots, a significant number of socialists of every persuasion reacted with hostility to the August meeting's ratification of unity of action. This was particularly the case in the centre–south zone where hostility to the PCE and to the stance of the Lamoneda executive were running hand in hand by mid-1938.[82] The fact that the Republican zone had physically been split in two in April 1938 had also exacerbated the problem by increasing the sense of isolation and defencelessness ('desamparo') of the socialist base in the centre–south zone.[83] The common factor of controversy throughout the committee meeting was what was termed the 'disloyalty' of the Communists in their dealings with Spanish socialists – either collectively or individually. Indeed, the PCE central committee's own prophetic view of the situation, derived from confidential regional reports made to it, was that the fast developing anti-communism of many reformist socialists on the ground was driving them back into the arms of the *Caballeristas*.[84] And it was socialist alienation from the national leadership which precipitated the formation on 30 June 1938 of the Organización Interprovincial Socialista (Toledo–Badajoz–Ciudad Real–Córdoba). One of the principal functions of this body was to gather data on communist abuses in both the army and civilian life in the centre–south zone. All the socialist federations involved in the initiative (Badajoz's resided in Ciudad Real) had first-hand experience of the persecution of both socialists and anarchists by communist commissars.[85]

As Vidarte recognised, the ever-increasing hostility of rank-and-file socialists towards the PCE in the centre–south zone which eventually found its mascot or symbol in Prieto the retrospective 'victim' of April 1938, was a time bomb which would finally explode after the loss of Cataluña in 1939, causing the socialists of Madrid and Valencia to join forces with Colonel Casado in his armed opposition to the Negrín government.[86]

The rising wave of rank-and-file anti-communism was closely bound up with PCE sectarianism. The party's recruitment policy was an aggressive one. Its practitioners did not shrink from employing crude appeals to avarice or personal ambition on the one hand and outright coercion and physical violence on the other. Although such excesses were always publicly condemned by the Communist Party's national leadership, this did not satisfy the rank-and-file socialists who were frequently the victims of such tactics. The anti-communism of the base was reflected in the discussions and resolutions of the August 1938 national committee meeting.[87] Yet Lamoneda still defended the concept of unity of action with the PCE and argued for the maintenance of the joint party committees. Criticism of communist behaviour came not only from those who were hostile to Lamoneda's policy towards the PCE. Rafael Henche, for example, the president of the Madrid provincial socialist federation and general secretary of Artes Blancas, representative for New Castile on the party's national committee and a firm supporter of Lamoneda, was forthrightly critical of the reality of socialist–communist relations at the grass roots. And the provincial socialist federation in Valencia – Lamoneda's reformist showpiece and a salutary warning to the left – called at the August national committee for the severing of the joint party committees.[88] By August 1938, a division was becoming apparent within reformist socialist ranks between those who, though hostile to the PCE's behaviour, understood the rationale which underlay Lamoneda's policy, or at least were prepared to continue giving him the benefit of the doubt, and those whose anti-communism was about to spill over into outright opposition to the socialist executive.

At root, the rift in Spanish socialist ranks was the inevitable outcome of the political dilemma which had confronted the PSOE since July 1936. The needs of war dictated socialist–communist unity to reinforce the Popular Front on which Republican resistance rested, but unity had meant the very real erosion of the PSOE. To many of its leading cadres, it seemed as if the PSOE was sacrificing its very existence as a political party in order to ensure the Republic's survival.[89]

The tension within the PSOE which would render futile all attempts to rebuild the internal unity of the organisation, was no longer the product of a quasi-ideological divide between the parliamentary reformists and the syndical 'left'. By the end of 1937, the *Caballeristas* had virtually been excluded from the political life of the Republic at war. Partly as a result of Lamoneda's campaign against the socialist left in the provincial federations, partly as a result of the impact on Largo's supporters of his personal withdrawal from the political arena, the PSOE reformists could claim victory in the party battle. But the satisfaction Prieto and the reformist camp derived from their successful isolation of the socialist left was short-lived. In a sense, victory had come too late. The reformists' triumph belonged to an old battle whose imperatives had been rendered meaningless by the military coup itself. The fact of civil war had radically altered the balance of political forces. By late 1937 and throughout 1938, the centre of tension in the PSOE was provided by the competing claims of socialist identity and the demands of the war effort. The latter required that the Socialist and Communist Parties – leaderships and militants – should work in harness, no matter how great the provocation from aggressive PCE proselytism which aimed to create a single, mass class party – along the lines of what the JSU constituted for the youth movement. The risk, as Spanish socialists perceived it, was that victory in the war might be achieved at a terrible price – the liquidation of the socialist movement.

In spite of his awareness of the dangers involved for the PSOE, Lamoneda nevertheless supported unity of action consistently. As the policy which had underpinned the PSOE's wartime strategy since the beginning of 1937, he always regarded it as the only rational response to the practical needs of Republican defence. Indeed, for Lamoneda the primary objective in neutralising the party left was itself to prevent the undermining of his joint action strategy. Until the end of 1937 Lamoneda was supported – tacitly but unconditionally – by Indalecio Prieto who shared his understanding of the crucial importance to the war effort of collaboration between the PSOE and the PCE. Prieto, however, passed from the firm advocacy of socialist–communist unity in the summer of 1937 to virulent and public opposition to the PCE by the beginning of 1938. This undeniably erratic behaviour reflected Prieto's growing personal political crisis whose most extreme manifestation was his intense and debilitating pessimism over the war's outcome. This assumed grave proportions with the loss of the north, which also provoked Prieto's estrangement from the Republic's Soviet advisers and the PCE. In Prieto's eyes, neither was committed unconditionally to a Republican victory. Rather they were concerned to stage military actions as show cases for PCE initiative and efficiency. Ultimately, Soviet aid was not sufficient to win the war for the Republic. And if it was *not*, then, in Prieto's view, it was being purchased at too high a price – namely the political eclipse of the PSOE by the PCE.

During the war as before it, however, the desire for personal political revenge provided a powerful motivating force in Prieto's case. For it was only *after* his departure from Negrín's cabinet that Prieto publicly 'discovered' the damage wrought by Popular Frontism to the political autonomy of the Republic. The April 1938 cabinet crisis suffered serious distortion as it was subsequently written into Prieto's seamless script of anti-communist conspiracy. According to this, Prieto's exclusion was the major objective of the cabinet reshuffle – rather than one product of a much deeper political crisis which, by opposing mediators and resisters, threatened to shatter the political unity of the loyalist camp and thus to sink entirely the war effort. In the event, as we have seen, the resolution of the April crisis, with the rapid inclusion of the UGT and the CNT in Negrín's government, provided a much-needed boost for the resistance camp, which Prieto himself then set about undermining by his behaviour at the PSOE's national committee meeting in August 1938.

Prieto's adoption of a high-profile anti-communist stance placed an increasing distance between him and the PSOE executive. The latter, for the time being, continued to support Lamoneda, who, in turn, committed the Socialist Party to Negrín's resistance policy and to unity of action with the PCE. But the national committee meeting in August revealed the extreme fragility of socialist unity. The violent sectarianism and organisational rivalry which had created such tension between the socialist and communist grass roots surfaced at the August meeting, where the acute shortcomings of unity of action *in practice* were exposed. The antagonism felt by centre–south zone socialists towards the PCE – exacerbated by their sense of physical isolation in a zone bounded by hostile territory and the sea – was about to spill over into opposition to the Lamoneda executive itself. It was this sentiment which the general secretary's opponents in the PSOE were able to exploit. The fact that by the last quarter of 1938 the internal opposition to Lamoneda included the supporters of both Largo Caballero and Prieto – previously the bitterest of enemies – demonstrates clearly how the strains of war had provoked the complete atomisation of the Spanish socialist movement.

8 The atomisation of reformist socialism

By the end of 1938 the Spanish socialist movement was irremediably split. There were simply no grounds for compromise between the advocates of resistance to the last and those who favoured a negotiated peace. By 1938 the PSOE contained fervent groups of both. In the last analysis, socialist unity was finally shipwrecked on the bitterest controversy of the civil war. To each camp, the other represented the worst kind of traitor. For those who were in favour of what they believed was a feasible mediated peace, the resisters were wantonly irresponsible, in bondage to the siren voice of the Communist Party and its advisers. To those who championed resistance, theirs was the only road open to a peace settlement with guarantees. The mediators were either treasonous capitulators or guilty of criminal naivety because they did not understand Franco's desire for an unconditional surrender, to be followed by a victory of vengeance. Hence the paradox, tirelessly proclaimed by its most eloquent exponent, Negrín, that the only true road to peace was via continued resistance. Without political guarantees, the civilian populace of the loyalist zone would suffer as much if not much more from the 'peace of Franco' as from the maintenance of the war effort. It was Negrín's particular gift that he could see this clearly at the time. This capacity to rise above the complexity, confusion and tragedy of his immediate reality firmly establishes Negrín's stature as a statesman, although his recognition as such in the annals of Spanish socialism is now long overdue.[1]

Negrín had always understood that the Republic's fate ultimately rested on factors outside its control. Its position could be improved only by a significant shift in international political perspectives. Since his appointment in May 1937, Negrín had therefore done his utmost in the diplomatic sphere to change the perceptions of the British and French governments, to convince them of the fundamental untenability of appeasement. But by the summer of 1938, with the worsening military situation at home and the Western democracies' determination to avoid a confrontation with the Axis powers, Negrín was forced to rethink his strategy.

The prime minister was obliged to consider the 'unthinkable' –
namely that he would have to sound out the possibility of a mediated
settlement. But he had very firm views about how any such approach
should be made. Negrín was convinced that Franco would not cede
anything which he believed he could take in the short or medium
term by military conquest. Hence Negrín's fundamental belief that
for negotiation to yield positive results, the Republic had to entrench
itself, it had to negotiate from a position of maximum strength –
which meant maintaining all-out resistance. In order to do this it
was vital that the morale of both combatants and civilians should be
maintained. This, in turn, dictated that any pre-mediation discussions should be pursued in the utmost secrecy. On this point Negrín
was adamant. The credibility of the entire war effort was at stake.
Thus, for example, when a matter of days after his departure from
the defence ministry, Prieto suggested that an approach to the
Nationalist government be made to test out the possibility of negotiation, the prime minister was only prepared to sanction it on
condition that Prieto would accept sole, personal responsibility
should the affair come to public knowledge. Prieto was reluctant to
accept these conditions, according to Negrín, because it impugned
his prestige and reputation.[2] Prieto himself always maintained that
Negrín simply vetoed his initiative. But Negrín's account fits with
Prieto's own behaviour over the post of minister without portfolio. In
refusing Negrín's conditions, Prieto no doubt also had in mind the
rebuff suffered by the socialist leader, Julián Besteiro at Negrín's
hands when, in May 1937, he had undertaken, at President Azaña's
personal request (but without Negrín's knowledge), to sound out the
willingness of the British to mediate.[3] Negrín himself met the Duke of
Alba in Zurich early in September 1938, but the encounter produced
no concrete results. Indeed, through his own soundings, Negrín had
come to the conclusion that there was absolutely no real possibility of
negotiation because Franco himself was determined to secure an
unconditional surrender.[4]

It was in these very bleak circumstances that Ramón Lamoneda
made a final attempt to prevent the total atomisation of the Socialist
Party via the creation of a new party leadership. At the PSOE's
national committee meeting in August 1938 he proposed the election
of a new national executive. Lamoneda's goal was to achieve some
measure of reconciliation – even if only symbolic – on the eve of the
PSOE's fiftieth anniversary by incorporating representatives of
every socialist tendency into the new leadership body. First and
foremost, Lamoneda proposed that the PSOE's three historic
leaders – Besteiro, Prieto and Largo Caballero – should be

reintegrated into the national executive.[5] Apart from Prieto, who was to retain his ordinary executive post, they would have the status of *vocales natos* (honorary members), as would those socialists holding ministerial office. Besteiro and Largo, as ex-presidents of the party, would have the right to vote, the acting ministers would not. So it is clear that as well as attempting to create an image of party unity, the measure was designed to tighten the links between the party and the government. It reflected Lamoneda's awareness that both the authority of the party and its future role were at stake. If the timely 'call to order' went unheeded then the party would be heading for total atomisation and certain political oblivion, 'yesterday party unity was a cherished aim, today it is an order'.[6] In the interests of reconciliation and unity, there was also a call from the leadership that the ASM should show willing and annul the long-standing expulsion of Andrés Saborit, Julián Besteiro's lieutenant.[7] But whilst good will and reconciliation were the order of the day in 1938, Ramón Lamoneda also issued a warning, to be repeated later on. Persistent dissidence and factionalism would not be tolerated within the party.[8] Not surprisingly, however, the three historic leaders refused to contemplate their reintegration into what they considered to be an alien executive body. Largo made his total disaffection from the socialist leadership clear. In his view, it had connived with the PCE in the campaign to present him as vain and incompetent. In his reply, while attempting to persuade Largo to change his mind ('for the sake of the party'), Lamoneda countered that the PSOE leadership had also suffered much public defamation at the hands of the party left. And he concluded, tellingly, that the left was merely reaping its own harvest of 'bolshevisation'.[9] Notwithstanding Largo's own stubbornness, however, his lieutenant Rodolfo Llopis was, according to Azaña, in favour of Lamoneda's proposal.[10]

The controversy surrounding the September 1938 elections to the national executive demonstrated that Lamoneda had failed in his plea. In the Levante, where there was much long-standing opposition to Lamoneda, the holding of the long-delayed elections for a regional representative to PSOE's national committee in May 1938 sparked off another round of left/reformist mutual recrimination over the choice of candidate.[11] Then in September, Lamoneda's Levante opponents accused him of seeking a rubber stamp from the socialist membership for his own choice of national executive without permitting any discussion of alternative candidates. A number of socialist groups altered the candidacy list by inserting their own preferences for some of the posts. Whether this was always a sign of considered dissidence, or merely a reflection of the same desire for

socialist unity which had inspired Lamoneda's attempt to reinte-
grate Prieto, Besteiro and Largo Caballero cannot be ascertained
from the voting returns themselves. However, such alterations, for
whatever motives, meant the immediate disqualification of the
returns, of which there were a considerable number.[12] Given the
divisions within the socialist organisation as a whole, the various
returns excluded or disqualified on technical grounds in September
1938 naturally provided fertile ground for further accusations of
Lamoneda's partisan and dictatorial tendencies. There was certainly evidence of much confusion among the base and one group,
Benicul de Júcar (Granada) even refused to accept the resignations
of the former executive members until their reasons had been made
clear. Cataluña was naturally excluded from this election process.
Its exclusion, an inevitable consequence of its absence from the
party's national committee, was a further indication of the PSOE's
total eclipse in the region since the creation of the PSUC in July
1936.

The electoral returns from the PSOE base, which ratified the list
presented to the national committee, were published in *El Socialista*
on 20 September 1938.[13] Alejandro Otero, as the new vice-president,
replaced Jiménez de Asúa, at that time still the Republican ambassador in Prague, whose opposition to Negrín's policies was of long-
standing and well known among the socialist hierarchy.[14] Equally
opposed to Lamoneda and Negrín, Fernando de los Ríos, the
Republican ambassador in Washington, was replaced as an ordinary member of the executive by Antonio Huerta, who had come to
work on the editorial team of *Adelante* after the PSOE executive
regained control in July 1937.[15] Prieto, determined to play no part in
the internal life of the PSOE and alienated from Lamoneda, refused
to take up his post, although listed in the press. Ricardo Zabalza, a
leading *Caballerista* and general secretary of the Socialist Landworkers' Federation (FNTT), ignored the fact that he had ever been
elected, playing no part in the life of the executive.[16] His attitude
hardly came as a surprise. In the first place, he was extremely close
to Largo Caballero and saw Lamoneda as the chief architect of his
decline. Moreover, as FNTT general secretary, Zabalza was hostile
to the Lamoneda executive because it had collaborated with the
PCE. This was seen as a betrayal, because throughout the war the
FNTT was forced to fight tooth and nail to defend its collectives
against the onslaught from the communist-controlled agriculture
ministry which sought to return as much land as possible to private
hands.[17]

In all there were four new appointments to the PSOE executive in

September 1938, Otero and Huerta, as listed above, and Zabalza and Martínez Gil to replace Bugeda and de Gracia.[18] Lucio Martínez Gil, the veteran *Besteirista* and former leader of the FNTT, was in fact a third choice after Besteiro's lieutenants, Saborit and Trifón Gómez, had both refused to join the national executive committee.[19] In seeking to recruit prominent members of the PSOE's disaffected factions – factions which had, moreover, previously been each other's enemies as well, Lamoneda was attempting to stamp a symbolic image of unity on the national leadership in order to boost party morale in the dark days of autumn 1938. But the negative reactions of leading *Caballeristas* and *Besteiristas* alike only highlighted what a thankless task Lamoneda had taken on. By 1938 the divisions were too deep. The Spanish socialist movement had been atomised. The channels of communication within the PSOE were virtually closed.

Lamoneda's attempts to create a symbolic party unity, on the basis of a new integrated executive committee, had probably been nigh on doomed from the start. By the summer of 1938, relations between Negrín and the veteran socialist leaders Prieto and Besteiro were already beyond repair. Divided as both men were from the prime minister over the issue of resistance versus mediation, the final rupture occurred in June 1938. As the Nationalists battled on in the Levante, with their sights set on conquering Castellón, Negrín left Barcelona for a tour of the centre fronts. In the murky political climate of the Catalan capital, where inconclusive political intrigue and speculation were rife, his absence gave rise to a host of rumours over the possible formation of a new government of pro-mediation elements. Both Besteiro's and Prieto's names were linked to the initiative, whereupon Negrín returned precipitately from his tour of the centre fronts. There followed his notorious comments to the press about being 'drawn back by the buzzing of flies'. Bitterly angry, Negrín added that Barcelona was 'a political mud hole' (*charca política*). 'If the people and the troops only knew the sort of things that were going on, they would sweep all of us politicians away.'[20] Both Besteiro and Prieto were stung by the violence of the prime minister's words, which they interpreted as a personal attack. In a sense, though, neither ought to have found Negrín's virulence particularly surprising. Julián Besteiro had never made any secret of his hostility to Negrín, whom he considered a communist puppet. From Madrid, where he had been in self-imposed exile since the start of the war, Besteiro had, in June 1938, openly declared his willingness to form a new Republican government.[21] Indeed from April 1938 onwards, both Besteiro's and Prieto's names had been linked consistently with a variety of republican-inspired intrigues. Although these remained inchoate, the guiding idea was always to oust Negrín as the main obstacle to mediation with the Nationalists.

Ramón Lamoneda, in his attempt to rebuild unity in the party, had sought, unsuccessfully, to suppress Negrín's comments in June 1938. Equally unavailing was his last ditch attempt to reincorporate both Prieto and Besteiro into the party at an executive meeting on 15 November 1938.[22] Both Lucio Martínez Gil, the veteran *Besteirista* and former leader of the FNTT, and the *Prietista* executive member, Francisco Cruz Salido, were equally unsuccessful in their own efforts to convince their respective mentors to reinvolve themselves in the party. Besteiro had been further alienated by the barrage of PCE-inspired press abuse which had greeted his arrival in Barcelona in November. The main purpose of his mission was to discuss with Azaña the dire material plight of the capital, with its starving and demoralised population. But, in the light of his June declarations, Besteiro was accused of coming to the city to pursue the object of loyalist capitulation with an assortment of disaffected republicans and Catalan nationalists.[23] While there is no doubt that these sort of ideas had been in the air since June,[24] and that Besteiro was morally supportive, the extent to which there was any concerted conspiracy or active preparation before 1939 is very unclear. But such was the virulence of the attack in November that Besteiro renounced his intention of meeting Azaña, for fear of adding fuel to the flames. Instead he met the PSOE executive. Ironically, it was Besteiro himself who, unwittingly, both encapsulated the PSOE's dilemma and vindicated Lamoneda's own wartime strategy of tactical *rapprochement* to the PCE. At the November meeting he emphasised, simultaneously, both his own visceral anti-communism – which precluded him from participating in the life of the executive – and the need, for the sake of the Republican war effort, for the PSOE and the PCE to present a common front.[25] It is startling that such a comment should have been made by someone who never ceased insisting that Negrín had sold out to the Communist Party. Besteiro's peculiar blindness, and the inconsistency it reveals, is a most graphic illustration of the acuteness of the socialist crisis.

From the changes in the constitution of the national executive, it becomes clear that by the last quarter of 1938 the tensions created by the war, and particularly by the increasingly gloomy international perspective, had substantially eroded the coherence of the PSOE's leadership cadres. By the time of the Munich accord at the end of September only a minority of the national executive felt any commitment to the policies of the Negrín government. With the Republican

Cortes due to gather at San Cugat del Vallés on 1 October 1938, the PSOE's parliamentary party met in full session on 29–30 September in order to prepare. As the major vote on the agenda in the Cortes was that of the assembly's confidence in Negrín as prime minister, the meeting of socialist deputies was inevitably a stormy one. The *Caballeristas* gave vent to their anger at what they saw as Negrín's anti-socialist policies. Cresenciano Bilbao even went as far as to allege that the entire Republican army was under PCE control, with the result, added Carlos Rubiera, that at the front it was dangerous to admit to being a socialist. There was a strong feeling in the parliamentary party, extending beyond the party left, that Negrín should remove the communist Antonio Cordón from his post in the under-secretaryship of war. But Negrín's response, delivered via José Prat, his prime ministerial under-secretary, was an unequivocal negative. In the end, thirty-seven deputies, including Bugeda, Anastasio de Gracia, Jiménez de Asúa, Bilbao and Belarmino Tomás voted for the government, while only the *caballerista* core of eleven abstained – Araquistain, Cerezo, Díaz Castro, Galarza, Ginés Ganga, García García, García Muñoz, Hernández Zancajo, Llopis, Rubiera and Zabalza.[26] The unfailing energy and determination of Lamoneda ensured that, publicly at least, both the party executive and the parliamentary party continued to back Negrín. Lamoneda gave particularly short shrift to the *Caballeristas* who complained that the parliamentary party was being bypassed by the PSOE executive and that Negrín was guilty of a criminal disregard for the will of the Cortes. Inclining in favour of Negrín's view that the exceptional circumstances of the war made inevitable the short-circuiting of the normal apparatus of democratic government, he accused the left of opportunism. Lamoneda argued that the supreme function of both the PSOE executive and the parliamentary party at such a time was to back the government to the hilt, and to do so unconditionally.

In the event, the Republican Cortes in session at San Cugat del Vallés voted to express its full and unconditional confidence in the Negrín government. Anything less and Negrín had sworn to resign. The fact that Prieto chose not to exploit the latent hostility to Negrín felt by the republican groups and by many of his fellow socialists, indicates his own determination to avoid having the political responsibility for ending the war devolved upon himself. The vote of confidence in Negrín, given that it ran counter to the general feeling in the Cortes, itself reflects the political bankruptcy of those opposing the prime minister. In spite of increasing opposition to Negrín in cabinet session by the end of 1938,[27] among socialist leaders the feeling was ever more prevalent that the fight to restore unity in the socialist movement was a futile one. The die was already cast. Indeed, those opposing Negrín and Lamoneda certainly did not want to dislodge them. This surely stemmed in part from fear of the impending and dreadful responsibility which would descend on the socialist leadership when Republican defeat became a reality.

Ramón Lamoneda's control of the socialist executive has since the end of the civil war, been the subject of considerable controversy. He has been viewed as a crypto-communist, working within the executive to benefit the PCE and its ambition of unity with the PSOE. This view was given a spurious credibility because Lamoneda had once been a member of the PCE in the 1920s. His closeness to Negrín during the war, his outstanding support for the prime minister's policies – unconditional in public if not in private – and his identification with Negrín in exile have also contributed to this image of subservience. Lamoneda is thus portrayed as the party's 'man of straw',[28] fulfilling within the Socialist Party a role equivalent to that commonly perceived to have been played in government by Negrín. In the intensely bitter post-war period, Lamoneda had to endure a veritable flood of 'hate mail' in which opinions such as the following (from a socialist refugee in France) abounded: '... all of the crimes and murders perpetrated against Spanish socialists by your cronies from 1921 – you're implicated in them all – in fact, perhaps that's the very reason why you joined the PSOE again afterwards, so that you could go on serving "the cause" ...'[29] Socialists hostile to the general secretary would often adduce his left socialist leanings and collaboration with Alvarez del Vayo during the early 1930s as proof of his 'treason' during the war. They conveniently forgot, however, that interspersed in time there lay a close friendship and political collaboration between Prieto and Lamoneda.

Lamoneda, like Negrín was a protégé of Indalecio Prieto's. It is well known that Negrín and Prieto became friends during the first period of the Republic after the former had been elected as deputy for Las Palmas (Canary Islands).[30] What was less commonly appreciated, however, is that Lamoneda, whose dynamism and energy had first attracted Prieto, was chosen and groomed by the latter after the May 1936 cabinet débâcle to manoeuvre within the party organisation against the left.[31] Between 1934 and 1936 Lamoneda and Negrín also came together as, respectively, secretary and vice-president of the socialist parliamentary party.[32] And after May 1937 it was Lamoneda as 'anchor man' who

ensured the consolidation of relations between the party and the
government. Through his efforts the PSOE became totally identified with Negrín's cabinets, and the reformist political philosophy
which held them together was essentially based on the same idea of
inter-class alliance previously championed by Prieto.[33] Lamoneda
consistently defended the Popular Front as a democratic rather
than a class-based front.[34] Although, after the experience of the
war, he had no illusions about the Socialists' republican allies,
admitting publicly that the PSOE was once again sustaining faint-
hearted liberals, as it had done between 1931 and 1933. But there
was a note of bitterness, as he declared that the wartime socialist
commitment was even greater because they had now sacrificed
many of the prospects of radical social and economic change to
procure, 'with their own blood', the lowest common political denominator they shared with their middle-class allies – the military
defeat of Franco.[35]

In spite of the political disadvantages which the Socialists had to
cope with, it was under Negrín's premiership that the process of
institutionalising the PSOE as the party of government was undertaken. The Socialists supplied cadres to run the state bureaucracy at
every level. Most prominent, however, were the ministerial under-
secretaries and their staff: José Prat in the presidency, Jerónimo
Bugeda in the finance ministry, Vidarte and Rafael Méndez in
interior, Julián Zugazagoitia in the defence ministry, along with
Francisco Cruz Salido (navy/air subsecretariat), Alejandro Otero
(armaments) and Trifón Gómez (supplies).[36] According to the conventional wisdom, the increasing isolation and frustration of these
socialist office-holders in 1938 was caused by the PCE's ruthless
drive for hegemony. In reality, however, both phenomena were
symptoms of the internal collapse of the Spanish socialist movement
under the pressures of the war.

By late 1938, Lamoneda came as close as he felt he could to
declaring publicly that the needs of the war, or rather of a Republican victory, demanded 'silence' and forbearance from the socialist
base. What such a silence meant in reality was turning a blind eye to
the PCE's more unacceptable political methods. 'We must not speak
of hypocrisy but rather of discretion.'[37] The PCE's behaviour at the
time of the POUM leaders' trial in late October 1938 tested the
patience of some socialists to the limit. Paulino Gómez Saez, the
Basque socialist who had replaced Julián Zugazagoitia as interior
minister in April 1938, had imposed a blanket press ban on reports of
the trial. The PCE's circumvention of his interdict drove him to the
point of resigning. The Communist Party saw fit to disseminate

clandestine publications virulently criticising the POUM in the usual terms, as 'trotskyist traitors'. This episode also increased the tension between Negrín and the PSOE executive. The prime minister was inclined to ignore the PCE's activities, but Lamoneda, under pressure from the socialist base, forced him to take a tougher line.[38]

The implementation and effects of the practical unity initiatives between the PSOE and the PCE, as championed by Lamoneda throughout the war, need to be scrutinised carefully for what they reveal both about the nature of socialist–communist relations on the ground and Lamoneda's political strategy. But no detailed scrutiny can sustain the wild and emotional accusations of crypto-communism levelled against the PSOE's general secretary in the bitter period of the immediate post war. His strategy, *vis-à-vis* the PCE and its strident campaign at both grass roots and national level for organisational unity with the PSOE, was an immensely subtle and complex balancing act by which he sought to satisfy both the requirements of a Republican victory and the claims of the PSOE to a separate, 'historic' identity. Indeed as Gabriel Morón, who acted as sub-editor of *El Socialista* in the later stages of the war, pointed out, the official party press was itself far from uncritical of government policy. Yet Lamoneda did not interfere with its editorial line.[39]

Indeed, one cannot really judge his 'unity' strategy to have been bankrupt in itself, as so many embittered socialists did from the bleakness of exile. Military and political defeat certainly rendered all Lamoneda's efforts futile because the Republic was swept away. But the historian some fifty years on, far from assessing Lamoneda's strategy of joint committees and common action with the PCE as flawed and irresponsible, must seek to understand its rationality and necessity, given the severe international constraints within which the political leaders were obliged to organise a war effort in which the very survival of the Spanish Republic was at stake. Ramón Lamoneda knew as well as the rest of the socialist executive how far relations between the socialist and communist bases had deteriorated in some areas of the centre–south zone. However, it was his personal conviction that these genuine problems could best be overcome by maintaining the joint party committees rather than by abandoning them. He refused to abandon the policy, carrying both the national committee decisions of July 1937 and August 1938 in his favour by the sheer force of his personal determination. There was always the suspicion that those who argued from the socialist ranks against the maintenance of the policy were covert or incipient factionalists. And it was true that the *Caballeristas* were seeking to make political capital out of burgeoning hostility to the PCE.[40] But even apart from the problems posed by the socialist left, it was Lamoneda's view that the maintenance of practical unity with the PCE cadres constituted an excellent lesson in internal party discipline and one from which the socialist collectivity could usefully profit after the literally disintegrating experience of the 1930s.[41]

Yet there can be no doubt that Lamoneda was no misty-eyed political naif where the procedure and techniques of the PCE were concerned. Naturally nothing of his hard-headed assessment is evident in his public speeches during the war, since this would have effectively undermined his own policy towards the PCE. Nevertheless, Lamoneda was the ideal person to negotiate for the PSOE on the national joint party committee in that he remained unmoved and unswervable in his objectives in spite of the barrage of threats, complaints, pathos and insults which were the staple content of the committee meetings.[42] Moreover the needs of war precluded any obvious back-tracking on the long road to unity, both because of the negative propaganda impact which it would have on the PSOE and, even more crucially, because of the deleterious effect which it would have on the availability of Soviet aid. In the final analysis, Lamoneda's genuine concern over the unity of the two parties also had much to do with his understanding of the post-war period and his conviction that if unity did not become a reality, in spite of all the practical problems, and no single strong proletarian party emerged after the conflict, then both Socialists and Communists would find themselves displaced from the centre of political power.[43]

But there was an overriding problem here. The socialist left's reluctance to accept the idea of joint party committees (from immediately after their foundation in April 1937), was increasingly finding an echo among the socialist base throughout the centre–south zone, as a consequence of the latter's daily experience of PCE sectarianism. And Lamoneda's attitude here unfortunately only compounded the problem. According to Araquistain – albeit not the most neutral of commentators – Lamoneda simply did not appreciate the sense of 'desamparo' (defencelessness or vulnerability) felt by socialists in the centre–south zone after the division of Republican territory in April 1938.[44] By the end of 1938 the zone was a powder keg for which the so-called Piñuela affair provided the spark. On 10 November 1938 the Murcian socialist, Fernando Piñuela, political commissar in the centre zone since December 1937, was dismissed by Jesús Hernández, the former communist education minister and then chief of the commissariat for the centre–south zone army group. To this event can be traced the beginning of the end of the attempt to make socialist–communist unity of action work. Yet Hernández's action was no more flagrant than in a good many other cases. Its impact can only be understood as the last straw.[45]

Immediately after Piñuela's dismissal was known, the socialist executive called upon Negrín to reinstate him. But the prime minister was not prepared so to do and nor was he prepared to appoint as Piñuela's replacement any of the socialists that the national executive subsequently recommended to him.[46] In the event, Edmundo Domínguez, the vice-president of the UGT executive, was nominated by Negrín. Although a socialist, his sympathy for the PCE aggravated the growing anti-communism in the centre–south zone. The removal of Piñuela provoked the final breakdown of the joint party committee structure, whilst Domínguez's appointment in turn provoked a mass resignation of other socialist commissars in the centre army out of solidarity with Piñuela. This infuriated Negrín who saw it as an act of gross indiscipline and irresponsibility, given the grave circumstances of the war.

The affair also introduced further tensions into the relations between the prime minister and the socialist executive. The latter, while agreeing that the mass resignation of socialist commissars was indefensible, made a case for leniency because of the circumstances in which it had occurred and the long previous history of heavy-handed communist proselytism and unbounded aggression against socialists, especially in the army. Indeed, by the end of 1938 the socialist executive was increasingly worried by the spread of a virulent hostility to the PCE throughout the centre–south zone. Their fear of sparking off a civil war within a civil war was one important factor which eventually decided the executive against pressing further for the reinstatement of Piñuela. 'As soon as someone raises the flag of anti-communism, the majority of the working class in the centre–south zone will follow them like a shot. Our Party has attracted a lot of discontented people and we're being landed as a result with many who aren't socialists.'[47] Equally, Piñuela's *caballerista* faith and also the fact that the socialist commissars who had resigned after his dismissal had been encouraged to do so by the ASM, tended to reduce the Lamoneda executive's desire to oppose Negrín because it was tantamount to backing the factional interests it had fought so long and hard to subdue. Nevertheless, there was a very real fear among executive members that the PSOE leadership could not win whatever it chose to do: 'If this sort of outrage continues to be perpetrated against socialist comrades, the Party as a whole will revolt against the government and the national executive committee.'[48]

The problem of socialist rebellion over the Piñuela affair spread rapidly through the provincial socialist organisations in the Levante – where there was fertile ground for this new outrage to take root. In Albacete, particularly, long-standing grievances made the socialist organisation receptive to the events in Madrid. Given the acute tensions in Albacete, this response, in turn, intensified the general impact of the Piñuela affair.[49] In Murcia too, where Piñuela had been both secretary of the socialist group and mayor, there was also a considerable amount of discontent. As in Madrid, so in the Levante organisations, Piñuela had become for many socialists, both at the grass roots and in the provincial hierarchies, a symbol of their own victimisation or of their own anger and fear over PCE sectarianism.[50] Piñuela was the 'fair' political commissar, tolerant of a heterogeneity of political opinions who had been swept aside on a pretext because he opposed the PCE's drive for ideological homogeneity and organisational hegemony. Although the issue had effectively split the PSOE's national executive, on 11 January 1939 a vote was taken and those in favour of petitioning Negrín directly to reinstate Piñuela – namely Otero, Albar and Francisco Cruz Salido, veteran socialist, journalist and colleague of both Zugazagoitia and Prieto – were defeated.[51] Instead it was agreed that Cruz Salido, Albar and Cordero should go to Madrid to attempt to calm the situation and to persuade the socialist commissars who had submitted their resignations to retract them. It was, however, only a piecemeal solution which dealt with the symptoms without ever attacking the cause of the malady. The pressure in the centre–south zone, and in Madrid especially, would eventually be released by the Casado coup (March 1939) which, by ousting Negrín, finally put an end to Republican resistance. This was, in effect, much more than a rebellion of the republican military. To understand its deep-rooted and prior *civilian* dimension one must look to the degeneration of relations between socialists and communists and to the climate of intense hostility which existed between the PCE and considerable sections of the socialist base in the enclosed centre–south zone by the end of 1938.[52]

It was grass roots anti-communism in the centre–south zone which cemented the alliance between the supporters of Largo Caballero and Indalecio Prieto and the hitherto isolated *Besteiristas*, whose common objective was to unseat Negrín and thence to initiate peace negotiations. The fact of such an alliance forced Negrín to rely increasingly on the PCE's cadres as the only political force still unreservedly committed to resistance. The net result of this was, unsurprisingly, to intensify opposition to Negrín inside his own party. But this opposition depended for its effectiveness on the strength of anti-communist feeling at the socialist grass roots. To understand why this was so immense by the end of 1938 one must look beyond the PSOE itself to developments in the trade union federation (UGT), during the war.

PART IV
The Dispute in the UGT

9 The battle for control of the union and the eclipse of the socialist left 1937–1938

The withdrawal of the socialist left from government as a result of the cabinet crisis of May 1937 had clearly marked the beginning of a concerted attack on the *Caballeristas'* remaining power bases. The assault was mounted by a PSOE executive significantly strengthened by the verdict of the July 1937 national committee meeting and supported to the hilt by the PCE. The object of the attack was to silence Largo Caballero and his supporters, to exclude them and their disruptive influence from the political life of the Republic at war.[1] It was to achieve this that the socialist left had been ousted from the PSOE's provincial federation in Valencia and from the leadership of the parliamentary party, on which, prior to July 1936, it had enjoyed majority control. The erosion of the *Caballeristas'* power base also meant reduced press access – which in itself accelerated the process of political disintegration. The loss of *Adelante* was inevitable once the reformist socialists had regained control of the provincial executive in Valencia. But most damaging of all for the left socialists was their loss of control over UGT newspapers such as *Claridad* (Madrid), *Las Noticias* (Barcelona) and *La Correspondencia de Valencia*. It is the erosion of the *Caballeristas'* position within the union organisation, that supposed bastion of left socialism, which we must now consider. For, by the summer of 1937, the PSOE reformists' central target for attack had become the UGT's national executive itself.

In all, the battle lasted seven furious months. On 28 May 1937 the UGT's national committee first censured its own national executive – led by Largo Caballero himself – for the line it had taken during the May cabinet crisis. By January 1938, Largo Caballero's executive had suffered its final defeat – with both national and international recognition being granted to the new UGT executive led by the Asturian miners' leader and PSOE president, Ramón González Peña.

The union executive which it replaced had been elected in January 1934. Headed by Largo himself as general secretary, its election had set the seal on the *Caballeristas'* ascendancy in the UGT.[2] Anastasio de Gracia was president and José Díaz Alor vice-president. Pascual Tomás took over as administrative secretary, Felipe Pretel as treasurer, and Ricardo Zabalza, Manuel Lois, Mariano Muñoz, Amaro del Rosal, Carlos Hernández Zancajo and Antonio Génova were elected as ordinary members. The election of this executive had signified victory for those in the union who believed that both the PSOE and the UGT should take advantage of the new opportunities for political action and involvement which the Second Republic had opened up. On this point all the members of Largo's executive were in agreement. Indeed it was this issue which had clinched their victory. Their rivals in the union, identified with the veteran socialist leader, Julián Besteiro, had lost out in 1934 mainly because their insistence that both the PSOE and the UGT should remain aloof from the republican experiment was out of sympathy with rank-and-file sentiment.

By 1937, however, the unanimity of Largo's executive had been broken to reveal two very different, indeed mutually antagonistic, conceptions of where political action ought to be leading both the PSOE and the UGT. By 1937, the UGT executive was critically split in its attitude to the Spanish Communists. Indeed, the controversy had already produced one casualty. Anastasio de Gracia's resignation from the union presidency in January 1936 had been the result of his disapproval of the *Caballeristas'* cultivation of the PCE in the pre-war period. By 1937, de Gracia's fears about the PCE's motives and methods had been realised. A whole series of events had brought home the painful truth that the PCE was set on absorbing socialist cadres: the loss of the socialist youth organisation to the PCE, the Communist Party's aggressive wartime campaign to absorb the PSOE rank and file, and even closer to home, the effective loss of the UGT's cadres in Cataluña which PSUC control of the UGT's Catalan secretariat necessarily implied. As a result, all the old guard *caballerista* unionists on the executive – men such as Díaz Alor, Pascual Tomás and, of course, Largo himself, had come round to de Gracia's way of thinking. Concerned to protect the political hegemony of Spanish socialism and, above all, its monopoly within the UGT, by 1937 they found themselves opposing those executive members who, with clear communist sympathies, still favoured the unification of the PSOE and the PCE.

The pro-communist bloc on the executive committee was constituted by three members: Amaro del Rosal, of the white-collar credit and finance union, Felipe Pretel, the UGT treasurer and leader of the entertainment and leisure workers' union, and Antonio Génova of the carpentry and woodworkers' union. Whilst continuing to advocate the unification of the Socialist and Communist Parties, they were also in favour of something which was even more anathema to their union colleagues; namely a policy of positive discrimination in order to increase communist representation in the UGT hierarchy. The split in the UGT executive committee demonstrates perfectly the major internal contradiction of the *caballerista* power base, which would eventually lead to its being eroded and destabilised from within. For the pro-communist bloc on the UGT executive was to play a major role in the October 1937 victory of the new González Peña union executive as we shall see.

The division in the UGT became overt on 17 May 1937. The fact that the UGT executive did not issue a public declaration of support for Negrín's new government was taken as proof of the *Caballeristas'* intention to boycott the new administration. The edition of *El Socialista* for 18 May, reporting the resolution of the cabinet crisis, implicitly criticised the *Caballeristas'* position by carrying declarations of support for Negrín. These came from the *prietista* sections of the UGT in Vizcaya, Guipúzcoa and Santander, and also from the newly elected federal executive of the UGT in Valencia. This was elected after its *caballerista* predecessor had resigned in the aftermath of the PSOE coup in Valencia.[3] The UGT's provincial committees in the Basque provinces also criticised Largo's 'política personalista', declaring that he was not 'insustituible' (irreplaceable).[4] In the following days the Socialist Party press carried an ever-increasing number of declarations of solidarity with the Negrín government from individual sections of the UGT's national federations, and the publication of these in the socialist press would continue throughout the months of the union dispute. The Catalan secretariat of the UGT likewise published a very early declaration of support for the government.[5] The *caballerista* executive, beginning to fight back against the attacks, referred scathingly to this as yet further proof that it was merely an adjunct of the PSUC, the Communist Party of Cataluña, and therefore entirely alien to the Spanish UGT.[6] By 20 May, the first signs of an organised movement against Largo and his supporters had appeared when the union executive received a request from six industrial federations to convene an extraordinary session of the full national committee.[7] Conscious of the mounting crisis in the UGT, Pascual Tomás convened a special meeting of national committee delegates for the 26th of the month at which Largo was to explain the executive's position over the May cabinet crisis. Well aware that both the PCE and the PSOE reformists were mobilising support in the UGT in order to challenge

Largo's authority, the union executive took the precaution of rigidly limiting the agenda of the meeting. Its object in so doing was to protect itself against any surprise attack from hostile national delegates.

In the event, the meeting proved every bit as stormy as Pascual Tomás and Largo had feared. The general secretary delivered a marathon speech to the gathering, *in camera*. Lasting over five hours, it dealt mainly with his own interpretation of the May government crisis and its aftermath.[8] The ensuing debate confirmed the hostility of a majority of the national committee's delegates. The sort of criticisms which had already appeared in the press were repeated. Largo was accused of personalising political issues in a way which was wantonly damaging to the war effort. But as well as calling upon the executive for a clear statement of its support for the Negrín government, the matter of communist representation on the UGT national executive was raised. José Rodríguez Vega, of the printers' union, a colleague of Ramón Lamoneda's (who had, likewise, briefly been in the PCE in the 1920s), pressed Largo and his supporters for a statement on this.[9] But the meeting broke up inconclusively.

Two days later, however, the UGT's national committee met in the absence of the executive and censured it, by 24 votes to 14, both for its conduct during the May crisis and for refusing explicitly to support a government in which Largo was not both prime minister and head of a unified defence ministry.[10] Ominously for Largo and the socialist left, a majority of the delegates also expressed the desire to re-establish the traditional relationship with the national executive of the PSOE. This second national committee meeting on the 28th had been arranged by Felipe Pretel, Amaro del Rosal and Antonio Génova, the pro-communist members of the UGT executive and their action marked the beginning of an overt split in the executive itself.

Also apparent were the beginnings of the struggle to control *Claridad*, the *Caballeristas'* main newspaper. It was a struggle which Largo's supporters would eventually lose.[11] In May 1937, the erosion of the *Caballeristas'* position was signalled when Carlos Hernández Zancajo was replaced as editor of *Claridad* by Isidro R. Mendieta. The formal responsibility for this decision was that of the workers' control committee in charge. A by-product of the revolution, the committee had been running the newspaper since the early days of the war. Behind this committee, however, the influence of Amaro del Rosal was clearly discernible. He had been a member of *Claridad*'s pre-war editorial board – along with the newspaper's joint owners – Luis Araquistain and Carlos de Baraibar. But it was through his close relationship with the workers' control commitee that Amaro del Rosal achieved a considerable degree of control over *Claridad*'s output during the war.[12] The change in editors in May had the effect of strengthening its pro-unity line. However, it was not until after June 1937, with the battle raging for control of the UGT, that *Claridad*'s editorial line became overtly critical of the socialist left. Nor can it be a coincidence that the newspaper's hostility to the leaders of the socialist left should have coincided with Amaro del Rosal's own forced resignation from the UGT executive in June.[13] By August, he was spearheading what would eventually be a successful campaign to deprive Araquistain and de Baraibar of the legal ownership of *Claridad*.[14]

Having passed the vote of censure against Largo's executive on 28 May, a majority of the national committee delegates called upon the executive to convene a full meeting of the UGT's national committee to cover an extensive agenda.[15] This request was instantly denied by Largo and his colleagues in order to gain time to plan their countering tactics. It seemed to the *Caballeristas* that they were surrounded by political enemies. Although the PCE's criticism of Largo in the aftermath of the May crisis had been expected, in the Communist Party press he was presented as public enemy number one, castigated both for his opposition to Negrín and to working-class unity. Largo's supporters in both the party and union organisation, outraged by the virulence of the personal attack on him, did their best to refute the PCE's accusations. But it is undeniable that the PCE's propaganda had exposed the vulnerability of the socialist left's position. By affirming that support for Negrín and loyalty to the Republican cause were indivisible, the PCE had successfully assumed the moral high ground. In the midst of a draining war, in which the Republic was being starved of international aid, the simplicity of the PCE's central case, that unity equalled strength, gave it a powerful popular appeal. The socialist left was thus forced onto the defensive. The reaction of the ASM is a good example of the left's dilemma. Its executive committee was prepared to denounce the PCE for its violent rhetoric against Largo. But, fearful of being accused of treasonous opposition to the Republican government by the Communist and Socialist Party press, it also issued a declaration of support for Negrín.[16]

Largo was not, however, entirely alone with his supporters on the union executive in that Ricardo Zabalza, executive member and general secretary of the UGT giant, the landworkers' federation (FNTT), had firmly pledged his own continuing allegiance and that of his union. But Largo Caballero and the old guard apparently had no strategy for dealing with the spreading dissent. The opposition's tactics clearly aimed at undermining the left's bases of support in the union and party until it was safe to oust Largo and his supporters from the UGT's national executive. Thus, with the Largo executive still in place, the dispute ground on through the spring and early summer, with meetings between the PSOE and the UGT executives, between Negrín and the delegates of the UGT national committee majority[17] and, even less happily for the *Caballeristas'* position, between the prime minister and the general secretary of the CNT, Mariano R. Vázquez, who also offered the government the formal support of his organisation.[18]

As the socialist left came increasingly under siege in both the union and the party, it was evident that the left's opponents in the UGT comprised two distinct political groups. Ultimately these had different political objectives, but they converged in their desire to neutralise the *Caballeristas'* power base in the union. One focus of opposition was naturally the reformists in the PSOE, associated with Prieto and the Lamoneda executive's struggle to regain organisational control of the party in the Republican zone. For this group, the erosion of the socialist left in its union stronghold was, for all that it was consistently denied in the party press, merely an extension of the dispute in the PSOE. The fact that the reformists felt confident enough to extend the battle to the union, supporting those opposed to Largo Caballero and the old guard, reflects the favourable outcome of the July 1937 national committee meeting in Valencia which had seen the strengthening of PSOE executive authority. Indeed, it would appear that, as early as August 1937, the PSOE reformists had already determined to remove Largo as general secretary of the UGT. Azaña, in his memoirs, records Negrín's own view that Largo's quasi-opposition to his government dictated his removal. This would defuse any statement or speech which Largo might choose to make at the forthcoming meeting of the Cortes (1 October 1937). The meeting was held back until after Largo's removal had been effected in order to render it impossible for him to lay claim to speak for a million Spanish workers – a claim which might have done a great deal to damage the government's credibility.[19]

The real dynamic of the opposition in the UGT, however, was provided by the unitarist tendency. This term defines those *ugetistas* who, through their communist affiliation or their general political sympathies, favoured the reorganisation of the leadership cadres, and especially of the national executive, to achieve a much higher level of communist presence therein. It was hardly a new line, and, as before, the debate always centred around a form of positive discrimination which would, first and foremost, raise representatives of the PCE to membership of the national executive. It hardly needs stressing that the essential precondition of this was the removal of Largo Caballero. Neither the reformist socialists nor their supporters in the UGT were particularly keen to grant the PCE favoured access to the UGT hierarchy. Indeed in Asturias, always the stronghold of the *Prietistas*, the political current was moving in the opposite direction. In April 1937 at the UGT's provincial congress, the socialist candidacy won outright victory, defeating the joint socialist–communist unity slate with a majority of 75,000 votes.[20] However, such was the determination of the PSOE reformists to carry their purge of the left into the union, because therein lay its political strength, that, effectively, they were pulling in the same direction as the unitarists. As a result, the PCE was able to gain a firm foothold in the organisational hierarchy of the UGT – something which had hitherto been denied it. By 1 October 1937 the PCE would have achieved its long-cherished aim, when, under the presidency of the *prietista* miners' leader Ramón González Peña, the new UGT leadership allocated the Communists two posts on the union's national executive commitee. This was made possible precisely because of the PSOE leadership's determination to remove control from the socialist left.

By the beginning of August 1937 Largo's executive had disowned both *Claridad* in Madrid and *Las Noticias* in Barcelona as official UGT newspapers.[21] However, in both cases the initiative was short-lived. The Catalan UGT's secretariat immediately claimed the Barcelona paper and where *Claridad* was concerned, after several months of polemic between pro- and anti-unitarist factions, August saw the beginning of a series of unitarist manoeuvres, coordinated largely by Amaro del Rosal. He had been expelled in June 1937 from the UGT executive for his orchestration of the national committee's campaign against Largo. Soon after this, his efforts on *Claridad*'s behalf would produce a resounding unitarist victory. Ironically, it was the very fact that *Claridad*, like other Madrid newspapers, had been taken over by a workers' committee in July 1936 which made it possible to remove the newspaper from the *Caballeristas'* control. Petitioned by Amaro del Rosal on behalf of the collective, the Negrín government recognised the workers' committee and legalised the expropriation of the newspaper.[22] Thus, the collectivisation of the left's newspaper effectively meant its loss as a *caballerista* mouthpiece.

With the left socialists increasingly under siege in the UGT, Araquistain and Carlos de Baraibar, as the owners of *Claridad*, were involved in a legal dispute with the workers' committee over ownership of the newspaper's printing machinery. On 10 November, resurgent bourgeois justice paradoxically found in favour of the workers and against the claims of private property. It was a perfect opportunity for the unitarist editorialists to criticise the pretensions of the newspaper's 'magnates' ('los elegantes caballeros de industria'), and their attempt to 'swindle' the workers of *Claridad*.[23] *Adelante* had by this time already been appropriated by the PSOE executive, which took it over on 26 July when the *caballerista* provincial executive was removed from power in Valencia. *La Correspondencia de Valencia* would remain in the hands of the socialist left until the end of November 1937, although by the beginning of October the party reformists had begun to rein it in. The interior minister, the reformist socialist Julián Zugazagoitia, suspended the paper briefly at the beginning of October.[24] A journalist himself and one time editor of the official PSOE newspaper, *El Socialista*, Zugazagoitia had reason to feel enmity towards the left and its press. The bitter editorial battle between *El Socialista* and *Claridad* in 1936 had been another facet of the factional strife inside the Socialist Party in the pre-war period.

It was no coincidence that the unitarist opposition in the UGT began seriously to be orchestrated just as the left's bid for a place on the PSOE's national committee was defeated. This failure spurred the left's opponents on. The *Caballeristas* were strong in the UGT, but not overwhelmingly so. Moreover, the political coalition now facing them was formidable. The *Caballeristas* stalled for time, borrowing tactics which Lamoneda had successfully employed against them at the PSOE's July national committee meeting.[25] But there was a crucial difference. Lamoneda's attentism derived from a position of strength, whereas the socialist left already had their backs to the wall.

As the calls for an extraordinary national committee meeting continued unabated, the *caballerista* executive rapidly resorted to the battleground it knew best – the minutiae of union statute – in order to fend off the unitarist attack. Given that the socialist left was most at home in matters of union bureaucracy, it is hardly surprising that, under threat, the executive should have withdrawn to such a terrain. It not unreasonably judged it to be the best chance of winning through against the ever-growing strength of the unitarist opposition within the UGT. However, in the event, the veterans' chosen weapon, the *Organización General*, or party statutes, proved double-edged. A series of inconsistencies and tactical errors meant that eventually it was turned against the Largo executive itself, to remarkable and quite deadly effect.

Early in August 1937, in an effort to 'discipline' the industrial federations which were leading the opposition to his executive, Largo Caballero proceeded to suspend Artes Blancas (bakers and confectioners) and to expel a number of other sections from the UGT. Those expelled, it was claimed, had dues arrears. The left argued that, according to union statute, this gave the executive the right to annul their membership.[26] Artes Blancas was a more difficult case because its dues had already been paid up to the beginning of 1937. However, it was the first industrial section to have its rights effectively suspended after its general secretary, Rafael Henche, a member of the PSOE national committee and a supporter of Ramón Lamoneda, had publicly criticised the behaviour of the UGT executive at a meeting on 8 August.[27] The division between *Caballeristas* and unitarists had been confirmed by the Largo executive's absence from a political meeting on 18 July called to mark a year of war. Since President Azaña had spoken there, the reformist socialists, the unitarists and the PCE all seized upon this absence as evidence of an explicit denial of support for the Negrín government, and therefore of the left's 'treason'.[28] The latter's semi-withdrawal from public life at this time was undoubtedly a reflex of defence in the face of growing political isolation, compounded by the PCE's hostile press campaign.[29] Largo had already written to the PCE's politburo to express his 'incompatibility' with their tactics. The left's absence from the 18 July multi-party meeting thus derived from this 'incompatibility'. In such circumstances, Largo saw Rafael Henche's criticisms of his executive as an act of personal betrayal as well as a breach of union discipline. Henche had made a *public* declaration, hence the suspension of his union from the UGT. Largo consistently maintained, in his defence of the UGT, that its absence from the meeting was simply a convenient stick with which to beat the socialist left for reasons which were quite other than those stated.[30]

But by this point it was rather late for Largo and his collaborators to be singling out Henche and Artes Blancas. Some twenty-nine other industrial sections had also emerged into open opposition by joining the call for a meeting of the national committee to be convened by the Largo executive.[31] On apprehending this, Largo proceeded to expel a further nine sections from the UGT, ostensibly for dues arrears, but as everyone was well aware, for their 'insubordination'.[32] The reality behind the expulsions was made doubly clear to all by the evident inconsistencies of the Largo executive's policy of exclusion.[33] As was pointed out in the party and union press – which by September 1937 was virtually all unitarist except for *La Correspondencia de Valencia* – there were many unions with dues arrears which

the national executive chose not to tackle – either because they were
sympathetic or because they had maintained some degree of distance from the dispute.

The expulsions and suspensions continued to increase as the
unitarist attack entered a dual phase in September. On the first of
the month the UGT majority called for an extraordinary meeting of
the national committee to be convened within a period of seven days
in accordance with article 33 of the statutes.[34] On 10 September, in
the absence of any reply from Largo's executive, the national committee delegates published an agenda for the meeting for which they
continued to petition.[35] There was mounting activity on the unitarist
front. Meetings of UGT delegates were convened by Amaro del
Rosal in Madrid (23 September) and Valencia (24 September).
Significantly, the Madrid meeting was held in the PSOE's headquarters, while the Valencia gathering was effectively a full national
committee meeting, with thirty-one federations in attendance.[36]
Under increasing pressure then, Largo and his colleagues finally
agreed to an interview with national committee representatives. It
took place on 25 September and the unitarist delegation comprised
Rodríguez Vega (printers), Septién (local government workers),
and Antonio Pérez (railway workers). Their message was a simple
one; a forty-eight hour ultimatum. The executive was to call a
meeting of the UGT's national committee within this period, or the
majority members of the national committee would act without it on
their own account. The union executive, still borrowing the tactics of
its opponents in the Socialist Party, claimed that, before it could
consider calling a national committee meeting, it would require the
delegates to obtain accreditation from their respective industrial
federations.[37]

The socialist left was, meanwhile, rapidly losing its last foothold
in both the party and the socialist press. On 30 September, in a
reformist coup, Largo Caballero and Rodolfo Llopis were replaced
on the executive of the socialist parliamentary party by Ramón
González Peña and José Prat.[38] For the socialist left the writing on
the wall was entirely clear. Having failed with the delaying tactic of
accreditation, Largo Caballero proceeded, amazingly, to expel a
further sixteen industrial sections from the union, whereby he
finally achieved the suspension or expulsion of the thirty-one UGT
federations which had attended the informal national committee
meeting in Valencia on 24 September. In the *Caballeristas'* rarified
logic, this expulsion would prevent a 'statutory' convocation of a
national committee meeting by the majority of its delegates who
were, henceforward, no longer members of the UGT.[39] This piece

of tactical lunacy precipitated Largo's final collapse. On 1 October, the day after the left's ejection from the leadership of the PSOE's parliamentary party, the majority members of the UGT's national committee met to elect a new UGT executive. Led by Ramón González Peña as president, it symbolised the political triumph of the PSOE reformists over the socialist left in the latter's union stronghold.

There was, however, a price to be paid for this victory. It had proved possible to defeat the left because of the collaboration of reformist socalists, unitarists and communists. But the PCE had put a price on its collaboration: namely that the Communist Party should be directly represented on the UGT's national executive. So, in the autumn of 1937, for the first time ever in the fifty-year history of the organisation, trade union leaders who were card-carrying members of the PCE took their places on the UGT's supreme leadership body. Out of a total membership of eleven, the PCE had two executive posts. These were filled by César Lombardía of the teachers' federation and by veteran union leader, Daniel Anguiano (petroleum industry). But the PCE's strength on the new González Peña executive was in fact greater than that number suggests. Of the remaining eight members (excluding the president himself and the PCE's members), three more were intensely pro-communist, namely Amaro del Rosal, Felipe Pretel, and Antonio Génova.[40] As a result, political power on the executive was very finely balanced. This would come to be important in the future, once the interests of the socialist and communist members on the executive began to diverge. From the perspective of 1 October 1937, however, one thing was very clear: the *Caballeristas* were not alone in their readiness and ability to use the machinery of the union bureaucracy.

The most effective of the unitarists' weapons, however, was the valuable propaganda they were able to make out of the *caballerista* executive's expulsion of the Asturian miners union from the UGT at the beginning of September 1937. It is very difficult to see what the *Caballeristas* hoped to gain by expelling the S M A – whose foremost leader was also president of the PSOE. It is hard to appreciate why it was not apparent at the time to the Largo executive that, by expelling the Asturian miners, it would be bestowing upon the opposition an enormous gift in terms of potential hostile propaganda. The war in the north was at its height, indeed by September 1937 it was reaching its bloody conclusion, and the Asturian miners, the heroes of October 1934, were once again in the front line of the struggle against fascism in Spain. Both the Socialist and Communist Party press and the union newspapers made full use of what was a tactical

blunder of epic proportions. The following extract from *Claridad* of 9
September 1937 captures the force of the unitarist propaganda
which did so much damage to the *caballerista* cause:

> . . . as fascism bayonets its way into Asturias, ravaging its legendary
> people, the national executive of the union, as its only gesture of en-
> couragement to the Asturians to continue the struggle, has offered to
> the miners . . . expulsion from the UGT, isolation from the community
> of their class brothers.

In that the battle for control of the UGT pitched Largo Caballero –
the immense symbol of working-class sacrifice and honesty – against
the legend of Asturias, it ought to have been a clash of Titans. In the
event, however, the *Caballeristas* gave the game away. The national
executive insisted, in the face of unitarist criticism, that it was not the
rank and file of the miners' union which had been expelled but only
the federation's insubordinate hierarchy – the former reverting to
the status of direct affiliates to the UGT's national executive.[41]
Largo's explanation, however, convinced very few. Nor could it
repair the damage done by hostile press propaganda. It was the
other face of the legend of October 1934, working-class unity rather
than revolution, which defeated the socialist left in its union
stronghold.

For the reformists in the PSOE, October 1934 had revealed the
hollowness of the left's revolutionary pretensions. The real revolution had occurred in the Asturian heartland which was *prietista*, and
Prieto himself had subsequently used the prestige of the Asturian
miners' leaders, and especially of Ramón González Peña, to very
good effect against the left in the party dispute. In the June 1936
elections to the PSOE executive, Prieto had consciously pitted
González Peña's reputation against Largo's in the battle for the
presidency.[42] In 1937, again, in the union dispute, which was really
an extension of the party's, Prieto's presiding will can be discerned
behind the shape of the new UGT executive elected on 1 October by
the UGT majority.[43] Once again González Peña and the powerful
symbolism of Asturian unity stood against Largo and the old guard
of the union, a fact which was not lost on the former general
secretary.[44] Asturias had been fashioned into a myth and wielded
against the socialist left: 'Asturias, land of titans', 'the shadow of
October', 'Asturias, generous and sublime', 'the epitome of solidarity'.[45] But there was little that the socialist left could do to counter an
enormously successful reformist tactic.

The conclusion to this chapter came then on 1 October 1937.
Faced with the stonewalling of Largo's executive and its effective

refusal to call a national committee meeting, the majority members took matters into their own hands. First they tried – and failed – to gain access to UGT headquarters. Largo and his 'rump' executive (Hernández Zancajo, Díaz Alor, Mariano Muñoz, Pascual Tomás and Ricardo Zabalza), plus assorted sympathisers had barricaded themselves inside.[46] These sympathisers included José Bullejos, the ex-general secretary of the PCE and his collaborator, Manuel Adame, both of whom were regular contributors to the monthly theoretical review, *Spartacus*, published by the Alicante socialist federation from June 1937. This became a vital forum for the left socialists because by mid-1937 there were very few such channels left.[47] This virtual siege of the UGT's headquarters also explains Largo's absence from the Cortes session.[48] But, in the event, the left's resistance was to no avail. Having failed to gain access, the national committee delegates, representing thirty-one of the forty-two federations, convened itself on the landing outside, whence it soon adjourned to the headquarters of the Federación Gráfica. There the new union executive was duly elected.[49]

Adelante's headline for 1 October ran: 'Pablo Iglesias expelled!' – a reference to Largo's expulsion of the Federación Gráfica, on which the founding father of Spanish socialism had built his party. This signalled the beginning of a concerted attempt to undermine Largo's moral credibility. The presence of Felipe Pretel, the fellow-travelling treasurer on Largo's old executive, was also crucial to the unitarists' success in that he oversaw the transfer of funds to the new executive, which could also count on the influence of the government.[50] Largo himself claimed that Negrín had personally intervened, via the finance ministry, to deny his executive access to banked union funds. But when on 3 October, *El Socialista* published the headline, 'La UGT reconquistada' it was only partly true. While the national executive had effectively been retaken from what *Adelante* had described as the 'rump' executive, the UGT as a whole was far from united behind it – for all the stirring propaganda of the unitarist press. The debate – the battle even – between Largo's partisans and the unitarists was to continue throughout 1938.

Yet it was not Asturias alone, or the expulsion of the SMA, which wrecked the *Caballeristas'* case. They had also failed to wage anything like a consistent battle on the organisational front. The executive had expelled and suspended a number of industrial sections for dues arrears, but not only was their statutory right to do so brought into question,[51] but more significantly, it was demonstrably the case that the executive had been very partial in its choice of which federations to expel. The accounts in the unitarist press repeatedly indicated the discrepancies and gave examples of federations which still enjoyed full membership of the UGT despite having arrears equal to or worse than other industrial federations which had suffered expulsion.[52] More scandalously still, the unitarists were able publicly to retail in the press accounts of the various abortive attempts by the expulsees to pay off their dues arrears at UGT headquarters. These included the efforts of Amador Fernández, president of the S M A, who vainly tried to present the UGT executive with 50,000 pesetas donated by Prieto.[53] But Largo's executive always managed to avoid receiving payment. This was never a direct refusal. But by leaving the office unattended, except by clerical staff, or by claiming a variety of other practical impediments to the acceptance of dues, for example, Carlos Hernández is supposed to have adduced a dearth of the appropriate vouchers, the executive managed to maintain the dissident majority in a state of what it claimed was lapsed membership.[54] Inevitably, the revelation of what was easily portrayed as scandalous triviality and deviousness in the middle of a draining civil war, did Largo's cause immeasurable harm. The endless and often very dubious manipulation of union regulations by Largo's executive clearly indicates that – beyond procrastination and stonewalling – *it had no strategy for dealing with the opposition.*

Thus, by 1 October, Ramón González Peña was president of both the PSOE and the UGT. His second triumph, however, was by no means a definitive one and it also had the effect of further embittering Largo because it served as a reminder of the party elections of June 1936 in which the reformist candidacy had triumphed by means of what the left believed could only have been blatant fraud. Azaña was almost certainly correct when he declared that Largo was not as powerful in the UGT as he supposed.[55] Nevertheless, he still wielded a considerable amount of influence and certainly sufficient to cause problems for the unitarist executive. On neither the union nor the wider political front could the opposition consider that it had entirely neutralised the socialist left. That this was well appreciated in unitarist spheres is clear from the continuing press attacks on the old UGT executive. Everything was called into question. First of all, the legitimacy of its election – for the Largo executive (if not Largo himself), had, like González Peña's, been elected by the UGT's national committee and not by a full congress.[56] Its supposedly lacklustre support of the government since May was constantly evoked, and, of course, there was always the old stand-by – Largo and his supporters were accused of harbouring a preference for union government. Likewise, grievances were aired over the *Caballeristas'* appropriation of union property from the headquarters at

Fuencarral, 93.[57] On every front, using every available argument, the unitarists had determined to sabotage the credibility of the left and in particular the moral authority of Largo Caballero himself, in order to consolidate the position of the González Peña executive. The UGT unitarists and the reformist socialists had a great advantage given that state power was held by those sympathetic to their cause – with Juan Negrín and Julián Zugazagoitia holding the premiership and the interior ministry respectively. In the first instance, Zugazagoitia had given permission for the dissenting UGT majority to assemble as a meeting of national committee delegates.[58] After the election of the new executive, Largo and his colleagues found that their correspondence was being diverted. Also, as they complained vociferously, they were unable to gain access to banked union funds because these had been frozen and instructions issued that their cheques were not to be honoured.[59] It was also a notorious fact that the Republic's security forces were used on various occasions to enforce the will of the party executive against *caballerista* dissidence and more specifically to ensure the repossession of party press and headquarters.

One of the most powerful and successful propaganda weapons used by both the Communist Party and the reformist socialists against the socialist left was that of the 'syndical pretensions' of the UGT leadership. It was claimed that the latter aspired to form a union government by means of which the UGT and the CNT would supplant the political parties, usurping their traditional hegemony in the political sphere.[60] This was a critical line which had been consistently sustained from the beginning of 1937 by the PCE.[61] The PSOE executive rapidly followed suit as a means of intensifying its attack on the party left. Moreover, the fact that in the aftermath of the political crisis in May 1937, the UGT and the CNT jointly signed an inter-union pact, tended to fuel the suspicions and fears of the political parties.[62] Yet this pact, signed on 29 July 1937 by Largo's executive and the national committee of the CNT, was above all a defensive one. It had come far too late to constitute a serious initiative which might have challenged the political parties' control of the state. The two unions, in different ways the 'victims of May', were closing ranks against both the erosion of Largo's influence in the UGT and against the threat to the CNT implicit in the outcome of the Barcelona May Days. But they were uniting from a position of weakness not strength.

Nevertheless, the UGT–CNT pact was viewed with considerable suspicion by the unitarist opposition in the UGT. They were fearful that it might inspire rogue political initiatives – as a circular produced by the building federation at the end of October 1937 implicitly made clear. This stressed that practical cooperation ought to be the keynote of the union agreement. The joint committees established under its terms were not to discuss general political issues but only professional matters and questions of practical cooperation between UGT and CNT workers. Nor, the circular insisted, could any agreements 'of a general nature' reached by the UGT–CNT joint committees have any binding force on the UGT federation's base, which had at all times to adhere to the directives of its own, *unitarist* national committee.[63]

Undoubtedly, the experience in 1936 of state collapse, popular revolution and the rise to prominence of workers' committees had badly shaken all the national political leaderships, those of the proletarian parties included. Indeed it had created an indelible impression on both the PCE and the PSOE. However, it is difficult to sustain that either the CNT or the UGT posed a serious threat to the hegemony of the political parties in respect of the possession of public state power. Ideology apart, the very structure of both union organisations constituted an overriding impediment to any successful conquest of the state. Organisational structure itself goes much of the way to explaining the unions' failure to make a revolution during the first weeks of the war when a vacuum of power existed. The degree of autonomy and decentralisation on which the UGT, as much as the CNT, operated rendered extraordinarily difficult the concentration, coordination and centralisation of power essential to efficient state administration – especially in wartime.[64]

Moreover, the concept of a union bloc to challenge the parties presupposes an ideological convergence between the UGT and CNT which simply did not exist. Whatever the practical difficulties involved, there was a strong current in the CNT which aspired to transplant the union organisation as a model for that of the state. The UGT leadership, however, never jettisoned its traditional understanding of the trade union as subordinate to the political party. Of course, by political party the *Caballeristas* meant the PSOE and it was control of this which they sought. This, however, was a far cry from cherishing dreams of syndicalising the state. Largo was not set upon launching the UGT on a course which would eclipse the PSOE. Not even under the concerted attack of the political parties in the spring of 1937, when the party press was proclaiming the imminence of union government in strident tones, would Largo and the CNT advance very far along this road. Equally, the socialist left's preoccupation with reconquering control of the PSOE leadership during the war provides more than sufficient evidence of a belief in the pre-eminence of the party. In one respect at least, Largo Caballero was correct in his famous speech in October 1937 in the Teatro Pardiñas – when he declared that the whole campaign against the socialist left as the purveyors of union government was a red herring which had conveniently obscured the real sources of the confrontation. It had served as a public justification for the ousting of the socialist left, undertaken by socialists and communists for a variety of different motives.

In the case of both the PCE and the PSOE, the collision with the *Caballeristas* was the product of an acute organisational rivalry rather than of fundamental ideological difference. This, insofar as it existed, lay most tangibly between the left socialists and the anarchists, rather than between the *Caballeristas* and the PSOE or the PCE. Where the PCE was concerned, the PSOE left stood opposed to its drive to absorb the socialist base, both in the UGT and via the formation of the single class party ('partido único'). For the PSOE reformists, the accusation of *sindicalismo* was an excellent way of attacking the left which was still bidding for control of the *party* organisation. Thus, an organisational rivalry, such as the division in the PSOE had always been at root, maintained in the civil war the appearance of ideological difference which it had assumed in the period of the Second Republic. The internal division of Spanish socialism itself also lent superficial credibility to the parties' 'sindicalista' accusations. This split meant that in both of Largo's governments, left socialists and reformists were seen as representing different political entities, one of which was a trade union. Moreover, Largo Caballero confirmed his close identification with the UGT by his conduct during the May 1937 cabinet crisis. Immediately he had apprised Azaña of events, it was to the union executive that Largo had recourse in order to discuss possible solutions to the crisis. By seeking out its support at such a crucial political moment, Largo effectively strengthened the impression that he was premier in his capacity as general secretary of the UGT, rather than as a PSOE militant. However, an editorial which appeared in the Alicante socialist federation's theoretical review, *Spartacus*, on 1 September 1937 came as close as any other publication to an explicit declaration of the real, organisational nature of the division within Spanish socialism:

> When it is claimed, for example, that in the course of the Spanish revolution the UGT has been more of a vanguard than the PSOE, this is not because the UGT is a trade union, but because the men who lead it have made it much more than an instrument to achieve material improvements for the workers. They have turned it into an instrument of

social revolution. . . . As members of the UGT, then, it is our duty to
revitalise the Party, by conquering the party leadership.[65]

It is also worth pointing out how the blurring of distinctions
between party and union was sustained during the war partly
because of the degree to which, historically, political and union
functions had always overlapped very considerably between the
PSOE and the UGT. Before the First World War the national
leaderships of the two organisations had almost always been one and
the same.[66] However, in both the north and the south of Spain it was
also true that the overlap between union and party functions was
very great. In the south, very often the UGT sections considered
themselves to be Socialist Party sections, and indeed functioned as
such, without, however, ever becoming formally affiliated to the
party.[67] Strictly speaking, of course, the UGT remained 'non-
denominational'. However, by the 1930s, with the arrival of the
Republic, sudden and rapid mass political mobilisation itself had an
enormous impact on the nature and function of the UGT. 'The
UGT, the mass of workers concentrated in its sections, has in these
last few years taken an enormous step, by becoming involved in
political action . . .' Thus opined Manuel Cordero, veteran trade
unionist and socialist leader, writing in 1932 of the effect of the
Second Republic on the UGT.[68] He forecast that the way forward
would necessarily involve the union in action of a political nature in
that, with the arrival of a democratic system, the route of political
struggle was for the first time genuinely open to the Spanish
proletariat which had previously been restricted to fighting for
improvements in the union sphere alone. Of course, Cordero was not
consciously seeking to describe a conflict of interests between party
and union, but rather to identify areas for future cooperation between the two. Nevertheless, the dispute which broke the socialist
movement so dramatically in the 1930s was, at root, the product of
an abiding tension in the PSOE between workerist (*obrerista*) and
parliamentary political (*político*) tendencies, which crystallised as an
organisational rivalry during the Second Republic. It is this tension
which explains the real origins of political party versus *sindicalismo*.
Within the socialist organisation it was not a dispute between those
who favoured party hegemony and the advocates of union government, but rather a battle over who was to control the party.

The experience of revolution at the beginning of the civil war, of
spontaneous, grass roots revolution it must be remembered, had
been equally traumatic for the national leadership of the UGT. It too
had temporarily lost control of its rank and file, in that the factory

committees – whether they were CNT or UGT inspired or coopera-
tive ventures – were not a response to national union directives.
UGT minutes betoken a particular hostility to joint UGT–CNT
initiatives, as throughout the second half of 1936 the national executive struggled desperately to regain control of its membership. This
was the political reality behind such abstract declarations as 'our
lives are of little value, but the patrimony of the UGT is priceless'.[69]
When the local federation in Málaga informed the national executive of the likelihood of its merging with the local CNT, if only to gain
access to weapons, the executive replied absolutely forbidding any
such initiative.[70] The UGT was primarily concerned to reassert its
authority over the UGT factory committees.[71] Implicit in the entire
propaganda production of the most prominent veteran UGT leaders
from 1936 to 1938 was the absolute need to re-establish hierarchical
control.[72] The speeches of all the *caballerista* leaders echoed Largo's
own reformism, his defence of the Popular Front, his insistence on
the national Republican government as sole legitimate authority
('único rector'). Anarchist commentators themselves have pointed
out that, as premier, Largo invested much more energy in bringing
the CNT into government than he did in establishing the basis of an
inter-union alliance such as the CNT sought.[73] For Largo, the
unions were the tools of government authority, they were not independent of it. It was their task to administer not direct. Centralisation (i.e. nationalisation) was essential for the war effort rather than
as an abstract political principle. Likewise, collectivisation was
important primarily as a means of rationalisation in certain areas in
order to boost production for the war effort. It was not an agent of
magical transformation and there were situations where it ought not
to be attempted, for example, where concerns were economically
weak or verging on the non-viable. So Largo Caballero was concerned to enact policies which he saw as practicable in the short or
medium term, rather than affirming an ideological choice. The
medium-term objective was national economic reconstruction, the
short term, strengthening the war economy.[74]

Had the *Caballeristas'* ideological stance been as it was presented in
the unitarist press, that is, in the Socialist and Communist Party
press, then the tremendous difficulties experienced by the UGT in its
relations with its anarchist counterpart during the war would never
have arisen. The fact that the left socialist leadership could not meet
the anarchist organisation on common ground, was, as has already
been outlined, one of the major reasons for the *caballerista* collapse in
May 1937. But enmeshed with the ideological issue was the no less
thorny and crucial question of escalating organisational rivalry

between the two. This was not something born of the war,[75] however, during the conflict the pre-existing rivalry erupted into extremely violent clashes, some of the worst of which occurred in Cullera (Valencia).[76]

The eventual *rapprochement* between the UGT and the CNT, which the pact of July 1937 signified, was really of little practical use to either organisation. The basis for the agreement, signed at the end of the month, was an extremely negative one. It sprang solely from the dire political straits in which the *Caballeristas* suddenly found themselves. With virtually no preparatory overtures to the CNT leadership, Largo's union executive, apprised of the rout of the socialist left in Valencia and of the loss of *Adelante* to the reformist socialists, hastened to seal an interim agreement with the anarchist organisation. Its objective was to avoid being forced into a political ghetto. The terms of the resulting agreement, which could only be signed provisionally by the UGT leadership, pending full national committee approval, were innocuous in the extreme. Fundamentally a non-aggression pact designed to improve relations between the UGT and CNT memberships, it stressed the need for practical cooperation between the two unions. Nevertheless, the timing of the pact and the fact that it sought to establish a national network of joint UGT–CNT committees at every level throughout Republican Spain, caused warning bells to sound inside the political parties. Their leaderships suspected this initiative as a covert attempt to relaunch the unions on a political career. The PCE was particularly critical. It claimed that the union agreement contained a hidden agenda: namely, that Largo and the CNT, as the 'losers' in May 1937, would work together to oust the leadership of the PSOE.[77]

By July 1937, it was in fact too late for the socialist left to use the inter-union agreement to relaunch itself politically. But it probably did have inchoate ambitions of this kind. It is difficult, otherwise, to make sense of the sudden adoption of anarchist faith by leading *Caballeristas*.[78] An article such as Araquistain's, 'La misión histórica de los sindicatos y los partidos políticos', first published in *Timón* (Barcelona), the theoretical anarchist review, in July 1938, but written a year earlier, only becomes politically coherent when one links the expression of new-found revolutionary faith on the part of the *Caballeristas* to their attempts in the summer of 1937 to forge an alternative political line to that of the PSOE-controlled government.[79] Hence the *textual* resurgence of the revolutionary interpretation of the war and its objectives. But in spite of the nervousness this produced in the PSOE and the

PCE,[80] the revolutionary rhetoric was no more than a futile final salvo. *For the left had no alternative strategy with which to confront the Popular Front bloc.*

It was partly to guarantee the political demobilisation of the UGT–CNT opposition that the assault on Largo's position in the UGT was undertaken.[81] By installing a new, reformist socialist-led national executive in the UGT, and then using it to negotiate a new inter-union agreement with the CNT, the Popular Front parties finally succeeded in exorcising the trade union threat to their political pre-eminence. It is in this context that the UGT–CNT unity of action pact, eventually signed in March 1938, must be analysed. Although this was publicised at the time as a consolidated version of the pact originally signed by Largo's executive in July 1937, the agreement was in fact an entirely separate exercise, with quite different objectives. In July 1937, Largo had been inspired by political considerations. The resulting pact had been intended as a political vehicle for the socialist left. In 1938, however, the object of the parties, and primarily the PSOE and the PCE, in overseeing the UGT–CNT unity of action pact, was to enshrine the terms of the unions' political *demobilisation* in a way which would be binding on both organisations.

It was in December 1937 that Ramón González Peña's new UGT executive first approached the CNT's national committee with the object of negotiating a common action initiative similar to the one signed by the PSOE and the PCE in August 1937.[82] The UGT leadership's intention here was twofold. First, negotiating the pact would help consolidate its own authority within the socialist trade union. Second, by absorbing the *Caballeristas'* initiative, the UGT unitarists sought to ensure that the pact could never serve as a potential focus of political discontent or opposition to the policies of the Negrín government. By January 1938, the undermining of the *caballerista* pact had begun with the preliminary agreement permanently to transfer the UGT–CNT national joint committee, established under the conditions of the July pact, to Barcelona, which was the UGT unitarists' stronghold.[83] By the middle of the month local joint committees were also being established.

From even the most cursory perusal it is clear that the basis of the March 1938 agreement was labour policy in the narrowest possible sense.[84] The final draft, hammered out between the UGT and CNT delegates, represented a serious defeat for anarchist ideology. The CNT deferred in every respect to the statism of the socialist union. The UGT's negotiators were César Lombardía (PCE), Amaro del Rosal and the UGT's vice-president, Edmundo Domínguez.

Significantly, all three were very closely identified with Negrín's philosophy that all political and economic power should be concentrated in the hands of central government. The March 1938 agreement was essentially a blueprint for disciplining both production and the producers. The unions were finally reduced to the role of managers of production, entirely dependent on the centralised state apparatus, an instrument for the channelling of government policy and propaganda – themselves determined by the political parties. The union pact also ratified the concept of a national network of joint committees, first established under the July pact, laying down provision for them along the lines of the norms first established for those between the Socialist and Communist Parties in April 1937. The parallel between the party and union strategies once again underlines the resurgence of the Popular Front line of the political parties. Paradoxically, then, the formal reincorporation of both the UGT and the CNT into the Popular Front alliance on 1 April 1938,[85] as a result of the union pact, signified their subjugation by the political parties. The unions were not being admitted to the alliance as equal or autonomous political agents. Joint UGT–CNT committees were to exist on a par with the joint party committees at national, regional, provincial and local level and also in work places.[86] However, the function of these committees, as stipulated in the agreement, again reflected the philosophy of political demobilisation which lay behind the union pact. The control committees, so-called because it was their function to supervise all aspects of the production process, were in fact almost all quality control bodies. The entire text as approved by the UGT and the CNT stressed the unity of the working class and its wholehearted support for the government's war effort.

All in all, the pact of March 1938 testified to a remarkable evolution within the anarchist leadership. In the space of less than two years – since the Zaragoza congress of May 1936 – the CNT's political line had undergone a sea change. It was no longer even apparently an anti-parliamentary, anti-statist monolith. The internal crisis of the anarchist organisation, intensified by the war, had brought the *políticos* to prominence. Analysing this transformation in pragmatic terms, it constituted the CNT's acceptance of the resurgent order of Popular Front symbolised by the Negrín government.[87] Propelled by the *políticos*, the anarchist organisation's formal adhesion to the Popular Front pact – both the CNT's and the FAI's – symbolised this 'historic compromise', while also paving the way for the anarchists' re-entry into government.[88] When Indalecio Prieto resigned from the cabinet in April 1938, thus necessitating its reorganisation, Negrín would grant the CNT a single representative in government.

Once the March 1938 pact had been ratified by the leaderships of the two organisations, a series of public meetings was immediately organised to publicise its conditions. At these meetings, which were held at strategic points throughout the Republican zone – in Valencia, Madrid, Barcelona, Castellón, Almería and Ubeda,[89] CNT and UGT leaders vied with each other in their declarations of loyal support for the Negrín government. García Pradas, speaking in Madrid, spoke of a 'revolutionary workers alliance', but *to support the government*. There was no longer any question of the unions exercising political power in their own right. From the contents of the joint committee minutes in the Madrid building federation during 1938, it is clear that discussion – in unitarist controlled federations at least – was successfully channelled in the direction of professional and practical issues. But, doubtless, the extreme pressure of deteriorating material conditions played a considerable part here too. And this raises another important function of the factory and workplace-based committees: the bolstering of an increasingly fragile morale and the motivation of the workforce in the desperate battle for production.[90] As the shortage of manpower at the front intensified and it was necessary to conscript older and younger age-bands, the UGT–CNT joint committees would also assume this task. In all the party and union newspapers the need to concentrate on practical issues was repeatedly emphasised. Abstract ideological debate was deemed a luxury unaffordable in wartime.

The Significance of the Unitarist Victory in the UGT

The most obvious and immediate consequence of the October 1937 *caballerista* defeat at executive level was that for the first time ever there were communists on the national executive of the UGT, and, moreover, they had been elected indirectly by the national committee rather than by a union congress. The UGT's new executive, elected on 1 October 1937, was as follows: president, Ramón González Peña (PSOE/miners); vice-president, Edmundo Domínguez (PSOE/building federation); general secretary, J. Rodríguez Vega (PSOE/printers); assistant secretary, Amaro del Rosal (PSOE/banking and finance); treasurer, Felipe Pretel (PSOE/entertainment and leisure industry) and it included Ezequiel Ureña (PSOE/chemical industry), Claudina García, (PSOE/garment and hatters), Antonio Pérez (PSOE/railways), Antonio Génova (PSOE/

woodworkers), César Lombardía (PCE/teachers' federation) and
Daniel Anguiano (PCE/petroleum industry) as ordinary members.[91] A PCE report on the UGT for 1938 affords a special executive
category to both Amaro del Rosal and Felipe Pretel: it denominates
them, somewhat euphemistically, as 'unitary current socialists'.[92]
The implications of a unitarist executive were to be tremendously
far-reaching. Similar attempts would be made to transform the
hierarchies of the national federations of industry as well as the
national structure of the UGT. But it seems likely that, in both cases,
most of the PCE's influence was exerted at the national rather than
the regional or local level.[93]

The campaign against the remaining dissident unions which still
recognised the Largo Caballero executive was stepped up. This was
achieved by actively encouraging unitarist trends within these union
organisations at the national, provincial and local level. The remaining dissident federations and their representatives on the new unitarist-dominated UGT national committee were as follows: Wenceslao
Carrillo (iron and steel), Elias Riego (office workers), Vélez (paper
industry), R. Mira (hairdressers), R. Diego (chemical industry),
Carlos Hernández Zancajo (transport federation) and Ricardo
Zabalza (FNTT). Largo himself interpreted the ousting of his executive as the final success of communist currents which had been
openly pressing from early 1937 for the direct inclusion of communist representatives on the UGT's national executive. As with the
PSOE so in the UGT, the root of the tension between socialists and
communists can be traced back to 1921. The repercussions of the
political schism which saw the emergence of the PCE were felt in the
union. In 1922 the UGT congress had expelled fifteen unions for
refusing to approve the expulsion of the communist delegates in the
highly charged atmosphere which followed the assassination of a
worker.[94] One of the expulsees was 'El Baluarte', the Madrid iron
and steel section, which again suffered expulsion during the 1937
dispute for its unitarist stance. The plenum of the PCE's central
committee in March 1937 had called for a special congress or a
national committee meeting in the UGT to elect a new national
executive which would include communists.[95] Alternatively, it was
suggested, PCE representatives could simply be appointed to the
existing executive committee.[96] This proposal had, of course, been
instantly vetoed by Largo's union executive which argued that direct
appointments were alien to the principle of grass roots democracy
which had always prevailed in the UGT.[97] A second communist
tactic, since the plenum of the central committee of the PCE in
March 1937, had been to procure wherever possible the celebration

of congresses in individual industrial federations in the hope of getting communists elected, thus eventually rendering Largo's argument useless. As a result, *caballerista* UGT leaders in the industrial federations immediately began to resort to all sorts of accords and bureaucratic manoeuvres within the organisation to prevent communists gaining access to leadership posts. Of course, the PCE leadership was itself well aware of these manoeuvres.[98]

On 24 October 1937, the UGT's national committee, meeting in Valencia, and attended by thirty-three federations, unanimously approved the new González Peña executive. This marked the beginning of a dual attack on the dissidents in the UGT.[99] While unitarist candidacies were now being elected at both the local and provincial level in some places, pressure also began to be placed on the leaderships of the dissident federations to call individual national congresses in their respective industries. The aim was clearly to oust what were presented as 'atypical' national executives. Not unexpectedly, the unions which faced the greatest onslaught in this respect were Carlos Hernández Zancajo's urban transport federation, Wenceslao Carrillo's iron and steel federation and the socialist landworkers' federation, led by Ricardo Zabalza – all *caballerista* stalwarts.[100] Of these three, the position of urban transport's national executive was the least secure because its provincial federations in Madrid, Valencia and Barcelona were all unitarist.[101]

Between the election of the González Peña executive in October 1937 and the formal resolution of the union dispute at national level in January 1938, via the mediation of the French trade union leader, Léon Jouhaux, there was a great deal of dislocation and division within the UGT. Not only were the dissident federations hostile to the unitarists and vice versa, but within each camp there were provincial organisations which opposed the position of their national leaderships. For example, although the national executives of Artes Blancas and Tabaqueros were solidly unitarist, the provincial federations of both in Valencia – where considerable support for the left socialists remained – backed Largo's executive.[102] And the same pattern was present in Vestido y Tocado (garments and hatters). The teachers' union (FETE) was badly split. Its general secretary César Lombardía, one of the two communist members on the UGT national executive, led a unitarist majority on the FETE's national executive, while Rodolfo Llopis, Largo Caballero's lieutenant, was one of a dissident minority on the committee. The FETE's provincial federations were also split. Most favoured the unitarists, including Valencia and Madrid, but Teruel, Huesca, Cuenca, Murcia, Alicante, Córdoba and Extremadura were all to some extent hostile to the unitarist majority,[103] while in Ciudad Real the FETE was solidly *caballerista*.[104]

Both sides in the UGT dispute were keen to assume the moral high ground by proving that their opponents were intent upon splitting those federations where they did not prevail.[105] But, however one assesses the legitimacy of the two sides' claims, the result of the ensuing conflict was major organisational dislocation in the UGT.[106] This would scarcely have been affordable in any war, but it was verging on the suicidal, given the savage disadvantage at which the Republic was forced to operate.

A perusal of the UGT press reveals that there were latent conflicts in most industrial federations at most levels. But in some of the more extreme cases the unitarists' opponents threatened to establish, unilaterally, new, integrally socialist union sections. As a result they came into conflict with González Peña's executive.[107] Nor was the UGT structure itself free from these debilitating conflicts.[108] And as with the industrial federations, so here too it was in the Levante and the southern provincial federations that support for the *Caballeristas* was concentrated.[109]

Although the *Caballeristas* consistently refused to accept the legitimacy of the new UGT executive, in reality, by the time of its election the dissidents had already lost. The fact that its president was González Peña neutralised much potential criticism of the PCE's presence. Thus the symbolism of Asturias had finally deprived Largo of support. The *Caballeristas* had lost the political initiative and this inevitably settled matters in the union dispute. The socialist left had lost out completely in the PSOE, and control of almost all its newspapers was gone. By the end of October, the *Claridad* dispute had been settled in the courts with a decision unfavourable to the left. By the end of November, *La Correspondencia de Valencia* would also be appropriated in an operation which duplicated the loss of *Adelante*.[110] A new left socialist daily, *La Victoria*, was mooted but never materialised.[111]

Towards the end of October, and as a result of his speech on the 17th in the Teatro Pardiñas, Largo Caballero was personally silenced. The Pardiñas speech had been intended as the first of a series throughout Republican Spain. But Julián Zugazagoitia, the reformist socialist interior minister, imposed a blanket ban on public meetings in order to prevent a head-on collision between the *Caballeristas* and their unitarist opponents – who had also embarked on arrangements for a series of counter-meetings.[112] To ensure the effective implementation of his ban, Zugazagoitia instructed the security forces that Largo was to be kept in Valencia. As a result there occurred an unfortunate incident at Perelló when, on 22 October, Largo Caballero, Luis Araquistain, Rodolfo Llopis and Wenceslao Carrillo, *en route* from Valencia to Alicante, fell foul of a group of assault guards determined to implement their orders.[113] The group was obliged to return to Valencia. The incident gave rise to some considerable controversy and not a little embarrassment, as the left socialist presented it as evidence of clear political persecution and of Negrín's dictatorial tendencies. Largo argued that the government could legitimately suspend public meetings, but it had no right to prevent the free movement of a deputy of the Spanish Cortes. Perhaps, tactically, it was not very wise for the PSOE to be seen acting quite so heavy-handedly against fellow-socialists (though the ban was lifted on 24 October – two days after the incident). But, on the other hand, it might equally well be argued that Largo and the left had been determined to force the issue, since on 21 October, the night before the incident at Perelló, Zugazagoitia's deputy, Carlos de San Juan, had telephoned Largo to inform him of the ban.[114] Though this did not stop Araquistain complaining before the permanent deputation of the Cortes that Perelló constituted 'persecution' by the socialists in government who were afraid of Largo's continuing popularity. The general consensus of the meeting, however, was favourable to the government ban.[115]

The unitarists gained the full force of Republican legality when, on 28 November, the Negrín government formally recognised the González Peña executive.[116] Although the old executive and its supporters still called, unrealistically, for a full general congress of the UGT for December, the leadership dispute was about to be settled in quite a different way – with the intervention of the labour international (International Federation of Trades Unions, IFTU).[117] Its arbitration was initiated in circumstances which remain less than entirely clear. Both sides in the dispute were in contact with the International. But whereas the new Ramón González Peña executive seems simply to have apprised the IFTU leadership of its election, without entering into the controversy, Largo's supporters apparently saw fit to petition the International to intervene directly in the dispute. Quite possibly they feared that they had been pre-empted in this regard by their unitarist opponents.[118] Rodolfo Llopis, on Largo's behalf, visited the IFTU's Paris headquarters at the beginning of October 1937 to make the *Caballeristas'* case in person to general secretary, Walter Schevenels. Well aware of the anti-communist persuasions of his interlocutor, Llopis laid great emphasis on the presence of communists and fellow travellers on the González Peña committee.[119] The *Caballeristas'* actions infuriated their opponents. The left was accused of blatantly parading the divisions in the UGT. As Manuel Cordero opined in a letter to Wenceslao Carrillo after the war, Largo had destroyed his own reputation both inside and outside the country by irresponsibly exposing the divisions in the labour movement at such a delicate moment for Spanish democracy.[120] As a result of Llopis' endeavours, however, Schevenels agreed to discuss with his colleagues the matter of IFTU arbitration in the UGT dispute.

The first meeting with Léon Jouhaux and Paul Faure, as representatives of the International, took place at the beginning of December 1937 in Paris.[121] For the second round of discussions at the end of the month, Jouhaux and Walter Citrine, general secretary of the TUC, went to Barcelona. By 30 December a compromise solution was reached.[122] From this meeting, attended by both the Largo Caballero and the González Peña executives, by the representatives of all the national industrial federations and by those of the UGT provincial federations in the loyalist zone, there emerged an augmented national executive which included four *Caballeristas*. This was presented by the unitarists as a genuine compromise to heal the breach in the organisation. In reality, of course, the intervention of the pro-unitarist Jouhaux had effectively resulted in the consolidation of the González Peña executive.[123] The *Caballeristas* had at first refused to accept anything less than a representation which was equal to that of the unitarists on the executive, that is, a total of five appointees. However, Jouhaux had been discouraging, leaving them no ground for manoeuvre. The *caballerista* presence, four strong, with Pascual Tomás, Díaz Alor, Ricardo Zabalza and Carlos Hernández Zancajo, was thus from the start a token representation, an alienated minority. (Unsurprisingly, Largo himself refused a post on the new executive.)[124] Given the circumstances of the IFTU's arbitration it is hardly surprising that *Caballeristas* immediately gave the new executive up for lost. Indeed, henceforward, only Zabalza, and to a lesser extent, Carlos Hernández Zancajo would play any part in its life.[125]

Its mandate thus assured, the González Peña executive took immediate steps to suspend the unitarist-inspired general congress of the urban transport federation which had been scheduled for 10 January 1938.[126] The González Peña executive declared it was superfluous, since the dispute in the union had been settled at national level. Of course, very little had really been resolved. Indeed the fact that the national executive acted so rapidly to halt the transport congress itself suggests it was uncertain of its outcome. 1938 was to be a year in which the González Peña executive made a concerted effort to dam the wellsprings of the dispute by manoeuvring within the dissident industrial federations. In the early months in some cases, where it felt confident enough, the UGT executive would also call for general congresses to be held – although these were always carefully presented in the press as necessary for impeccably practical *raisons de guerre*.

The intervention of the labour international in the UGT dispute thus closed a phase which the May 1937 cabinet crisis had opened. The exclusion of the *Caballeristas* from government signalled the beginning of a campaign to destroy their power base in the UGT. This campaign saw reformist socialists and communists united in their efforts to this end – although the underlying motives which prompted their collaboration were markedly different.

At one level, the PSOE executive's determination to exclude the left from the union leadership can be explained in terms of the internal party dispute. Lamoneda's initiatives in the party were all geared towards re-establishing a strong and united PSOE via the imposition of national executive discipline. An integral part of this process was the conquest of national and provincial leadership bodies, not just in the *party* organisation, but in the socialist movement as a whole. Given that the *Caballeristas'* stronghold had always been the UGT rather than the PSOE, the reformists were bound to challenge the left's control there to ensure peace in the party – or rather to guarantee their own continued control therein. The reformists' sense of urgency over the conquest of the UGT was probably also increased by their awareness of the union federation's vital practical role in wartime, in the fields and factories. This was certainly the aspect stressed publicly by the reformists. Largo's distinct lack of enthusiasm for the Negrín administration – explainable entirely in terms of the internal socialist dispute – provided ready ammunition for the reformists' public campaign against his union leadership. Socialist and communist newspapers pointed to the UGT's lukewarm attitude towards the government as evidence of a near treasonous lack of concern for the Republican war effort itself. Thus was public opinion in the loyalist zone – and particularly that of the socialist rank and file – prepared for the leadership changes in the UGT in October 1937. The left's defeat in the UGT was an inevitable consequence of its total political isolation by May 1937. But the task of Largo's opponents was nevertheless facilitated by the fact that the *Caballeristas* chose to defend themselves by resorting to bureaucratic manoeuvres. It was relatively easy for Largo's opponents to discredit the left by presenting such tactics as the height of irresponsibility in the middle of a civil war.

The fact that the reformist socialists should have looked to the PCE for support in their battle against the *Caballeristas* in the UGT was entirely consistent with the PSOE's overall wartime strategy of socialist–communist alliance, cemented in April 1937 with the joint party liaison committee agreement. While both this agreement and the subsequent common action pact, signed in August 1937, had an obvious practical function – the consolidation of the Popular Front and the Republican war effort – they were also central to the reformists' strategy for combatting the socialist left. The hidden agenda of the August pact, to which both socialists and communists subscribed, was how to break the *Caballeristas'* hold on the UGT. The PCE was as eager to achieve this as Lamoneda, although for quite separate reasons.

In its Popular Frontist phase, the Spanish Communist Party was engaged upon a recruitment drive in both the political and union spheres. The PCE's bid for a decisive influence in the UGT – although successful in Cataluña, mainly because of the pre-war weakness of socialist organisation there – had clashed in the rest of Republican Spain with Largo Caballero's refusal to contemplate the co-option of communists onto the UGT's national executive. It thus became essential for the PCE to break the *Caballeristas'* hold on the union hierarchy in order to gain access to it. This was effectively achieved as a result of the joint reformist–communist campaign against the left's union leadership between May and October 1937. This campaign was thus sparked by an organisational rivalry – or rather by two distinct ones – not by conflicting ideologies. It is hard to identify any major points of divergence between the political practices of left socialists, reformists and communists. Ideological tensions – insofar as they existed – came rather between left socialists and anarchists. But even here the notion of ideological conflict has been over-stressed. Although an investigation of it necessarily falls outside the scope of this study, the CNT's praxis both before and during the civil war was far more pragmatic than purist. It is organisational rivalry which explains the fundamental failure of the *Caballeristas* and the CNT to reach a political agreement in time to challenge the Popular Front bloc.

The election of the González Peña executive in October 1937 appeared initially to be as much a victory for the reformist socialists as for the Communists. But the socialists soon discovered a major flaw in the strategy they had employed against the party left in the UGT. For whilst the objectives of anti-Caballero socialists and Communists had converged in the short term, the PCE's Popular Frontist strategy ultimately posed an inescapable organisational challenge to the PSOE as a whole. The political control of the organised Spanish working class was at stake. It is well known that during the civil war the PCE welcomed into its ranks the professional and commercial middle classes who sought protection against the social and economic upheaval of the revolution, as well as a political formation capable of efficiently channelling the Republican war effort. But such a party profile has necessarily to be explained as a unique product of the specific conditions of the civil war. The Spanish Communists must have perceived as clearly as their socialist counterparts that such 'circumstantial' communists would not remain in the PCE once victory against both the revolution and the Nationalists had been secured. The fact was that, in peace time, under normal political conditions, the PSOE and the PCE would, as mass parliamentary parties of the left, be competing for members. This rivalry was already evident in the battle being waged between the Socialists and Communists in 1938 for control of the UGT. It was this conflict which was to bring the *Caballeristas* – entrenched in some of the UGT's most powerful industrial federations – back to political prominence.

10 The caballerista old guard: entrenchment and resurgence

The fact that the *Caballeristas* had lost control of the UGT executive and most of the provincial secretariats by January 1938 did not mean that the left had been completely defeated. The UGT was a confederation of *semi-autonomous* industrial unions and the left still had a power base in some of the strongest of these. Throughout 1938 the Ramón González Peña executive and the UGT's unitarist national committee – backed by the majority of the national industrial federations – were ranged against the remaining dissident federations, or, more specifically, against their dissident leaderships.

Leading the attack was the UGT's unitarist-dominated national committee. This was composed as follows: out of a total of forty-two, there were ostensibly thirty-one socialists and eleven communists. However, an analysis of the composition of the socialist membership presents quite a different picture of the internal political balance. There were three unitary current socialists, including Virgilio Llano of Espectáculos Públicos; two PSUC members who were technically socialist, but effectively counted with the communists. There were eighteen socialists of the González Peña tendency, of whom four were sympathetic to the unitary trend, and finally there were eight *Caballeristas* on the national committee. This breakdown, which appears in a PCE report on the UGT for 1938, reveals the considerable amount of influence wielded by the Communist Party within the national committee. Once this analysis has been taken fully into account, rather than presenting 31:11 as a ratio of comparative strength, something in the order of 22:20 would be a more accurate assessment. Indeed, the González Peña socialists would only be able to count on the *Caballeristas* very late in the day, when, by the last quarter of 1938, the bitter divisions in the socialist movement, although far from forgotten, were effectively taking second place as a result of the increasing division between socialists and communists.[1]

The national committee's major targets in 1938 were the pro-Caballero leaderships of the iron and steel, landworkers (FNTT) and urban transport federations.[2] In the iron and steel federation the national executive supported Largo. In the FNTT the national committee and some of the executive, including general secretary Zabalza, supported him. In the urban transport federation, the national executive was split.[3] Especially in the case of the transport federation, opposition to the González Peña executive would come to be bound up in 1938 with the whole debate in the trade union international (IFTU) over the desirability of the Soviet trade unions' membership. We shall now consider in turn the internal battle in the FNTT and transport federations from late 1937 onwards.

The FNTT and the Defence of Caballerismo: 1937–1938

Just as the FNTT, for its enormous size alone, had been a crucial part of the *caballerista* power base in the Second Republic, so too it became the pivot of the socialist left's last stand between 1937–8 when it was subjected to the full onslaught of the unitarist attack in the UGT. At one level, the enduring *caballerista* faith of the FNTT is hardly surprising, given that its enormous membership was drawn mainly from the poor agrarian south. In those areas remaining to the Republic after the military coup of July 1936, the vast majority of the population, that is, the landless, remained as committed to the principle and practice of collectivisation as they had been before the war. For in the south, the class nature of the war remained extremely visible. Indeed, the fact that in the occupied zone the military rebels and *latifundistas* immediately began repossessing land which had been settled on the landless prior to the rising, intensified that commitment.[4]

During the war, an enormous battle was waged over agrarian collectivisation between the communist agriculture minister, Vicente Uribe, and the FNTT, and between the latter and the PCE at a local level. Largo Caballero himself, however, was a socialist leader in as reformist a tradition as Prieto or Negrín. He failed signally to defend the collectives against Uribe's policies. Yet in spite of Largo's defence of the Popular Front and the reformist political and economic order which it represented, nothing could quite shatter the union veteran's revolutionary mystique – which rhetoric alone had created between 1934 and 1936. An awareness of the pragmatic exigencies of the war and, above all, its vital international dimension, doubtless countered what might otherwise have been a much greater degree of FNTT disaffection from Largo and the socialist left. In the event, sustained by the belief that in a post-victory Spain they would find in Largo Caballero a champion for a full programme of collectivisation, the FNTT remained the socialist left's strongest support.[5] The fortunes of war placed the FNTT at the forefront of opposition to the PCE in the rural south.[6] For, by and large, it had been the Andalucian provinces where the CNT had exercised its greatest influence which had fallen to the military rebels at the beginning of the war and the areas where the FNTT was strongest, such as Jaén, which remained to the Republic.[7]

The consistent and enduring support for Largo Caballero in the FNTT's southern federations, indeed even growing support by late 1937, was to a considerable extent a reflection of the increasingly bitter dispute in the Socialist Party. It was mainly the southern provincial socialist federations which, since the reformists' victory in July 1937, had become alienated from Lamoneda's executive. Among such federations as Córdoba, Ciudad Real and Albacete, the *caballerista* faith had been of varying levels of strength when the reformists initiated their purge of the party organisation in the summer of 1937. However, what is certain is that the reformists' purge, coinciding as it did with the PCE's virulent criticism of Largo himself, effectively strengthened support in the party for the socialist left. Witness the remarks of Miguel Ranchal to Ramón González Peña: 'It pains me that you have done to this man exactly what his faction did to you, Prieto and Belarmino at the infamous Ecija meeting.'[8] Such comments did not necessarily indicate increased support for the radicalism associated with the *Caballeristas* before the war. Support for the left during the conflict was more a reflection of the distaste many socialists felt for the PCE's political methods. One could argue, thus, that Lamoneda's campaign against the party left – and particularly against Largo as its figurehead – was counterproductive. Far from healing the breach in socialist ranks, it deepened the divisions because Lamoneda appeared to be conniving at the PCE's defamatory campaign. Moreover, by attacking the pockets of support for Largo in the PSOE's southern federations, Lamoneda drove the party left to make common cause with Largo's supporters in the union. This tendency was also fuelled by Lamoneda's slow response to socialists' complaints over aggression in military units and pressure to make them join the PCE. A classic example of these tensions is to be found in the correspondence between Lamoneda and Zabalza.[9] Lamoneda's reply of 10 October displayed characteristic caution. He enjoined Zabalza to convince socialists to think before issuing such denunciations and reminded him that they should be writing to the PSOE executive, not to the FNTT. Zabalza's reply was sarcastic and angry. He accused Lamoneda of being 'obsessed with the correct procedures'. Accordingly, in the Republican south the links were tightened between the PSOE's provincial federations and those of the FNTT.[10] It was also in the FNTT that the first resurgent socialist youth sections began to appear. In February 1938 in Madrid a provincial committee of the Juventudes Socialistas of the FNTT was constituted with Rafael Henche as the president of its executive and Carlos Rubiera as secretary.[11]

By December 1937, when the left socialists were politically a spent force, and with the beginning of international mediation to settle the UGT dispute, it was the FNTT which still sought to defend their cause. Its national executive called for the reconstruction of the Workers' Alliance.[12] The FNTT also supported Largo's call for a general congress in the UGT as a means of resolving the crisis. It also observed, significantly, that the FNTT contained the 'absolute majority of the UGT's affiliates'.[13] The unitarist response, as so often in the UGT dispute, was to treat the FNTT leaders' support of the *Caballeristas* as unrepresentative of grass roots feeling.[14] Pressure on the pro-Caballero majority in the FNTT leadership was also exerted from within by FNTT president, José María Soler and by the Jaén national committee delegate, López Quero. Both were unitarists. Jaén socialists, including López Quero, had been much influenced by the PCE's line, forming the shortlived 'unified socialist party of Jaén' in August 1937.[15] However, in contrast to their approach to the other dissident industrial federations – iron and steel and urban transport – the unitarists were not keen to force a national congress in the FNTT. This would suggest uncertainty about its outcome, as well as the impossibility of contemplating a congress on such a scale in wartime.

The FNTT executive's defence of Largo Caballero clearly had much to do with its continuing commitment to the goal of collectivised agriculture. The defence of the *Caballeristas* in December 1937 coincided with the dispatching of further letters to Vicente Uribe to protest against the agriculture ministry's anti-collectivist campaigns. In this correspondence, the collectives were defended precisely as an effective means of providing and maintaining war supplies. The collectives were thus on the offensive. They were attacking head-on the communists' argument of practicality, expediency and *raison de guerre*, countering that the collectives constituted a positive defence of the national economy.[16] The proposed refloating of the *Alianza Obrera* also has to be understood in this context. It was seen as the only means of guaranteeing the conquests of the revolution, and above all the advances in collectivisation. To this same end, in December 1937 the FNTT's national committee

decided to establish a joint committee with its CNT counterpart. At
national level this would be presided over by Ricardo Zabalza
himself and organisation at the provincial and local level was under
way by May 1938.[17]

Communists versus Socialists: The Internal Battle in the FNTT

In the battle between the landworkers' federation and the PCE, and
also between socialists and communists within the FNTT, there was
a strong element of organisational rivalry, just as there was between
the Socialist and Communist Parties and within other individual
industrial federations.[18] Nevertheless, it was in the Spanish countryside where the struggle between socialists and communists was most
obviously the result of a bitter ideological division. There, the FNTT
was pitted not only against the PCE and its unions, but also against
the Republican state apparatus (that is, the Institute of Agrarian
Reform (IRA)), which the party also dominated. The IRA had been
established as a means of administering the 1932 Agrarian Reform
Law. But by 1937, given that its titular head was a communist, then
the organisation became the spearhead for implementing the Popular Front line in the Republican countryside.[19]

   At the March 1937 plenum of the PCE's central committee, the
general secretary of the PCE's provincial federation of peasant
smallholders in Valencia (Federación Provincial Campesina) outlined the Communist Party's dual strategy in the countryside. On
one hand it was organising a separate union initiative, while on the
other it was seeking to establish its own factions within the FNTT.
The PCE's federations were intended to foster Popular Frontism by
protecting the interests of peasant smallholders. The first was
created in Valencia in October 1936.[20] In order to function successfully, however, they depended, by definition, on the presence of a
substantial class of prosperous smallholders. Given Spain's agrarian
backwardness and her vast regional disparities, these peasant federations would only flourish inside the fertile Levante provinces where,
in spite of a history of turbulent relations with their socialist counterpart, they would eventually join the FNTT *en bloc* in the spring of
1938.[21]

   In Valencia in particular, there was a fairly fierce confrontation of
the UGT and the CNT with the PCE's peasant federation. While the
anarchist organisation was historically strong in the province, the
Federación Provincial Campesina had also grown apace as smallholders flocked to it to oppose the drive for socialisation championed

by the anarchist and socialist landworkers' federations.[22] In Valencia it was, by and large, the Republican peasantry who joined the PCE's provincial federation. Indeed, this had been formally sanctioned by both Izquierda Republicana and the Valencian Esquerra (Partido Valencianista d'Esquerra). However, many peasants formerly linked to the CEDA or to the old Partido Autonomista (Derecha Regional), had also joined the PCE and been allowed to do so in the full knowledge of their previous affiliations – something which had angered socialists in the area.[23]

The dispute in Valencia focused particularly on the issue of the export of the orange crop, with the PCE waging war in the name of the Valencian peasantry against the CNT–UGT joint committee which controlled both the collection of the crop and the port.[24] This became part of a larger battle between the unions and the resurgent central state. The representatives of the latter saw the attainment of a monopoly on exports as vital to the drive for supremacy and a more efficient war effort. In Valencia the UGT and CNT established the CLUEA (Consorcio Levantino Unificado de la Exportación Agrícola), to coordinate the collection and export of the orange crop. The unions and the CLUEA came up increasingly against state hostility, the dispute centring on the control of crucial foreign exchange – the maximalisation of which had been the CLUEA's objective.[25]

Nevertheless, the PCE was not merely offering help and support to those who were already evidently hostile to collectivisation for fear of losing their smallholdings. Its policy meant that in many areas where there was collectivisation that had genuinely been approved by a majority, the PCE set about fostering opposition to the whole system within the collectives themselves. This it did by seeking out those with grievances, as the 'weak link in the chain'. It was a notorious fact that the PCE cared little how trivial or dubious the complaint was, provided it could be turned to its purpose. For Zabalza and the FNTT, worst of all was the major role played by the agriculture ministry and especially the IRA delegations in the offensive against the collectives. In May 1937, Zabalza railed against their activities: 'It is today our dearest wish to consolidate the conquests of the revolution, above all, the FNTT's collectives, against which a host of enemies is appearing.'[26] He went on to point out how 'the reactionaries of yesterday and the unconditional supporters of the local political bosses (*caciques*) were actively being favoured by many of the IRA delegations against the interests of the collectives. But it was equally the case that the October 1936 collectivisation decree had damaged the collectives, not just by limiting

them but also because it offered every possibility to those smallholders and tenant farmers not directly implicated in the military
rising to possess in usufruct up to a total area of thirty-eight hectares
of land. As the FNTT pointed out, although this seemed fair in
principle, in reality it rendered impossible the creation of collectives
in some areas where there were a great many landless labourers.[27]

The FNTT's provincial federation in Badajoz was particularly
angry at the behaviour of the IRA delegation. This had arrived
in January 1937 and had subsequently employed its best efforts
dividing up, according to the principles of 'reparto' (division for
individual use), land, livestock, everything which had already been
collectivised. Naturally the result was that the PCE won over all the
rightists in the region who had previously gone to ground. Speculation began to reappear and there were even pueblos such as Higuera
de la Serena (Badajoz) where the IRA had actively supported those
who had assaulted the collectives. Most notorious of all was the
incident in Garbayuela, where the IRA delegate handed a large
estate back to its former owner whose political credentials were of the
most dubious kind.[28] As a result, Ricardo Zabalza called upon the
minister to restructure the IRA delegations so as to include representatives of both the FNTT and the CNT, thereby returning to the
norm of the early days of the Institute's existence in the first years of
the Republic. His protest, however, was to no avail.

The confrontation between the FNTT and the PCE was rooted in
the very nature of the Popular Front as espoused by the PCE. This
involved treating as allies all those individuals and class groups who
had not actively supported the military rising. Translated to the
countryside this meant respecting and protecting the private
property of groups and individuals who had been the eternal class
enemies and exploiters of the agricultural labourers. As a policy this
was fundamentally unacceptable to the FNTT. Indeed there was
pressure inside the FNTT to extend collectivisation. At the FNTT's
national conference in June 1937 there were demands for the modifi-
cation of the October 1936 decree so that it would be possible to
confiscate not only land belonging to those directly implicated in the
military rising, but also the land of 'those who, to date, we consider
as the enemies of the working class'.[29] Given that the Communists
were on the one hand insisting that all collectivisation had to be
entirely voluntary, while on the other actively fostering the desires of
the peasantry for *reparto* because it accorded with the Popular Front
strategy, it is hardly surprising that the clash between the FNTT
and the PCE and the IRA should have been so fierce or so enduring.[30] It was not that the socialist left advocated the wresting of land

from the peasantry. However, it emphasised that the political loyalty of the individual smallholder, both to the Republic and to a new economic and social order, had always to be the deciding factor, and, equally, it was made quite clear that a specific order of priorities existed. The collectives had to be nurtured and supported by all the technical and material advantages available so that collectivisation would be seen to be the most rational and efficient means of agricultural exploitation.

At the other end of the agricultural spectrum from Valencia, with its large body of prosperous smallholders, is the case of a province such as Jaén (Andalucía), one of the major areas of *latifundia* in Spain. There the FNTT was powerful and the concept of collectivisation deeply rooted and central to the agenda for political and economic change long before the civil war erupted.[31] In that Jaén, unlike much of the agrarian south, remained in Republican hands until the very end of the war, it provides a perfect means of analysing communist tactics and objectives in the Spanish countryside. Such an analysis tends also to debunk the PCE's own declarations that it was not hostile to collectivisation *per se*, but simply to its doctrinaire application in inappropriate situations where there was a great risk of alienating a substantial peasantry to the detriment of productivity and, therefore, of the war effort. In Jaén, as a detailed study of the province during the civil war period has shown, the PCE actively subverted efficiently organised socialist or joint socialist–anarchist collectives by supporting a minority of smallholders and wealthier peasants against the interests of the majority.[32] In the Levante, as a fertile area of small-scale agricultural exploitation, although the issue remains open to debate, it was possible for the PCE to make a reasonable case for its defence of smallholders in terms of the needs of production and the sake of the war effort. However, in the south the PCE's underlying hostility to the collectives gave the lie to the claim that it was acting in an objectively correct manner, in the spirit of Popular Front, according to the needs of the existing situation. In Jaén during the civil war the Communist Party used a variety of tactics, the objective of which was always the same – to discredit, erode and eventually to destroy the collectives as ideologically alien and, moreover, for the most part, *beyond the control of the party*.

It was, of course, far more difficult for the PCE to discredit collectivisation in the Republican south because it was mainly socialist-based. The usual accusations of 'syndical egoism' or 'terrorism' and the era of the 'new *caciques*' which were constantly being levelled against the CNT in Aragón were of no use.[33] This is not to imply that the accusations against the CNT were necessarily justified or accurate, but rather that certain incidents which had occurred, such as the violent clashes between UGT and CNT affiliates at Cullera (Valencia) in February 1937, together with the activities of the 'uncontrollables' in the early months of the civil war had created an environment in which such charges appeared credible.[34] In the case of the socialist collectives, however, the PCE had need of much subtler weapons. Thus what the PCE set out to do in Jaén was to increase its own influence in order to domesticate radical collectivist doctrine, and indeed to subvert its practical manifestation, the collectives, in favour of cooperatives.

In Jaén during the war there were three main ways in which the PCE sought to undermine the socialist or joint FNTT–CNT collectives. First, by means of the provincial IRA delegations in which its influence, as in the agriculture ministry itself, was significant. Second, by the implementation of the voluntary JSU work brigades whose task it was to carry the Popular Front line to the countryside and especially to the smallholding peasantry. And thirdly and most directly of all, by massive propaganda in favour of the creation of cooperatives as a replacement for the collectives. The cooperatives were presented as a 'logical' alternative to the collectives and, naturally, as more efficient. But in that the PCE realised that the concept of collectivism was too deeply rooted in Jaén to be effectively destroyed outright, the party was particularly concerned to infiltrate the existing collectives and thus to modify them qualitatively from within in what amounted to a kind of counter-revolutionary entryism.[35] But in so doing, the PCE in Jaén itself contributed to the 'inefficiency' it was always so quick to bring up whenever collectivisation was mentioned. By fostering the development of small collective 'groups' and by both fomenting and supporting the often petty grievances of small groups or individuals within the existing collectives it effectively provoked destabilisation, demoralisation and fragmentation in the latter.[36]

By late 1937, the PCE had achieved considerable successes in advancing its political line in the province, most notably in the degree of influence exercised by the party over the leadership of the Jaén socialist federation. In mid-August 1937, the Jaén socialists united briefly with the PCE in the Partido Socialista Unificado de Jaén. The unification was reversed immediately by the PSOE's national executive.[37] But that it should have occurred demonstrates the tremendous influence which the PCE exerted over the provincial socialist leadership. The latter espoused the superiority of cooperatives over collectives with a conviction which was as fierce as the PCE's. At the FNTT's provincial congress in September 1937, in the presence of 80,000 affiliates and the agriculture minister, Vicente Uribe, the Jaén socialist leadership joined the provincial PCE in condemning collectivism as 'wasteful', declaring the family wage to be extremely harmful because it destroyed the workers' incentive to produce more. The anti-collectivist position of the socialist leadership in the province was ultimately responsible for the rift between it and the socialist/FNTT base, with its intensely collectivist faith. Indeed, at the September congress, the socialist leadership, in criticising collectivisation, was in fact attacking proposals which had been put forward by its own rank and file.[38] There was thus a growing division between the directives of the socialist leaders in Jaén and the reality of collectivisation being enacted and defended by its own rank and file right until the end of the war.

1938 saw the landworkers' federation at the national level go on to the offensive in order to defend the collectives. In April it published a book entitled *A year of collectivisation in Extremadura*. This attempted to demonstrate the practicality and efficiency of collectivisation through the presentation of a variety of general provincial reports and detailed studies of individual collectives. Its content and approach were both eminently practical, but the political point was made implicitly with the pictures of the dead southern socialist leaders, Nicolás de Pablo, Pedro Rubio, Adolfo Bravo, Antonio Pulgarín which were intercalated with the text.[39] These men had died in a war which had a profound class content. To deny or reverse the radical social and economic changes which had occurred in the Republican south would be to render their deaths meaningless. Collectivisation was the patrimony of the southern dead. The act of printing their pictures was a silent affirmation that they had not died to protect the status quo of 1931. Zabalza referred to the campaign against the collectives and the way in which a revanche of rightists and the property-owning classes was occurring in the Republican countryside, courtesy of the PCE:

> ... turning Spain into a country of smallholders ... and to this end taking advantage of the fact that our most committed comrades are fighting at the front – men whose rage would know no bounds if, on their return, they discovered that all their efforts and sacrifices had only served to consolidate the dominance of their eternal enemies, *who, to add insult to injury, can now boast membership of a proletarian party*.[40]

In April 1938, Ricardo Zabalza, as general secretary of the FNTT, also launched, with the backing of the CNT, an attack on the PCE's campaign in various provinces to create a network of 'small collectives' or 'collective groups' which meant, in practice, the dissolution of the real collectives.[41] By the second half of 1938, the FNTT–CNT joint committees were increasingly challenging the PCE's argument that the collectives were an unaffordable political luxury which had disrupted the rhythm of production. In Jaén and elsewhere, the FNTT and CNT gradually began to defend their rank and file's continuing commitment to collectivisation by reasserting its central importance, as rooted both in ideology and pragmatism.[42]

It is possible to gauge accurately the FNTT's political weight in the UGT from the considerable attention which the González Peña leadership devoted to developments in the landworkers' federation. For while it is true that the *Caballeristas* were never organised to any degree which could have justified their opponents' accusations of 'faction', the FNTT in 1937–8 was central to such left socialist reorganisation as occurred within the UGT. The FNTT's provincial federations maintained regular contact within the remaining *caballerista* provincial socialist federations which were, again, all located in the centre–south zone – Badajoz (displaced), Ciudad Real, Albacete, Alicante, Córdoba (displaced). Close cooperation had also been established between FNTT leaders such as Zabalza and Romero Solano, left socialists such as Baraibar – who had not previously been directly connected with the union sphere – and even ex-communists such as José Bullejos were active in the FNTT.[43]

The major attempt to turn the FNTT into a *caballerista* bulwark came to the attention of the unitarists on the UGT executive at the beginning of 1938 – just after its consolidation *in situ* courtesy of Jouhaux's mediation. The *Caballeristas'* tactic, as befitted past masters of the art of manipulating the union bureaucracy, consisted of tapping the enormous source of membership numbers in the 'catch-all' category of Oficios Varios (Miscellaneous Trades). In those areas where the FNTT, and therefore the *Caballeristas*, were strong, the sections of Oficios Varios were being decanted into the FNTT *en masse*, enormously increasing the size of the landworkers' federation. The socialist left was in a sense attempting to repeat, by this calculated manipulation, the experience of spontaneous expansion in the FNTT during the pre-war Republican period which had so boosted its strength.[44] The object in increasing the FNTT's size to the maximum possible was to make the union decisive in all the UGT's deliberations, and ultimately to allow it to defeat the unitarist line at the first ordinary general congress of the UGT after the war.

This was not an unreasonable plan, given that membership size certainly counted. In the UGT, unlike the Socialist Party, the votes of both delegates and national committee members were weighted in accordance with the numbers they represented. They were not, as in the case of the party, nominal votes. Thus Largo Caballero had sought to confront the unitarists with the argument that the crucial piece in the game being played for control of the UGT was the FNTT, and that since he was assured of its support, then ultimately he would reconquer the UGT. Indeed, it was undoubtedly the case that the *Caballeristas* did control some of the largest industrial federations in the UGT, even if one discounts the Oficios Varios strategy. However, it is unlikely that without the latter tactic this could ever have amounted to a clear majority, as the *Caballerista*, Justo Martínez Amutio claimed in 1975.[45] The figures for UGT membership published in April 1938, while they do indeed record the enormous size of the FNTT and the fact that the iron and steel and urban transport federations were also among the heavyweight[46] federations, do not bear out Martínez Amutio's claim that the three together constituted 55 per cent of the total membership. The UGT figures for April 1938 give a total union membership of 1,904,569, within forty-four national federations of industry, comprising a total of 7,215 sections across the Republican zone. If one uses the data given in the analysis of industrial federations (see table pp. 219–20 below), as a basis for calculating the sum total of FNTT, urban transport and iron and steel as a percentage of the total membership of the UGT, then these three federations together add up not to 55 per cent, but to 43 per cent of the total membership: a substantial percentage indeed, but not the clear majority claimed.[47] Of course, the situation as regards Secciones Directas, in which Oficios Varios would be included, was by no means clear. Undoubtedly the *Caballeristas* would have contested that many of the sections listed under Secciones Directas already belonged to the FNTT and thus that the unitarist executive's figures were not accurate because they did not reflect this. Nevertheless, even the figure of 700,000 for the FNTT in the spring of 1938, as recorded by the UGT leadership, was staggering, especially if compared with the CNT's Federación de Campesinos with a total membership at that time of some 200,000. Its size can truly be appreciated if one considers that by 1938 the FNTT alone was more than twice the size of the total remaining agricultural affiliation of the I F T U, which was 308,000.[48]

These developments in the FNTT and the absorption of so many sections of Oficios Varios were, naturally, a matter of no small concern to the leadership of the UGT, especially as Oficios Varios constituted one of the most numerically substantial components of the union. The national executive rapidly sought to undo the damage, or potential damage, by seeking to dissolve the link between the FNTT and those members of Oficios Varios who were not agricultural workers. However, although a census enquiry was instituted within the FNTT to clarify the situation, it was known in advance that most of the areas where such an amalgamation had occurred were rural areas and thus that many of the workers in such sections – and probably the majority – would indeed be engaged in agriculture. As a result, the UGT leadership was only able to take remedial action in a minority of cases – either by obliging the workers concerned to join the relevant national industrial federation or by creating a new network of Oficios Varios.[49]

The unitarists pressed consistently for national congresses in the UGT's other dissident federations, in the belief that the result would be an overwhelmingly hostile plebiscite which would force the resignations of their pro-Caballero national leaderships. Such pressure was applied vigorously to the iron and steel and the urban transport federations, of which Largo Caballero's intimates, Wenceslao Carrillo and Carlos Hernández Zancajo were, respectively, leaders.

The Battle in the Urban Transport Federation: 1937–1938

In March 1937 Carlos Hernández Zancajo had thrown down the gauntlet in an editorial in *La Correspondencia de Valencia*. In it he explicitly accused the PSUC of usurping the authority of the UGT's national executive inside Cataluña.[50] Indeed, from its formation, the Catalan secretariat had been at odds with Largo Caballero's national executive and mainly beyond the latter's control. In December 1936, Largo's executive itself directed all national executives of the industrial federations to send representatives to Barcelona to examine the agreements and resolutions of their Catalan sections.[51] Hernández Zancajo claimed that the Catalan secretariat was intercepting correspondence from local UGT sections which ought to have been sent to the national executive in Valencia. But he was finally jolted into public criticism by his outrage at the style of the regional congress of his own urban transport federation, held in mid-March 1937 in Barcelona. He complained that the Catalan section had been totally monopolised by the PSUC, with its communist insignia – to such an extent that there was no visible evidence that the union was still affiliated to the UGT.[52] The result of such statements had been extremely stormy scenes at the congress which were then deliberately concealed in the congress reports published in *Las Noticias*, the UGT's Catalan mouthpiece. As a result, Hernández Zancajo refused to recognise the authority of the congress and announced the dissolution of the urban transport federation's regional secretariat. He gave the Catalan sections thirty days to affiliate directly to the national transport federation. Those who did not comply were no longer to be considered its members.[53]

Carlos Hernández Zancajo's intense hostility to the Communists' control of the UGT in Cataluña, which amounted to a virtual declaration of war, in addition to his long-standing political collaboration with Largo Caballero, meant that the growing confrontation of unitarists and *Caballeristas* within the transport federation was seen by González Peña as a particular danger to the stability of the UGT. Within the transport federation, the national executive's continued support for Largo, even after Jouhaux's intervention, led to the unitarist fractions – which included the provincial committees of Valencia, Toledo, Aragón, Madrid and Cataluña – banding together as a pro-congress committee to try to force a decision from their national executive.[54] The unitarists subsequently took matters into their own hands by publishing notice of a congress scheduled for 10 January 1938.[55] However, it was the González Peña executive itself which vetoed this, adducing the mediation of the labour international as sufficient settlement of the union dispute. This decision reflected González Peña's desire to avoid aggravating the already bitter divisions in the transport federation, as well as his reluctance to pursue a course of action which might significantly strengthen the unitarists' hand.[56]

By August 1938, Carlos Hernández Zancajo had become the target of the collective wrath of both the PCE and the unitarists on the UGT's national committee who were incensed by his 'insubordination'.[57] The position of his national executive was considered to be one of open rebellion because it had imposed a virtual boycott on the UGT's national executive, neither answering its correspondence nor attending meetings of the national committee. The transport executive's relations with its CNT counterpart – established under the conditions of the March 1938 union pact – were said to be hampering the government's drive towards centralisation and the militarisation of transport. It is thus to August 1938, when transport was militarised, that one can trace the beginnings of a concerted PCE–unitarist campaign which was designed to oust Hernández Zancajo by the gradual erosion of his control inside the union.[58] His opponents set about achieving this in two ways. First they launched a denunciatory press campaign. Second, within the national federation itself, the unitarist sections, and principally therefore the Catalan sections, were mobilised in an internal propaganda campaign designed to undermine Hernández Zancajo's authority.

The line followed by the González Peña executive over national congresses was hardly more consistent than Largo's had been over the expulsion of industrial federations. Staunchly unitarist federations were allowed to hold congresses: for example, Espectáculos Públicos held a national congress in Valencia in February 1938.[59] Unsurprisingly, the sessions were a showpiece of unitarist faith with exhortations from the delegates to forge a single class party and to labour ceaselessly against the 'enemies of unity'. There were also references to the need to open up the union to all the workers in the industry whatever their political affiliation or lack of it. Thus, with the ascendancy of the unitarists in the UGT there was a clearer articulation of the line championed by the PCE in the JSU, namely, the massification of the organisation which envisaged the inclusion of Catholic organisations.[60] Indeed, in February 1938 the González Peña executive effectively rescinded the instructions of its predecessor relating to post-18 July membership of the UGT. A circular issued by Largo and his colleagues in April 1937 had directed that new members be debarred from holding all official posts in the union. The González Peña executive, however, took the line that this was simply a recommendation. This effectively removed a major obstacle to the ambitions of the PCE to greater influence in the UGT, and it came as a further blow to the left. For, already in December 1937, it had lost out in the numbers war when Ramón Lamoneda agreed to the incorporation into the Catalan secretariat of all *ugetista* refugees in the region.[61]

The UGT executive elected on 1 October 1937 was itself far from monolithic, however. A temporary alliance had been forged because of the convergence of reformist socialists and unitarists over a shared primary objective – the liquidation of *caballerista* influence in the UGT. Nevertheless, the two groups were driven by very different motives. PSOE policy towards the PCE in the union sphere had clearly been designed to complement the joint party committee initiative. However, once the Largo executive had been defeated and the intervention of Léon Jouhaux had consolidated González Peña's position, outright differences and hostilities began to emerge within the national executive. The flavour of the conflict can be gauged from the following extract from a secret report on the UGT, prepared for the PCE's central committee by Amaro del Rosal while he was still technically a *socialist* member of the union executive.

> The national executive is still a far from homogeneous body. In its sessions discussion is plagued by contradictions because it has no firm guiding principle. There exists a fairly strong anti-communist element. At executive meetings I'm able to keep this sector in check – by resorting to the convincing argument that, as the UGT is composed of workers of

various political tendencies, the leadership cannot openly declare a sectarian position. Something else which gives certain executive members pause for thought is the reminder that the national executive symbolises working-class unity, that its *raison d'être* is its unity policy, that it is this which guarantees it the support of the workers – indeed it was for this reason that it was elected.[62]

Ramón González Peña for one was increasingly concerned about the PCE's increasing inroads into the UGT's hierarchy:

Often, when it has been necessary to fill the post of president, secretary or whatever in this or that union section – there have been, say, half a dozen communists present at the assembly – but as they move like lightning, suddenly one has proposed another. We haven't really paid much attention to a post here and a post there. After all, everyone was continually talking about 'unity' . . . so, anyway, we didn't oppose such elections. But now it's too late. In some federations, like, for example, the petroleum workers and teachers, the Communists have majority control.[63]

By mid-1938 the central committee of the PCE in its own internal reports was criticising both the socialist-led national executive of the union and the majority of the national federations of industry for the inadequacy of their response to the *Caballeristas*. Indeed it is quite clear that by the middle of 1938 the PCE leadership was waking up to the fact that there was a certain *caballerista* resurgence, or at least an entrenchment, occurring within the UGT:

A substantial weakening has occurred in the leadership of all national industrial federations – except for those headed by the *Caballeristas* who are working methodically to consolidate their positions. In those federations where we have conquered posts over the last couple of years, not only are we not extending our influence but we are also seeing it eroded – and in other unions we just cannot consolidate our position at all.[64]

Equally, relations between socialists and communists on the executive were becoming more difficult because it was known that both Indalecio Prieto and Ramón González Peña had ceased, very early on in 1938, to support congresses in those federations with dissident leaderships because they were afraid that the likely conclusion of the *Caballeristas'* ejection would be their own defeat in the union at the hands of the unitarists.[65] For the same reason, they were also determined that both the president and the general secretary of the UGT should be socialists, regardless of the unity policy.[66] In a sense, the experience of the socialists of the Prieto– Peña 'line' was the converse of the left socialists' in the period

1935–6. The *caballerista* power base had always been the union: in it their control was absolute because their understanding of the intricacies of its bureaucracy was also absolute. The union merger of December 1935 had been both a symbolic and a very real triumph for the veteran union bureaucrats of the UGT. In spite of their protests, the communist negotiators had been obliged to accept, not a unification, as they insisted upon terming it, but rather the absorption of the CGTU's members by the socialist giant.[67] Under the terms of the agreement the UGT gave no quarter nor advantage to the communist entrants. As a result, before the war the communists were scarcely able to breach the defences of a UGT hierarchy controlled with consummate ease and skill by the socialists. In the railway federation, for example, new members were granted only gradual access to posts in the union hierarchy: one year before they were eligible for any post, two years before zone office and four before access to the executive could be considered.[68] This effortless supremacy in the union, however, made the *Caballeristas* over-confident and spurred them on to attempt political conquest, whereupon they fell foul of the organisational skills of the PCE in the political arena. The result was *confusionismo* and the trickling of the socialist base into the PCE via the sort of grass roots unity initiatives already described. As a consequence of this, the new reformist executive of the PSOE launched an attack on the socialist left in both the party and the union in order to regain control of the socialist movement and to block the inroads being made into its base by the Spanish Communists. However, the reformist socialists were, for the most part, *políticos*, and not *obreristas*, that is, they were parliamentary socialists not union veterans. In purging the *Caballeristas* from the union, they effectively removed the only socialist group that had the capacity to challenge the PCE within the UGT. If the *Caballeristas* had been political novices, then the reformists, to their cost, were discovering that they were novices in the business of manoeuvring within the union in order to protect the hegemony of the PSOE.

The PCE, for its part, was determined to advance on all fronts in the UGT, and to defend the presence of communists at all levels from the growing hostility of the socialists. The PCE and the unitarists on the national executive of the UGT claimed to possess a popular mandate from the iron and steel federation, whose leadership, which included both Wenceslao Carrillo and Pascual Tomás, was a major focus of dissidence.[69] The PCE did have a great deal of influence in the union in Madrid, Valencia and Cataluña, but this was being increasingly challenged, as, by the middle of 1938, both Wenceslao

Carrillo and Pascual Tomás were fighting hard to regain lost positions. Tomás drummed up support in the Levante and succeeded in regaining control in Valencia for the *Caballeristas*. Wenceslao Carrillo, having been appointed as commissar of war in Madrid, also succeeded in regaining control of the local iron and steel federation. Thus there was a growing socialist fraction again within the hierarchy of the federation.[70]

The Spanish polemic over the status and influence of communists in the UGT took on an international dimension as the debate over Soviet trade union membership of the labour international began to gather momentum. The González Peña executive, from the time of its election, saw its single most important task as that of convincing the labour international to admit the Soviet trade unions to membership at the congress of the organisation in Oslo in May 1938. This was obviously far from being a point of abstract political principle in that it was fervently hoped by many Spanish socialists – and not only those of the unitarist persuasion – that the Soviet inclusion would force the labour international actively to intervene on behalf of the Spanish Republic. From within the IFTU the Soviet unions would be able to put far greater pressure on both the labour and socialist internationals to provide material aid instead of merely 'moral support' for the loyalist war effort.[71] The UGT leadership backed the call for Soviet entry at a special meeting of its national committee at the beginning of March 1938.[72] The majority vote was unsurprising, given the force of the argument of working-class unity as the best defence against fascism. But there were still dissenting voices: both Wenceslao Carrillo and Pascual Tomás of the iron and steel federation abstained from the vote.[73]

But the González Peña executive was under no illusions about the unequal nature of the task, given the tremendous weight of anti-communism in the IFTU. By the spring of 1938, the French and Spanish unions were thus cooperating closely in order to present the best possible case for Soviet membership at the Oslo congress.[74] But in spite of combined French and Spanish efforts, the Oslo congress voted overwhelmingly to exclude the Soviet trade unions from the IFTU. Even worse, it also voted to end all negotiations between the two sides.[75] This decision provoked a fierce reaction in the Republican press. The labour international was accused of hypocrisy and Walter Citrine, the TUC's general secretary, was severely criticised for toeing the British government's non-interventionist line.[76] Yet in spite of the crushing defeat at Oslo, the González Peña executive persisted in its efforts to ensure the homogeneity and solidarity of the UGT federations behind the proposal of Soviet integration in the

IFTU.[77] It had little choice in the circumstances. But inevitably this line would bring it into direct conflict with the dissidents, and most significantly with Carlos Hernández Zancajo and the urban transport federation.

Hernández Zancajo's battle with the Catalan section of his union continued throughout 1938, with the formation of a separate joint UGT–CNT committee for the urban transport federation in Cataluña. Meanwhile, the UGT executive continued to pressurise Hernández Zancajo's national executive to call a general congress in the transport industry. This was vital, so it was argued, to discuss how the union might best improve the efficiency of the national transport industry to boost its contribution to the war effort.[78] Exactly the same case was being put before the executive of the iron and steel federation and the González Peña executive's request was supported by unitarist federations within the industry itself, most notably by El Baluarte, Madrid's iron and steel federation.[79] But as the *Caballeristas* observed, it was highly suspicious that *only* the dissident federations were being requested to hold national congresses for what amounted to *raison de guerre*.[80] The tactic was an obvious one: the congresses were to be used to oust the rebels as 'unrepresentative' of rank-and-file opinion.[81] By the end of October 1938 the tension had mounted in the transport federation particularly, where the UGT executive and Carlos Hernández were at loggerheads because of his vote against Soviet membership of the IFTU at the international congress of transport federations in Luxemburg at the beginning of November.[82] UGT unitarists used Hernández's 'indiscipline' to increase the pressure on him to call a congress. The Catalan section of urban transport called repeatedly for the federation to be strengthened 'numerically and ideologically' by the inclusion of communists on the national executive.[83]

In the end it was the sustained campaign against Carlos Hernández in the unitarist press which finally caused the rest of his national executive to cave in before the demands of the UGT leadership.[84] On 10 December 1938, urban transport's national committee met and by 8 votes to 5, Carlos Hernández was removed, in his absence, from the post of general secretary.[85] By a majority of only one, the meeting resolved to seek reconciliation with the UGT and to convene an extraordinary congress in Albacete for 1 March 1939. At this it was planned to discuss the formal revision of the federation's attitude to the UGT executive and until such time the post of general secretary was to be left vacant. But this congress was never held. Political developments in the loyalist zone would soon render such an initiative superfluous.

The battle between the PSOE and the PCE for control of the UGT was being waged in deadly earnest. The reformist socialists in the UGT, like those in the PSOE, found themselves in an impossible position – caught between the PCE and the *Caballeristas*. The particularly unfavourable circumstances in which the civil war was occurring – the political isolation of the loyalists in the international arena and the collapse of the republican groups inside Spain – had dictated collaboration between the Socialist and Communist Parties and between socialists and communists in the UGT. The immense political leverage which the Soviet Union was able to exert by dint of its status as the Republic's sole major supplier of war aid had obliged the PSOE leadership to accept the PCE's Popular Frontist pro-unity initiative, and this in spite of the increasingly severe organisational rivalry between their respective cadres. For Popular Front, as a Comintern policy, came endorsed by the Soviet leadership. Had the PSOE turned its back on the PCE, it would have proved fatal to the Republican war effort. It is important to register this point. Not least because in spite of the *Caballeristas'* repeated accusations that the PSOE executive's alliance strategy with the PCE was aimed *purely* at defeating the party left, it is clear that the objective of unity of action, as pursued between the parties and in the UGT, lay far beyond such partisan concerns. The policy was a genuine and serious attempt to meet the vital needs of the war effort. González Peña's castigation of Hernández Zancajo for his anti-Soviet vote at the international congress of the transport federation has likewise to be viewed in this context. By autumn 1938 the reformists had no sectarian interest in sniping at the left's remaining bases in the UGT. The sheer desperation spawned by the hopelessness of the international climate goes much of the way to explaining González Peña's enforcement of a three-line whip over Soviet inclusion in the IFTU. By September 1938, any initiative which might have lessened the Republic's isolation – however slight its chances of success – was considered to be worth at least the attempt.

But growing anti-communist sentiment among the socialist rank and file in both party and union, sharpened by the PCE's aggressive recruitment policy, by the evident 'desocialisation' of the Catalan labour movement and by revelations of the political reality of youth unity, all steadily eroded the credibility and authority of the reformist socialist leadership in both the UGT and the PSOE. At the same time, from within those industrial federations which remained to them, the *Caballeristas* were working steadily to consolidate their position. It was their long-standing opposition to the PCE which explains the resurgence of support for the *Caballeristas* among the socialist rank and file.[86] As military defeat loomed large, the *caballerista* leaders would be the major beneficiaries of anti-communist feeling in the centre–south zone – although in the midst of Republican devastation, it was to be a bitter and futile victory.

Unión General de Trabajadores: Analysis of Membership by Industrial Federation

Comercio	15,621	(small traders)
Agua, Gas, Electricidad	15,000	(public utilities)
Artes Blancas	16,000	(bakers and confectioners)
Azucareros	1,926	(sugar refineries)
Carteros Urbanos	1,979	(urban postal service)
Carteros Post Rural	4,187	(rural postal service)
Cerveza, Hielo, Gaseosas	2,000	(beer/soft drinks industry)
Dependientes de Comercio	50,608	(shop assistants)
Correos	2,400	(post office workers)
Crédito y Finanzas	7,000	(bank workers)
Edificación	75,955	(building industry)
Empleados de Oficinas	29,917	(office workers)
Enseñanza	14,000	(teachers)
Espectáculos Públicos	20,000	(leisure and entertainment)
Industrias Farmacéuticas	4,500	(drug industry)
Farmacéuticos	1,200	(pharmacists)
Ferroviarios	50,274	(railwayworkers)
Gráficos	9,451	(printers)
Hostelería	14,825	(hotel and catering)
Juntas de Obras de Puertos	1,600	(dockworkers)
Madera	12,884	(wood/carpenters)
Manicomios y Hospitales	4,746	(asylums and hospitals)
Médicos	1,190	(doctors)
Mineros	30,448	(miners)
Municipios	14,109	(local government employees)
Papeleros	3,626	(stationers)
Peluqueros	4,641	(hairdressers)
Petróleos	6,000	(petroleum industry)
Piel	5,000	(leather industry)
Practicantes	1,800	(medical auxiliaries)
Productos Químicos	9,214	(chemical industry)
Radiotelegrafistas	400	(wireless operators)
Siderometalúrgicos	50,798	(iron and steel industry)
Seguros	7,000	(insurance workers)
Tabaqueros	10,000	(tobacco industry)
Teléfonos	4,957	(telephone workers)
Telégrafos	4,306	(telegraph workers)
Textiles	90,000	(textile industry)
FNTT	700,000	(landworkers' federation)
Toneleros	1,377	(coopers)
Transporte Marítimo	11,875	(maritime transport)
Transporte Urbano	50,755	(urban transport workers)
Vestido y Tocado	30,000	(garment and hatters)
Vidrio	1,000	(glass industry)
Secciones Directas	493,000	(directly affiliated sections)

The membership figures above were published in *La Correspondencia de Valencia*, 4 April 1938. The total UGT membership used in footnote 47, p. 294 below was calculated using the above figures. The sum total as published in *La Correspondencia de Valencia* is incorrect. This is possibly because of the omission from the published list of three other industrial federations whose memberships seem to have been included in the membership total as quoted. These federations as follows: *funcionarios de Estado* (civil servants) (11,000); *seguros y previsión* (insurance workers) (1,300) and *aviación* (5,000); Amaro del Rosal, *Historia de la UGT* (2), appendix IV, pp. 920–1.

PART V
Socialist–Communist Rupture

11 The Casado coup and the end of the war

By autumn 1938 the most tangible political reality in the centre–south zone was the massive hostility developing apace between socialists and communists. This would eventually lead to violent confrontations which destabilised the entire zone – and with it the loyalist war effort. Although the struggle between socialists and communists was being waged across the whole range of political organisations and at all levels of government administration in the Republican zone, the tension was particularly acute in the unified youth organisation. There, it was reaching the proportions of an internal civil war.

This conflict set the national leadership of the JSU – which was entirely loyal to PCE discipline and Popular Frontist policies – against the resurgent old-guard young socialists, many of whom had retained their *caballerista* faith. The latter, having hoist aloft the banner of anti-stalinism in the drive to re-establish an independent socialist youth organisation, were gathering about them an ever-increasing following from the socialist rank and file. By the middle of August 1938 the socialist left was openly advocating breaking up the JSU. This was first broached publicly by the ASM's secretary, the *Caballerista*, Enrique de Francisco, at a meeting of socialist trade unionists in Madrid on 21 August. He had been influenced by the violent anti-communism of young socialists in the capital who were eager to take direct action to restore socialist independence by assaulting the JSU headquarters in the city and re-establishing an integrally socialist leadership.[1]

The PCE and JSU leaderships were immediately aware of the threat which resurgent *caballerismo* posed to their own control and took steps directly to suppress the opposition. As Antonio Mije indicated in his report to the PCE's central committee on 22 August 1938, socialist dissidence in the JSU was concentrated predominantly in half a dozen provincial federations – Albacete, Alicante, Ciudad Real, Jaén, Valencia and Murcia. Hostile correspondence to

223

the JSU national executive was not, however, limited to these provinces. As a result, the communist counter-offensive was launched on two fronts. First, Santiago Carrillo was to convene the plenary session of the JSU national committee earlier than anticipated, in mid-November rather than December, as a forum in which to defend the 'autonomy and the unity of the youth organisation'. Meanwhile, Mije's report proposed moving rapidly against the nuclei of socialist dissidence in specific provincial youth federations. But it was the JSU national leadership which triggered the situation of open and violent rebellion at the November national committee meeting, by seeking to replace the socialist youth executives elected in autumn 1938 at provincial youth congresses in Albacete and Jaén. This, in turn, made irreversible the socialist–communist division throughout the entire youth organisation.

By the latter half of 1937 reports to the PSOE executive about socialist–communist relations across the entire centre–south zone were far from promising. But Albacete gave particular cause for concern. The PCE had a high profile in the area which was the major training centre for the International Brigades and an important military supply centre for the whole zone. In Albacete, the clash between 'old' young socialists and communists in the JSU would reach considerable physical violence in an atmosphere of tension and bitterness. But the youth organisation was not the only arena of dissent in Albacete. The *caballerista* PSOE federal executive in the province had threatened Negrín's presidential undersecretary, José Prat (one of its affiliates), with expulsion unless he was prepared to support its political line.[2] Gabriel Morón, the former wartime socialist governor of Almería, and by late 1938 the sub-editor of *El Socialista*, described the conflict as 'the first signs of the political tension which would produce the Casado coup'.[3] The JSU dispute in Albacete was sparked when the national youth executive sought to reinforce its authority by relieving the new socialist provincial executive of its post. In late October 1938, the national executive dispatched a delegate to the province to assume control, thereby not only riding roughshod over the authority of the recent provincial congress, at which the executive had been elected, but also ignoring the subsequent referendum in the province which had reinforced the congress decision.[4]

JSU executive member, Fernando Claudín, formerly of the UJC leadership, and described by the dissidents as the 'destripador de las juventudes' (the Jack the Ripper of the youth organisation), seized control of the JSU offices in Albacete even before the formal notice of disqualification had been published.[5] The use of elements sympathetic to the position of the national JSU executive tended to increase the bitterness of the divisions in the provincial organisations.[6] As a result of this unilateral action on the part of the JSU executive, Albacete's provincial youth committee, in plenary session, supported a vote of confidence in the deposed socialist executive and further recommended that another provincial congress be scheduled for mid-November in order to confront the national executive's delegates with the mandate of the provincial membership. Gradually socialist resistance to Carrillo and his colleagues was gathering momentum. The provincial leadership of the JSU in Alicante sent Albacete a declaration of solidarity and the calls for the rescheduling of the mooted August 1936 national youth congress – indefinitely postponed with the eruption of war – were growing apace. The young socialists envisaged that this congress should be preceded by a full session of the JSU national committee at which all the provincial organisations, including the dissidents, would have both 'a voice and a vote'. This national committee would elect a new national executive whose brief it would be to prepare the long-delayed national congress, which, in turn, would debate the fundamental problem of youth unity.[7] Carrillo and the national leadership, however, had other plans. While preparing the ground for a national committee meeting heavily weighted in their favour, they pressed on with the process of purging the dissidents from the provincial organisations.

Events in Jaén mirrored those in Albacete. The national executive stepped in to overrule the authority of the provincial youth congress after it had elected an integrally socialist executive in November 1938.[8] The dissidents were angry enough to consider storming the provincial headquarters to retake the executive by force. There was also a rumour circulating that the sympathetic socialist chief of the IX Army corps, Francisco Menoyo, was prepared to support them. There is no hard evidence that this would have extended to the provision of military muscle – but the mere existence of the rumour reflects the way in which the heightened political tension had led to a blurring of the distinction between the military and civilian fronts. This confusion had already been initiated by the outgoing unitarist youth executive in Jaén. In an effort to avoid being voted out at the November 1938 provincial congress, it had sought to have the votes of the Andalucian 'army clubs' included in the electoral returns. This practice, expressly forbidden by government decree, would effectively have meant granting voting rights over the affairs of the JSU in Jaén province to socialist and communist youth members from all over Republican Spain.[9]

The ambivalent attitude of the PSOE executive over socialist dissidence in the JSU was compounding the PCE's problems.[10] In fact, the task of maintaining a precarious equilibrium was rapidly becoming impossible for Ramón Lamoneda. As a result of the violence in Albacete, the PCE called a meeting of the Popular Front joint national committee, attended by Lamoneda and Lucio Martínez for the PSOE. Dolores Ibárruri, representing the PCE with Francisco Antón, unleashed a tirade of rhetoric calling for the castigation of the Albacete dissidents. The meeting inevitably ended in stalemate, with *El Socialista* reporting the probable breakdown of the Popular Front liaison committee.[11]

Throughout 1937 and even into 1938, the fear of playing into the hands of a resurgent left faction had produced in the PSOE executive such a level of inertia in respect of the JSU, that in practice the remains of the socialist youth had been abandoned to its fate. In the event, this 'fate' constituted exclusion from the JSU hierarchy. While the PSOE leadership's stance had prevented neither the emergence of young socialist dissidence nor its crystallisation around the old-guard *caballerista* nucleus, the irony was that many young socialists previously hostile to the socialist left were, by 1938, making common cause with the *Caballeristas*.[12] The latter had emerged as the champions of socialist independence, at the same time as young socialist exasperation with Lamoneda and the reformist leadership had increased across 1937–8. PSOE executive inertia was held to be mainly responsible for the severe erosion suffered by the socialist youth leadership cadres after the 1936 youth unification. This was indeed bitterly ironic, given that youth unity had been spearheaded by the Young Turks of the FJS whose political mentor had been Francisco Largo Caballero. The PSOE executive's call in August 1938 for the creation of a network of youth secretariats at provincial and local level met with little response.[13] By the summer of 1938 it was already too late for such initiatives. In the provinces, either the socialists' loss of control had resulted in disillusion and demobilisation, or, in those federations where the socialists had mounted a successful counter-attack, the battle had already reached new and violent levels so that there seemed little point in establishing a toothless administrative body which could offer no real solution to their problems.

Developments in the Murcian youth organisation provide a useful insight into the process of young socialist disaffection from the Lamoneda executive. The PSOE leadership consistently refused to provide high-profile support for the young socialists of the Murcian youth federation who, by September 1938, were under attack from the JSU national executive as the 'enemies of unity'. The young socialists feared – rightly as it turned out – that the JSU campaign would be used as an excuse to remove them from the leadership.

Back in August 1937 the provincial youth federation in Murcia in plenary session had elected an entirely socialist executive. This was something of a coup, because the previous committee had been communist-led. The initial recouping of control had been made possible with the help of the 'parent' socialist federation in the province. However, from the start the national youth executive had made it clear publicly that it would attempt to sabotage the new provincial executive.[14] By August 1938, as the battle in the youth organisation reached new levels of tension and violence, the Murcian socialists took the precaution of declaring the six most important members of the youth executive 'insustituible', and therefore exempt from military service.[15] When the JSU's national executive refused to support this request, the Murcians appealed to Lamoneda to intercede on their behalf by making specific representation to Negrín in the defence ministry. This request was refused and the socialist leadership in Murcia was subsequently mobilised.[16] In December 1938, as the JSU prepared to recoup control of the provincial youth executive, a violent confrontation occurred in Murcia. In a province where the socialist civil governor, Sánchez Hernández, was sympathetic to the dissidents, security forces surrounded the JSU headquarters in an attempt to force the restitution of a socialist youth executive.[17] This action reflects the overwhelming sense of desperation felt by many young socialists. It was a desperation compounded, moreover, by the belief that they had been abandoned by the PSOE. Indeed socialist alienation in Murcia had, by the end of 1938, gone beyond the youth organisation. As a result of what was perceived as the increasingly blatant sectarianism of military appointments in the province there occurred a blanket socialist withdrawal from the provincial and local joint party committees. The impact of Piñuela's removal was crucial here.[18] The last straw provoking the withdrawal from the joint party committees had been the transfer of the civil governor Sánchez Hernández to Almería after the incident outside the JSU provincial headquarters.[19] Although he was replaced by another socialist, the impression that he had been removed to placate the PCE only served further to embitter the already alienated socialist base in the province.

Once socialist dissidence in the JSU had exploded in the press, as it had done by the final months of 1938, it became impossible for the Lamoneda executive to ignore the crisis. Various articles by the *caballerista* vanguard consolidated the basis of the youth dissidents' case as a thoroughgoing criticism of both the ideological and organ-isational principles of the JSU.[20] Some, who were unsympathetic to the *Caballeristas*, feared that by splitting the JSU they would be handing the Socialist Youth back to the left – which had engineered the unification in the first place.[21] But most old-guard socialists did not think in these terms. Paramount was their concern to prevent the erosion of the movement's class basis implicit in the massification of the Popular Front and in the open door ('mano tendida') policy operative in the JSU. 'The unity of *all* youth?' asked *Nuestra Lucha* (PSOE/UGT) on 21 December 1938, objecting that unity was not possible with those who had assassinated workers during the 1936 construction strike.[22] The Alianza Juvenil Antifascista was rejected as a grave error. Socialists responded with increasing consternation to the PCE's concept of 'national union' as developed in the party's speeches in 1938. 'For Spain's liberty and independence, [we need] the unity of all Spaniards ... German and Italian fascism, control[s] a part of our patria, aided by a handful of traitors ... To benefit the foreign fascist exploiters, our unfortunate compatriots are compelled to work in the fields, mines and factories beneath the yoke of the occupying forces.'[23] The existence of a *civil* war was being virtually obliterated. Socialist anger was being fuelled by the realisation that the Popular Front line as proposed by the Communist Party had led to a denial of the civil war as a class war.

1938 saw the publication of a variety of pamphlets designed to explain how to organise the different kinds of clubs that constituted the base of the 'amplia organización de nuevo tipo' (a new type of mass organisation).[24] These pamphlets constantly stressed the apo-litical nature of the activities that such clubs should seek to foster. Youth organisers were encouraged to concentrate on the general educational and cultural improvement of their members. Sugges-tions included the formation of choirs and theatre groups, the hold-ing of youth festivals and literary competitions. Sports sections were to be set up as well as a general recreational division in each club or 'casa'. Overall, the reality outstripped any possible parody and was reminiscent of Serrano Poncela's ironic references back in March 1936 to the Scandinavian social democratic parties with their choirs and picnics.[25] Against all this, the youth dissidents demanded a return to the old FJS model. These demands, however, were expressed in terms of a return to the basis of the original youth unity pact of 1936 – which tends to suggest that the young socialists had never thought through the full implications of the massification which *had been stipulated as a policy objective in the original pact* that they referred to so nostalgically.[26]

In addition to ideological indignation, young socialists were not prepared to accept the Popular Front line as espoused by the JSU leadership because it would mean a certain end to socialist organisational pre-eminence in the youth movement. Ideological critique and pragmatic opposition were fused in the youth dissidents' campaign. The socialist youth rebellion in the provincial organisations of the centre–south zone was certainly provoked by their exclusion from the leadership cadres. This exclusion was reflected in the way the dissidents' press articles attacked the acute lack of internal democracy in the JSU. Indeed its democratic centralist procedure was now spectacularly evident in the dispossession of the youth executives in Albacete and Jaén. Policies were imposed from above. They were not the product of discussion or consensus of any kind. The passivity of the base was also facilitated by the sheer proliferation of bureaucratic layers in the JSU. This tendency – strenuously opposed by the socialist dissidents – was clearly in evidence by the time of the November 1938 national committee meeting. The proliferation of names on the executive committee at this meeting signalled its transformation into a central committee – thereby putting even more distance between the majority and the policy-making centre.[27]

The date of the JSU national committee meeting had been brought forward from December to November expressly to provide an arena in which to neutralise the threat posed by the youth dissidents. This was grave because in challenging the national executive's hegemony the dissidents were implicitly questioning the legitimacy of Popular Frontism. But faced with the growing rebellion of the socialist base, the unity strategy on which the Popular Front depended was obviously bankrupt. Nowhere was this more evident than at the JSU's national committee meeting held in Madrid from 24 to 28 November. Increasingly isolated but incapable of any measure of flexibility or compromise, the national leadership was determined to enforce organisational unity by sheer political force. Backing Negrín's Thirteen Points to the hilt, vehemently repeating the Popular Front line *circa* January 1937 the executive denounced the activities of the youth dissidents. It was at this meeting also that notorious leaflets were distributed denouncing the socialist civil governors of Albacete and Jaén, the socialist chief of the IX army corps, Francisco Menoyo, and as the final insult, Gómez Osorio, the civil governor of Madrid himself.[28] Predictably, they were labelled 'trotskyists' – a term used so indiscriminately that it had lost all meaning. The procedure adopted at the national committee meeting was a blatant exercise in the exclusion of the six provincial youth federations considered as centres of dissidence. Albacete, Jaén, Murcia, Alicante, Valencia and Ciudad Real did not attend because they had been invited in the capacity of 'spectators' only – which meant they had the right neither to intervene nor to vote.[29] In solidarity with them the two token socialists on the full youth executive elected in September 1937, Martín Cantal and Alfonso Rodríguez, immediately resigned, declaring that the executive's dictatorial behaviour disqualified in advance any resolutions which the assembly might formulate.[30] The November meeting elected four socialists to the new national committee – José Lacomba, Tomás Huete, Pascual Sánchez and Ezequiel Ureña. The high-handed manner in which this was effected – with neither the PSOE executive nor, in some cases, the appointees themselves being consulted in advance – doomed the initiative from the start. Lacomba and Huete were disqualified by the PSOE executive and both Sánchez and Ureña, the latter associated with the PSOE's youth secretariat, personally declined.[31] Moreover, the threats to purge all dissidents from the JSU made during the meeting only served to exacerbate the situation.

The deterioration of relations between socialists and communists had, in reality, far outstripped the youth leadership's perception of the situation. In Albacete and in Jaén, there existed effectively two parallel provincial federations and two sets of affiliates as a result of the war being waged between the national executive and the socialist dissidents it wished to oust.[32] Even in what were considered as the bastions of youth unity, the press reflected the divisions which were emerging ever more visibly in the JSU.[33] All over, socialists dissatisfied by their experience of youth unity were beginning to make their voices heard.[34] By 1938 the secretiveness which had initially surrounded the JSU leadership's change of political allegiance in November/December 1936 was generating anger among JSU socialists, as the full consequences struck home about the pledge which Santiago Carrillo had made, unilaterally, of their own political futures.[35]

For the best part of two years this anger had been contained for the sake of the war effort as a whole. For, whatever the reality of organisational unity, it was undeniable that the JSU formed the backbone of the Republican army. A majority of young socialists therefore heeded the PSOE executive's warning that by breaking up the JSU they would be dealing a death blow to Republican resistance. By late 1938, however, in many of the press declarations made by young socialists it was stressed that two years of 'silence and forbearance' was more than enough.[36] Their justification of that lengthy silence revealed that the Socialist Youth too had internalised and retained the basic principle of *pablismo* – namely the primacy of working-class unity. The weight of socialist tradition also made them instinctively cautious. Rebellion against the JSU leadership was a traumatic affair because at least in part many young socialists felt it was aimed against an organisation which was, historically, their own. When the revolt finally occurred in 1939, the old guard socialist youth found it necessary to invoke the 'spirit of rebellion' of their founder, Tomás Meabe, thus legitimising their opposition to 'unity' by reference to the traditions of their movement. The struggle against Carrillo and the youth executive was justified as a crusade to reconquer or salvage an integrally *socialist* youth organisation as the alienated patrimony of the PSOE.

The Casado Coup

On 3 March 1939 the official gazette of the defence ministry (Diario Oficial) published details of a series of military promotions made by Negrín, in a last-ditch attempt to bolster his authority in the centre–south zone. By and large, those promoted were leading communist officers. These appointments aroused great hostility among Negrín's opponents. But, in reality, they did little to strengthen the position of either the premier or the PCE.[37] Negrín was already in a minority position in his own government. After the fall of Cataluña in the first week of February, active support for continued resistance was limited to Uribe and Alvarez del Vayo. The prime minister's authority had suffered a further blow as a result of the political and constitutional crisis precipitated by Azaña's resignation as Republican president on 27 February 1939. This was provoked by France and Britain's simultaneous recognition of the Nationalist government. But the government crisis was compounded by the fact that vice-president Martínez Barrio, Azaña's constitutional successor, refused to take office unless he was granted powers to end the war. The constitutional structure of the Second Republic was collapsing. In such conditions, Negrín's determination to resist an unconditional surrender meant that he had little choice but to rely on the only military and political formation still unreservedly committed to the war; namely the Spanish Communist Party.

But in the burgeoning anti-communism of the centre–south zone, the news that Negrín intended promoting leading communists to the Republic's key military posts precipitated the very loss of control which he had sought to avoid. Widespread anti-communist reaction throughout the zone involved both civilians and military personnel.

On 4 March an extremely confused rising took place at the Cartagena naval base, involving both anti-communist Republican groups
and fifth column Falangists. Jesús Hernández, the former education
minister and now commissar general for the centre–south zone,
dispatched troops who managed to suppress the rising. But in the
panic and confusion the Republic lost its navy. Under orders from its
commanding officer, Admiral Buiza, who opposed continued resistance, the fleet set sail for North Africa where it was interned by the
French at Bizerta pending delivery to Franco.[38]

The centre of the reaction against Negrín's military appointments
was, however, Madrid. Since late February, Colonel Segismundo
Casado, the Republican commander of the centre army who
opposed Negrín's policy of out-and-out resistance, had been negotiating in the capital with like-minded civilian political leaders – and
principally with the veteran socialist, Julián Besteiro.[39] The object of
these secret talks was to establish a national defence junta to seize
power from Negrín for the purpose of ending the war on the best
terms possible. Casado was, all along, driven by the mistaken belief
that Franco would be prepared to negotiate with a fellow army
officer and that it had only been Negrín's reliance on communist
support and the presence of the PCE in the Republican cabinet
which had caused the previous deadlock. At any event, it was the so-
called Casado coup of 5 March, which, by effectively terminating
Republican resistance, put an end to the civil war itself.

The Casado affair has always been defined as a rebellion, first and
foremost of the Republican military – that is of professional officers
in the main – against the near communist hegemony in the
Republic's military command structure. In reality, however, the
Casado affair was much more than a military rebellion. What
occurred in Madrid was the culmination of a series of developments
throughout the centre–south zone. As Luis Araquistain commented:

> . . . the rebellion which defeated the Negrín government was not only a
> military one – it was also a civilian rising. *As a result of the civilian reaction,*
> the National Defence Council emerged. This was not a military junta –
> the only officers present were Casado and, if you like, Miaja. All the
> other members were representatives of political parties and union organ-
> isations, amongst which figured our own PSOE and the UGT. Whether
> we like it or not, whether these developments were positive or negative –
> this is the incontrovertible reality of what occurred.[40]

And over this much at least, Araquistain and Lamoneda concurred.
'The end of our war was *preceded* in the centre–south zone by a large-
scale purge [of communists] initiated by most of the national leader-

ships of the political parties.'[41] The coup signified the convergence of diametrically opposed political and social interests against a Communist Party which, by 1939, was entirely isolated from the other political groups in Republican Spain.[42] For whilst the PCE had alienated anarchists and socialists both by its policies and its aggressive proselytisation techniques, it had equally failed to retain the allegiance of its middle-class power base by 'failing' to deliver the military victory on which the political commitment of the bourgeoisie had ultimately always depended. The Casado rebellion thus constituted the final stage in the break-up of the Spanish Popular Front whose foundations had been eroded over time as relations between the PSOE and the PCE deteriorated. The military confrontation between 5 and 14 March in Madrid, examined below, was merely the crystallisation of a much wider civilian movement in the Republic's political rear. This, since the last quarter of 1938, had ranged anarchists, socialists – both young and old – and republicans against the PCE which was perceived as excessively influential in the military cadres, political organisations and governmental bodies of the Republican zone.

The onset of the political crisis which would prepare a climate propitious for Casado's coup can be traced back to the physical division of the Republican zone by the Nationalist armies at Viñaroz (Levante) in April 1938. This meant the separation of the centre–south zone from the Republican government and the national leaderships of the political parties and labour organisations, which were based in Barcelona until the fall of the city in January 1939. This sense of physical separation was transformed with dangerous ease into a feeling of political isolation and of moral desertion.[43] Particularly badly affected in this respect was the socialist rank and file in the zone. Frustration and bitterness had long been accumulating at what was seen as Lamoneda's excessive tolerance of PCE aggression. This tipped over into outright anger once centre–south zone socialists became convinced that the PSOE leadership was indifferent to their welfare. The word most frequently employed by socialist militants to describe their feelings of defencelessness was 'desamparo'. Most of the criticism was aimed directly at Lamoneda personally. Ricardo Zabalza, who, because of his FNTT status and public hostility to the PCE, had received numerous accounts of abuses from aggrieved socialists, was savagely sarcastic, accusing Lamoneda of a wanton disregard for the fate of party members:

> You say in your letter that the Party is concerned about all these matters, in spite of the amount of time you waste dealing with all this 'factional

wrangling'. We are eternally grateful for such fine concern and hope very
much that it begins to yield results – not least for the sake of so many of
our socialist comrades, FNTT affiliates included, who, doubtless
because of over-active imaginations, feel themselves to have been abandoned, and go in fear of their lives as a result of the excessive friendliness
of a brother party.[44]

Araquistain too criticised Lamoneda's aloofness: 'As a proof correc-
tor, [he] would have been superb: but he's as cold as ice. He feels
neither the agony of our country nor the needs of our party.'[45] The
fact that the Lamoneda executive departed for France after the
collapse of Cataluña in February 1939 only turned a suspicion into a
bitter conviction for many of the socialists trapped in the centre–
south zone – surrounded only by Nationalist territory and the sea.
Indeed Lamoneda's lengthy absence from the centre zone, which
lasted from April 1938 until the end of the war – apart from specific
tours to give speeches – in effect handed his opponents control of the
socialist movement there. But the desperation and chaos of the times
blurred former political allegiances. Not all the ASM members who
ended up supporting Casado were *Caballeristas*. This group included,
for example, Lamoneda's colleague, Rafael Henche.[46]

In such an unfavourable climate, war weariness soon produced a
profound demoralisation among the civilian population of the zone.
This resulted both from the sheer physical exhaustion consequent on
thirty months of cumulative material deprivation, and from the
despairing contemplation of an ever-bleaker international horizon.
This had reached its nadir at Munich in September 1938, when not
only Czechoslovakia but also the Spanish Republic was sacrificed on
the altar of appeasement. Faced with such bleak prospects, both
domestically and internationally, many erstwhile middle-class and
military supporters of the PCE were, moreover, engaged in a rapid
reassessment of the political stakes. The PCE ceased to be considered a political saviour, providing protection against a feared
social revolution, and the most likely means of winning the war.
Instead it had become the abiding obstacle to a negotiated settlement with Franco and the oligarchic interests which he represented.
In the face of working-class exhaustion and a wavering and discontented middle class, the PCE found itself unable to mobilise any
section of the population behind a rapidly disintegrating Popular
Front.[47] The socialist, Antonio Ramos Oliveira, commented afterwards on the general mood of passive expectancy into which the
coup had erupted. 'The Defence Council scarcely encountered opposition. It had an overwhelming advantage – given the passivity of its
enemies and the anxiety and expectation of the general populace.'[48]

Weakened thus, the PCE had to confront the mounting hostility of the socialist and anarchist movements whose vast accumulated store of resentment at the PCE's drive for political hegemony was unleashed by the imminence of virtually certain military defeat. Declarations of political 'incompatibility' with the PCE were made across the board by all the loyalist political forces as soon as news of Casado's rebellion in Madrid had reached the other provinces of the centre–south zone. These declarations had a clear precedent in the withdrawal of the socialist youth from the JSU and the definitive suspension of the PSOE/PCE joint party committees in Albacete, Alicante, Valencia, Ciudad Real and Murcia:

> Casado certainly didn't initiate the rebellion. Before he acted militarily, our socialist sections had initiated a civilian coup. I suppose you know that in Albacete the socialists took action, and then all the republicans and the CNT followed their example. It was decided unanimously not to allow the military command of the zone to be delivered to Negrín's communist appointee . . .[49]

In the early hours of 5 March, Colonel Casado rebelled against the Negrín government from his command post in the capital. The prime minister, dining at his residence in Elda (Alicante) with the majority of his ministers after a cabinet meeting, learned of the coup attempt by radio, although Casado was soon in contact with him directly by telephone. The colonel sought to legitimise the defence council by reference to the strategic and moral bankruptcy – indeed to the non-existence – of the Negrín government, the collapse of the entire edifice of the Republican state and the sheer impossibility and moral indefensibility of continuing the war. At the beginning of February, when Negrín had publicised his three conditions for a negotiated peace at the last wartime session of the Republican Cortes at Figueras, the anti-resistance camp had felt certain that mediation was imminent.[50] For Negrín, however, his three conditions – Spanish territorial independence, no reprisals against those who had fought for the Republic and a national plebiscite over the future form of government – were not intended as a face-saving device, still less as a coded signal that he was ready to surrender. The prime minister was not prepared to treat *unless* the terms of his conditions were met. As a minimum requirement, Franco had to guarantee that no reprisals would be taken against the population of the Republican zone. As no such assurance was forthcoming, Negrín saw no alternative but to maintain the resistance.

The Negrín government's peripatetic and atomised existence

following the fall of Cataluña – with some of the cabinet based in Madrid while Negrín established himself in splendid isolation in Alicante – had also undermined its authority, thus increasing Casado's credibility. Nor was Negrín's isolation purely a matter of his physical location. The prime minister's oft-quoted 'dependence' on the PCE was a direct function of the fact that, by the end of January 1939, political support from his cabinet was virtually non-existent. Apart from Uribe and Alvarez del Vayo, none of Negrín's ministers – and that included the socialists Ramón González Peña and Paulino Gómez Sáez – believed in the feasibility of Republican resistance.

The constitution of the Madrid-based 'national defence council', whose declared objective was to negotiate an 'honourable peace' with Franco – that is, one with guarantees – was immediately publicised as the following: president: General Miaja; foreign affairs/vice-president: Julián Besteiro; interior: Wenceslao Carrillo (ASM/PSOE); defence: Casado; finance: González Marín (CNT); justice: Miguel San Andrés (Izquierda Republicana); education and health: José del Río (Unión Republicana); public works: Eduardo Val (CNT); labour: Antonio Pérez (UGT). The Partido Sindicalista was also represented in the person of Sánchez Requena, as secretary to the council.

But in response to the constitution of the defence council on the fifth, there occurred a communist counter-rebellion in Madrid which unleashed an internal civil war in the city. For almost a week (7–12 March) the capital was the scene of intense fighting between Casado's forces and a number of communist-led units.[51] Of the four corps which constituted the centre army, three were commanded by professional officers who were PCE members – Barceló (I), Bueno (II) and Ortega (III).[52] In Madrid, therefore, Casado could count only on the IV army corps – commanded by the anarchist Cipriano Mera.[53] The communist commanders – most notably Colonel Barceló and Major Ascanio (Ortega's second-in-command) – were motivated not so much by a desire to resist the capitulationary option as by an instinctive fear of the anti-communist purge which Casado's triumph would inevitably unleash throughout the centre–south zone. Indeed the fact that in Madrid and throughout the rest of the territory remaining to the Republic Casado's adherents were driven by a virulent and vengeful hostility to Negrín and his supporters, rather than by the desire to secure for the junta the right to attempt mediation with Franco, lent a good deal of credence to such fears. Sheer panic was often the order of the day:

New authorities were established – with no basis whatever in constitutional legality. No matter how arbitrary, all means were deemed acceptable. Casting aside all common sense and logic and responding to what can only be described as an impulse of collective madness, there occurred a massive purge of the civilian authorities [throughout the Republican zone] – as if the [Casado] rebels were assuming control in conditions of normality. They seemed oblivious of the fact that they were at several days' distance from the hecatomb which they themselves had provoked.[54]

Some socialists were shockingly blunt about the function of Casado's coup. For example, Molina Conejero, the reformist socialist and civil governor of Valencia, who had played a leading role in ousting the *Caballeristas* from control of the provincial socialist federation in July 1937 declared: 'We are being asked to liquidate the PCE as a political party in order to end the war. If the PS[OE] were asked to make this sacrifice it would willingly comply. What difference can it make whether you're wiped out now or in a fortnight's time when the fascists take control?'[55] It is true, however, that neither for Madrid, the Levante or the south is there any evidence that there was a central command operating to coordinate the actions either of pro- or anti-Casado forces.

The communist resistance in arms in Madrid was thus as much an instinctive reflex of self-defence in a city where socialist–communist confrontation had reached crisis proportions even before the coup occurred.[56] Indeed, both the communist-led military units and the PCE's political cadres seem, in the wake of Casado's rebellion, to have acted instinctively throughout the centre–south zone in the absence of Comintern instructions. Whilst the overwhelming impression is one of a general Comintern decampment, it is still not clear whether any or all of the PCE cadres were in receipt of specific orders *not* to resist the defence council forces. The young communist commander, M. Tagüeña, claimed that orders were received actively to refrain from intervening against the *Casadistas* in Madrid.[57] Togliatti referred to orders from the politburo to the party in Madrid to resist. But this seems suspect, and somewhat at odds with his observation about the passivity of communist units on the Levante front – that they did not intervene to aid their comrades in Madrid because no one instructed them to.[58] Moreover, Togliatti's version of the Madrid events (he was not present), is wildly off-target in general. An all-encompassing, if excessively neat, anti-stalinist explanation of the PCE's inaction faced with the Casado conspiracy is provided by the historian Joan Estruch. He suggests that it was a direct result of the volte-face in Soviet foreign policy.[59] But given the chaotic state of communications in the centre–south zone after

Casado's rebellion (and even Togliatti could not be everywhere) it seems extremely unlikely that Comintern instructions not to resist could have been as perfectly relayed as Estruch suggests.

What is certain, however, is that no preventative measures had been taken in the capital to forestall any attempted coup – the danger of which PCE reports for February 1939 were clearly sensitive to.[60] In Madrid, communist resistance only emerged *after* the arrest of the PCE leadership. Even then, it did not encompass all the communist forces in the capital. Only Barceló's and Bueno's corps intervened, (Major Ascanio commanding corps II as a result of Bueno's illness). Antonio Ortega's corps did not intervene. He would later act as a mediator during the negotiations for a truce between the defence junta and the communist forces. On the other fronts, all the PCE's forces maintained a neutral stance.[61] Apart from the question of orders or the lack of them, this passivity can also be explained more simply in terms of the understandable reluctance of many of the communist cadres to initiate a futile fratricidal battle from which only Franco could emerge the victor.

By its limited resistance, it is true that the PCE was able to establish a basis for bargaining with the defence council forces in order to obtain the release of communist detainees.[62] In Alicante, for example, UGT adhesion to the defence council was accepted by the Communists in order to secure the release of Rafael Milla, secretary of the local UGT federation.[63] By resisting, time was also gained both to organise the evacuation of its cadres and to prepare the party for clandestinity.[64] It seems likely that the decision of the Madrid communists to treat with the defence council was motivated as much by an awareness of their own isolation as it was by any assessment of the relative military strength of Casado's forces in the capital.[65] This isolation, created by the vacuum left by the Comintern advisers, was compounded by the final departure from Spain first of the Negrín government on 6 March and almost immediately after of the bulk of the PCE leadership.[66] These departures may well have been justified, given that *casadista* forces were closing in rapidly on Elda (Alicante) where the prime minister's temporary headquarters were located at 'posición Yuste'. Nevertheless, Negrín's departure gave a tremendous political advantage to Casado and his supporters.

The PCE had created of the Republican capital a legendary symbol of antifascist struggle and a military stronghold. Yet by 1939 Madrid had become 'a trap which everyone sought to escape while there was still time'.[67] The outcome of the Casado affair reflected the fundamental weakness of the PCE's political – as opposed to military – base. Indeed, in the tense conditions of February–March 1939 some socialists had feared that the PCE would attempt to use the army units it controlled to defend its political position.[68]

It was visceral anti-communism in the ASM which led various of its leading members into plotting with Casado. Indeed the ASM became the nexus of the civilian conspiracy. Talks were held in its headquarters between Besteiro, Carlos Rubiera, Wenceslao Carrillo, Angel Pedrero (the anti-communist head of the Madrid SIM) and Cipriano Mera, anarchist commander of the centre army's IV corps.[69] Wenceslao Carrillo was approached towards the end of February 1939 by fellow socialist, Orencio Labrador, who was acting as Casado's intermediary.[70] Enrique de Francisco was also involved and through his contacts with members of the Socialist Youth, he was left in no doubt about the stance that most Madrid socialists would adopt over the Casado affair. Relations between the socialist and communist bases in the capital were probably the worst in the Republican zone. Taking a lead from the veterans of the ASM, Largo Caballero's stronghold, the joint committee structure had been virtually inoperative throughout the second half of 1938 which meant that, formally, the two parties had no direct contact with each other.[71]

The five days of fighting in Madrid saw a confrontation between socialists and communists whose violence was unprecedented even taking into account the levels of hostility in the civil war. The assault led by young socialists on the JSU provincial headquarters at Núñez de Balboa, 62 was probably the most violent of all the seizures of JSU headquarters which occurred throughout the centre–south zone.[72] Apart from Madrid, young socialists also assaulted the JSU headquarters in Valencia, Alicante and Almería, ousting the provincial executive committees, whereupon integrally socialist leaderships were re-established.[73] In the case of Ciudad Real, all membership granted after 18 July 1936 was annulled – with the proviso that those of 'good will' might reapply, but could expect to be subjected to the rigorous selection procedure necessary to re-establish the 'fabric and content' of the old socialist youth federation.[74] Once the socialist elements had reasserted their authority in the provincial bodies of the JSU in the wake of Casado, the old-guard leaders, such as Sócrates Gómez, Antonio Escribano and José Martínez summoned provincial youth delegates to a national committee meeting in Madrid. There they would proceed to re-elect a full committee for the new Federación Nacional de Juventudes Socialistas. This national committee would oversee the formal disqualification of the JSU national committee – apart from its two socialist members – Alfonso Rodríguez and Martín Cantal – who had already resigned in protest in

November 1938. They joined the new youth committee.[75] Gradually thereafter, JSU influence in Madrid province was dismantled.[76]

Nor was the violent exclusion of the PCE limited to the youth organisation. Throughout the centre–south zone communist civil governors were removed and PCE militants ousted from all levels of local and provincial administration, from Popular Front committees and from the union hierarchies of both the UGT and individual industrial federations.[77] Communist radios, the PCE equivalent of the PSOE's agrupaciones (groups), were forced to adhere to the defence junta in many areas. Others disbanded for fear of reprisals against members, for example in Denia, Callosa and Elda (Alicante). In many places PCE headquarters were assaulted and ransacked and communist militants arrested by pro-Casado military or security forces. This occurred in Almería, Ciudad Real, Alicante, Jaén and Córdoba provinces.[78] In Valencia and Alicante, the party newspapers – *Verdad* and *Nuestra Bandera* respectively – were also suppressed.[79] Togliatti was also arrested briefly in Alicante, along with Checa and Claudín, but fortunately they managed to secure release fairly rapidly.[80] In short, the PCE was being dismembered as an organisation. This process of neutralisation was intended by the Casado Junta as a means of establishing for itself a set of credentials acceptable to Franco in order to facilitate future negotiations. The hostility of Spanish socialists towards communists was further fuelled by various incidents during the Madrid conflict. The assault on the ASM headquarters by a unit under the command of the communist commissar Conesa, later to be executed by the defence council for his part in the counter-rising, left the premises devastated and three PSOE militants dead. A number of prominent socialists were taken hostage to El Pardo, including the civil governor himself, Gómez Osorio. After the communist capitulation, a common grave was discovered there which was found to contain the body of the socialist commissar Angel Peinado Leal.[81] Equally many communists in the capital and elsewhere met their deaths at the hands of socialists which perpetuated the cycle of violence.[82]

Whilst the Casado coup was targeted against the political and military influence of the PCE, it also brought about the final rupture of organisational unity in the Spanish socialist movement – both party and union. In the UGT, the Casado coup had profound repercussions at every level of the organisation in the centre–south zone. The unitarist national executive had for some time been the target of virulent criticism from socialists, in both the union and the party, who were hostile to Negrín and his policy of resistance. Increasingly in 1938 the government had come to rely on the UGT as one fundamental bulwark of resistance, providing as it did both practical and moral support.[83] The very fact that the UGT leadership was so identified with the government aroused the hostility of a number of UGT federations which adduced this close relationship as proof of the ascendancy of communists and unitarists in the UGT hierarchy. Such federations and union sections – often where *Caballeristas* had retaken the high ground, as in Madrid – were only too ready to involve themselves in the Casado conspiracy. The local union federations in Madrid, Alicante, Murcia and Albacete were numbered among the most active in this respect, and, therefore, the most hostile to the González Peña executive. After the Casado coup, it was these federations which took the lead in opposing the UGT's national executive.

Only six members of the UGT's national executive were located in the centre–south zone when the Casado rebellion occurred: Ramón González Peña himself – present as much in his capacity as justice minister – Edmundo Domínguez (vice-president), Rodríguez Vega (general secretary) and three ordinary members, Antonio Pérez, Claudina García and Ricardo Zabalza.[84] The remainder were located in Toulouse, along with the national committee. Though supportive of their colleagues in the centre–south zone and generally favourable to Negrín's resistance policy, they were unable, at such a distance, to offer effective opposition to the pro-Casado forces in the UGT who were determined to elect a new national executive committee shorn of all unitarist traces.

This determination was only increased by the fact that the UGT executive was, in the main, out of sympathy with Casado and his aims. In Madrid so hostile was the socialist organisation to the union's national executive that neither Domínguez nor Rodríguez Vega was able to make the least impact. *Claridad* was taking a pro-Casado line. Its new editor, the virulently anti-Negrinist[85] Javier Bueno, rejected Rodríguez Vega's appeal to him not to aggravate further the divisions in the union. Unable thus to exercise a restraining influence, Rodríguez Vega left for Valencia where the anti-unitarists were demanding a national committee meeting.[86] In the immediate aftermath of the Madrid rebellion, the *Casadistas* in the UGT were determined to cast the union leadership in their own image: hence the demands for a national committee meeting in Valencia. This began on 17 March and witnessed extraordinary scenes of violent confrontation, with pistols brandished and assassination threats made against Rodríguez Vega.[87] As a result, Rodríguez Vega, in some considerable peril, and aware of the precarious position of Domínguez who had remained in Madrid, accepted that the UGT should appoint a representative to the defence council. Such were the circumstances of Antonio Pérez's selection as labour councillor. His appointment as UGT representative on the Madrid defence council was very much a matter of accepting the *fait accompli* of Casado's coup in an attempt to prevent the total dismemberment of the UGT.[88] Pérez reluctantly complied with his mandate. And his would be the only junta vote against the death sentence for the communist commanders Barceló and Conesa.[89] In some places PCE cadres and trades union leaders argued for the tactical wisdom of accepting the defence council's authority in an attempt to prevent the massive expulsion of communist union members.[90] In spite of this, however, card-carrying members of the PCE, both in the UGT and within individual industrial federations, were obvious targets for the *Casadistas* throughout the centre–south zone. Expulsions occurred at local and provincial level. Even a formal adherence to the defence council, however, failed to satisfy the anti-unitarist opposition in the UGT. A subsequent session of the national committee in Valencia on 25 March – called to agree guidelines for the evacuation of UGT cadres – had to be abandoned amid further violence. Thereafter the *Casadistas* took matters into their own hands, electing a new UGT executive committee to replace González Peña's. The anti-Negrín executive included the veteran *Besteiristas*, Trifón Gómez and Andrés Saborit – as well as Largo Caballero's lieutenant, Rodolfo Llopis.[91]

The election of a new UGT leadership in Madrid in the last days of the Republic effectively completed the new socialist trinity. For 20–21 March also saw the election in Madrid of a new PSOE executive. The edition of *El Socialista* for the twentieth published notice of a meeting in Madrid of PSOE delegates from the provincial federations of the centre–south zone 'to discuss the situation arising from the absence of the national executive'. Significantly, this was held in the FNTT's Madrid offices.[92] At this meeting the following executive was elected: president: José Gómez Osorio†; vice-president: Wenceslao Carrillo; general secretary: Pascual Tomás; vice-general secretary: Gómez Egido; minutes secretary: Ricardo Zabalza†; ordinary members: Trifón Gómez, Fernando Piñuela†, Antonio de Gracia†, Carlos Rubiera†, José López Quero, Francisco Ferrándiz Alborz. Piñuela, as the socialist commissar dismissed in November 1938, was the archetypal 'victim' of PCE sectarianism. Antonio de Gracia was civil governor of Jaén and López Quero general secretary of the FNTT in Jaén. Ferrándiz Alborz came from the Alicante socialist federation. He was also appointed the new editor of *El Socialista*.[93] This executive –

intended as an exile leadership – was decimated by the Nationalist repression.[94]

As is clear from its constituent names, this new PSOE executive represented the resurgence of *Caballeristas* and *Besteiristas* riding the wave of grass roots anti-stalinism in the centre–south zone which had swept away Lamoneda, shipwrecking his unity strategy.[95] Nearly all the new executive members were either old-guard left socialists – the majority associated with the ASM – or else they came from Besteiro's camp, for example the veteran railway union leader, Trifón Gómez and Gómez Osorio, civil governor of Madrid. The latter was also the father of Sócrates Gómez, a leading JSU dissident and one of the founders of the new socialist youth federation.[96]

For the Madrid socialists connected with the defence junta their action symbolised the 'redemption' of the 'historic' party of Pablo Iglesias, vitiated by PCE aggression, at which the Lamoneda executive had connived: '. . . in spite of its very recent election two days ago, the PSOE executive's authority is indisputable – based on its loyalty to the historic mission that has always defined our Party. Today the PSOE has regained its true identity – as Spanish and socialist'.[97] With the hecatomb looming, this obsession with party tradition and heritage is immensely revealing of the self-image of many old-guard socialists and of their perception of what had happened to the PSOE during the civil war. In the eyes of the Madrid-based executive, the authority of Lamoneda's executive, vastly diminished by the negligent and irresponsible policies it had pursued during the war, had finally been forfeited by its physical desertion of the Republican zone – and therefore symbolically of the Republic – in its final crisis. The Lamoneda executive had been based in France since the fall of Cataluña in February 1939. It had rapidly disclaimed any connection with Casado's defence junta. But it had done this in a low-key way which reflected its wish not to exacerbate the division in the socialist movement, given that the council was an accomplished fact and there were other prestigious socialists closely associated with it. The 'more in sorrow than in anger' tone adopted by Lamoneda contrasted sharply with the PCE's strident denunciations of *casadista* socialists as traitors and imperialist agents.[98] But as Lamoneda remarked, it was nevertheless ironic – if not also symbolic – that the self-styled socialist left should have regained control of the PSOE executive amid the wreckage of a devastated Republic and a shattered socialist movement.

The Casado rebellion had thus finally precipitated what had been threatening for nearly three years of civil war: the complete and utter shattering of the unity of the Spanish socialist movement. In the savage bitterness of the immediate post-war exile, the responsibility for both the Republic's political decomposition and its military defeat would be the subject of a vicious polemic among the atomised ranks of Spanish socialism. As the organisation which embodied the Second Republic's reforming ideal, it was bitterly ironic that the PSOE should have inherited real political power only after the outbreak of a civil conflict whose imperatives radically altered the political agenda, ultimately burying that ideal. It was an indication of the PSOE's pivotal importance too that it should have endured within itself the disintegrating effects of the severe political contradictions of the Popular Front strategy.

Appendix 1

PSOE wartime executive committees

	JUNE 1936	AUGUST 1938
President	Ramón González Peña	re-elected
Vice-president	F. Jiménez de Asúa	Alejandro Otero
General secretary	Ramón Lamoneda	re-elected
Vice-secretary	Juan Simeón Vidarte	re-elected
Administrative secretary	Francisco Cruz Salido	re-elected

MEMBERS:

I. Prieto	A. de Gracia	I. Prieto
M. Cordero	M. Albar	M. Cordero
F. de los Ríos	J. Bugeda	M. Albar
		Antonio Huerta
		R. Zabalza
		L. Martínez

'HONORARY' MEMBERS:
Julián Besteiro
F. Largo Caballero
J. Negrín
J. Alvarez del Vayo
P. Gómez Sáez

UGT Wartime Executive Committees

OCTOBER 1937

President	A. de Gracia	R. González Peña
Vice-president	J. Díaz Alor	Edmundo Domínguez
General secretary	F. Largo Caballero	J. Rodríguez Vega
Administrative secretary	Pascual Tomás	A. del Rosal
Treasurer	Felipe Pretel	F. Pretel

MEMBERS:

R. Zabalza	Mariano Muñoz	A. Génova
Amaro del Rosal	Carlos Hernández Zancajo	Ezequiel Ureña
		Claudina García
Manuel Lois	Antonio Génova	Antonio Pérez
		César Lombardía (PCE)
		Daniel Anguiano (PCE)

JANUARY 1938 ADDITIONS:

P. Tomás
R. Zabalza
J. Díaz Alor
C. Hernández Zancajo

First (Provisional) JSU Executive Committee

(SEPTEMBER 1936)

General Secretary	Santiago Carrillo (FJS)
Organisation	Trifón Medrano (UJC)
	José Laín (FJS)
Press	S. Serrano Poncela (FJS)
	Fernando Claudín (UJC)
Militia	Federico Melchor (FJS)
	José Cazorla (FJS)
	Segismundo Alvarez (UJC)
Youth	Paulina Odena (UJC)
Administration	Luis Cuesta (UJC)
Trade unions	Manuel Vidal (UJC)
Women	Aurora Arnaiz (FJS)
Sport	Justo Rodríguez (UJC)
Young Pioneers	J. José Renales (UJC)
International Affairs	Alfredo Cabello (FJS)

JSU Executive Committee

JANUARY 1937

General Secretary S. Carrillo, *Vice-Secretary* T. Medrano, *Organisation* J. Laín, *Press* F. Claudín, *War Production* M. Vidal, *Agriculture* S. Alvarez, *Military Secretary* J. Cazorla/F. Melchor, *International Affairs* A. Cabello/L. Cuesta/ S. Serrano Poncela.

JSU Executive

SEPTEMBER 1937

S. Carrillo, J. Laín, F. Claudín, M. Vidal, S. Alvarez, J. Cazorla, F. Melchor, A. Cabello, Antonio Bueno (PCE), Trinidad Torrijos (PCE), Josefina López (PCE), Clemente Ruiz (PCE), Agustín Nieto (PCE), Ignacio Gallego (PCE), Martín Cantal (PSOE), Alfonso Rodríguez (PSOE).

JSU Executive

S. Carrillo, J. Laín, F. Claudín, M. Vidal, S. Alvarez, J. Cazorla, F. Melchor, A. Cabello, S. Serrano Poncela, T. Torrijos, J. López, A. Nieto, I. Gallego, J. Rodríguez (PCE), Isidro Mendieta (PSOE), J. Sarcan (PCE), M. Tagüeña (PCE), Victor Velasco (PCE), José Lacomba (PSOE), Tomás Huete (PSOE), Pascual Sánchez (PSOE), Ezequiel Ureña (PSOE), Eloisa Villalba (PSOE), J. M. Jiménez, Antonio Hidalgo.

ASM Executive Committee
(ELECTED MARCH 1936)

President F. Largo Caballero, *Vice-president* J. Alvarez del Vayo, *Secretary* Enrique de Francisco, *Vice-secretary* Wenceslao Carrillo, *Administrative secretary* P. Tomás, *Members* Rodolfo Llopis, Luis Araquistain, C. Hernández Zancajo, R. Zabalza, J. Díaz Alor, Juan Gómez Egido.

Appendix 2

Dramatis personae

ADAME (MANUEL) ex-member of PCE executive, supported Largo Caballero during the war.

AGUIRRE (JOSÉ MARÍA) Largo Caballero's politico-military secretary.

ALBAR (MANUEL) PSOE executive member throughout war.

ÁLVAREZ DEL VAYO (JULIO) fellow-travelling member of socialist left, appointed foreign minister by Largo in September 1936 and again by Negrín in April 1938.

ANGUIANO (DANIEL) communist member of UGT executive elected October 1937 and veteran leader of petroleum federation.

ARAQUISTAIN (LUIS) close collaborator of Largo Caballero, Republican ambassador in Paris (September 1936–May 1937), member of ASM executive.

ASENSIO (GENERAL JOSÉ) Largo's under-secretary of war (September 1936–February 1937).

AZAÑA (MANUEL) Republican President, leader of Izquierda Republicana.

BARAIBAR (CARLOS DE) leading left socialist, Largo Caballero's choice to replace General Asensio as under-secretary of war, co-owner of *Claridad* with Araquistain.

BESTEIRO (JULIÁN) veteran, Madrid-based socialist leader (PSOE president 1925–32, UGT president 1925–34), one of the PSOE's few theoreticians and leader of reformist unionists who lost control of UGT executive to the *Caballeristas* in January 1934.

BUGEDA (JERÓNIMO) reformist socialist, PSOE executive member (June 1936–August 1938), subordinate of Negrín's in finance ministry.

BULLEJOS (JOSÉ) ex-general secretary of PCE, supported Largo Caballero during the war.

CABELLO (REMIGIO) PSOE vice-president, died April 1936.

CANTAL (MARTÍN) one of two socialist members of JSU executive (September 1937–November 1938).

CARRILLO (SANTIAGO) leader of FJS before war, JSU general secretary, public order delegate on Madrid defence junta (November 1936), member of PCE.

CARRILLO (WENCESLAO) leading left socialist, member of ASM, Largo's UGT executive and a national leader of iron and steel federation, appointed by Largo as D.G. of Security in Madrid, member of Casado's defence junta (March 1939).

CASADO (COLONEL SEGISMUNDO) Republican army officer, his rebellion against Negrín ended the war.

CASARES QUIROGA (SANTIAGO) Republican premier (May–July 1936).

CEREZO (ENRIQUE) member of the JSU's Valencian federation and supporter of Largo Caballero.

CLAUDÍN (FERNANDO) young communist leader, member of JSU executive.

CODOVILA (VITTORIO) (alias Medina), Comintern delegate in Spain.

COMPANYS (LUIS) president of the Generalitat.

CORDERO (MANUEL) veteran union leader and PSOE executive member, collaborated closely with R. Lamoneda.

CRUZ SALIDO (FRANCISCO) *prietista* member of PSOE executive, editor of *Adelante* after reformist take-over, appointed by Negrín to navy/air sub-secretariat.

CUESTA (LUIS) communist member of JSU executive, killed in accident, February 1937.

DÍAZ (JOSÉ) general secretary of PCE.

DÍAZ ALOR (JOSÉ) close collaborator of Largo Caballero, vice-president of UGT executive until October 1937, national executive member of the bakers' and confectioners' federation, and of ASM executive.

DOMÍNGUEZ (EDMUNDO) elected UGT vice-president in October 1937, leader of construction union, unitarist sympathies, appointed by Negrín in November 1938 to replace Piñuela as socialist political commissar in centre army.

FRANCISCO (ENRIQUE DE) leading left socialist, ex-general secretary of PSOE and acting general secretary of ASM.

GALARZA (ANGEL) ex-Radical Socialist, appointed interior minister by Largo Caballero (September 1936–May 1937).

GANGA TREMIÑO (GINÉS) Alicante socialist, leading supporter of Largo Caballero.

GARCÍA (CLAUDINA) member of UGT executive elected October 1937, and of garment and hatters federation.

GÉNOVA (ANTONIO) unitarist member of UGT wartime executives.

GIRAL (JOSÉ) Republican premier (July–September 1936), leading member of Izquierda Republicana, close personal friend of Azaña.

GÓMEZ (SOCRATES) socialist youth dissident, instrumental in re-emergence of independent socialist youth federation, Madrid, March 1939.

GÓMEZ (TRIFÓN) *besteirista* union leader (railway workers). Appointed by Negrín as head of supplies sub-secretariat in defence ministry.

GÓMEZ EGIDO (JUAN) left socialist, member of ASM, of Madrid provincial socialist federation and of PSOE executive elected in Madrid (March 1939).

GÓMEZ OSORIO (JOSÉ) socialist civil governor of Madrid at end of war, elected PSOE president, March 1939.

GÓMEZ SAEZ (PAULINO) Basque socialist, appointed interior minister by Negrín, April 1938.

GONZÁLEZ PEÑA (RAMÓN) reformist leader of Asturian miners' union, elected president of PSOE (June 1936) and UGT (October 1937), appointed justice minister by Negrín (April 1938).

GRACIA (ANASTASIO DE) UGT president and member of PSOE executive, served as minister of trade and industry and of labour in Largo's two cabinets.

GREGORI member of JSU's Valencian federation and supporter of Largo Caballero.

HENCHE (RAFAEL) president of Madrid socialist federation, general secretary of bakers' and confectioners' union, regional delegate for New Castile on PSOE national committee, supporter of Lamoneda.

HERNÁNDEZ (JESÚS) communist education minister until April 1938, then chief political commissar for centre army.

HERNÁNDEZ ZANCAJO (CARLOS) president of FJS before the war, fervent *Caballerista*, member of UGT wartime executives, general secretary of urban transport federation.

HUERTA (ANTONIO) elected to PSOE executive, August 1938, regional delegate for Basque Country on PSOE national committee.

IBÁRRURI (DOLORES) (*La Pasionaria*) leading member of PCE politburo.

JIMÉNEZ DE ASÚA (LUIS) socialist law professor, Republican ambassador in Prague during war, vice-president of PSOE (June 1936–August 1938).

LAMONEDA (RAMÓN) elected PSOE general secretary in June 1936 in reformist coup, prime mover in internal party purge against socialist left, architect of joint action strategy between PSOE and PCE during war.

LARGO CABALLERO (FRANCISCO) veteran socialist trade union leader and maximum leader of socialist left, Republican premier and war minister (September 1936–May 1937), UGT general secretary until October 1937.

LOIS (MANUEL) member of Largo's UGT executive.

LOMBARDÍA (CÉSAR M.) FETE general secretary and communist member of UGT executive elected October 1937.

LÓPEZ QUERO) Jaén socialist, unitarist regional delegate on FNTT national committee.

LLOPIS (RODOLFO) Largo Caballero's presidential under-secretary and a member of FETE national executive.

MARTÍNEZ AMUTIO (JUSTO) member of *caballerista* socialist federation in Valencia, appointed civil governor in Albacete by Largo Caballero, Levante regional delegate to PSOE national committee.

MARTÍNEZ BARRIO (DIEGO) leader of centrist Unión Republicana, vice-president of Republic.

MARTÍNEZ DASI (SALVADOR) member of JSU's Valencian federation and supporter of Largo Caballero.

MARTÍNEZ GIL (LUCIO) *besteirista* leader of FNTT, elected to PSOE executive, August 1938.

MAURÍN (JOAQUÍN) left-communist, leader of Bloc Obrer i Camperol and co-founder of POUM.

MEDRANO (TRIFÓN) communist youth/JSU leader, killed in accident, February 1937.

MÉNDEZ (RAFAEL) Asturian socialist, appointed to interior ministry staff by Negrín.

MÉNDEZ ASPE (FRANCISCO) Negrín's Left Republican subordinate in finance ministry, appointed minister, April 1938.

MENDIETA (ISIDRO) unitarist socialist, became editor of *Claridad*, May 1937, elected to JSU executive, November 1938.

MENOYO (FRANCISCO) left socialist commander of IX army corps.

MIAJA (GENERAL JOSÉ) Republican army officer, head of Madrid defence junta (November 1936) and of Casado's defence junta (March 1939).

MIJE (ANTONIO) member of PCE politburo.

MOLINA CONEJERO (MANUEL) reformist socialist leader of Valencian (city) socialist group and civil governor of Valencia, Levante delegate to PSOE national committee.

MORÓN (GABRIEL) FNTT leader from Córdoba, former *Prietista* who supported Lamoneda and Negrín during the war, appointed interim Director General of Security in 1937, later editor of *El Socialista*.

MUÑOZ (MARIANO) member of Largo's UGT executive, leader of hotel and catering federation.

NEGRÍN (JUAN) right-wing socialist, finance minister in Largo's cabinets, Republican premier, May 1937–March 1939.

NIN (ANDRÉS) left–communist, co-founder of POUM, abducted and assassinated by Soviet agents in aftermath of Barcelona May Days.

OTERO (ALEJANDRO) Granada socialist and former Cortes deputy, appointed under-secretary for armaments by Negrín, elected vice-president of PSOE, August 1938.

PEINADO LEAL (ANGEL) general secretary of National Union of Socialist Union Groups (UGSS), killed during socialist–communist infighting in Madrid after Casado coup.

PÉREZ (ANTONIO) member of UGT executive elected October

1937, leader of railway federation and UGT representative on Casado defence junta.

PÉREZ (LEONCIO) member of JSU's Valencian federation, supporter of Largo Caballero.

PESTAÑA (ANGEL) former CNT leader, founder of Partido Sindicalista.

PIÑUELA (FERNANDO) left socialist political commissar in centre army, dismissed by Jesús Hernández, November 1938.

PRETEL (FELIPE) UGT unitarist, treasurer on UGT national executives throughout the war.

PRIETO (HORACIO) ex-general secretary of CNT, Mariano R. Vázquez's *éminence grise*.

PRIETO (INDALECIO) leader of reformist socialists, navy and air minister in Largo's cabinets and war minister in Negrín's until April 1938, member of PSOE executive from which increasingly disaffected after mid-1938.

PUENTE (ENRIQUE) president of Madrid socialist youth (JSM) and founder of *La Motorizada*, the PSOE youth militia.

RANCHAL (MIGUEL) left socialist member of PSOE's Cordoban federation.

RÍOS (FERNANDO DE LOS) law professor from Granada, moderate socialist close to Prieto, Republican ambassador in Washington during war, member of PSOE executive until August 1938.

RODRÍGUEZ (ALFONSO) socialist member of JSU executive (September 1937–November 1938).

RODRÍGUEZ VEGA (JOSÉ) general secretary of UGT executive elected October 1937, leader of printers' federation.

ROSAL (AMARO DEL) fellow-travelling member of Largo's union executive, played major role in unitarist conquest of UGT's national leadership in October 1937, leader of banking and credit workers' federation.

ROSENBERG (MARCEL) Soviet ambassador to Spain, recalled May 1937.

RUBIERA (CARLOS) left socialist, secretary of Madrid socialist federation and under-secretary to Galarza in interior ministry.

SABORIT (ANDRÉS) Besteiro's lieutenant, leader of the printers' federation, expelled from the ASM in January 1936 for his editorship of the *besteirista* newspaper *Democracia*.

SERRANO PONCELA (SEGUNDO) FJS/JSU executive member, increasingly opposed to S. Carrillo and PCE.

SOLER (JOSÉ MARÍA) Jaén socialist and unitarist president of FNTT.

TOGLIATTI (PALMIRO) general secretary of Italian Communist Party and Comintern's number one in Spain.

TOMÁS (BELARMINO) *prietista* leader of Asturian miners' federation (SMA).

TOMÁS (PASCUAL)   old-guard *Caballerista*, member of UGT executive, leader of iron and steel federation.

TUNDIDOR (JUAN)   member of JSU's Valencian federation, supporter of Largo Caballero.

UREÑA (EZEQUIEL)   UGT national committee delegate for chemical federation, socialist youth member associated with Lamoneda's youth secretariat, elected to JSU executive in November 1938, but declined post.

URIBE (VICENTE)   communist agriculture minister during war.

VÁZQUEZ (MARIANO R.)   CNT general secretary during war.

VIDARTE   (JUAN-SIMEÓN)   PSOE   executive   member, appointed by Negrín as under-secretary in interior ministry.

ZABALZA (RICARDO)   UGT executive member and FNTT general secretary, maximum supporter of Largo Caballero.

ZUGAZAGOITIA (JULIÁN)   reformist socialist interior minister (May 1937–April 1938), appointed by Negrín as defence under-secretary.

Appendix 3

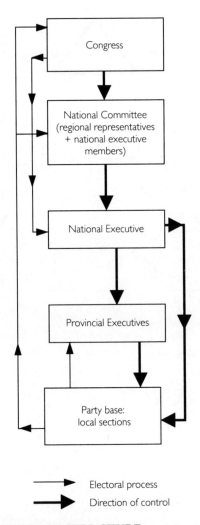

Electoral process
Direction of control

PSOE: ORGANISATIONAL STRUCTURE

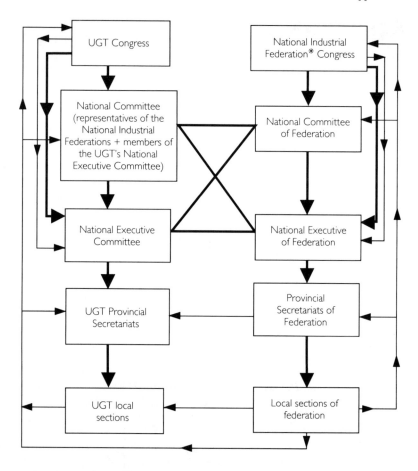

Electoral process

Direction of control

Channels of communication rather than control

*   This structure – paralleling the UGT's – existed for each component National Federation of Industry in the UGT.

UGT ORGANISATIONAL STRUCTURE

Notes

Introduction

1 For the rise of the 'renovated' PSOE, R. Gillespie, *The Spanish Socialist Party: A History of Factionalism* (Oxford, 1989). For perspectives on the transition, P. Preston, *The Triumph of Democracy in Spain* (London 1986), S. Balfour, *Dictatorship, Workers and the City. Labour in Greater Barcelona since 1939* (Oxford, 1989).

2 For an account in English of the PSOE's early years, see P. Heywood, 'The Labour Movement in Spain before 1914' in Richard Geary (ed.), *Labour and Socialist Movements in Europe before 1914* (Oxford, New York, Hamburg, 1989).

3 Serious conflict between the party and union has only recently re-emerged over the general strike of 14 December 1988, see S. Juliá (ed.), *La Desavenencia. Partido, sindicatos y huelga general* (Madrid, 1989).

4 B. Bolloten, *The Grand Camouflage: The Spanish Civil War and Revolution, 1936-39* (New York, 1961). A new version of this appeared in 1979. *The Spanish Revolution: The Left and the Struggle for Power during the Civil War* (Chapel Hill). A third version, vastly augmented, was published posthumously in Spain, *La Guerra Civil española: revolución y contrarrevolución* (Madrid, 1989). In 1991 it will be published in the United States and Britain, under the title, *The Spanish Civil War: Revolution and Counterrevolution*.

1 Internal divisions in the Spanish socialist movement 1934–1936

1 J. J. Morato, *El Partido Socialista Obrero* (Madrid, 1918), *passim*; G. Meaker, *The Revolutionary Left in Spain 1914–1923* (Stanford, 1974), pp. 11, 14, 114–15, 192–9; José Andrés Gallego, *El socialismo durante la Dictadura (1923–1930)* (Madrid, 1977); M. Contreras, *El PSOE en la II Républica: Organización e ideología* (Madrid, 1981), chapter 1.

2 P. Preston, 'The Origins of the Socialist Schism in Spain 1917–31' in *Journal of Contemporary History*, 12, no. 1, 1977, 101–32; also P. Preston, *The Coming of the Spanish Civil War* (hereafter *CSCW*) (London, 1978), chapter 1; S. Juliá, 'Corporativistas obreros y reformadores políticos: crisis y escisión del PSOE en la II República' in *Studia Histórica*, no. 1

(4), 1983, 41–52; G. Morón, *El Partido Socialista ante la realidad política de España* (Madrid, 1929).

3 Paul Preston, *CSCW*, p. 196.

4 I. Prieto, *Discursos fundamentales* (Madrid, 1975), pp. 169–70.

5 'In our country, which is politically so backward, we socialists must *replace* the progressive bourgeoisie', interview in *Le Populaire* (Paris), 17 January 1931; cf. also 'Discurso en el cine Pardiñas, *El Socialista*', 6 February 1934, in *Discursos fundamentales*, p. 185, also p. 279.

6 For eye-witness accounts/personal testimony of the Asturian October, see M. Grossi, *La insurrección de Asturias* (Valencia, 1935, repr., Gijón, 1979); J. Canel, *Octubre rojo en Asturias* (Madrid, 1935); N. Molins y Fábrega, *UHP. La Revolució Proletaria d'Asturias* (Barcelona, 1935); Amaro del Rosal, *1934. El movimiento revolucionario de Octubre* (Madrid, 1984). Modern accounts include, B. Díaz Nosty, *La comuna asturiana* (Bilbao, 1974), A. Shubert, *Hacia la revolución. Orígenes sociales del movimiento obrero en Asturias 1860–1934* (Barcelona, 1984), F. I. Taibo, *Octubre de 1934* in *Historia General de Asturias* (Gijón, 1978), vols. VII and VIII; see also Jackson *et al.*, *Octubre 1934. Cincuenta años para la reflexión* (Madrid, 1985).

7 F. Largo Caballero, *Notas históricas de la Guerra en España (1917–1940)* ms., Fundación Pablo Iglesias (hereafter FPI). First part published as *Francisco Largo Caballero: Escritos de la República* (ed. S. Juliá) (Madrid, 1985), pp. 42–158.

8 F. Largo Caballero, *Escritos*, p. 150 n. 51; also P. Preston, *CSCW*, pp. 123–4.

9 Amador Fernández to Juan Pablo Garcia, Brussels, 29 August 1935 in I. Prieto *et al.*, *Documentos socialistas* (Madrid, 1935), pp. 217–21. Also in Largo Caballero, *Notas históricas*, pp. 175–9.

10 For the habitually difficult relations between the PSOE and its youth wing, I. Prieto, *Documentos socialistas*, pp. 50–2, and his 'Discurso a la escuela socialista de verano de Torrelodones', 9 August 1933, in *Discursos fundamentales*, p. 177; E. Conze, *Spain Today* (London, 1936), pp. 32–3. For the young socialists' case, M. Bizcarrondo, 'Democracia y revolución en la estrategia socialista de la Segunda República' in *Estudios de Historia Social*, nos. 16–17 (1981), p. 307.

11 R. Viñas, *La formación de las Juventudes Socialistas Unificadas (1934–1936)* (Madrid, 1978), pp. 36, 157.

12 Amaro del Rosal was expelled from the PSOE in 1946. For his formal declaration of allegiance to the PCE, see his article, 'Quiero un puesto de combate en el Partido Comunista', *Nuestra Bandera*, June–July 1948.

13 Luis Araquistain, 'Largo Caballero, ante los jueces' in *Leviatán*, no. 20, January 1936, *Leviatán (Antología)*, ed. P. Preston (Madrid, 1976), pp. 266–77; Largo Caballero, *Notas históricas*, p. 123.

14 J. Díaz, 2 June 1935, the Monumental cinema, Madrid, cited in *Tres años de lucha*, 3 vols. (Toulouse, 1947, edn used, Barcelona, 1978), (I) pp. 42–43.

15 P. Preston, *CSCW*, pp. 127, 132.
16 R. Henche, intervention during youth report discussion, National Committee meeting, 17–21 July 1937, stenographic record, p. 132, in the PSOE's Archivo Histórico de Moscú, hereafter, A H-(M).
17 R. Lamoneda, 'El secreto del anticomunismo', ms, personal archive, FPI.
18 S. Juliá, 'The origins and nature of the Spanish Popular Front' in M. S. Alexander & H. Graham (eds.) *The French and Spanish Popular Fronts: Comparative Perspectives* (Cambridge, 1989), p. 30; also J. S. Vidarte, *El bienio negro y la insurrección de Asturias* (Barcelona, 1978), pp. 396–8; P. Preston, *CSCW*, p. 135.
19 S. Juliá, 'Sobre la formación del Frente Popular en España', *Sistema*, 73, July 1986, 67–81.
20 Marta Bizcarrondo, 'De las Alianzas Obreras al Frente Popular' in *Estudios de Historia Social*, nos. 16–17, January–June 1981, p. 97.
21 Cf. J. Díaz, speech, Oviedo, 5 July 1936, *Tres años de lucha* (I), p. 270.
22 M. Contreras, *El PSOE en la II República*, pp. 156–7; S. Juliá, *La Izquierda del PSOE (1935–1936)* (Madrid, 1977), pp. 82–6; 'Sobre la formación', p. 78; P. Preston, *CSCW*, pp. 144–5; A. Blas Guerrero, *El socialismo radical en la II República* (Madrid, 1978), pp. 55–61.
23 S. Juliá, *La Izquierda*, pp. 84–9.
24 G. Mario de Coca, *Anti-Caballero* (Madrid, 1936, edn used, Madrid, 1975), pp. 131–2; P. Preston, *CSCW*, pp. 145–6.
25 For details of the referendum, *Claridad*, January 1936, 20th to end of month. The voting returns, declared to be 'unofficial', as follows: Largo Caballero 21,927; Remigio Cabello 127; Jiménez de Asúa 93; Prieto 72; Julián Besteiro 55; Ramón González Peña 47 and various other candidates received fewer votes, A H–22–2.
26 PSOE national committee minutes, 25 May 1936, A H–24–1.
27 A H–22–2.
28 Popular Front signatories to the electoral pact of 15 January 1936 as follows: PSOE, UGT, FJS, PCE, POUM, Izquierda Republicana (Azaña), Unión Republicana (Martínez Barrio) and Pestaña's Partido Sindicalista. For pact, S. Juliá, *Orígenes del Frente Popular en España: 1934–1936* (Madrid, 1979); also H. Graham & P. Preston (eds.) *The Popular Front in Europe* (London, 1987).
29 P. Preston, *CSCW*, pp. 146–9.
30 P. Preston, *CSCW*, p. 148; electoral correspondence and campaign lists, AHM.
31 J. S. Vidarte, *Todos fuimos culpables*, 2 vols. (Barcelona, 1978) (I) pp. 38–9; R. Lamoneda, A H–24–1.
32 UGT executive minutes, 6, 19 March 1936, FPI; also Marta Bizcarrondo, 'De las Alianzas Obreras al Frente Popular'.
33 Vidarte's letter, 14 March 1936, UGT executive minutes, 19 March 1936.
34 J. S. Vidarte, *Todos* (I), p. 99.

35 See, for example, the socialist group of Vicálvaro, Canillas y Canilejas (Madrid) to the PSOE executive, complaining about the re-emergence of the 'caciques de toda la vida' (the agents of the old dynastic parties, or, more generally, class exploiters), March 1936, AH–17–20.

36 A. Shubert, 'A reinterpretation of the Spanish Popular Front: the case of Asturias', in Alexander & Graham, *The French and Spanish Popular Fronts*, pp. 213–25.

37 Largo's reply, UGT executive minutes, 19 March 1936.

38 *Ibid.*

39 See Jesús Lozano, *La Segunda República: imágenes, cronología y documentos* (Barcelona, 1973), pp. 213–14; P. Preston, *CSCW*, p. 184.

40 R. Viñas, *La formación*, p. 160; F. Claudín, *Santiago Carrillo: crónica de un Secretario General* (Barcelona, 1983), pp. 36–9.

41 Santiago Carrillo and Carlos Hernández Zancajo were also nominated as youth representatives.

42 President – F. Largo Caballero; vice-president – J. Alvarez del Vayo; Secretary – E. de Francisco; vice-secretary – W. Carrillo; administrative secretary – P. Tomás; ordinary members – L. Araquistain, J. Díaz Alor, J. Gómez Egido, C. Hernández Zancajo, R. Llopis, R. Zabalza. See also, P. Preston, *CSCW*, p. 191; J. S. Vidarte, *Todos* (1), p. 66.

43 ASM members included Ramón Lamoneda, Juan Negrín and Luis Jiménez de Asúa. For others, G. Mario de Coca, *Anti-Caballero*, pp. 192–4; P. Preston, *CSCW*, p. 146.

44 For a detailed analysis of this period and the manoeuvres surrounding the call for a congress, S. Juliá, *La Izquierda*, pp. 124–38, particularly pp. 132–3.

45 See ASM correspondence with the national executive 1935–6, AH–17–1. For opposition to the reformist executive see the cases of Almería 7 March, 27 May 1936, AH–13–3 and Alcira (Valencia), AH–0–12. For Alcira, S. Juliá, *La Izquierda*, pp. 124, 137.

46 Call for the congress, in *El Socialista*, 9 March 1936, see also G. Mario de Coca, *Anti-Caballero*, pp. 194–6.

47 See Ciudad Real (city group) correspondence with the national executive, March 1936, AH–7–21; G. Mario de Coca, *Anti-Caballero*, p. 194; S. Juliá, *La Izquierda*, pp. 126–7.

48 ASM correspondence, AHM, 10 March, 7 April 1936; S. Juliá, *La Izquierda*, p. 129.

49 The ASM to the PSOE's national executive, 18 March 1936, ASM correspondence, AHM.

50 S. Juliá, *La Izquierda*, p. 129.

51 For conditions of youth pact signed in Moscow on 15 March by Santiago Carrillo (FJS) and Trifón Medrano (UJC), R. Viñas, *La formación*, pp. 57–8, 145–6.

52 J. S. Vidarte, *Todos* (1), p. 59.

53 B. Bolloten, *The Spanish Revolution. The Left and the Struggle for Power during the Civil War* (Chapel Hill, 1979), p. 132.

54 Serrano Poncela's article 'Comentarios al Congreso', published March 1936 in *Renovación*, repr. in R. Viñas, *La formación*, pp. 140–4. Serrano on the origins and nature of youth unity, in 'Algunos datos estadísticos', youth secretariat correspondence, AHM.

55 H. Graham & P. Preston (eds.) *The Popular Front in Europe*, pp. 3–4.

56 M. Wolf, 'Unamos las fuerzas de la nueva generación', report to the VI congress (Joven Guardia, n.p., 1937), quoted R. Viñas, *La formación*, pp. 112–37.

57 F. Claudín, *Santiago Carrillo*, p. 45, R. Viñas, *La formación*, p. 59.

58 Such unifications occurred all over Spain, R. Viñas, *La formación*, p. 55; F. Claudín, *Santiago Carrillo*, p. 41.

59 R. Viñas, *La formación*, pp. 146–55.

60 B. Bolloten, *The Spanish Revolution*, p. 132; Carrillo's speech, in *Mundo Obrero*, 6 April 1936.

61 'The knowledge brought tears to his eyes. I witnessed the scene personally', Amaro del Rosal in the margin of p. 36 of the copy of G. Morón's *Política de ayer y política de mañana* (Mexico, 1942), held by the FPI. F. Claudín, *Santiago Carrillo*, p. 45, places this meeting in December 1936.

62 B. Bolloten to L. Araquistain, 1947–9, Correspondencia de Luis Araquistain, Archivo Histórico Nacional (hereafter, LA/AHN), legajo 25, B162–168; R. Viñas, *La formación*, p. 145.

2 The break-up of the socialist unity and the coming of the civil war

1 Santos Juliá, *La Izquierda*, p. 324.

2 Largo Caballero's election as president of parliamentary party, 16 March 1936; P. Preston, *CSCW*, p. 191. For list of PSOE deputies in 1936, M. Contreras, *El PSOE en la II República*, pp. 183–93.

3 P. Preston, *CSCW*, pp. 191–2; J. S. Vidarte, *Todos* (I), pp. 120–4; S. Juliá, *La Izquierda*, p. 324.

4 S. Juliá, *La Izquierda*, pp. 129–30, 132–3; P. Preston, *CSCW*, p. 198; J. S. Vidarte, *Todos* (I), pp. 192–3.

5 P. Preston, CSCW, p. 192; J. S. Vidarte, *Todos* (I), pp. 119–22.

6 For Azaña's position, *ibid.* (II), p. 664.

7 Qualities displayed in abundance in speeches such as 'La conquista interior de España', made at Cuenca on 1 May 1936, see Prieto, *Discursos fundamentales*, pp. 255–73.

8 Vidarte, *Todos* (I), p. 147; P. Preston, *CSCW*, p. 193.

9 'Here begins the real responsibility that Prieto as a clear-sighted statesman cannot evade.' G. Morón, *Política*, pp. 52–5 (p. 54). For a contrary view, L. Romero Solano, *Vísperas de la guerra de España* (Mexico, 1947), pp. 160–1.

10 Stenog. record of discussion, AH–24–1. For the row over the postponement, S. Juliá, *La Izquierda*, pp. 130–1.

11 Felix Morrow, *Revolution and Counter-Revolution in Spain* (New York, 1938, 3rd edn used, London, 1976), p. 38; G. Morón, *Política*, pp. 61–2.

12 J. S. Vidarte, *Todos* (i), pp. 193–6; S. Juliá, *La Izquierda*, p. 116; M. Contreras, *El PSOE en la II República*, p. 158; P. Preston, *CSCW*, pp. 198–9.

13 Vidarte, *Todos* (i), pp. 194–5; G. Morón, *Política*, pp. 60–3.

14 Cf. the left's behaviour at the time of the elections for party president in January 1936. The *caballerista* candidacy for June 1936 elections as follows, Largo Caballero (president); Julio Alvarez del Vayo (vice-president); de Francisco (general secretary); Pascual Tomás (administrative secretary); Luis Araquistain, Rodolfo Llopis, Carlos Hernández Zancajo, Ricardo Zabalza, José Díaz Alor and Juan Gómez Egido (ordinary members). This was the line-up which, in March, had defeated the reformist candidacy to take the ASM executive.

15 For the computed voting returns from AHM, Alfredo Pastor Ugena, *La Agrupación Socialista Madrileña durante la Segunda República*, 2 vols. (Madrid, 1985) (ii), pp. 555–635.

16 S. Juliá, *La Izquierda*, pp. 132–4, 324–5.

17 Results in *El Socialista*, 1 July 1936, returns in AH–22–1, AH–22–2.

18 J. S. Vidarte, *Todos* (i), pp. 206–8; S. Juliá, *La Izquierda*, pp. 119, 306–8; P. Preston, *CSCW*, pp. 198–9.

19 S. Juliá, *La Izquierda*, pp. 134–6, 306–8; M. Contreras, *El PSOE en la II República*, pp. 158–9.

20 Martínez Amutio, 'Contribución a la historia del PSOE', *Tiempo de Historia*, no. 9, August 1975, 29–37. For the Ecija events see also, S. Juliá, *La Izquierda*, p. 324; P. Preston, *CSCW*, p. 198; Romero Solano, *Vísperas de la guerra de España*, p. 207; G. Morón, *Política*, pp. 63–4.

21 Almería correspondence 1935–9, AH–13–43, 7 March, 27 May 1936; Alcira, AH–0–12, 27 May 1936.

22 S. Juliá, *La Izquierda*, p. 124; F. Morrow, *Revolution and Counter-Revolution in Spain*, p. 38.

23 ASM correspondence, January–May 1937, AH–17–2, for the ASM's status as a 'shadow executive'. G. Morón, *Política*, p. 63 and M. Cordero's letter to W. Carrillo, 19 June 1939, p. 5, Cordero's exile correspondence, AH–25–6.

24 (50 per cent plus one vote), S. Juliá, *La Izquierda*, pp. 134–5; J. S. Vidarte, *Todos* (ii), p. 208.

25 S. Juliá, *La Izquierda*, pp. 135–6; P. Preston, *CSCW*, p. 146.

26 S. Juliá, 'De la división orgánica al gobierno de unidad nacional', *Anales de Historia* (ii) (Madrid, 1987), p. 230.

27 Cf. the PCE leadership's reluctance to accept Largo's designation of communist ministers in September 1936. B. Bolloten, *The Spanish Revolution*, p. 122.

28 For the genesis and development of the Workers' Alliance, and 'socialist imperialism', P. Preston, *CSCW*, pp. 117–20; M. Bizcarrondo, 'De las Alianzas Obreras al Frente Popular', pp. 83–104, also M. Bizcarrondo

(ed.) *Octubre del 34: reflexiones sobre una revolución* (Madrid, 1977), *passim*; S. Juliá, *La Izquierda*, pp. 202–16.

29 B. Bayerlein, 'El significado internacional de Octubre de 1934 en Asturias. La Comuna asturiana y el Komintern' in G. Jackson *et al. Octubre 1934. Cincuenta años para la reflexión*, pp. 25, 29, 39.

30 For socialist attitudes to the AA.OO., J. Díaz, *Tres años de lucha* (1), pp. 177–8, 179. For the Workers' Alliances (AA.OO.) after October 1934 and the left socialists' attitude, M. Bizcarrondo, 'De las Alianzas Obreras al Frente Popular', pp. 90–3. This includes details of how and where they occurred. For greater detail PCE archive, microfilm XIII (170), 'relación de Alianzas Obreras y Campesinas' dated variously throughout 1935.

31 PCE report, 9 December 1935, PCE archives, microfilm XIII. (The letter from Sevillian socialists, dated 5 April 1935 and signed by FJS, UGT and FNTT.)

32 PCE report, 9 December 1935, PCE archives, microfilm XIII. For Alicante, see also Salvador Forner, *Industrialización y movimiento obrero. Alicante 1923–1936* (Valencia, 1982).

33 Cf. M. Bizcarrondo, 'De las Alianzas Obreras al Frente Popular', p. 90; S. Juliá, *La Izquierda*, pp. 212, 214.

34 See P. Preston, *CSCW*, pp. 19, 54, 61, 70, 94, 208; M. Contreras, *El PSOE en la II República*, pp. 53–5, 114–21.

35 S. Juliá, *La Izquierda*, pp. 217, 253.

36 For anarchist activities in Madrid, S. Juliá, *Madrid 1931–1934. De la fiesta popular a la lucha de clases* (Madrid, 1984).

37 S. Juliá, *La Izquierda*; P. Preston, *CSCW*, also 'The Origins of the Socialist Schism in Spain 1917–31' and 'The Struggle Against Fascism in Spain: Leviatán and the Contradictions of the Socialist Left, 1934–6', *European Studies Review*, vol. 9, 1979, 81–103; M. Bizcarrondo, *Araquistain y la crisis socialista de la II República/Leviatán (1934–1936)* (Madrid, 1975), also 'Democracia y revolución en la estrategia socialista en la Segunda República', 227–459 and 'La crisis socialista en la Segunda República', *Revista del Instituto de Ciencias Sociales*, no. 21, 1973; A. Blas Guerrero, *El socialismo radical en la II República*; A. and I. Aviv, 'Ideology and Political Patronage: Workers and Working Class Movements in Republican Madrid 1931–4', *European Studies Review*, vol. 2 (1981), 487–515 and 'The Madrid Working Class, the Spanish Socialist Party and the Collapse of the Second Republic (1934–36); *Journal of Contemporary History*, vol. 16 (1981), 229–50; J. M. Macarro Vera, 'Causas de la radicalización socialista en la Segunda República', *Revista de Historia Contemporánea* (Seville), no. 1, December 1982, 178–224.

38 S. Juliá, *La Izquierda*, pp. 2–3, 288–9.

39 For the phenomenon of bureaucratic reformism, J. Andrade, *La burocracia reformista en el movimiento obrero* (Madrid, 1935), *passim*; S. Juliá, *La Izquierda*, pp. 289–304. See also R. Lamoneda's acid criticism of Largo's political inconsistency, in 'El secreto del anticomunismo', ms. notes in

Lamoneda's personal archive, A R L F– 166–40, FPI, for example, 'The truth is that Caballero is an old chameleon who has changed political direction more than enough times but who has been very fortunate never to have had anyone seriously take him to task about it. For all his famed principles, he's stood for and against everything.'

40 S. Juliá, *La Izquierda*, pp. 219–22; for the UGT in the Ministry of Labour, cf. A. and I. Aviv, 'Ideology and Political Patronage'.

41 S. Juliá, *La Izquierda*, p. 235 for the resolutions on the Popular Front of various CNT assemblies. For the most ready of all acceptances, see the Asturian e.g., Adrian Shubert, 'The Popular Front in Asturias' in Alexander & Graham, *The French and Spanish Popular Fronts*, pp. 213–25.

42 S. Juliá, *La Izquierda*, pp. 204–5, 214–15.

43 *Ibid.*, pp. 246–7. For socialist incomprehension of the anarchist mentality, S. Juliá, *La Izquierda*, pp. 224, 239 and W. Carrillo, *Claridad*, 23 November 1935.

44 S. Juliá, *La Izquierda*, p. 247.

45 For the conditions of the union pact mooted by the CNT in January 1936, John Brademas, *Anarcosindicalismo y revolución en España (1930–1937)* (Barcelona, 1974), p. 161. For the union/party division S. Juliá, *La Izquierda; Madrid 1931–1934: De la fiesta popular a la lucha de clases* and 'Partido contra sindicato', *Anales de Historia* (2) (Madrid, 1987), pp. 341–2.

46 For a definition, F. Claudín, *The Communist Movement* (Harmondsworth, 1975), p. 218.

47 Union relations in Madrid and the escalating conflict of the Republican period, S. Juliá, *Madrid. De la fiesta popular a la lucha de clases*.

48 *Solidaridad Obrera*, 16, 17 July 1936.

49 4,592 (23.5 per cent) of *ugetistas* voted to continue the construction strike, as against 14,940 who were in favour of a return to work, S. Juliá, *La Izquierda*, p. 260.

3 The appointment of the Largo Caballero government

1 M. Contreras, *El PSOE en la II República*, pp. 147–9; 160–1. ASM dominance in the early period was more the result of the PSOE's infrastructural weakness elsewhere than of any centralising ethos.

2 UGT minutes, 16, 17 July 1936 (FPI). Ricardo Zabalza (FNTT) also remained in Spain, but in Cádiz.

3 The UGT's Casas del Pueblo were centres with a dual function. They provided the local sections of the industrial federations with organisational back-up, whilst also acting as social and cultural centres for the workers.

4 UGT minutes, 16, 17 July 1936. For a misleading account of this incident, Amaro del Rosal, *Historia de la UGT de España 1901–1939* (2 vols.) (Barcelona, 1977) (1), pp. 487–8; Lamoneda's intervention

during 'Posición Política' report at the July 1937 PSOE national committee meeting, stenograph record. For left and reformist acute mutual suspicion, Vidarte, *Todos* (i), p. 95.

5 Largo Caballero, *Mis Recuerdos* (Mexico, 1954, edn used, Mexico, 1976), pp. 153–4 and Amaro del Rosal, *Historia de la UGT*, p. 490 (i); M. Tuñón de Lara 'El significado político del Frente Popular', *Estudios de Historia Social*, nos. 16–17 (1981), p. 126; S. Juliá, *La Izquierda*, p. 132.

6 R. Lamoneda: PSOE national committee meeting, 1937, stenog. record, p. 84. UGT obstruction also highlights the growing rivalry between the party and union blocs.

7 S. Juliá, *La Izquierda*, pp. 289–304.

8 For details of this crowded period, see Vidarte, *Todos* (i), pp. 259–82; G. Jackson, *The Spanish Republic and the Civil War 1931–1939* (Princeton, 1965), pp. 231–46; also R. Carr, *Spain 1808–1975* (Oxford, 1982), pp. 653–5, from whom the quote is taken.

9 B. Bolloten, *The Spanish Revolution*, p. 188; Vidarte, *Todos* (i), p. 476; also L. Araquistain to Largo Caballero, 24 August 1936, AHN/LA, leg. 32/30a.

10 R. Lamoneda, 'Circular a los militantes del PSOE', August 1939, in *Ramón Lamoneda. Ultimo secretario general del PSOE designado en España. Posiciones políticas – documentos – correspondencia* (Mexico, 1976), p. 228; B. Bolloten, *The Spanish Revolution*, p. 188.

11 Amaro del Rosal, *Historia de la UGT* (ii), pp. 493–6; Largo Caballero, *La UGT y la Guerra*, speech October 1937 (Valencia, 1937), p. 14, also *Mis recuerdos*, p. 166; R. Llopis, 'Las etapas de la victoria' in *Spartacus*, 1 October 1937, p. 4.

12 A. Vélez (pseud. for J. M. Aguirre), *Informaciones*, 9 November 1977, states that Azaña's preference was for Prieto to form a government; Araquistain to Largo, 24 August 1936, LA/AHN.

13 Prieto's exasperation at Azaña's 'chronic procrastination', reported by A. Vélez, *Informaciones*, 10 November 1977; Azaña's sentiments in his *Obras completas*, 4 vols. (Mexico, 1966–8) (iii), p. 495. *Ibid.* for his unavailing attempts to form a coalition government from conservative republicans to the PSOE on 20 July. Also Vidarte, *Todos* (i), pp. 476–7. Giral's resignation forced the issue, p. 501; see also Azaña, *Obras* (iv), pp. 592–3.

14 Araquistain's letter in his correspondence, leg. 32/30a.

15 *Guerra y Revolución en España 1936–1939*, 4 vols. (Moscow, 1967–78) (ii), pp. 45–6.

16 B. Bolloten, *The Spanish Revolution*, pp. 119–20.

17 B. Bolloten, *The Spanish Revolution*, pp. 120–1; Vidarte, *Todos* (ii), p. 615; for the 'desgaste' ('erosion') of the socialist left, A. Ramos Oliveira, *Historia de España*, 3 vols (Mexico D.F., n.d.) (iii), p. 312.

18 B. Bolloten, *The Spanish Revolution*, p. 121; *Claridad*, 4 September 1936.

19 Vidarte, *Todos* (i), p. 481.

20 Araquistain to Largo Caballero, 24 August 1936.

21 For the events of May 1936, P. Preston, *CSCW*, pp. 191–2; Vidarte, *Todos* (I), pp. 117–24; Lamoneda's intervention, 'Posición Política' report, July 1937, PSOE national committee meeting; *El Socialista* editorial, 19 October 1937. This was the first public criticism by the PSOE executive of Largo's behaviour in September 1936.

22 Lamoneda, before the party's national committee in July 1937, declared that only three people had known in what circumstances Largo had been offered the premiership – Azaña, Giral and Largo himself, PSOE national committee, July 1937, stenog. record, p. 85. Also M. Cordero to W. Carrillo, 19 June 1939, AH–25–6; Vidarte, *Todos* (I), pp. 480–2.

23 M. Azaña, *Obras* (IV), p. 603.

24 Vidarte, *Todos* (I), p. 481, (II), p. 678; B. Bolloten, *The Spanish Revolution*, p. 121.

25 Prieto's speech, Egea de los Caballeros (Aragón), 19 May 1936, *Discursos fundamentales*, p. 282.

26 J. Zugazagoitia, *Guerra y vicisitudes de los españoles* (Buenos Aires, 1940, edn used, Barcelona, 1977), p. 178.

27 G. Morón, *Política*, p. 85.

28 R. Lamoneda, 'Circular a los militantes del PSOE', p. 228.

29 For speeches, Vidarte, *Todos* (I), pp. 321–2. For Prieto's pessimism, Alvarez del Vayo to Araquistain, 2 February 1937, LA/AHN, leg. 23, no. 112a; G. Morón, *Política*, p. 84; J. Gorkín, *Caníbales políticos. Hitler y Stalin en España* (Mexico, 1941), p. 220.

30 R. Lamoneda, 'Notas del Grupo Parlamentario', ARLF–166–40.

31 For a breakdown of the September cabinet, B. Bolloten, *The Spanish Revolution*, pp. 122–3.

32 Vidarte, *Todos* (I), pp. 480–4.

33 A. Vélez (J. M. Aguirre), *Informaciones*, 8, 9, 10 November 1977; also Aguirre, LA/AHN, leg. 71/no. 22, p. 22.

34 L. Araquistain, *Sobre la guerra civil y en la emigración* (Madrid, 1983), pp. 146–52.

35 Araquistain to Norman Thomas, *Sobre la guerra*, pp. 51, 174.

36 Vidarte, *Todos* (II), p. 862.

37 Prieto's doubts about Asensio in letter to Araquistain, 13 February 1953, LA/AHN, leg. 36, no. 252. For Galarza, 'who, unfortunately for us, saw fit to join our party', cf. Vidarte, *Todos* (II), p. 673; also A. Vélez, *Informaciones*, 9 November 1977.

38 Vidarte, *Todos* (II), p. 655.

39 Galarza had desperate problems securing a passage to Mexico after the war, his letter to Araquistain, leg. 29, nos. 13–17. There he drew close to Negrín and his socialist and communist supporters, sharing a public platform with them (Negrín, Lamoneda, Alvarez del Vayo and Rodríguez Vega, *Por la República contra el plebiscito* (Mexico, 1945)). Along with the above and other leading socialists, Galarza was expelled from the PSOE in 1946 as a 'communist sympathiser'.

40 Vidarte, *Todos* (II), p. 656; UGT executive minutes, 23 October 1936.

Also report from provincial socialist federation of Murcia to Lamoneda executive, 14 April 1937.

41 G. Morón, *Política*, p. 77.

42 Vidarte, *Todos* (II), pp. 661–2.

43 J. M. Aguirre to L. Araquistain, 28, February 1937, LA/AHN, leg. 23, no. A 28a, sheet 3, which relates Largo's comments to his two ministers.

44 *Historia de la UGT* (II), p. 527.

45 UGT executive minutes 1936–37. Home searches, 23 October, 24 December 1936. CNT behaviour in Cartagena and Aragon, 1 October 1936. The PSOE federation in Alicante, for example, wrote to the UGT executive. For references to clashes between UGT and CNT militants, January–April 1937, R. Lamoneda, report on unification at July 1937 PSOE national committee meeting, AH–24–2, pp. 125–6.

46 For example, the remarks of Juan Tundidor, a member of the FJS old guard, at congress of Juventudes Socialistas de España, Toulouse, 21–2 April 1945. Conference report published by JJ.SS., Mexico. Tundidor presents the Socialist Youth leadership which forged the unity pact as a group of ambitious individuals blinded by the 'prizes' offered them.

47 Claudín, *Santiago Carrillo*, p. 44. For the polemic in the socialist movement over the departure from Madrid, ASM executive minutes, 7–8 August 1937. The leading *Caballeristas* left the ASM in the hands of an interim committee. The 'desertion' of Madrid became another barbed weapon in the PSOE dispute. Serrano Poncela recalled how Santiago Carrillo had referred to the 'shameful' way in which the PSOE had abandoned the capital – Poncela to Ramón Lamoneda, 21 July 1939, AHM. For this polemic also, C. Fernández, *Paracuellos del Jarama: ¿Carrillo culpable?* (Barcelona, 1983) and J. Aróstegui & J. A. Martínez, *La Junta de Defensa de Madrid* (Madrid, 1984), pp. 131–2.

48 Claudín, *Santiago Carrillo*, p. 45; R. Viñas, *La formación*, p. 54.

49 UGT executive minutes, 17 December 1936.

50 UGT minutes, 15 September 1936; Largo Caballero, *Notas históricas*, p. 258.

51 UGT minutes, 22 November 1936; also Amaro del Rosal, *Historia de la UGT* (II), p. 603.

52 See also Hernández Zancajo, executive minutes, 4 February and Pretel, 25 February 1937 (p. 34), also minutes 4 March.

53 28 February 1937, p. 2 (my italics).

54 Lamoneda's comments in 'Posición Política' report, PSOE national committee meeting, July 1937, stenog. record, pp., 85–6; also G. Morón, *Política*, p. 72.

55 Vidarte, *Todos* (I), p. 482, (II), p. 620.

4 Political realignments inside the socialist movement

1 R. Viñas, *La formación*, p. 64 for the executive list in full.

2 B. Bolloten, *The Spanish Revolution*, pp. 134–6; R. Viñas, *La formación*, pp. 64–8.

3 Martínez Dasi, 'Conference or Congress?', *Adelante*, 7 May 1937, outlines the techniques used to 'stagemanage' the conference; Leoncio Pérez, 'El Pleito Juvenil ¿son las JSU independientes? ¿pueden serlo?', *Adelante*, 12 May 1937. Also minutes of the youth report at the PSOE national committee meeting, July 1937, stenog. record. Claudín, *Santiago Carrillo*, p. 50; R. Viñas, *La formación*, pp. 65–8.

4 F. Largo Caballero, *Notas históricas*, pp. 254–5. Cf. also socialist disquiet at the PCE's repeated use of the ambiguous term 'pueblo' (people/nation), Antonio Escribano, secretary of the JSU federation in Alicante, *Spartacus*, no. 3 (1937), pp. 13–16 and Sócrates Gómez, speech, 'Los jóvenes socialistas y la JSU', Madrid, 9 September 1938, p. 24.

5 S. Carrillo, introductory speech at JSU conference, January 1937, *La conferencia de la nueva generación heroica, libre y estudiosa* (Valencia, 1937), p. 13.

6 Title of Carrillo's closing speech at the January 1937 youth conference. 'We want unity, we want it with the young republicans, young anarchists and young catholics who are fighting for liberty . . . we know that such unity cannot be based on marxist principles.' Carrillo, *La conferencia de la nueva generación*, pp. 49–50; cf. also Carrillo to the plenary session of the PCE, 24–6 September 1937; M. Vidal, *La juventud en la Guerra y en la Revolución* (JSU, 1938).

7 P. Preston, *CSCW*, pp. 92–130.

8 S. Carrillo, *La conferencia de la nueva generación*, p. 19 (see also p. 50).

9 S. Alvarez, *La juventud y los campesinos* (Valencia, 1937), p. 6.

10 Trifón Medrano, 'Hombres nuevos y nuevos cuadros', *La Conferencia de la nueva generación*, p. 4.

11 Cf. *JSU de España: nuestra organización y nuestros cuadros* (n.p., 1937).

12 S. Carrillo: 'En marcha hacia la victoria'; F. Melchor: 'Organicemos la producción'; José Lain: 'Por un ejército regular, disciplinado y fuerte'; S. Alvarez: 'La juventud y los campesinos'; I. Gallego: 'El problema campesino en Andalucía' in *La conferencia de la nueva generación*.

13 JSU shock brigades were also extended to industry, F. Melchor, 'Organicemos la producción', pp. 12–14. Also Carrillo's opening speech, p. 39. There was growing friction with socialist and anarchist workers who saw the initiative as a further attempt at political monopolisation by the PCE.

14 S. Alvarez, 'La juventud y los campesinos', pp. 12–15; cf. also I. Gallego, 'El problema campesino en Andalucía', p. 4.

15 S. Alvarez, 'La juventud y los campesinos', p. 12. Also, B. Bolloten, *The Spanish Revolution*, p. 217.

16 Socialist youth dissidence centred on the Valencian JSU federation, e.g. Leoncio Pérez, Juan Tundidor, Enrique Cerezo, Salvador Martínez Dasi and Gregori, *El Socialista*, 4 January 1937.

17 '. . . we have found our party', S. Carrillo, speech, 'La juventud, factor

de la victoria', to the plenary session of the PCE's central committee, 6–8 March 1937, Valencia.

18 Cf. many references in socialist exile correspondence to the Communists' 'betrayal' of the conditions of youth unity. E.g. Henri Lafayette to S. Carrillo, n.d., LA/AHN, leg. 42, no. 67. Also report to the Second International on the Socialist Youth in the JSU, 12 June 1939, LA/AHN, leg. 72, no. 13; the resolutions of the congress of the JJ.SS. de España, 21–22 April 1945, Toulouse (Mexico, 1945) (FPI). For the war period itself, cf. vi congress of Cordoban provincial socialist federation (Pozoblanco), January 1939 for accusations regarding the PCE's 'perversion' of the youth unity pact, AHM.

19 Figures for Madrid province in *El Socialista*, 17 May 1937; for the mobilisation of the JSU, S. Carrillo, 'La juventud, factor de la victoria'.

20 Serrano Poncela to Lamoneda, 25 May 1939, AHM.

21 Report to the Second International on Socialist Youth in the JSU.

22 Aguirre to Araquistain, 28 February 1937; see also M. Koltsov, *Diario de la guerra española* (Madrid, 1978), p. 352: 'Everyone speaks ill of Largo Caballero: his enemies shout from the rooftops while his supporters whisper criticism.'

23 *CNT*, 6 January 1937, 'Our most urgent priority is to secure the UGT–CNT pact.' CNT ambitions, Aguirre to Araquistain, 28 February 1937; S. Juliá, 'Partido contra sindicato', pp. 333, 337–41.

24 R. Lamoneda, July 1937 PSOE national committee meeting, stenog. record; also his speech in the Monumental Cinema, 27 June 1937, *Cuatro discursos sobre la unidad* (Madrid, 1937?); M. Cordero to F. García, (n.d. but 1939), correspondencia de M. Cordero, AH–25–6; *Guerra y revolución* (III), p. 53.

25 Examples of union group unification, credit and finance, shoemakers, in both Madrid and Valencia, *El Socialista*, 2 May 1937; joint 'unity' papers, *Unidad* in Alcira (Valencia) and *Vida Obrera* in Albacete. For other initiatives and the executive's attitude, R. Lamoneda, speeches on 27 June 1937 in the Monumental and 1 August 1937 in the Cine Bilbao, in *Cuatro Discursos*, pp. 6–7 and 28–9 respectively.

26 A. Peinado Leal, general secretary of the federation of socialist union groups, *El Socialista*, 3 March 1937. The PCE's undemocratic proselytism in the unions criticised in *El Socialista*, 14 March 1937.

27 *El Socialista*, 14 March 1937.

28 Socialist representatives on the national GSS/GOSR joint committee: A. Peinado Leal and J. Rodríguez Vega of the printers' federation and future UGT general secretary.

29 R. Lamoneda, editorial, *El Socialista*, 28 March 1937.

30 G. Morón, *Política*, pp. 61–2; Vidarte, *Todos* (i), pp. 480–2; R. Lamoneda, 'Circular a los militantes del PSOE', p. 228.

31 *Claridad*, 6 January 1937 for the signatories, as follows, Largo Caballero, Araquistain, Alvarez del Vayo, Galarza, Carlos de Baraibar, Rodolfo Llopis, Pascual Tomás, Amaro del Rosal, Díaz Alor, M. Lois, J. M.

Aguirre, F. Pretel, Mariano Muñoz, Ogier Preteceille, Wenceslao Carrillo, Carlos Rubiera, Valeriano Casanova, Carlos Hernández Zancajo, Luis Menéndez, Ricardo Zabalza, Enrique de Francisco, Ginés Ganga, Miguel Villalba, Salvador García, Luis Romero Solano, Aurelio Almagro, Cresenciano Bilbao, Campos Villagrán, Isidro Escandell, Menéndez Ballesteros, Pedro García, Alejandro Peris, Francisco Menoyo, Moreno Mateo.

32 *Guerra y revolución* (III), p. 53.

33 *Ibid.*, p. 55.

34 Inconclusive UGT–CNT conversations (between UGT national executive and CNT national committee) over unity of action from December 1936 to January 1937, *El Socialista*, 7 March 1937: J. Peirats, *Los anarquistas en la crisis política española* (Buenos Aires, 1964, repr. Madrid, 1976), p. 295.

35 See above chapter 3, p. 64 n. 45 and below chapter 4, p. 82 n. 51. Further references to UGT–CNT clashes at the July 1937 PSOE national committee, Marcen's intervention, stenog. record, p. 93.

36 R. Lamoneda, unification report, PSOE national committee meeting, July 1937, stenog. record, p. 125; also his 'notas del grupo parlamentario', A R L F–166–40.

37 *Guerra y revolución* (III), p. 54.

38 M. Tuñón de Lara, 'El significado político del Frente Popular', p. 126.

39 Cf. Spanish socialists to their communist counterparts in January 1935: 'The Communist International is interested in fostering closer relations with socialist parties, not because they may be rightist or leftist, but because they control the masses.' PCE archive, microfilm, XIV, 181, p. 5.

40 Minutes of ASM interim committee, 25 March 1937, AHM.

41 J. Martínez Amutio, *Chantaje a un pueblo* (Madrid, 1974), p. 211.

42 R. Llopis, *Spartacus*, 1 October 1937, p. 5.

43 So the Almansa (Albacete province) socialist group informed Lamoneda, group's correspondence, AHM. Also *Vida Obrera* – 'órgano de unificación marxista' (Albacete), August 1937.

44 S. Juliá, *La Izquierda*, pp. 173–84, esp. pp. 181–2.

45 Ramón Lamoneda, July 1937 PSOE national committee meeting, stenog. record, pp. 123–4; also Llaneza and Rafael Henche's interventions, pp. 120 and 130 respectively. Also, *Guerra y revolución* (III), pp. 51–2.

46 See below, chapter 6.

47 Editorial *El Socialista*, 25 February 1937; also *El Socialista*, 30 December 1937.

48 His view is reinforced by report of an extraordinary plenary session of the PSOE's Valencian federation, 10–11 July 1937, A H–2–7.

49 For Ecija, Lamoneda, stenog. record, July 1937 national committee meeting; chapter 2 above, p. 39 n. 20. P. Preston, *CSCW*, p. 198; G. Morón, *Política*, pp. 63–4.

50 Minutes of youth report, PSOE national committee meeting, Valencia,

July 1937, stenog. record, p. 84. Also, Lamoneda's comments in speech at JSU meeting, Monumental Cinema (Madrid), 27 June 1937, *Cuatro discursos sobre la unidad*, p. 4.

51 For UGT–CNT internecine warfare in Valencia, Málaga and Barcelona, G. Jackson, *The Spanish Republic and the Civil War*, p. 285. For Cullera incidents, A. Bosch Sánchez, *Ugetistas y libertarios: (guerra civil y revolución en el país valenciano 1936–1939)* (Valencia, 1983), pp. 111, 122; also UGT executive minutes for 1 October 1936, 12 January, 4 February 1937.

52 Henche, July 1937 national committee meeting, stenog. record, pp. 130–4.

53 B. Bolloten, *The Spanish Revolution*, pp. 350–2.

54 A. Llaneza, stenog. record, pp. 134–6. Sánchez Román symbolised the extreme conservative wing of Spanish republicanism.

55 Almería, provincial correspondence, 1938. Although the SIM was PCE-controlled in many areas – such as Almería – this was not the case everywhere. In Madrid, for example, the PCE was not in control, UGT minutes, 29 December, 1938.

56 Henche, PSOE national committee, July 1937, stenog. record, p. 131.

5 The socialist left: crisis and collapse

1 J. Peirats, *Los anarquistas en la crisis política española*, pp. 257–62; Amaro del Rosal, *Historia de la UGT* (II), p. 735. For the *políticos'* attempt at orienting the CNT and the organisation's internal crisis during the war, César M. Lorenzo, *Los anarquistas españoles y el poder* (Paris, 1972).

2 C. M. Lorenzo, *Los anarquistas españoles*, p. 229, quoting from the FAI's peninsular plenum, Valencia, July 1937.

3 See above chapter 3, p. 64 n. 45 and chapter 4, p. 82 n. 51.

4 See J. Peirats, *La CNT en la revolución española*, 3 vols. (Paris, 1971) (I), pp. 233–4, (II), p. 57.

5 Amaro del Rosal, *Historia de la UGT* (II), p. 603. For UGT–CNT friction, B. Bolloten, *The Spanish Revolution*, p. 184 (n. 16).

6 E.g. letter from president of Oficios Varios to PSOE national executive, 15 June 1937, provincial correspondence, Zaragoza, AHM. Also Pascual Tomás' speech celebrating 50th anniversary of PSOE, August 1938.

7 S. Juliá, 'Partido contra sindicato', pp. 336–45.

8 See above chapter 4, p. 78 n. 36.

9 S. Juliá, 'De la división orgánica al gobierno de unidad nacional', p. 236.

10 Prieto's speech, Egea de los Caballeros (Aragón), repr. in I. Prieto, *Discursos fundamentales*, pp. 274–84.

11 Largo Caballero to the Socialist Youth International, 8 May 1939, exile correspondence of the Secretariado Juvenil, AHM.

12 Letter to Tillett in B. Bolloten, *The Spanish Revolution*, p. 118; interview with Reichmann, Vidarte, *Todos* (II), p. 613.

13 F. Urales (pseud.) was the father of Federica Montseny, CNT Minister of Health and Social Security in Largo's second cabinet. His first letter to Largo in *Adelante*, 12 January 1937, the second plus Largo's reply in *El Socialista*, 12 February 1937.

14 Pascual Tomás' interview with Largo, 17 December 1936, UGT minutes.

15 For southern collectivisation, Luis González Garrido, *Colectividades agrarias en Andalucía: Jaén (1931–1939)* (Madrid, 1979), *passim*; Grandizo Munis, *Jalones de derrota, promesa de victoria* (Mexico, 1948, edn used, Madrid, 1977), pp. 414, 423, 428–31.

16 F. Largo Caballero, *Notas históricas*. For socialist collectives, see below, chapter 10, pp. 198–210.

17 B. Bolloten, *The Spanish Revolution*, pp. 330–2; Largo Caballero, *Mis recuerdos*, pp. 211–12; L. Araquistain, 'El comunismo y la guerra de España' in *Sobre la guerra*, p. 216; (del Vayo's German expertise was unnecessary as Rosenberg and Largo could communicate in French). J. Martínez Amutio, *Chantaje a un pueblo*, p. 215; A. Vélez (Aguirre), *Informaciones*, 11, 14 November 1977.

18 Stalin's first letter in *Guerra y revolución* (II), pp. 101–3, also in Vidarte, *Todos* (II), pp. 652–4. The second letter (dated 4 February) was delivered by hand by Marcelino Pascua, the Republic's ambassador in Moscow, *El Socialista*, 12 February 1937, also L. Araquistain, *Sobre la guerra*, p. 240.

19 R. Llopis, *Spartacus*, 1 October 1937, pp. 6–7; *El Socialista*, 14 February 1937; B. Bolloten, *The Spanish Revolution*, p. 341.

20 B. Bolloten, *The Spanish Revolution*, pp. 327–9, 338–40; J. Alvarez del Vayo, *Freedom's Battle* (London and New York, 1940).

21 A. Vélez, *Informaciones*, 9, 14 November 1977. Prieto to Araquistain, 13 February 1953, LA/AHN, leg. 36 no. 252. For a critical view of Asensio as a capable opportunist, J. Gorkín, *Caníbales políticos*, p. 215. Later on in the war and afterwards Asensio was associated with Negrín's camp, Martínez Amutio, *Chantaje a un pueblo*, p. 160; also Asensio's article defending the SERE, *España Libre*, 26 April 1940.

22 R. Llopis to Araquistain, 20 February 1937, leg. 33/LL 8a; J. Zugazagoitia, *Guerra y vicisitudes*, p. 241; for the Rosenberg incident, B. Bolloten, *The Spanish Revolution*, pp. 328–9; F. Largo Caballero, *Mis recuerdos*, p. 181; S. Juliá, 'Partido contra sindicato', p. 335. Carlos de Baraibar's capabilities would also be subjected to insidious press speculation as part of the campaign. For de Baraibar's experience of the PCE thereafter, B. Bolloten, *The Spanish Revolution*, pp. 350–2.

23 Julio Mateu, *La obra de la Federación Provincial Campesina* (Barcelona, 1937).

24 First issue of *Adelante* appeared 2 February 1937. The opening editorial criticised the 'partisan politics' of others.

25 Llopis to Araquistain, 20 February 1937, LA/AHN. Del Vayo was expelled from the PSOE at the end of the war, ASM *expediente*, March 1939. Also B. Bolloten, *The Spanish Revolution*, pp. 137 (and n. 3), 354–5.

26 Interviews reported in *El Socialista*, 27 February 1937; Aguirre to Araquistain, 28 February 1937; R. Llopis in *Spartacus*, 1 October 1937, pp. 6–7.

27 Largo Caballero, 'Ante el panorama político y social de España', *Claridad*, 27 February 1937; Vidarte, *Todos* (II), p. 662.

28 M. Azaña, *Obras* (IV), pp. 591–2.

29 Discussion at the July 1937 PSOE national committee meeting, stenog. record, p. 97; B. Bolloten, *The Spanish Revolution*, p. 432.

30 G. Brenan, *The Spanish Labyrinth* (Cambridge, 1943, edn used, Cambridge 1976), pp. 305, 313; S. Juliá, 'Partido contra sindicato', p. 336.

31 N.I.C. decision, 8 March 1937, *Guerra y revolución* (II), p. 233.

32 R. Llopis to Araquistain, 4 March 1937, LA/AHN.

33 The campaign against the 'politicisation' of the unions was waged across a variety of articles in the socialist press January–May 1937. Cf. 'Neither a trade union organisation without an ideological motor nor a Socialist Party without its union base.' Lamoneda's circular to the socialist sections, *El Socialista*, 28 March 1937. For PCE's line, *Guerra y revolución* (III), pp. 60–1.

34 The draft cabinet proposals in letter from Llopis to Araquistain, LA/AHN, leg. 33/LL 6a. This is the source of the ministerial allocations described in the following section.

35 B. Bolloten, *The Spanish Revolution*, p. 188.

36 The other reformist socialist minister suggested was Anastasio de Gracia (Labour).

37 I.R. had two ministers – Supply and one without portfolio. U.R. held Communications.

38 Vidarte, *Todos* (II), p. 678.

39 Negrín's speech to the Cortes, 30 September 1938, *El Presidente del Consejo de Ministros del Gobierno de Unidad habla para todo el pueblo español* (Valencia, 1938), p. 4.

40 *Ibid.* and cf. his view, expressed via his subordinate in the finance ministry, Jerónimo Bugeda, 'the war is over for us the day the last gold-peseta is spent'. Bugeda's economic report, PSOE national committee, Valencia, July 1937, stenog. record, pp. 46–7; Mariano Ansó, *Yo fui ministro de Negrín* (Barcelona, 1976), p. 151; *Epistolario Prieto y Negrín* (Paris, 1939), p. 40.

41 Bolloten, *The Spanish Revolution*, p. 138; R. Lamoneda, 'Circular a los militantes del PSOE', p. 227; Vidarte, *Todos* (I), pp. 480–2. Otero served later as Negrín's under-secretary of armaments, José Fernández Castro, *Alejandro Otero: el médico y el político* (Madrid, 1981), p. 108.

42 E.g., J. Gorkín, *España, primer ensayo de democracia popular* (Buenos Aires, 1961), p. 109; A. Vélez, *Informaciones*, 16 November 1977.

43 Formed in July 1936 out of four smaller parties (USC, the Catalan

sections of the Socialist and Communist Parties and the Partit Catalá Proletaria), and termed the United Socialist Party of Cataluña, it was really the Catalan equivalent of the PCE, see Bolloten, *The Spanish Revolution*, pp. 376–8.

44 For the complex political situation in Cataluña before and during the May Days, Bolloten, *The Spanish Revolution*, pp. 368–430. Also, S. Juliá, 'Partido contra sindicato', p. 342.

45 There is a vast bibliography on the 'revolution versus war' debate. For a reappraisal of the debate and its implications, R. Fraser, 'Reconsidering the Spanish Civil War', *New Left Review*, no. 129, September–October 1981, 35–49. For a distinctive focus on the political conflict in the Republican zone, J. Aróstegui, 'La República en guerra y el problema del poder', *Studia Histórica*, vol. 3, no. 4, 1985, 7–19; also vol. 2 of *Anales de Historia* which is devoted to 'Socialismo y Guerra Civil'.

46 Azaña, *Obras* (IV), pp. 591–3.

47 Bolloten, *The Spanish Revolution*, pp. 433–4; *Guerra y revolución* (III), pp. 79–80.

48 'Caballero always claimed to have been "kicked out by the Communists", which was in part true, since everyone kicked him out, from Azaña to Martínez Barrio.' R. Lamoneda, 'el secreto del anticomunismo', p. 6.

49 Vidarte, *Todos* (II), pp. 665–6.

50 Bolloten, *The Spanish Revolution*, pp. 435–7 and notes for details of the operation and estimations of its feasibility.

51 *Guerra y revolución* (III), pp. 80–1.

52 Full cabinet list, *Guerra y revolución* (III), p. 81. I.R. held two ministries, Public Works and Propaganda; U.R. had one, Communications/Merchant Navy.

53 Vidarte, *Todos* (II), p. 665.

54 *Ibid.*, pp. 665–6; *Guerra y revolución* (III), p. 82 for PSOE's note in *El Socialista*, 18 May 1937. In general, and in spite of the AHM, it is difficult to shed new light on the May crisis *directly*. For the PSOE executive's unilluminating account of its role, July 1937 PSOE national committee, Valencia, stenog. record, pp. 88–91.

55 For PCE's response to Largo's draft cabinet, its note, 17 May 1937 repr. in *Guerra y revolución* (III), pp. 81–2, also p. 83.

56 CNT's communiqué, *Guerra y revolución* (III), pp. 82–3; also J. Peirats *La CNT en la revolución española* (II), pp. 182–3 and C. M. Lorenzo, *Los anarquistas españoles*, p. 220.

57 UGT minutes, 13 May 1937.

58 UGT minutes, 15 May 1937, p. 90.

59 UGT minutes, 13 May 1937.

60 UGT minutes, May 1937, p. 91(b) italics mine.

61 Vidarte, *Todos* (II), pp. 662–3, 678–9.

62 An example of such a partisan interpretation of the May crisis in R. Llopis, 'Las etapas de la victoria', *Spartacus*, 1 October 1937, pp. 4–7.

63 Lamoneda, PSOE national committee, July 1937, stenog. record, p. 83.

6 Ramón Lamoneda confronts the PSOE left

1 Lamoneda defends his own policies in *Adelante*, 5 February 1938. On the need for iron discipline, Elche speech (Alicante), 30 October 1938, *Avance* (Alicante) 6 November 1938. Also speeches, Cine Monumental, (Madrid) 27 June 1937, p. 9; Teatro Principal (Valencia) 8 July 1937, pp. 22–3; Cine Bilbao (Madrid), 1 August 1937 pp. 26–7, 30, 34–5.
2 Araquistain to R. González Peña, 15 July 1939, LA/AHN, leg. 29.
3 G. Morón, *Política*, p. 109.
4 R. Lamoneda's speech in Baza (Granada), *La Correspondencia de Valencia*, 24 March 1937; also Lamoneda's interview in *Le Peuple* (Brussels) 1 January 1938, PCE, microfilm xix, 232.
5 Cf. Bugeda's economic report to July 1937 PSOE national committee.
6 Lamoneda, *Glosa de los acuerdos del Comité Nacional del PSOE* (Madrid, 1938) pp. 15–16.
7 Some examples, *El Socialista*, 13 January, 2, 9 February 1937 for extracts from Lamoneda's speeches in Republican south. Also speech in Cine Bilbao (Madrid), 1 August 1937, and 26 September 1937 in Baza (Granada), both in *Cuatro discursos sobre la unidad*, pp. 33–5 and 46 respectively. Also, *Glosa de los acuerdos del C.N. del PSOE*, pp. 5–6.
8 See below, chapter 9.
9 Minutes of meetings, *Memoria de la actuación de las federaciones provinciales socialistas* (Ediciones Meabe, Valencia, 1937).
10 R. Henche, PSOE national committee meeting, July 1937, stenog. record, p. 69.
11 Provincial attendance varied from meeting to meeting (18 May to 27 July), details, *Memoria de la actuación*, pp. 4–5, 11, 21, 32.
12 *Memoria de la actuación*, p. 8.
13 M. Contreras, *El PSOE en la II República*, pp. 161, 165.
14 *Memoria de la actuación*, pp. 23–4.
15 *Memoria de la actuación*, p. 22.
16 Socialist-led provincial executive there included Gregori (general secretary), Juan Tundidor (organisation), Enrique Cerezo (administration) and Salvador Martínez Dasi (culture), *El Socialista*, 4 January 1937.
17 The '*rincones* Largo Caballero', (literally 'corners') – details of dissident youth activity here from Lamoneda's youth report to PSOE national committee, July 1937, stenog. record, pp. 112–22. Also AH–24–4.
18 Henche (New Castile), Solar (Old Castile), Azorín (Andalucía), Llaneza (Asturias/Léon), Marcén (Aragón), Ferretjans (Balearics), Amutio (Valencia). This calculation omits Huerta (País Vasco), who was still a sub. in 1937, and N. Vázquez who was absent.
19 For a very subjective account, with little resemblance to the stenog. record, J. Martínez Amutio, *Chantaje a un pueblo*, pp. 66–71.
20 R. Lamoneda, stenog. record, p. 26.

21 Celebrations for PSOE's 50th anniversary scheduled for 22–28 August – the date of the party's foundation being taken not as 1879, but as 1888, the year of the first party congress. *Adelante*, 27 July 1938; *El Socialista*, 25 August 1938.

22 A. de Gracia's letter of resignation, 20 February 1936, UGT minutes; S. Juliá, *La izquierda*, p. 92.

23 Vidarte, *Todos* (I) p. 482, (II) p. 620.

24 Youth report, July 1937 stenog. record. De Gracia's opposition, pp. 112–22.

25 *El Socialista*, 19 February 1937. Also, Serrano Poncela, 'Algunos datos estadísticos', youth sec. corresp., AHM, p. 4 (where Cuesta is wrongly listed as a socialist).

26 S. Carrillo, *Somos la organización de la juventud* (Valencia 1937).

27 G. Morón, *Política*, p. 166; Vidarte, *Todos* (I) p. 482.

28 De Gracia's opposition to Prieto's suggestion of socialist–communist fusion, Vidarte, *Todos* (II), p. 621.

29 Bugeda's speech, *El Socialista* (Madrid), 20–1 July 1937, J.S. Vidarte, *Todos* (II), p. 622.

30 PSOE executive correspondence with de Gracia, July–October 1937, AH–62–18.

31 R. Lamoneda, 16 October 1938, *Glosa de los acuerdos del C.N. del PSOE*, pp. 18–21 (p. 18); also *Cuatro discursos sobre la unidad*.

32 'El PSOE. Su moral', *Avance* 7 August 1938.

33 R. Lamoneda, *Avance*, 4 July 1938, '¿Cuál es el deber de los Socialistas?', '. . . we are a serious party and we know that one or two years cannot constitute a historical tradition'.

34 G. Morón, *Política*, p. 79.

35 AHM correspondence, Madrid province – Fuencarral's socialist group and the national executive, 8, 16 September 1936; *El Socialista*, 6 March 1937; closing speeches at August 1937 Ciudad Real provincial PSOE congress, AH–8–8.

36 'Socialistas conscientes', *Adelante*, 26 January 1938; 'Nuestro Partido, organización y orientación', *Avance* 17 September 1938.

37 The security argument in Ciudad Real congress, August 1937, closing speeches, p. 75; also, Molina Conejero to Círculo Socialista de Mestalla (Valencia), *Adelante* 5 April 1938 and M. Cordero, *Avance* (Ciudad Real) 11 June 1938.

38 FNTT delegates, Badajoz provincial secretariat, arguing that post-18 July affiliates should have neither the right to intervene nor to vote' ('ni voz ni voto'), *La Correspondencia de Valencia*, 6 April 1938.

39 Almería, report on the province, March 1938, AH–13–63, p. 80. For 'actions not words philosophy', as one of many examples see closing speeches, August 1937 PSOE provincial socialist congress, Ciudad Real, AH–8–8, pp. 68, 80; cf. also 'We have never plastered the insignia of our Party over walls – but let those who have seen us act bear witness for us.' *Avance*, 10 June 1938.

40 Meeting of 19 July, *Memoria de la actuación*, pp. 29, 33; circular from Valencian socialist federation, with congress agenda, 20 July 1937, in Játiva group correspondence (Valencia), AHM.

41 Full agenda, *Memoria de la actuación*, pp. 31–2.

42 R. González Peña's letter and the possession order, *Memoria de la actuación*, p. 35.

43 F. Largo Caballero, *La UGT y la guerra*. p. 25. Cf. also, J. Martínez Amutio, *Chantaje a un pueblo*, pp. 225–7.

44 Federación Socialista Valenciana – circulares/manifiestos 1936–8,), pp. 674–5.

45 Bracketed are the wartime locations of the federations' HQs.

46 Jaén provincial correspondence, 8, 13 July 1937, AH–10–47.

47 *El Socialista*, 6, 8 August 1937.

48 His letter to González Peña, 5 October 1937, AH–25–2.

49 15–17 August 1937, AH–13–37 (Badajoz correspondence).

50 The reference is to UGT national committee meeting of 28 May 1937, see below, chapter 9, pp. 169–70.

51 Unification details in Jaén provincial correspondence, August 1937. Also, L. Garrido González, *Colectividades agrarias en Andalucía: Jaén (1931– 1939)*, (Madrid, 1979), pp. 78–81.

52 *El Socialista*, 21 August 1937; Jaén provincial correspondence, 23 August 1937.

53 Correspondence, April–June 1938, AH–14–12.

54 *El Socialista*, 2 November 1937; Ranchal's criticism in Amutio, *Chantaje a un pueblo*, p. 69.

55 R. Henche, PSOE national committee, July 1937, stenog. record, pp. 78–9.

56 Under-secretary, September 1936–May 1937, Vidarte, *Todos* (II), pp. 674–5.

57 Letter, signed by Henche and Cuevas, to *El Socialista*, 12 June 1937, Madrid correspondence, 1936–8, AH–17–25.

58 See chapter 9 below.

7 **The purge of the party left and the growing crisis in the reformist camp**

1 PSOE national committee meeting, July 1937, stenog. record, pp. 82–3.

2 M. Tuñón de Lara, 'El socialismo español en la guerra civil', *Anales de Historia* (1) (Madrid, 1986), p. 284; also minutes of PSOE parliamentary party, AH–18–7.

3 The other proposers of the motion were: Sapiña, José Prat, García Cubertoret, Saiz, Ruiz Lecina, Aliseda, Longueira, Muñoz de Zafra, Alvarez Resano, Pasagli, Alvarez Angulo, Lorenzo, Labín and three more illegible signatures.

4 Full text of proposal in AH–18–17 (minutes of PSOE parliamentary party 1936–9). The italics are mine. The proposal accorded with PSOE

regulations, see M. Contreras, *El PSOE en la II República*, pp. 172–3, 306.

5 See below chapter 9.
6 PSOE list of socialist minority (dated January 1939), compiled by R. Lamoneda, general correspondence, AH–18–10. But M. Contreras, *El PSOE en la II República*, p. 179, lists only ninety-two seats obtained by the PSOE in February 1936.
7 Almagro (Granada), Bilbao (Huelva), Blanco (Córdoba), Campos (Cádiz), Carrillo (Córdoba), Castro (Córdoba), Fernández Ballesteros (Seville), García Muñoz (Alicante), Guerrero (Murcia), Peris (Jaén), Pradal (Almería), Romero Solano (Cáceres), Sosa (Badajoz), Tomás (Murcia), Zabalza (Badajoz), Cerezo and Escandell (Valencia), Ganga and Villalta (Alicante). For the enduring nature of the *Caballeristas'* support in the Republican south, and especially in the FNTT, see below, chapter 10.
8 M. Azaña, *Obras* (IV), p. 746; Mª R. Ripollés Serrano, 'Francisco Largo Caballero 1869–1946. Biografía política de un socialista español' (unpublished doctoral thesis, Facultad de Derecho, University of Valencia, 1979), FPI, Madrid, p. 868.
9 Minutes of the ASM executive committee, 7, 8 August 1937. *El Socialista* 10 August, reports plenary meeting of the ASM committee, attended by Largo, De Francisco, Llopis, Díaz Alor, Pascual Tomás, Wenceslao Carrillo, Luis Araquistain, Carlos Hernández Zancajo and apologies from Ricardo Zabalza.
10 Amaro del Rosal, *Historia de la UGT* (II), pp. 648, 710–11; *El Socialista* editorials 9, 10 September 1937.
11 'La ASM enjuicia la política del PCE', ASM circulars 1935–7, AH–16–53 (n.d., but post-August 1937).
12 *El Socialista*, 9, 10 September 1937.
13 Lamoneda, PSOE national committee, July 1937, stenog. record, p. 83.
14 For Largo's meetings, Ripollés Serrano, 'Francisco Largo Caballero', p. 867; also *El Socialista*, 10 August 1937.
15 Largo Caballero was otherwise engaged on 1 October, under siege inside UGT HQ. M. Koltsov, *Diario de la guerra española*, p. 509; also chapter 9 below.
16 Largo Caballero, *Notas históricas*, pp. 1272–1300. Galarza's comment, 'Ir a la C.E. a pedir ¿qué? ¿Armonía? Ni nos la dan, ni nos interesa'.
17 J. Gorkín, *Caníbales políticos*, p. 168; Ripollés Serrano, 'Francisco Largo Caballero', p. 869; Bolloten to Araquistain, 5 July 1947, LA/AHN, leg. 25, no. B162.
18 Llopis to Araquistain, 8 August 1939, 16 March 1940 leg. 23/no. 20.
19 For these restrictions, see details of Perelló incident, below, chapter 9, pp. 192–93.
20 Minutes of parliamentary party, 14 January 1938, AH–18–8.
21 Largo Caballero, *Notas históricas*, pp. 1284–1300.
22 Discussion of reports on international situation presented by Jiménez

de Asúa and Azorín at PSOE national committee meeting, July 1937, stenog. record, pp. 33–45.

23 Prieto's interview with H. Dubois, *El Socialista*, 1 September 1937; *El Socialista*, 11 September 1937.

24 Vidarte, *Todos* (ii) pp. 620–1; B. Bolloten, *The Spanish Revolution*. p. 364, G. Morón, *Política*. p. 107, C. Lorenzo, *Los anarquistas españoles*, p. 313 n. 2.

25 Letter to Felipe García, n.d. but 1939 post-war, corresp. de M. Cordero, A H–25–6. Also, M. Albar's reference to Prieto's stillborn suggestion, at the August 1938 PSOE national committee meeting, *El Socialista* (Barcelona), 10 August 1938, p. 3; R. Lamoneda, 'El secreto del anticomunismo', ARLF, FPI, p. 6.

26 Vidarte, *Todos* (ii), p. 621. The reference to Largo is to his proposal in the spring of 1936.

27 Vidarte, *Todos* (ii) p. 622.

28 Vidarte, *Todos* (i) p. 538; see also R. Llopis to L. Araquistain, 24 April 1956, leg. 33, no. 84; Amutio, *Chantaje a un pueblo*, pp. 64, 107.

29 L. Araquistain to Vidarte, *Todos* (ii), p. 593. Cf. Lamoneda, 'Prieto, the master of ceremonies, welcoming Rosenberg, playing up to him . . .' Lamoneda 'El secreto del anticomunismo'.

30 Vidarte, *Todos* (ii), pp. 593, 623, 821, 843; G. Morón, *Política*, pp. 106–7; B. Bolloten, *The Spanish Revolution*, p. 364.

31 Vidarte, *Todos* (ii) pp. 335–6, 372–7.

32 Cf. Prieto's letter to the PSOE executive, 30 March 1938, CE/CN correspondence, A H–23–1, referring to his 'quebranto' (demoralisation), over the loss of the north.

33 José Antonio Aguirre, *Informe del Presidente Aguirre al gobierno de la República sobre los hechos que determinaron el derrumbamiento del frente del Norte* (Bilbao, 1978), pp. 353–62.

34 Irujo to Prieto, 1, 4 April 1937.

35 Both Prieto's and Irujo's resignations rejected by Negrín, 21 June 1937, *Informe del Presidente Aguirre*, p. 177. See also unsigned, undated report, *Las causas de la pérdida de Bilbao: unos datos olvidados en la nota del ministro de defensa*, Araquistain's correspondence, leg. 71, 25B (almost certainly written by Araquistain himself). This is critical of Prieto's self-defence published in *El Socialista*, 30 October 1937. Also letter from Araquistain to González Peña, 15 July 1939, leg. 29.

36 L. Romero Solano, *Vísperas de la guerra de España*, p. 133. For Prieto's problematic impulsiveness. R. Llopis to L. Araquistain, LA/AHN, 7 August 1953.

37 Internal correspondence executive/national committee 1936/9, 7 October 1937, A H–23–1.

38 Lamoneda, 'El secreto del anticomunismo'. Prieto was the 'past master of opportunism and sophistry'.

39 R. Lamoneda, 'Circular a los militantes del PSOE' in *Posiciones políticas*, p. 227; G. Morón, *Política*, pp. 89–92; cf. also Togliatti, 'Problemas del

CC del PCE', *Escritos sobre la guerra de España* (Barcelona, 1980) p. 156.
40 I. Prieto, *Cómo y por qué salí del Ministerio de Defensa Nacional* (Mexico, 1940), pp. 56–60; G. Morón, *Política*, pp. 93–100, 100–4.
41 J. Gorkín, *Caníbales políticos*, pp. 220–2.
42 R. Lamoneda, 'Circular a los militantes del PSOE', p. 229; G. Morón, *Política*, p. 107.
43 See chapter 9 below.
44 J. Gorkín, *Caníbales políticos*, p. 65.
45 *España, primer ensayo*, p. 71.
46 *Epistolario Prieto y Negrín*, pp. 26–8, 67–8; G. Morón, *Política*, pp. 83, 86.
47 PCE report for March 1938, microfilm xx, 238, p. 5; Vidarte, *Todos*, (ii), pp. 820–2; Azaña's desire for mediation, P. Togliatti, *Escritos*, pp. 153–4, 192–4; for fears about Republican capitulation, pp. 156, 190–1. Prieto's campaign to involve Britain in mediation, Vidarte, *Todos* (ii), pp. 820–1, 854. His campaign against the PCE's influence in the army, see B. Bolloten, *The Spanish Revolution*, pp. 463–4 and *Guerra y revolución* (iv), pp. 68–72.
48 The received wisdom most notably in B. Bolloten, *The Spanish Revolution*. For the PCE's doubts about Negrín, Togliatti, *Escritos*, pp. 154–5.
49 For the PCE's fear of 'defeatism', P. Togliatti, *Escritos*, p. 157; J. Estruch, *Historia del PCE (1920–1939)* (i) (Barcelona, 1978), pp. 112–14.
50 For Prieto's campaign, B. Bolloten, *The Spanish Revolution*, 463–4; J. Hernández, *Yo fui un ministro de Stalin* (Mexico, 1953); *Guerra y revolución en España* (iv), pp. 68–72. J. Hernández's two articles criticising Prieto's defeatism, published March under pseud. Juan Ventura, see J. Zugazagoitia, *Guerra y vicisitudes*, p. 393; Vidarte, *Todos* (ii), pp. 843, 847–8. Prieto, *Cómo y por qué*, pp. 48–50 and *Epistolario*, pp. 72–9.
51 I. Prieto, *Cómo y por qué*, p. 30.
52 For the demonstration of 16 March, B. Bolloten, *The Spanish Revolution*. p. 467–8; P. Togliatti, *Escritos*, p. 193; J. Hernández, *Yo fui un ministro de Stalin*, p. 161; I. Prieto, *Epistolario*. pp. 105–8; J. Zugazagoitia, *Guerra y vicisitudes*, pp. 389–90.
53 Negrín's remarks to José Prat in J. Zugazagoitia, *Guerra y vicisitudes*, pp. 395–6.
54 Zugazagoitia's comments to Negrín: 'Don Juan let's call a spade a spade. At the front they are assassinating socialists because they have refused to join the Communist Party'; for Zugazagoitia's disillusion in the *secretaría general* of the defence ministry, letter to PSOE executive, 19 December 1938, Prieto, *Epistolario*, p. 100; Vidarte, *Todos* (ii), pp. 854–5; I. Prieto in *Cómo y por qué*, pp. 47–8.
55 Vidarte *Todos* (ii), p. 849; M. Tuñón de Lara, 'El socialismo español en la Guerra Civil', p. 286.
56 Prieto's interview with Horacio Prieto, Segundo Blanco and Galo Diez, I. Prieto, *Como y por qué*, pp. 65–6; Vidarte, *Todos* (ii), pp. 849–50; J. Zugazagoitia, *Guerra y vicisitudes*, p. 401; P. Togliatti, *Escritos*, p. 195.

57 Prieto himself admits he told Negrín to replace him if need be, *Cómo y por qué*, p. 46; also R. Lamoneda, 'Circular a los militantes del PSOE', p. 228; J. Zugazagoitia, *Guerra y vicisitudes*, pp. 396, 402–3; Vidarte, *Todos* (II), p. 849; *Epistolario*, p. 8.

58 *Ibid.* p. 8.

59 *Ibid.* p. 47.

60 Full cabinet in *El Socialista*, 6 Apr. 1938, repr. in *Guerra y revolución* (IV), p. 77. The list as follows: premiership and defence (Juan Negrín); interior (Paulino Gómez Sáez) (PSOE); foreign ministry (Julio Alvarez del Vayo) (PSOE); justice (Ramón González Peña) (PSOE/UGT); labour and social security (Jaime Ayguadé) (Esquerra); education and health (Segundo Blanco) (CNT); communications and transport (Bernardo Giner de los Ríos) (Unión Republicana); public works (Antonio Velao) (Izquierda Republicana); agriculture (Vicente Uribe) (PCE); finance and economy (Francisco Méndez Aspe) (Izquierda Republicana); ministers without portfolio (José Giral) (Izquierda Republicana) (M. Irujo) (PNV). PSOE executive's declaration of support for Negrín's new government in *El Socialista* (Madrid), 7 April 1938, repr. *Guerra y revolución* (IV) p. 137.

61 Vidarte, *Todos* (II), p. 670.

62 J. Zugazagoitia, *Guerra y vicisitudes*, pp. 290–5; for Nin see also, Vidarte, *Todos* (II), pp. 731–3.

63 J. Zugazagoitia, *Guerra y vicisitudes*, pp. 404–5; Vidarte, *Todos* (II), p. 829. Paulino Gómez had acted as Zugazagoitia's special envoy in Barcelona, prior to the transfer there of the Republican government in October 1937, Vidarte, *Todos* (II), p. 681.

64 The FAI considered the level of ministerial representation to be deeply humiliating. But a month later they ratified Negrín's Thirteen Points along with the CNT.

65 For a detailed analysis of developments in the UGT and CNT, see below, chapter 9.

66 Amaro del Rosal, *Historia de la UGT* (II), pp. 666–78; for the predominance of unions over parties in 1930s Spain, S. Juliá, 'The origins and nature of the Spanish Popular Front' in Alexander & Graham, *The French and Spanish Popular Fronts*. For the battle in the CNT, C.M. Lorenzo, *Los anarquistas españoles*. For union pact, J. Peirats, *La CNT en la revolución española* (III), pp. 36–41.

67 Negrín, *Epistolario*, p. 8 and Vidarte, *Todos* (II), p. 849, for Negrín's intention to retain Prieto in his cabinet. Prieto refers to Negrín's intention, suggested via Zugazagoitia, to split Public Works and Railways between him and Giner de los Ríos, *Cómo y por qué*, p. 59; Vidarte *Todos* (II), p. 854; also *Guerra y revolución* (IV), p. 75; B. Bolloten, *The Spanish Revolution*. pp. 467–8.

68 For Prieto's 'Nota de despedida', see *El Socialista*, 7 April 1938; R. Lamoneda, 'Circular a los militantes del PSOE', p. 227.

69 As G. Morón notes, *Política*, p. 121; also Vidarte, *Todos* (II), p. 849.

70 Prieto's speech published as *Cómo y por qué*.
71 Correspondence published as the *Epistolario*, cited above.
72 For views of Prieto's performance, J. Zugazagoitia, *Guerra y vicisitudes*, p. 414; G. Morón, *Política*, pp. 118–21; Vidarte, *Todos* (ii), p. 858. For August 1938 PSOE national committee meeting, *Guerra y revolución* (iv), p. 136; PSOE executive minutes 1932–9, A H–20–4 and Vidarte, *Todos* (ii), pp. 844–52.
73 Negrín to Prieto, 23 June 1939, *Epistolario* pp. 23–5; J. Zugazagoitia, *Guerra y vicisitudes*, pp. 395–6; *Guerra y revolución* (iv), pp. 74–5. Prieto's response, *Epistolario* and *Cómo y por qué*, pp. 69–70. Cf. also Zugazagoitia, *Guerra y vicisitudes*, pp. 402–3.
74 Vidarte, *Todos* (ii) pp. 843, 858.
75 R. Lamoneda, 'Circular a los militantes del PSOE', p. 230; G. Morón, *Política*, pp. 119–20; *Guerra y revolución* (iv), p. 136.
76 *El Socialista*, 11 October 1938.
77 Cf. I. Prieto, *Discursos en América* (Mexico, 1944), p. 172.
78 G. Morón, *Política*, p. 120; cf. also Prieto's letters to the PSOE executive, 18, 28 April 1938, executive/national committee correspondence, A H–23–1.
79 Rafael Henche and Ramón Lamoneda attended the Belgian congress, 4 June 1938, A H–23–1, also Prieto, *Epistolario*, p. 11; *Guerra y revolución* (iv), p. 108; executive minutes, 6 October 1938, A H–20–4; also minutes for 18 October 1938, A H–23–1.
80 R. Lamoneda, 'El secreto del anticomunismo'; cf. G. Morón, *Política*, p. 55, 'In the cold light of day, Prieto was just another republican in a Republic of republicans who were as lavish with words as they were short on action.'
81 The meeting's agenda, A H–24–12; also *Guerra y revolución* (iv) pp. 37–9; for the approval of unity of action, Vidarte, *Todos* (ii), p. 858; *El Socialista*, 12 August 1938 (Madrid). For reports of the sessions, *Avance* (Ciudad Real) 10, 11, 12 August 1938.
82 P. Togliatti, *Escritos*, pp. 245, 274.
83 Vidarte, *Todos* (ii), p. 858; L. Prieto, *Epistolario*, p. 92.
84 PCE archive, microfilms, xvii (214), xx (238). For proof of this in parliamentary party, M. Tuñón de Lara, 'El socialismo español en la Guerra Civil', p. 288. For anti-communist and anti-Lamoneda feeling rife among socialists in the centre–south zone, provincial socialist correspondence 1937–8, for Albacete, Ciudad Real, Toledo; also *Claridad* correspondence (23 September 1938), A H–25–20.
85 Letters from the PSOE executive, 13 August A H–8–13 and 25 May, A H–7–21 1938, fuelled the provinces' alienation.
86 For the run-up to Casado, *Todos* (ii), p. 843. For socialist rebellion, see below chapter 8; also Tuñón de Lara, 'El socialismo español en la Guerra Civil', pp. 286–7. For the Casado coup, see below, chapter 11.
87 Constitution of national committee in Lamoneda's list, July 1938, A H–24–13.

88 Vidarte, *Todos* (II), p. 858.
89 This conflict articulated by various socialists, including R. González Peña, PSOE executive meeting, 15 November 1938, AH–20–5.

8 The atomisation of reformist socialism

1 Cf. S. Juliá, 'El socialismo español en busca de su historia', *El País*, 5 December 1982.
2 *Epistolario*, pp. 12–13, 53.
3 G. Jackson, *The Spanish Republic and the Civil War*, pp. 441–3.
4 Vidarte, *Todos* (II), p. 844. For Negrín's soundings in Zurich, Jackson, *The Spanish Republic and the Civil War*, pp. 53–4 and Vidarte, *Todos* (II), pp. 857–67, 909.
5 *Guerra y revolución* (IV), pp. 139–40.
6 Lamoneda, August 1938 national committee meeting, *Avance* (Ciudad Real), 12 August 1938; see also speeches, Cine Bilbao (Madrid) 1 August 1937, in *Cuatro discursos sobre la unidad*, p. 34 and 16 October 1938, *Glosa de los acuerdos del C. N. del PSOE*, pp. 30–1.
7 This dated from January 1936. For Saborit affair, see correspondence between him, the ASM and the PSOE executive, in A. Pastor Ugena, *La Agrupación Socialista Madrileña durante la Segunda República* (II), pp. 263–74, 384–401.
8 Cf. *Glosa de los acuerdos del C.N. del PSOE*, p. 30; also letter from Lamoneda to Largo, 17 September 1938, AH–23–1.
9 Largo's refusal in letter to the PSOE executive, 28 September 1938 AH–23–1; Lamoneda's reply, 10 October 1938.
10 Azaña, *Obras* (IV), p. 895.
11 Albacete, provincial correspondence, AH–12–2.
12 Returns in AH–24–14; for detailed returns see AH–21–2/3.
13 Repr. in *Guerra y revolución* (IV), pp. 139–40.
14 After Munich (September 1938), Jiménez de Asúa formed part of the Spanish delegation to the United Nations, Vidarte, *Todos* (II), p. 864, where it states, erroneously, that Jiménez de Asúa remained PSOE vice-president.
15 AH–19–11 (press correspondence).
16 Zabalza's letter declining post, 3 November 1938, his correspondence AH–23–17.
17 For the FNTT vs PCE, see chapter 10.
18 For full executive list, see Appendix 1, p. 245.
19 G. Morón, *Política*, p. 112.
20 *The Times*, 21 June 1938. J. Zugazagoitia, *Guerra y vicisitudes*, pp. 440–4, for the reactions of all three men.
21 Zugazagoitia, *Guerra y vicisitudes*, pp. 443–4.
22 A report of Lamoneda's interview with Besteiro in Madrid in *El Socialista* (Barcelona), 22 October 1938.
23 Zugazagoitia, *Guerra y vicisitudes*, pp. 488–90; Togliatti, *Escritos*, p. 236.

24 Zugazagoitia, *Guerra y vicisitudes*, pp. 440–1.
25 Executive minutes, 15 November, AH–20–5.
26 For the PSOE and Cortes meetings, Zugazagoitia, *Guerra y vicisitudes*, pp. 483–7; Tuñón de Lara, 'El socialismo español en la Guerra Civil', pp. 288–9; PSOE parliamentary party minutes, AH–18–7.
27 Togliatti, *Escritos*, p. 236.
28 L. Romero Solano, *Vísperas de la guerra de España*, p. 177 ff.
29 18 July 1939, AH–64–11.
30 Vidarte, *Todos* (II), p. 860.
31 *Ibid.* (I), pp. 194–5; G. Morón, *Política*, pp. 60–3, 110.
32 Romero Solano, *Vísperas de la guerra de España*, p. 177; Vidarte, *Todos* (I), p. 196.
33 Lamoneda, speeches in Cine Bilbao (Madrid) 1 August 1937, and in Baza (Granada), 26 September 1937, in *Cuatro discursos sobre la unidad*, pp. 34 and 38 respectively.
34 *Glosa de los acuerdos del C.N. del PSOE*, Teatro Chueca, 16 October 1938, pp. 9–10, 14–15, 42–3, extracts also in *Claridad*, 17 October 1938.
35 Lamoneda, *Glosa de los acuerdos del C.N. del PSOE*, p. 10.
36 Zugazagoitia, *Guerra y vicisitudes*, pp. 388, 417; *Epistolario*, p. 100, Vidarte, *Todos* (II), pp. 670–1.
37 Lamoneda's frank speech in Elche (Alicante) 30 October 1938, *Avance*, 6, 7 November 1938, as one of several speeches made during his autumn tour of centre–south zone (Madrid, Guadix, Ciudad Real, Murcia, Granada, Almería).
38 P. Togliatti, report, 21 May 1939, *Escritos*, pp. 232–3.
39 G. Morón, *Política*, pp. 114–15.
40 Cf. comments at the meeting of left socialist deputies, prior to Cortes session of 1 October 1937. 'The feeling of disgust and outrage is reaching crisis point. We must make use of it to turn the situation in the Party to our advantage. The time is ripe.' F. Largo Caballero, *Notas históricas*, p. 1283.
41 Speeches in Cine Bilbao, Madrid, 1 August 1937, pp. 27–8; Baza (Granada), 26 September 1937, p. 45. Also unification report and discussion at July 1937 national committee meeting, stenog. record, and *Glosa de los acuerdos del C.N. del PSOE*, pp. 18–19.
42 G. Morón, *Política*, pp. 111–14.
43 Lamoneda, unification debate, July 1937 national committee meeting, stenog. record.
44 Araquistain to González Peña, 15 July 1939, LA/AHN, leg. 29; national executive circular, 27 April 1938, Valencian provincial correspondence 1936–8, *Circulares y manifiestos 1936–38*, AHM.
45 For the abysmal state of socialist–communist relations on the Madrid front, Togliatti, *Escritos*, pp. 241, 252, 274.
46 Otero, Huerta and Albar had discussions with Negrín, executive minutes 11 November, 1 December 1938, AH–20–4. Also *Guerra y revolución* (IV), pp. 163–5.

47 A Huerta, PSOE executive minutes, 11 November 1938.
48 M. Cordero, PSOE executive minutes, 7 November 1938; for ASM involvement and for discontent spreading to the Levante, PCE report, Pedro Checa, 17 November 1938, microfilm XVIII, 222.
49 Albacete provincial socialist correspondence, July–December 1938, AH–12–2. Also Isidro Mendieta's comments on the province, 23 September 1938, '. . . now that Albacete is becoming ever more the hub not only of road and rail communications, but also the touchstone of political developments.' Correspondence *Claridad*/Mendieta 1937–8, AH–25–20.
50 *Nuestra Lucha* (UGT/PSOE, Murcia), 21 December 1938.
51 PSOE executive minutes, 1932–9, AH–20–4. For the split in the UGT executive over Piñuela affair, UGT minutes, 29 December, 1938.
52 For the Casado affair, see below, chapter 11.

9 The battle for control of the union and the eclipse of the socialist left 1937–1938

1 Largo Caballero to Díaz Alor, 14 August 1938, AHN (sección Guerra Civil, Salamanca, henceforward AHN/SGC), carpeta no. 780; also, F. Largo Caballero, *Mis recuerdos*, pp. 215–17.
2 Largo Caballero had himself been elected as general secretary by congress in October 1932, see Amaro del Rosal, *Historia de la UGT* (I), pp. 350–3, 366–7 and P. Preston, *CSCW*, pp. 105–6.
3 *Adelante*, 11 September, 3 October 1937; *La Correspondencia de Valencia*, 27 September 1937; *El Socialista*, 5 October 1937. For the UGT's organisational structure, see Appendix 3, p. 256.
4 *El Socialista*, 19 May 1937.
5 *Claridad*, 21 May 1937.
6 Vidiella's counter-attack in *Claridad*, 10 August 1937.
7 UGT minutes, 20 May 1937.
8 *Claridad*, 27 May; *El Socialista*, 28 May 1937; see also, Manuel Cordero to Wenceslao Carrillo, 19 June 1939, p. 9, corresp. de M. Cordero, AH–25–6. Also, Largo Caballero, *Mis recuerdos*, p. 215. The agreements of this meeting were never published, see Díaz Alor and Largo Caballero, *A las organizaciones de la Unión General de Trabajadores de España*, 4 October 1937 (AHN/SGC). But for a version of the agenda and agreements, see *Hospitales, sanitarios y similares: posición política y sindical de la federación* (n.p., n.d.), pp. 1–10, 29.
9 *Adelante*, 17 October 1937.
10 *Claridad*, 29 May 1937.
11 Carlos Hernández's complaints about *Claridad*'s editorial line, UGT minutes, 11 February 1937.
12 Amaro del Rosal, *Historia de la UGT* (II), p. 648; M. Bizcarrondo, *Araquistain y la crisis socialista*, pp. 419–20.
13 *Claridad*, 26 June 1937; for the precise circumstances, UGT minutes

17, 24 June, 1 July 1937. Rosal retained the backing of his union, the unitarist *Créditos y Finanzas*. He was thus appointed as their national delegate to the UGT's national committee (see UGT minutes, 19 August 1937), but the Largo executive stalled his instatement.

14 For more on the *Claridad* dispute, see below, pp. 173–174.

15 *Claridad*, 29 May 1937; M. Tuñon de Lara, *Historia de Espana* (IX) (Barcelona, 1981), p. 366.

16 The ASM was internally split, see *Claridad* report, 29 September 1937.

17 Delegation as follows: Rodríguez Vega (printers' union), Edmundo Domínguez (building workers), Antonio Septién (local government employees), Antonio Pérez (railway workers), Cesar Lombardía (teachers' union) (FETE), *El Socialista*, 30 May 1937.

18 *Claridad*, 1 June 1937.

19 M. Azaña, *Obras* (IV), p. 746; M. Koltsov, *Diario de la guerra española*, p. 509; Largo Caballero, *Notas históricas*, pp. 1276–7.

20 Voting was 87,000 to 12,000 in favour of the socialist candidacy, Vidarte, *Todos* (II), p. 616; For the tensions between Asturian socialists and communists prior to the congress, A. Llaneza, quoted above chapter 4, p. 83, n. 54.

21 *El Socialista*, 1 August 1937; also *Claridad* correspondence 1937–8, A H–25–20.

22 By 25 August the *Gaceta de la República* recognised the workers' committee as legal owners of the paper.

23 *Claridad*, 10 November 1937; for the dispute, M. Bizcarrondo, *Araquistain y la crisis socialista*, pp. 419–20.

24 *El Socialista*, 3 October 1937; José Peirats, *La CNT en la revolución española* (II) (Paris, 1971) p. 294.

25 *Adelante*, 17 July 1937.

26 UGT minutes, 31 August 1937.

27 *Adelante*, 13 August 1937.

28 For example of unitarist outrage, *Hospitales, sanitarios y similares*, p. 29. Their case was refuted by Largo in circular to the UGT base, *A las organizaciones*, 4 October 1937 (AHN/SGC).

29 *Frente Rojo*, 10 July 1937.

30 Largo Caballero, *La UGT y la guerra*, October 1937; Largo to Díaz Alor, 14 August 1938 (AHN/SGC, carpeta 780).

31 *Claridad*, 27 August 1937. At the forefront of the call were Artes Blancas and Espectáculos Públicos, see *Hospitales, sanitarios y similares*, pp. 34–6.

32 The nine federations were: FETE, Crédito y Finanzas, Piel (leather workers), Vestido y Tocado, Petróleo, Agua–Gas–Electricidad (utilities), Telefónica, Espectáculos Públicos (leisure and entertainments) and the Sindicato Minero Asturiano (miners) *Adelante*, 8 September 1937.

33 M. Cordero to W. Carrillo, 19 June 1939, p. 10.

34 'The National Committee will meet whenever a majority of its dele-

gates considers it necessary.' For national committee delegates and agenda, *Claridad*, 1 September 1937.

35 *Adelante*, 10 September 1937.
36 *Hospitales, sanitarios y similares*, p. 20; *Adelante*, 24 September 1937.
37 *Hospitales, sanitarios y similares*, p. 31; Largo Caballero, *La UGT y la guerra*, p. 28; *A las organizaciones*. This duplicated Lamoneda's request to the dissidents at the July 1937 PSOE national committee meeting.
38 *El Socialista*, 1 October 1937; see above, chapter 7.
39 *Hospitales, sanitarios y similares*, p. 33. A press communiqué detailing the expulsions was issued by Largo on the evening of 30 September.
40 For full executive list and comment, see below pp. 189–90; also Amaro del Rosal, *Historia de la UGT* (II), p. 674.
41 Largo Caballero, *La UGT y la guerra*.
42 F. Largo Caballero, *Mis recuerdos*, pp. 146–7; Vidarte, *Todos* (I), p. 193.
43 *El Socialista*, 2 October 1937.
44 The unitarist line in *Claridad*, 15 September 1937 and Largo's response to this 'opportunism' in *La UGT y la guerra*, p. 27.
45 *Claridad*, 20 September 1937.
46 M. Cordero to W. Carrillo, 19 June 1939, p. 10, for sarcastic references to Carrillo's 'heroism', pistol in hand, behind the 'barricades'. See also *Hospitales, sanitarios y similares*, pp. 20–6.
47 M. Bizcarrondo, *Araquistain y la crisis socialista*, p. 411.
48 M. Koltsov, *Diario de la guerra española*, p. 509.
49 A. Vélez (Aguirre), *Informaciones*, 14 November 1977; full details of the byzantine circumstances in which the so-called 'ejecutiva de la escalera' (executive on the staircase) was elected, in Amaro del Rosal, *Historia de la UGT* (II), pp. 666–78.
50 J. Peirats, *La CNT en la revolución española* (II), pp. 293–4. For the battle over funds, Largo Caballero, *Notas históricas*, pp. 1220, 1226; *La UGT y la guerra*, pp. 24–9.
51 For article 9 of the UGT statutes and Largo's alleged abuse of it, *Hospitales, sanitarios y similares*, p. 29.
52 UGT minutes, 23 September 1937; *Claridad*, 23 September, *El Socialista*, 2 October 1937, pointing out that five of the 'legal' federations also had dues arrears.
53 *Adelante*, 21 September 1937.
54 *Claridad*, 21 September 1937; *Hospitales, sanitarios y similares*, p. 30. For a tremendously bureaucratic, jesuitical defence of the executive's behaviour, Largo Caballero, *A las organizaciones*.
55 Azaña, *Obras* (IV), p. 596.
56 *El Socialista*, *Adelante*, 16 October 1937, refuted by Largo in *La UGT y la guerra*, p. 23.
57 *Adelante*, 27 October 1937; Edmundo Domínguez in *Claridad*, 1 November 1937. Largo argues 'tit for tat' in *La UGT y la guerra*.
58 *Hospitales, sanitarios y similares*, pp. 20–6.
59 Largo Caballero, *Mis recuerdos*, p. 218; *La UGT y la guerra*, pp. 29–30.

For the new executive's negotiations with Negrín and Zugazagoitia for access to UGT funds and property, UGT minutes, 16, 19 October 1937.

60 For a resumé of the main thrust of this campaign, directed equally against the CNT, S. Juliá, 'Partido contra sindicato', pp. 340–2.

61 Cf. speeches by JSU leaders at the National Youth Conference, January 1937. Also, A. Mije, *El papel de los sindicatos en los momentos actuales* (Valencia, January 1937); J. Díaz at the March 1937 plenum of the PCE's Central Committee, in *Claridad*, 3 March 1937 and his anti-union line is maintained in the PCE's history of the civil war, *Guerra y revolución* (III), pp. 60–1. Note also that it was Pretel who first queried the exact relationship between the UGT and Largo's supporters in the government, UGT minutes, 25 February, 4 March 1937.

62 Text of the July 1937 pact in J. Peirats, *La CNT en la revolución española* (II), pp. 268–9.

63 'Concerning the UGT–CNT joint committees', October 1937 (Building Federation) (AHN/SGC, carpeta 1558, Madrid).

64 S. Juliá, 'De la división orgánica al gobierno de unidad nacional', p. 237.

65 Editorial, 'Sindicalismo y política', p. 2.

66 Enrique de Santiago, *La UGT ante la revolución* (Madrid, 1932), pp. 123–4; S. Juliá, 'Indalecio Prieto: un líder político entre dirigentes sindicales', p. 26.

67 M. Tuñón de Lara, *El movimiento obrero en la historia de España* (Madrid, 1972), p. 648; M. Cordero, *Los socialistas y la revolución* (Madrid, 1932), p. 365.

68 *Ibid.*

69 Pascual Tomás, *La UGT: Columna de la Victoria*, speech, UGT provincial congress, Valencia, November–December 1936.

70 UGT minutes, 9 December 1936.

71 Declaration of iron and steel federation, *El Socialista*, 5 March 1937.

72 E.g. Pascual Tomás, *La UGT: Columna de la Victoria*, p. 10; also his speech reported in *El Socialista*, 9 January 1937 emphasising the need to abstain from making economic demands for the duration of the war. Also, P. Tomás, speech in Ciudad Real, *Avance*, 6 June 1938 and 'La nacionalización de las industrias de guerra', *Spartacus*, September/October 1938, pp. 19–21.

73 J. Peirats, *La CNT en la revolución española* (II), p. 58.

74 Cf. P. Tomás, 'El problema de las incautaciones' in *La UGT: Columna de la Victoria*.

75 B. Bolloten, *The Spanish Revolution*, p. 184.

76 Relations were in general better in the south (e.g. Jaén) than in the Levante or in Aragón. But there were still incidents, for e.g. those involving Maroto's anarchist militia column in Almería, J. Peirats, *La CNT en la revolución española* (II), pp. 66–8. Also, G. Morón, *Política*, pp. 73–7.

77 *Guerra y revolución* (III), pp. 60–1.

78 Largo Caballero, in *La UGT y la guerra*, often has his remarks taken completely out of their political context.

79 M. Bizcarrondo, *Araquistain y la crisis socialista*, pp. 422–3; Araquistain, *Sobre la guerra civil*, p. 48. Also C. Hernández Zancajo, 'La tarea ingente del movimiento sindical español' in *Spartacus*, 1 October 1937, pp. 15–18.

80 In *Claridad*, 14 August 1937, the PSOE executive explicitly forbade socialist sections and provincial federations to make pacts with other political forces.

81 Cf. British observers' comments that Negrín's main task was to prevent the UGT 'patching up its quarrel with the CNT with a view to winning its way back to power.' Foreign Office, general correspondence, Spain, May 1937, w9561/1/41.

82 Decision to approach CNT taken at UGT executive meeting, 24 October 1937; *Hospitales, sanitarios y similares*, p. 66; also *El Socialista*, 15 December 1937.

83 *Adelante* 7, 14 January 1938; *El Socialista*, 23 March 1938. The national committee was constituted as follows: president and vice-president (Horacio M. Prieto and Roberto Alfonso, CNT), secretary and vice-secretary (J. Rodríguez Vega and C. Lombardía, UGT).

84 Signed 12–13 March. For a detailed comparison of UGT and CNT proposals and a severe criticism of the CNT's, J. Peirats, *La CNT en la revolución española* (III), pp. 29–50.

85 *La Correspondencia de Valencia*, 1 April, *El Socialista*, 2 April, *Claridad*, 3 April 1938.

86 *Adelante*, 27 March 1938.

87 Cf. the similar pragmatism displayed by the CNT in the face of the overwhelming popularity of the electoralism represented by the Popular Front pact of February 1936.

88 C.M. Lorenzo, *Los anarquistas españoles*, pp. 234–7.

89 Reports in *Claridad*, 25, 27 March 1938 and *El Socialista*, 29 March 1938.

90 Comité de Enlace UGT–CNT Hostelería y Cafetería (UGT) Alimentación e Industria Gastronómica (CNT) (Madrid), *El Socialista*, 12 April 1938.

91 *El Socialista*, 2 October 1937.

92 PCE report (PCE microfilm XVII, 213) – undated, but post-January 1938 as it lists the four *Caballeristas* appointed under the terms of Jouhaux's settlement, see below, p. 194; cf. Amaro de Rosal, *Historia de la UGT* (II) p. 732; also Togliatti, *Escritos*, p. 243.

93 Togliatti suggests the unitarist/PCE influence in both the UGT and individual industrial federations was mainly at national level, *Escritos*, p. 243.

94 G. Meaker, *The Revolutionary Left in Spain 1914–1923*, pp. 454–5.

95 Speeches by José Díaz and A. Mije, 'Por una potente industria de guerra'.
96 A. Mije, 'El papel de los sindicatos en los momentos actuales'.
97 F. Largo Caballero, *A las organizaciones*.
98 M. Adame, 'Otro documento histórico del Partido Comunista', *Spartacus*, November 1937, p. 17 for reference to PCE's politburo report, 27 March. See also C. Hernández Zancajo, 'La tarea ingente del movimiento sindical español', *Spartacus*, 1 October 1937, pp. 15–18.
99 For meeting of 24 October (agenda and reports), *Hospitales, sanitarios y similares*; *El Socialista*, 28 October 1937, *Adelante*, 16, 30 October 1937.
100 For the formation and activities of 'pro-congress' committee in the transport federation, cf. correspondence with UGT executive, November, December 1937, AH–56–29.
101 *El Socialista*, 5 October 1937, *Adelante*, 21 October 1937. In October 1937, both *Adelante* and *Claridad* carried numerous articles calling for a national congress of the iron and steel federation.
102 *Adelante*, 21 December 1937.
103 *El Socialista*, 2 July 1937.
104 *Adelante*, 3 November 1937.
105 *Hospitales, sanitarios y similares*, p. 22.
106 AH–57–49/62 for avalanche of conflicting replies to Largo's call for a general UGT congress in December 1937. These came from all areas of the Republican zone (except Cataluña), though in most cases the *ugetistas* ended by calling on Largo and González Peña to reach a compromise.
107 *El Socialista*, 6 May 1938.
108 For UGT's structure, see below, Appendix 3, p. 256.
109 Cf. remarks in Albacete's *Vida Obrera*, 2 October 1937: 'We declare out and out war on this illegitimate executive. No truce with those who have divided the UGT. Viva Largo Caballero! Viva Pablo Iglesias!' Although the unitarists did score some successes in the Levante and south as late as the end of 1937; e.g. autumn elections of joint executives in Alicante and Baza (Granada), *Adelante*, 23 October, 6 November 1937; J. Peirats, *La CNT en la revolución española* (II), p. 294.
110 The appropriation of *La Correspondencia de Valencia* in *Claridad*, 30 November 1937. Togliatti's 'forecasting' of this, in his letter to Dimitrov & Manuilsky, 15 September 1937, *Escritos*, p. 147.
111 A. Huerta to Ramón Lamoneda, October 1937, press correspondence, AH–19–11.
112 Vidarte, *Todos* (II), pp. 746–7; Largo Caballero, *Mis recuerdos*, p. 221.
113 Largo Caballero, *Mis recuerdos*, pp. 220–3; Largo Caballero to Azaña, 23 October 1937, AHN/SGC, carpeta 780.
114 Largo Caballero, *Mis recuerdos*, p. 221; Vidarte, *Todos* (II), pp. 746–7.
115 L. Araquistain's speech before the *Diputación Permanente de las Cortes*, 2 November 1937. LA/AHN, leg. 71/1.
116 Amaro del Rosal, *Historia de la UGT* (II), p. 677.

117 Circular from Largo Caballero to the federations of the UGT, 1 November 1937 (AHN/SGC); *Claridad*, 21 December 1937 reported that a majority on the FNTT's national committee supported the congress call.

118 In *Mis recuerdos*, p. 218, Largo accuses his opponents of calling in the IFTU. But in the more reliable, documentary-based *Notas históricas* (p. 1220) Largo simply refers to the fact of intervention. The UGT minutes for 1 and 2 October 1937 refer only to González Peña's letter to IFTU *informing* it of the change in leadership. It seems plausible that the left, learning of this communication, *then* decided to approach the IFTU with its version of events. Schevenels' letter of 19 November 1937 to Rodríguez Vega, calling the executive to the Paris meeting, also suggests Largo as the initiator of IFTU intervention, AH–57–2.

119 Llopis' report, 19 October 1937, AH–57–63. His interview with Schevenels took place on 13 October. According to Stols, the IFTU's admin. secretary, the González Peña executive had made no approach about the UGT dispute. Rather oddly, Largo's accusations are repeated uncritically by Amaro del Rosal, *Historia de la UGT*, pp. 677–8.

120 M. Cordero to W. Carrillo, 19 June 1939, p. 10. For communist anger at IFTU intervention, *Nuestra Lucha* (JSU, Murcia), 29 November 1937, AH–57–2, which also accuses Largo's camp of initiating the proceedings.

121 *Claridad*, 27 November 1937.

122 *El Socialista*, 28 December 1937; *Adelante* and *Claridad*, 30 December 1937; Largo Caballero, *Mis recuerdos*, pp. 218–19.

123 Amaro del Rosal, *Historia de la UGT* (II), pp. 726–7.

124 Largo Caballero had believed his closeness to Jouhaux would favour the *Caballeristas*, M. Cordero to W. Carrillo, 19 June 1939; A. del Rosal, *Historia de la UGT* (II), p. 731.

125 UGT minutes, 20 January 1938. The absence of the *Caballeristas* was noted here and on subsequent occasions, e.g. 2, 10 February, 24 March 1938.

126 UGT minutes, 6 January 1938, see below, chapter 10, p. 211.

10   The *caballerista* old guard: entrenchment and resurgence

1 PCE microfilm XVII, 213.

2 For the transport federation, UGT minutes, 13 December 1937, 6 January 1938.

3 For urban transport, *Adelante*, 21 October 1937. Its new provincial executive in Valencia was pro-González Peña, *Adelante*, 5 October 1937.

4 For collectivisation in the Republican south, L. Garrido González, *Colectividades agrarias en Andalucía*.

5 For the clashes between the FNTT base and the PCE in the south,

Adelante, 12 February 1937; for confrontations between the FNTT and the PCE in Serena (Badajoz), Ripollés Serrano, 'Francisco Largo Caballero', p. 712.

6 For PCE hostility to Zabalza, Togliatti, *Escritos*, p. 243.

7 L. Garrido González, *Colectividades agrarias*, pp. 32, 102.

8 Miguel Ranchal (Cordoban provincial federation) to R. González Peña, 5 October 1937, in latter's correspondence, 1937, AH–25–2, p. 2.

9 September–November 1938, AHM.

10 For links between other PSOE federations and the FNTT, J. Peirats, *La CNT en la revolución española* (II), p. 294.

11 The full executive as follows: R. Henche (president), Mariano Prados (vice-president), Fermín García (general secretary), Carlos Rubiera (administrative secretary), Francisco Umanes (treasurer) and León García (propaganda secretary).

12 *Adelante*, 21 December 1937; cf. also *Spartacus*, September 1937, p. 12.

13 FNTT note to press (n.d., but late 1937), AH–58–1.

14 *Adelante*, 18, 19, 21 December 1937.

15 Interview with Soler, *Adelante*, 3 November 1937.

16 *Adelante*, 22 December 1937.

17 *Adelante*, 19 May 1938.

18 For problems in Jaén between the FNTT and PCE, L. Garrido González, *Colectividades agrarias*, chapters 5 and 7. Also extensive correspondence between FNTT sections/federations in centre–south and PSOE executive concerning PCE infiltration into collectives to counter FNTT influence, AH–72–12.

19 During the war, the IRA's director general was Enrique Castro Delgado (PCE).

20 Julio Mateu, 'La obra de la Federación Provincial Campesina' at the plenum of the PCE's central committee, 5–8 March 1937, Valencia.

21 A. Bosch Sánchez, *Ugetistas y libertarios*, pp. 340–8; see also UGT minutes, 24 June 1937 for the cases of Alicante and Valencia, *La Correspondencia de Valencia*, 15 February 1938 for Alicante FNTT accord.

22 According to FNTT report, 55.8 per cent of the surface area in Valencia was given over to smallholdings, *La Correspondencia de Valencia*, 15 February 1938.

23 B. Bolloten, *The Spanish Revolution*, p. 225. For the PCE's success in the Levante provinces, V. Uribe's speech to PCE central committee plenum, March 1937.

24 J. Mateu, 'La obra de la Federación Provincial Campesina'.

25 *Ibid.*; A. Bosch Sánchez, *Ugetistas y libertarios*, pp. 117–23, 336–40; also W. Bernecker, *Colectividades y revolución social: el anarquismo en la guerra civil española 1936–1939* (Barcelona, 1982), pp. 123–6; also the economic report at the PSOE national committee meeting, July 1937.

26 Interview with R. Zabalza to *Adelante*, reproduced in *Solidaridad Obrera*, 28 May 1937. Also R. Zabalza's letter to the agriculture minister, V. Uribe, in *Adelante*, 29 May 1937.

27 *Por la revolución agraria*, FNTT pamphlet, June 1937 (Biblioteca Nacional), p. 42.

28 For complaints about the behaviour of the IRA's delegates in Badajoz province in the pueblos of Baterno, Medellín, Talarrubio, Peñalsordo, Herrera del Duque, Navalvillar and Puebla de Alcocer, *Adelante*, 29 May 1937; the case of Garbayuela also quoted in B. Bolloten, *The Spanish Revolution*, pp. 225–6, and notes, pp. 533–4.

29 *Por la revolución agraria*, p. 44.

30 For PCE hostility, see also the replies of various provincial FNTT executives to *Adelante* questionnaire, *Adelante*, 17, 20 June 1937.

31 Cf. Justo Vila Izquierdo, *Extremadura: La Guerra Civil* (Badajoz, 1983), p. 119; L. Garrido González, *Colectividades agrarias*, p. 101.

32 For a study of agrarian collectivisation in Jaén, the growth, influence and tactics of the PCE, L. Garrido González, *Collectividades agrarias*, *passim*, for the 'interests of the majority' in the province, p. 99.

33 E.g. V. Uribe's speech to PCE plenum, Valencia, March 1937.

34 For Cullera and other incidents, A. Bosch Sánchez, *Ugetistas y libertarios*, pp. 111, 122, 133–4.

35 For a detailed analysis of all three tactics. L. Garrido González, *Colectividades agrarias*, pp. 63–82.

36 B. Bolloten, *The Spanish Revolution*, pp. 228–9.

37 See above chapter 6, p. 122; also L. Garrido González, *Colectividades agrarias*, pp. 78–9.

38 The FNTT's provincial congress, 19 September 1937, L. Garrido González, *Colectividades agrarias*, pp. 75, 77.

39 *La Correspondencia de Valencia*, 5 April 1938.

40 Interview in *Adelante*, reproduced in *Solidaridad Obrera*, 28 May 1937, with a clear reference to the PCE's activities.

41 *Avance*, 5 April 1938.

42 R. Zabalza on the 'new way' in the countryside, *Avance* (Alicante), 25 December 1938 and 16 December for 'Las dos batallas' *against* Franco and *for* production, cooperation and collectivism, as the only way to eradicate *caciquismo* and class exploitation in the rural south: 'the solution lies in developing new modes of production and exchange which will render superfluous both middle men and capitalists'.

43 See PCE report on the FNTT (1938), as part of a general report on the UGT, which refers to the *Caballeristas'* consolidation of their position in the FNTT and also to Zabalza's 'aparato caciquil', i.e. the left's power base in the FNTT's provincial federations, PCE microfilm XVII, 213.

44 For details of the FNTT (1931–6), P. Preston, *CSCW*, p. 19; also P. Preston, 'The agrarian war in the south' in P. Preston (ed.) *Revolution and War in Spain 1931–1939* (London, 1984), pp. 165–6. FNTT–UGT pamphlet, *Un siglo de acción sindical nos respalda* (FPI, 1977). For the FNTT's dramatic expansion rate in 1936, UGT minutes, 1936, e.g. 23 April, 7, 21, 28 May, 11, 25 June, 9 July 1936; 28 January, 25 February, 25 March, 28 April, 16 September 1937.

45 'Contribución a la historia del Partido Socialista Español' in *Tiempo de Historia*, August 1975, pp. 29–37.

46 Togliatti acknowledged that this 'heavyweight' opposition was a serious obstacle to the unitarists' plans. Togliatti, *Escritos*, p. 243.

47 The calculation is as follows: (a) total membership 1,887,569*
(b) total FNTT
iron and steel   801,553
urban transport
(b) expressed as a percentage of (a)   = 42.5 per cent
* See note on p. 220.

48 Figures from Bullejos' article, *Avance* (Alicante) 13 August 1938.

49 Amaro del Rosal, confidential report on UGT. For breakdown of UGT by industrial federation see table p. 219.

50 'El PSU a caballo de la UGT', *La Correspondencia de Valencia*, 25 March 1937.

51 UGT executive minutes, 9 December 1936; also 17 February 1937.

52 For his complaints about the 'massification' of the Catalan UGT, UGT minutes, 24 June 1937.

53 *El Socialista*, 26 March 1937.

54 *La Correspondencia de Valencia*, 4 January 1938.

55 *La Correspondencia de Valencia*, 8 December 1937, 6 January 1938.

56 *La Correspondencia de Valencia*, 7 January 1938.

57 Amaro del Rosal's report on the UGT to PCE central committee, 6 August 1938, PCE microfilm xvii, 209–13.

58 Amaro del Rosal's report on UGT to PCE, 6 August 1938: 'Vega himself admits that we can no longer tolerate Carlos Hernández's behaviour, that we must expel him.'

59 *La Correspondencia de Valencia*, 7 February 1938. But note, the Asturian regional federation opposed its national leadership, *El Socialista*, 17 September 1938.

60 Cf. Gregorio Sánchez at the plenum of the committees of the GSS and the GOSR, 13 March 1938, referring to the GOSR as organisations of the masses, independent of all parties, *Claridad*, 14 March 1938.

61 Minutes of PSOE/PCE comité nacional de enlace and PSOE executive minutes, AHM.

62 Informe sindical 'Muy Reservado', 6 August 1938, prepared for the PCE Central Committee by Amaro del Rosal, PCE microfilm xvii 209–13. For Amaro del Rosal's formal declaration of allegiance to the PCE see his article 'Quiero un puesto de combate en el Partido Comunista.' *Nuestra Bandera*, no. 28, June–July 1948.

63 Quoted in Largo Caballero, *Notas históricas*, pp. 1287–1300.

64 'Como se han aplicado los acuerdos del CN de la UGT', PCE report, n.d. (but post-April 1938), microfilm xvii, 213.

65 Report cited above, note 64, which refers in these terms to González Peña's suspension of the urban transport congress in January 1938.

66 PCE microfilm xx, 238; Togliatti, *Escritos*, p. 243.

67 S. Juliá, *La Izquierda*, pp. 171–84.
68 UGT executive minutes, 23 January 1936.
69 Amaro del Rosal, report to PCE central committee, 6 August 1938.
70 UGT minutes, 29 December 1938, for references to Madrid socialists presenting entirely socialist candidates for election to union committees. For details of the socialist rank and file's hostility to 'unity' candidacies at provincial UGT congress in Alicante, April 1938, F. Ferrándiz Alborz, *La Bestia contra España* (Montevideo, 1951), p. 65.
71 *El Socialista*, 26 April 1938 for harsh criticism of the IFTU.
72 Meeting 6–7 March 1938, *Claridad*, 24 February 1938 (for the agenda); *La Correspondencia de Valencia*, 7 March 1938.
73 *La Correspondencia de Valencia*, 7 March 1938.
74 *La Correspondencia de Valencia*, 16 February 1938. Rodríguez Vega represented the UGT on the CGT committee.
75 Amaro del Rosal and Rodríguez Vega attended on the UGT's behalf. Those in favour of Soviet entry were France, Spain, Mexico, Czechoslovakia and Norway.
76 *La Correspondencia de Valencia*, 17 May 1938; cf. also, M. Cordero, discussion on international situation, PSOE national committee meeting, July 1937 (stenog. record).
77 *La Correspondencia de Valencia*, 17 June 1938, for UGT executive circular.
78 *El Socialista*, 26, 28 September, 1 October 1937.
79 The iron and steel federation in Cataluña had also created its own separate joint UGT–CNT committee, *El Socialista*, 28 September 1937.
80 *Avance* (Alicante), 29 September 1938. Also noteworthy is the massive influx of new transport sections into the Catalan secretariat (Barcelona, Tarragona, Lérida, Gerona), UGT minutes, 9 June 1938. The unitarists' hand was thereby strengthened *vis-à-vis* a future national congress.
81 An example of the pro-congress articles – 'Para orientar el transporte hace falta un congreso', *La Correspondencia de Valencia*, 15 February 1938.
82 Congress, 31 October–5 November 1938. Both the Spanish railway union and the maritime transport federation voted in favour. For letters from other UGT federations criticising Hernández Zancajo, UGT minutes, 24 November, 1 December 1938.
83 Luis Selgas, *Claridad*, 16 November 1938.
84 *Claridad*, 24 November 1938 for the UGT executive's circular referring to the circumstances of the transport congress. Cf. 'Vida sindical', *El Socialista* (Barcelona), 22 November 1938 for criticism of Hernández.
85 *El Socialista*, 21 December 1938.
86 Cf. Díaz Alor's reference to dissident pamphlets from Madrid circulating in Valencia, in letter to Largo Caballero, 17 September 1938, AH–23–1.

11   The Casado coup and the end of the war

1 A. Mije, report to PCE central committee, 22 August 1938, PCE archive, microfilm XVIII, 222. Socialist trade union groups existed

within the JSU with aim of reorienting socialist youth, cf. Togliatti, *Escritos*, p. 241.

2 Isidro R. Mendieta (ed. of *Claridad*), in letter, 28 September 1938, *Claridad*, correspondence, AHM.

3 Cf. also Domínguez's comments about the 'denso ambiente' (conspiratorial atmosphere), 1 January 1939, PSOE executive correspondence 1938–9, AH–25–1.

4 *Avance* (Alicante), 28 October, 2 November 1938.

5 *Avance* (Alicante), 19 November 1938, article by Cástulo Carrasco.

6 *Avance*, 28 December 1938, for article by Virginio Sánchez, 'Socialistas y mercaderes'. Also Alcantarilla (Murcia) in *Avance*, 24 November 1938 for a local (socialist) JSU section's nostalgia for the days 'before the movement was enslaved by the *consigna*' (central directive).

7 Letter from JSU in Callosa de Segura (Alicante), *Avance*, 3 November 1938.

8 *Adelante*, 12, 13 November 1938.

9 P. Checa, report to the PCE's central committee, 17 November 1938, PCE microfilm XVIII, 222.

10 Mije's report to the PCE central committee, 22 August 1938.

11 G. Morón, *Política*, pp. 111–13. No date is given for the meeting but the context places it in October 1938.

12 P. Togliatti, *Escritos*, p. 228. Hostile young socialists compared Lamoneda's tactics against the *Caballeristas* with the JSU executive's against the youth dissidents, for example, C. Carrasco's 'Consecuencias del "centralismo democrático"', *Avance* (Alicante), 19 November 1938.

13 Resolution of August 1938 PSOE national committee meeting, although secretariat idea was first mooted at July 1937 national committee. Claudín, *Santiago Carrillo*, p. 54.

14 For split in Murcian federation, R. Togliatti, *Escritos*, p. 149.

15 Socialist civil governor's report on Murcia province to PSOE executive, December 1938, provincial correspondence, AHM, relevant details, 17 August 1938.

16 Murcia, provincial correspondence, 12 September, 1938, AHM.

17 Cf. telegram to PSOE national executive from unitarist section in Murcia (capital), 19 November 1938, 'Police surrounding JSU HQ. Attempted assault to deliver HQ expelled factionalists.' Murcia, provincial correspondence.

18 Civil governor's report, December 1938.

19 Transfer ordered by socialist interior minister, Gómez Sáez, civil governor's report, December 1938.

20 For these see provincial newspapers, especially *Avance* (Alicante) in the last quarter of 1938, for example, 14 October (Verdú vs. Pascual Sánchez), 18, 22 October ('La Vieja Guardia contesta', by C. Carrasco, founder member of Ciudad Real JSU and member of Madrid socialist youth elected in March 1939), 28 October, 2, 3, 19, 30 November, 27 December 1938.

21 Evident in running debate in *Avance*, 11–19 October 1938.
22 Cf. also J. Tundidor, 'We are not interested in the unity of "all youth"', JJ.SS. congress, Toulouse, April 1945 (speeches pub. Mexico 1945).
23 PCE central committee resolution, May 1938. For more on 'unión nacional', J. Estruch, *Historia del PCE 1920–1939* (I), Appendix XIII, pp. 190–6.
24 *El Club: organismo de base de la JSU* and ¿Qué es una Casa de la juventud campesina? (JSU, 1938).
25 Serrano Poncela, *Renovación*, Madrid 1936.
26 Verdú, *Avance*, 21 October 1938. In the post-war period, in the correspondence of embittered socialists, references to the Communists' 'betrayal' of the conditions of youth unity abound, see, for example, H. Lafayette to S. Carrillo (n.d.) LA/AHN, leg. 42, no. 67.
27 For a list of those elected, *Adelante*, 1 December 1938; also Serrano Poncela, *Algunos datos estadísticos*, youth section correspondence, AHM, p. 5. Cf. Criticism made about incipient democratic centralism, PSOE national committee meeting, July 1937, youth report, stenog. record. Also, *El Socialista*, 21 November 1937.
28 *Avance*, 28 November 1938, *Adelante*, 1 December 1938. For further reports on the sessions, *Claridad*, 24, 26 November 1938 (for the agenda, *Adelante*, 6 November 1938).
29 *Avance*, 6 December 1938; also, letter from angry socialist militant to Lamoneda, JSU correspondence 1939, AH–26–8.
30 *Avance*, 4 December 1938; Rodríguez to Lamoneda, May 1939, AHM; also M. Cantal in *Avance*, 16 December 1938.
31 Serrano Poncela, *Algunos datos estadísticos*, p. 5; *Avance*, 25 December 1938. Full November committee in R. Casterás, *Las JSUC: Ante la Guerra y la Revolución (1936–1939)* (Barcelona, 1977), p. 331.
32 *Avance*, 7, 24 December 1938.
33 For example, 'La Unidad de la JSU', signed Machabla, *Adelante* (UGT, Almería), 23 October 1938.
34 'JSU. Mezcla que no llegó a la fusión', *Avance*, 20 September 1938.
35 See bitter criticism of S. Carrillo, in article cited in previous note; also in article by C. Carrasco, *Avance*, 29 October 1938; also Carlos de Baraibar, 'La traición del Stalinismo'.
36 For a perfect evocation of the wartime *pablista* ethos, see article by Francisco Cruz Salido, 'El silencio de las tumbas socialistas', *El Socialista* (Madrid), 11 December 1938.
37 Both Modesto and Lister were made generals but were not posted. Cordón (PCE), was made director general in the defence ministry. Bueno, Barceló and Galán (all PCE members) were made generals and Galán was appointed as the new head of the naval base at Cartagena to replace General Bernal. For these and other promotions listed in the *Diario Oficial*, see pages of gazette reproduced in R. Salas Larrazábal, *Historia del Ejército Popular de la República* (4 vols.), (Madrid, 1973), pp. 3399–3408, especially pp. 3399–3400. Etelvino Vega (PCE) was

appointed military commander in Alicante, *Guerra y Revolución* (IV), p. 298. For the enduring polemic over the extent and significance of these military appointments, Burnett Bolloten, *La guerra civil española: revolución y contrarrevolución* (Madrid, 1989), pp. 1039–48. General accounts of the last stages of the war are to be found in G. Jackson, *The Spanish Republic and the Civil War*, pp. 465–77 and, in greater detail, in B. Bolloten, *La guerra civil española*; H. Thomas, *The Spanish Civil War* (Harmondsworth, 1977), pp. 886–915. Specialised accounts in J.M. Martínez Bande, *Los cien últimos días de la República* (Barcelona, 1972); Ignacio Iglesias, *La fase final de la guerra civil: de la caída de Barcelona al derrumbamiento de Madrid* (Barcelona, 1977); personal accounts of the Casado affair by participants/eye witnesses include W. Carrillo, *El último episodio de la guerra civil española* (Toulouse, 1945); E. Domínguez, *Los vencedores de Negrín* (Mexico, 1940); J. García Pradas, *Como terminó la guerra de España* (Buenos Aires, 1940).

38 For events at Cartagena, see the general accounts cited above; also, L. Romero's detailed account, *Desastre en Cartagena* (Madrid, 1971).

39 Besteiro's role is mentioned in most general accounts, see also J. Zugazagoitia, *Guerra y vicisitudes*, pp. 569–70; Vidarte, *Todos* (II), p. 923.

40 L. Araquistain to R. González Peña, 15 July 1939, LA/AHN, leg. 29, n° G 181 (my italics).

41 R. Lamoneda, 'Manifiesto de la CE del PSOE' – Mexico, 15 November 1945, *El Socialista*, no. 10, January 1946 (my italics).

42 For abundant illustrations of this isolation see Togliatti's report, May 1939, *Escritos*, pp. 240–1, 245, 247, 258, 260, 266, 270–1, 274–6, 281; For an analysis, cf. J. Aróstegui, 'La República y el problema del poder', p. 19.

43 Togliatti, *Escritos*, pp. 231–2, 247. Both PCE and Lamoneda leaderships were held to be guilty here because they were based in Barcelona after the division of Republican territory. Cf. also G. Morón, *Política*, p. 140–1.

44 Zabalza to Lamoneda, 3 November 1938, Zabalza's personal correspondence, AHM.

45 Araquistain to González Peña, 15 July 1939.

46 Togliatti, report 21 May 1939, *Escritos*, pp. 273–4.

47 Togliatti, *ibid.*, pp. 225–305.

48 A. Ramos Oliveira, *Historia de España*, pp. 381–440.

49 L. Araquistain to R. González Peña, 15 July 1939; also Togliatti, report, *Escritos*, p. 228.

50 Togliatti, *Escritos*, p. 264.

51 *Guerra y revolución* (IV), pp. 307–17; M. Tagüeña, *Testimonio*, pp. 319–21.

52 M. Tagüeña, *Testimonio*, p. 307; M. Alpert, *El ejército republicano* (Paris, 1977), pp. 385, 387, 403.

53 *Ibid.*, pp. 307–8.

54 For a realistic description of the situation, Amaro del Rosal's preface to

the UGT minutes for 1939 (very imperfect and handwritten, AHM); also the final chapters of his *Historia de la UGT*, e.g. p. 910.
55 PCE microfilm xx, 238, frame 136.
56 The Francoist military historian, J.M. Martínez Bande concurs, see *Los cien últimos días de la República*, p. 186. For developments in Madrid, see also *Guerra y revolución* (IV), pp. 305–6.
57 *Testimonio*, pp. 319, 321. See also Jesús Hernández, *Yo fui un ministro de Stalin*, pp. 305–7.
58 Togliatti, *Escritos*, pp. 291–2 and cf. p. 293.
59 J. Estruch, *Historia del PCE (1920–1939)* (I), pp. 114–16.
60 PCE archive, xx, 238, frame 92, for example, details Casado's conspiratorial meetings with ASM leaders and Besteiro.
61 M. Tagüeña, *Testimonio*, p. 320; Togliatti, *Escritos*, p. 293.
62 Togliatti, *Escritos*, p. 320.
63 *Guerra y revolución* (IV), pp. 298–9.
64 PCE report, xx, 238, frames 101–2, 109, 135; Togliatti, *Escritos*, pp. 210–11, 295–7; E. Domínguez, *Los vencedores de Negrín*, p. 227. Also *Guerra y revolución* (IV), pp. 313–14, 316.
65 M. Tagüeña, *Testimonio*, p. 321; R. Carr, *The Civil War in Spain* (London, 1986), p. 245.
66 *Guerra y revolución* (IV), pp. 299–303.
67 M. Tagüeña, *Testimonio*, p. 306. For ASM involvement and that of non-*Caballeristas* such as Henche, also Togliatti, *Escritos*, pp. 273–4.
68 PCE, xx, 239, PSUC delegate's report, 20 April 1939; also Togliatti, *Escritos*, pp. 205, 207; *Guerra y revolución* (IV), p. 300 for a relevant extract from Delicado's report, 12 March 1939.
69 E. Domínguez, *Los vencedores de Negrín*, p. 105; PCE report to Negrín, 20 February 1939, xx, 238, frames 69, 135.
70 W. Carrillo, *El último episodio de la guerra civil española*, pp. 9–10; also Llopis to Araquistain, 16 June 1939, LA/AHN, leg. 33 n° 15. PCE report, March 1939, microfilm xx, 238, frame 92, dates ASM conversations with Casado from the time Negrín's government first left Spain after the fall of Cataluña and Azaña's resignation (27 February 1939).
71 Togliatti, *Escritos*, pp. 240–2, 252.
72 *Adelante*, 12 March 1939.
73 For Alicante: PCE microfilm xx, 238, frame 142, for Valencia, frame 136 and see also C. de Baraibar, 'La traición del Stalinismo', p. 79; for Almería, PCE, xx, 243.
74 *Adelante*, 8, 9 March 1939; *Avance*, 14, 17 March 1939.
75 PCE report, xx, 238, 14 March 1939; see also O. Salcedo, 'Posiciones y orientaciones de las Juventudes Socialistas' (Mexico, 1944), p. 13, which dates the meeting as 10 March 1939.
76 For example, by the dissolution of the 'Clubes del Soldado' and the replacement of the provincial executive of the Students' Union (FUE), *Claridad*, 23 March 1939.
77 Togliatti, *Escritos*, pp. 294, 297; PCE report, xx, 238, frame 120 for

'declaration of incompatibility' by Valencian Popular Front, 9 March 1939 (see also frames 134–5 and frames 141–2 and *El Socialista*, 22 March 1939 for Alicante's). Also *Guerra y revolución* (IV), pp. 318–19. For Almería where PCE HQ ransacked, xx, 238, 243. See also report by UGT general secretary, Edmundo Domínguez, 'Informe ante la CE en relación con su intervención en los hechos ocurridos en la zona centro', quoted by Amaro del Rosal, UGT minutes 1939, p. 95; *Adelante*, 18 March 1939, for details of exclusion of communists from Madrid's town council; *El Socialista*, 18 March 1939, report from the new socialist committee of 'El Baluarte', the local iron and steel federation, referring to its recovery from a 'fictitious communist majority', p. 2; *El Socialista*, 20 March 1939, circular from *Hospitales*' Madrid executive, apprising affiliates of expulsions of communists. Alongside this an article, 'Las 21 Condiciones: Dictadura que pretendía ejercer la Tercera Internacional' which lists the conditions, reminding readers of the PSOE's rejection of them in 1921.

78 PCE xx, 238, 243.
79 PCE xx, 238, frames 136, 141–2; Togliatti, *Escritos*, pp. 213–14.
80 Togliatti, *Escritos*, his report, 12 March 1939 from Valencia, pp. 203–5; also *Guerra y revolución* (IV), pp. 303–4.
81 W. Carrillo, *El último episodio de la guerra civil española*, p. 13; *El Socialista*, 24, 25, 26 March 1939; also *Guerra y revolución* (IV), p. 349.
82 Abundant references in PCE reports from centre–south zone, xx, 238, 239, 243. All centre–south zone provinces were affected. See also Togliatti, *Escritos*, p. 206; S. Carrillo's 'Los que entregaron Madrid: La Junta de Traición' in *Mundo Obrero*, no. 142, November 1948.
83 Togliatti, *Escritos*, pp. 242–3.
84 *Claridad*, 10 February 1939; Amaro del Rosal, UGT minutes 1939; also Amaro del Rosal, *Historia de la UGT* (II), p. 891.
85 For example, his article in *Claridad*, 7 March 1939, in which he described Negrín's Figueras speech on 1 February 1939 (that Barcelona could be held and the course of the war changed), as 'a scene straight out of a psychiatric clinic', and Negrín with his resistance policy as manifesting exalted delusions ('acentos de loco-Díos').
86 Zabalza arrived Madrid from Valencia bearing demands for a national committee meeting; UGT minutes, 1939; see also E. Domínguez, *Los vencedores de Negrín*, pp. 205–7; PCE report, xx, 238, frame 118.
87 UGT minutes, March 1939; also Amaro del Rosal, *Historia de la UGT* (II), pp. 891–2; E. Domínguez, *Los vencedores de Negrín*, pp. 266–7; PCE report, xx 239; also some details in *El Socialista*, 26, 28 March 1939; *Guerra y revolución* (IV), p. 327; Togliatti, *Escritos*, p. 296.
88 Letter from Rodríguez Vega to the UGT's national executive, 17 March 1939, in *Guerra y revolución* (IV), p. 293.
89 For Pérez, UGT minutes, March 1939. The UGT unitarists disowned Pérez's collaboration with the defence council as the product of undue duress, declaration, 23 March 1939, PCE xx, 248.

90 In Valencia, for example, PCE report, xx, 238, frame 135.
91 UGT minutes, March 1939; see also Amaro del Rosal, *Historia de la UGT* (II), pp. 891–2, 911–12. In the post-war period, the two UGT executives continued to function in exile until 1950.
92 F. Ferrándiz Alborz, *La Bestia contra España*, pp. 69–73.
93 Details of the new executive in *El Socialista*, 22 March, *Claridad*, 22 March, *Adelante*, 24 March 1939. See also, Ferrándiz Alborz, *La Bestia contra España*, pp. 72–3.
94 See editor's note to Largo Caballero, *¿Qúe se puede hacer?* (Paris, 1940), p. 22. (Also† in text). Also, Appendix C, p. 441, in R. Gillespie, *The Spanish Socialist Party. A History of Factionalism*, (Oxford, 1989).
95 One consequence of this in the immediate post-war period would be the expulsion from the PSOE of leading militants. Lamoneda was expelled along with Negrín, Angel Galarza and even Ramón González Peña. Less surprisingly, Julio Alvarez del Vayo and Amaro del Rosal were also expelled. (The *expedientes* are located in AHM.)
96 S. Gómez, *Los jóvenes socialistas y la JSU*.
97 'La nueva Ejecutiva', *El Socialista*, 23 March 1939; cf. also *El Socialista*, 24 March 1939.
98 The most notorious example of this was Santiago Carrillo's letter denouncing his father, Wenceslao Carrillo, as a traitor to his class and his people, for collaborating with the Casado junta. Letter dated 15 May 1939, published by the *Juventudes Socialistas* (Mexico), as a salutary warning of 'how stalinism defiles'.

Bibliography

Primary Sources

(i) Archivo Histórico Nacional (Madrid)
    Personal archive of Luis Araquistain, published catalogue for this
    archive, *Papeles de D. Luis Araquistain Quevedo en Archivo Histórico Nacio-
    nal* (Madrid, 1983)
(ii) Archivo Histórico Nacional – Sección guerra civil (Salamanca) Sec-
    ción político-social – (i) Madrid, (ii) Valencia
(iii) Archivo del Partido Comunista de España (Madrid) Republic/Civil
    War microfilmed documentation, 1935–40, films XIII–XXII (internal
    and inter-party correspondence; national, regional and local party
    and union minutes, reports, circulars and newspaper articles)
    PCE's supplementary catalogued holdings in manuscript and printed
    form: (a) Documents, 1936–9 (b) Speeches, reports, articles, 1935–45
    (c) Correspondence 1936–9
(iv) Fundación Pablo Iglesias (PSOE) (Madrid)
    Minutes of UGT national executive committee 1936–9; Moscow
    Historical Archive (PSOE archive, 1930–9); personal archive of
    Amaro del Rosal (AARD); personal archive of Ramón Lamoneda
    (ARLF); F. Largo Caballero, *Notas históricas de la guerra en España 1917–
    1940* (unpublished manuscript held by the FPI)
(v) Public Records Office (Kew, London)
    Foreign Office general correspondence: Spain 1937–9

Newspapers and Periodicals

Adelante (Valencia) (daily, February 1937 to March 1939)
Avance (Alicante) (daily, April 1938 to February 1939)
Avance (Ciudad Real) (daily, February 1938 to March 1939, imperfect run
    lacking November, December 1938 and January 1939)
Claridad (Madrid) (daily, July 1936 to February 1939) (NB. by second half
    of 1938, a seriously imperfect run)
La Correspondencia de Valencia (daily, 1937–8, very imperfect run)

The Manchester Guardian (daily, December 1936 to March 1939)
The New York Times (daily, September 1936 to March 1939)
El Socialista (Barcelona) (daily, September 1938 to January 1939)
El Socialista (Madrid) (daily, January 1937 to March 1939, increasingly imperfect run by summer 1938)
Spartacus (Alicante) (monthly), September 1937 to August 1938, April missing)
The Times (daily, September 1936 to March 1939)

In addition to the above continuous or partial runs of newspapers and periodicals, numerous short runs and odd copies were also consulted. These included:
Adelante (Almería)
Democracia (Jaén)
Frente Rojo (Barcelona)
Generación Roja (Castellón)
Informaciones (Madrid)
Mundo Obrero (Madrid)
Nuestra Lucha (Murcia)
Reconquista (Euskadi refugees)
Timón (Barcelona/Buenos Aires)
Trabajo (Guadix)
Treball (Barcelona)
La Vanguardia (Málaga)
Vestido (órgano de la Federación de Vestido y Tocado)
Vida Obrera (Albacete)

Printed Documents: Conference Reports, Agit-Prop, Pamphlets and Speeches (The following is a selective list)

Alvarez, Segismundo. *La juventud y los campesinos*, speech to JSU national conference, January 1937 (Valencia, 1937)
   Nuestra organización y nuestros cuadros (Valencia, 1937)
Baraibar, Carlos de. *La guerra de España en el plano internacional* (Barcelona, 1938)
Carrillo, S. *Amigos de la juventud, con motivo del 50 aniversario de la Fundación del Partido Socialista* (n.p., 1938)
   En marcha hacia la victoria, speech to JSU national conference, January 1937 (Valencia, 1937)
   La juventud, factor de la victoria, speech to PCE's central committee, plenary session 6–8 March 1937 (Valencia, 1937)
   Por la Alianza Nacional de la juventud (Madrid, 1937)
   Por una juventud victoriosa, speech to the JSU national committee, September 1937 (Madrid, 1937)
   ¡Salud a la juventud española!, speech 16 December 1938 (Valencia, 1938)

Somos la organización de la juventud, speech to JSU national committee meeting, 15–16 May 1937 (n.p., n.d.)

Carrillo, W. 'La verdad sobre el Consejo Nacional de Defensa', *Voces Socialistas* (Mexico, 1946)

Checa, Pedro. *A un gran partido, una gran organización* (Barcelona, 1937)
 Tareas de organización y trabajo práctico del partido (Madrid, 1938)

Claudín, Fernando. *La juventud española continua su lucha* (Mexico, 1940)

CNT. *Federación Regional de Campesinos de Andalucía* (congreso de constitución, memoria), Baza, 15–17 July 1937 (n.p., n.d.)

CNT–UGT. *Alianza CNT–UGT. Sus bases. Sus objetivos. Sus antecedentes* (Barcelona, 1938)

Communist International. *Unity for Spain* (correspondence between Communist international and the Labor and Socialist internationals, June–July, 1937) (New York, 1937)

Companys, L. *De Companys a Indalecio Prieto. Documentación sobre las industrias de guerra en Cataluña* (Buenos Aires, 1939)

Corralejo. *Nuestro Konsomol* (Madrid, 1937?)

Díaz, José. *Por la unidad, hacia la victoria*, speech to PCE Central Committee (n.p., 1937)

FAI. (Comité Peninsular) *Observaciones críticas a la dirección de la guerra y algunas indicaciones fundamentales para continuarla con más éxito*, August 1938, repr. *Timón*, January 1940 (Buenos Aires, 1940)

FNTT. *Cursillos en Valdepeñas. Lecciones teórico-prácticas* (Madrid, 1937?)
 Homenaje a Ricardo Zabalza con motivo del cuarto aniversario de su fusilamiento (Mexico, 1944)
 Un siglo de acción sindical nos respalda (Madrid, 1977)
 Por la revolución agraria: 2 comicios campesinos históricos (December 1936, June 1937) (Madrid, 1937)

Gómez, Sócrates. *Los jóvenes socialistas y la JSU*, speech, September 1938 (Madrid, 1938)

González, Regino. *La cooperación en el mundo* (given in Valdepeñas as part of a series organised by FNTT, 17–31 October 1937 (Barcelona, 1938)

González Peña, R. *Discurso pronunciado en el cine Bilbao de Madrid*, 1 August 1937 (Madrid, 1937)

González Peña, R. & Lamoneda, R. *La guerra y la unidad marxista* (Barcelona, 1937)

Hernández Zancajo, C. *Veinte años de revolución 1917–1937* (Madrid, 1938)

Hospitales, Sanitarios y similares (UGT). *Posición política y sindical de esta federación – documentos relacionados con el pleito interno de la UGT* (n.p., n.d.)

Instituto de Reforma Agraria. *La política del Frente Popular en agricultura* (Madrid/Valencia, 1937)

Jimeno, Arsenio. *Francisco Largo Caballero. Unos apuntes biográficos y tres conferencias* (Paris, n.d.)

JSU. *Clubes de educación de la JSU* (n.d., n.p.)
 Los clubes de la Juventud Socialista Unificada en el Ejército (Valencia, 1938?)

Cómo se forja la democracia campesina en España (Valencia, 1938)
Conferencia Nacional de Juventudes, collected speeches from JSU conference, January 1937 (Madrid/Valencia, 1937)
Las diez reivindicaciones de la juventud (Valencia, n.d.)
En el II aniversario de la unidad (Madrid, 1938)
La JSU en el campo (Valencia, 1938)
La JSU y la producción (Valencia, 1938)
La juventud en el Ejército Popular (Madrid, 1938)
Nuestra lucha por la unidad (Valencia, 1937?)
¿Qué es una brigada de choque? Los jóvenes socialistas unificados y las nuevas tareas (Valencia, 1937)
Lain, José. *Por un ejército regular, disciplinado y fuerte*, speech to JSU national conference, January 1937 (Valencia, 1937)
Lamoneda, Ramón. *Cuatro discursos sobre la unidad* (Madrid, 1937?)
El deber socialista. Manifiesto de la Comisión Ejecutiva del PSOE por R. Lamoneda y R. González Peña (Paris, 1946)
Glosa de los acuerdos del Comité Nacional del PSOE, speech, teatro Chueca, Madrid, 16 October 1938 (Madrid, n.d.)
El Partido Socialista en la República Española (Mexico, 1942)
Por la Reconquista de España – Unidad de lucha (Mexico, 1945)
Ramón Lamoneda. Ultimo secretario general del PSOE. Posiciones políticas – documentos – correspondencia (prologue by Amaro del Rosal) (Mexico, 1976)
Los sindicatos tienen que ganar la batalla de las fábricas, III Congress of the UGT in Cataluña, 13–18 November 1937 (Barcelona, 1937)
Landau, Katia. *Le stalinisme en Espagne: témoignages de militants révolutionnaires sauvés des prisons staliniennes* (Paris, 1938)
Largo Caballero, F. *El creador de la victoria: 3 fechas representativas en el balance de su obra* (Valencia, 1937)
Discursos a los trabajadores. Una crítica de la República, una doctrina socialista, un programa de acción (Madrid, 1934)
Discurso del presidente del Consejo de Ministros ... pronunciado en Valencia el 1 de febrero de 1937 (Madrid, 1937)
La UGT y la Guerra, discurso en el teatro Pardiñas de Madrid (Valencia, 1937)
Llopis, Rodolfo. *Etapas de la revolución española. Octubre de 34* (speech given in Paris, 9 October 1949) (Mexico, n.d.)
Nuestro Partido no galvaniza cadáveres ni dejará absorber, speech, Alicante, April 1937 (Valencia, 1937)
López Sevilla, E. *El PSOE en las Cortes Constituyentes de la República* (Mexico, 1969)
Mateu, Julio. *¿Qué es la Federación Provincial Campesina?* (Valencia, 1936)
La obra de la Federación Campesina (Barcelona, 1937)
Medrano, Trifón. *Hombres nuevos y nuevos cuadros*, speech to the JSU national conference, January 1937 (Valencia, 1937)
Melchor, Federico. *Organicemos la producción*, speech to the JSU national conference, January 1937 (Valencia, 1937)

Mije, Antonio. *El papel de los sindicatos en los momentos actuales* (Madrid/ Valencia, 1937)
   Por una potente industria de guerra (Barcelona, 1937)
Montiel, Francisco. *Por qué he ingresado en el Partido Comunista* (Barcelona, 1937)
Muñoz Arconada, F. *Carta abierta al Comité Peninsular de las Juventudes Libertarias* (Madrid, 1937?)
   La juventud en la defensa de Madrid, speech to the JSU national conference, January 1937, Valencia (Madrid, 1937)
Negrín, Juan. *Conmemoración del 19 de julio. Discurso de J. Negrín, y otros*, delivered in London, 20 July 1941 (London, 1941)
   Declaración del Excmo. Sr. presidente del Gobierno de Unión Nacional, Barcelona, 14 October 1938 (Barcelona, 1938)
   Un discurso (Mexico, 1942)
   Discurso del presidente del Consejo de Ministros don Juan Negrín, 26 February 1938 (Barcelona, 1938)
   Discurso pronunciado por . . . el día 3 de septiembre de 1945 en el Frontón, México (London, 1945)
   Discurso que el presidente del Consejo de Ministros y Ministro de Defensa Nacional, doctor Negrín pronunció por radio el día 27 de enero, afirmando la seguridad en la victoria (n.p., 1939)
   Documentos políticos para la historia de la República española. Dos discursos de Juan Negrín (Mexico, 1945)
   Dos discursos del presidente. Luchamos por España y venceremos. Mensaje a la democracia norteamericana, 24–31 December 1938 (n.p., n.d.)
   ¡España para los españoles! Discurso del presidente del Consejo de Ministros y Ministro de Defensa pronunciado en Madrid el 18 de junio de 1938 (Barcelona, 1938)
   El Gobierno de la República se dirige al país (Madrid, 1938?)
   Informe de . . . a los republicanos españoles, pronunciado en el palacio de Bellas Artes de la ciudad de México el día 1 de agosto de 1945 (London, n.d.)
   '*La política internacional, la República y la guerra española*', *Mundo Libre*, February 1943
   Pour une République libre et indépendante. Discours prononcé à Paris le 11 août 1946 (Paris, 1946)
   Premier Negrín's address to the League of Nations assembly, 18 September 1937 (n.p., 1937)
   El Presidente del Consejo de Ministros del Gobierno de la Unidad Nacional habla para todo el pueblo español (speech before Cortes, San Cugat del Vallés, 30 September 1938 (Valencia, 1938)
   Saludo y despedida del doctor Negrín a los combatientes de las Brigadas Internacionales que abandonan España (Madrid, n.d.)
   . . . una sola orden en cada conciencia: ¡Resistir para vencer! (Discurso pronunciado por el presidente del Gobierno de la República, camarada Negrín, la noche del 28 de marzo de 1938) (Madrid, 1938)
   Speech to the Council on Foreign Relations, 8 May 1939 (n.p., n.d.)

PCE. *Congreso de la Internacional Comunista (VII)* (speeches, resolutions) (Madrid, 1935)

El partido comunista por la libertad y la independencia de España: llamamientos y discursos (Valencia, 1937)

Programa de acción común para la creación del partido único del proletariado (Valencia, 1937)

Prieto, Indalecio. *¿Ablandamiento? La inútil deshonra* (n.p., n.d.)

El auxilio de América y América para la reconstrucción de España, speech, 9 October 1938 (Barcelona, 1938)

Cómo y por qué salí del Ministerio de Defensa Nacional. Intrigas de los rusos en España. Texto taquigráfico del informe pronunciado el 9 de agosto de 1938 ante el Comité Nacional del PSOE (Paris, 1939; Mexico, 1940)

Un discurso de Indalecio Prieto. Recuerdos y perspectivas, 28 August 1938 (Barcelona, 1938)

Discursos en América con el pensamiento puesto en España (Mexico, 1944)

Discursos fundamentales (Madrid, 1975) (ed. E. Malefakis)

Inauguración del Círculo Pablo Iglesias, de México, discurso (Mexico, 1940)

Palabras al viento (Mexico, 1969)

Prieto, Indalecio, et. al. *Documentos socialistas* (Madrid, 1935)

PSOE. *Federación provincial socialista de Badajoz, el Fascismo sobre Extremadura* (Madrid, 1938)

Federación provincial socialista de Valencia. Memoria de la actuación de las federaciones provinciales socialistas (Valencia, 1937)

Programa de acción común (Valencia, 1937)

República. Por la República contra el plebiscito. (Discursos) (speeches by Alvarez del Vayo, Galarza, Lamoneda, Negrín, Rodríguez Vega) (Mexico, 1945)

Rodríguez Vega, J. *Discurso de . . . Secretario general de la UGT.* III Congress of the UGT in Cataluña (Barcelona, 1937)

Rosal, Amaro del. *Conferencia pronunciada por el compañero . . . . el día 12 de enero de 1937 en Valencia* (Federación Española de Trabajadores del Crédito y de las Finanzas) (UGT) (n.p., n.d.)

Salcedo, O. *Posiciones y orientaciones de las Juventudes Socialistas* (Mexico, 1944)

Serrano Poncela, S. *La Conferencia Nacional de Juventudes. Guía de divulgación y de trabajo* (Valencia, 1937)

Sindicato Nacional de Trabajadores del Crédito y de las Finanzas, UGT. *Congreso extraordinario. Actas de las sesiones celebradas . . . durante los días 17 a 20 de septiembre de 1936* (Madrid, 1936)

Sindicato Nacional de Trabajadores del Crédito y de las Finanzas, UGT. *Pleno nacional ampliado, celebrado en Valencia durante los días 4 a 9 de abril de 1937. Informes, discusiones* (n.p., n.d.)

Tres conferencias pronunciadas por los compañeros Luis Guillén. Alfredo Lagunilla y Amaro Rosal (Barcelona, 1938)

Sindicato (Nacional) de la industria fabril, textil y anexos. Memoria de la decisión de la destitución de la C.E. de la UGT (Barcelona, 1937)

Sindicato Nacional de Trabajadores de Hospitales, Sanitarios y similares. Posición política y sindical de esta federación – documentos relacionados con el pleito interno de la UGT (n.p., n.d.)

Sindicato metalúrgico de Madrid ('El Baluarte'). *Resoluciones del Comité Nacional de la Unión General de Trabajadores* (Madrid, 1938)

Togliatti, Palmiro. *Las características de la revolución española* (Barcelona, n.d.)

Tomás, Pascual. *Conferencia ... organizado por el C.E. del GSS de ferroviarios con motivo del cincuentenario del primer congreso del PSOE* (Madrid, 1938)

    El deber de hoy: exhortación a nuestra retaguardia (Murcia, 1938)

    Discurso en el 'Gran Price' de Barcelona, el día 17 de enero de 1937 (Barcelona, 1937?)

    Perfiles de nuestra guerra, speech (Madrid, 1938)

    La UGT, columna de la victoria, discurso en el congreso provincial del secretariado de Valencia, UGT (Valencia, 1937)

    Unión General de Trabajadores en España y en el exilio (Toulouse, 1955)

UGT. *Federación Provincial de Valencia. UGT 1888–1938* (Valencia, 1938)

    Secretaría de Formación. Rasgos históricos de la Unión General de Trabajadores (Madrid, 1976)

UGT–CNT. *Programa de unidad entre UGT–CNT* (Barcelona, 1938)

Uribe, Vicente. *Los campesinos y la República: conferencia pronunciada el día 22 de enero de 1938, Valencia* (Valencia, 1938?)

    Nuestros hermanos los campesinos (Valencia, 1937?)

    La política agraria del partido comunista, speech, 4 July 1937, Valencia (Barcelona, 1937)

Vidal, M. *La juventud en la guerra y en la revolución* (n.d., n.p., [1938])

Wolf, Michael. *¡La unidad internacional de la juventud en defensa de España!*, speech to the JSU national conference, January 1937 (Valencia, 1937)

Memoirs, Diaries, Contemporary and Eye-witness Accounts, Theoretical Works by Protagonists

Abad de Santillán, D. *Contribución a la historia del movimiento obrero español* (Mexico, 1965)

    Por qué perdimos la guerra (Buenos Aires, 1940)

Adame, Manuel. *¿Qué es el bloque obrero y campesino?* (n.p., 1932)

Aguirre y Lecube, J. A. *De Guernica a Nueva York pasando por Berlín* (Buenos Aires, 1944)

    Informe del Presidente Aguirre al gobierno de la República sobre los hechos que determinaron el derrumbamiento del frente del Norte (Bilbao, 1978)

Alaíz, Felipe. *Indalecio Prieto: Padrino de Negrín y campeón anticomunista* (Toulouse, n.d.)

Albar, Manuel. *Cartas, artículos y conferencias de un periodista español en México* (Mexico, 1958)

Alonso, Bruno. *La flota republicana y la guerra civil de España* (Mexico, 1944)

    El proletariado militante (Memorias de un provinciano) (Mexico, 1957)

Alvarez del Vayo, J. *En la lucha. Memorias* (Mexico, 1975)

Freedom's Battle (London and New York, 1940)
The Last Optimist (London, 1950)
Andrade, Juan. *La burocracia reformista en el movimiento obrero* (Madrid, 1935)
Ansó, Mariano. *Yo fui ministro de Negrín* (Barcelona, 1976)
Araquistain, Luis. *El comunismo y la guerra de España* (Carmaux (Tarn), 1939)
  Franco y el comunismo (Uruguay, 1959)
  La intervención de Rusia en la guerra civil española (Paris, 1958)
  Mis tratos con los comunistas (Toulouse, n.d.)
  Sobre la guerra civil y en la emigración (ed. J. Tusell) (Madrid, 1983)
  La verdad sobre la intervención y no intervención en España (Barcelona, 1938)
Asensio, General. *El General Asensio: Su lealtad a la república* (Barcelona, 1938?)
Azaña, Manuel. *Los españoles en guerra* (Barcelona, 1977)
  Obras completas (4 vols.) (Mexico, 1966–8)
Baraibar, Carlos de. *Las falsas 'posiciones socialistas' de Indalecio Prieto* (Madrid, 1935)
  'La traición del Stalinismo', *Timón* (Buenos Aires, June 1940)
Barea, A. *La forja de un rebelde* (Buenos Aires, 1951)
Borkenau, Franz. *The Spanish Cockpit* (London, 1937; repr. Ann Arbor, 1963)
Bowers, Claude. *My Mission to Spain* (London, 1954)
Buckley, Henry. *Life and Death of the Spanish Republic* (London, 1940)
Buenacasa, M. *La CNT, los treinta y la FAI* (Barcelona, 1933)
  El movimiento obrero español 1886–1926 (Barcelona, 1928; Madrid, 1977)
  Por la unidad CNT–UGT. Perspectivas del movimiento obrero español (Mexico, 1964)
Bullejos, J. *La Comintern en España. Recuerdos de mi vida* (Mexico, 1972)
  España en la segunda república (Mexico, 1967)
  Europa entre dos guerras, 1918–1938 (Mexico, 1945)
  'Los últimos momentos de la guerra civil', *Mundo* (Mexico, October 1943)
Cánovas, C. S. *De Franco a Negrín pasando por el partido comunista: Historia de la revolución española* (Toulouse, n.d.)
  Durruti, Ascaso, la CNT y la revolución de julio (Toulouse, 1948)
Carrillo, W. 'En torno al trágico fin de nuestra guerra', *Timón*, 1, November 1939 (Buenos Aires)
  El último episodio de la guerra civil española (Toulouse, 1945)
Casado, S. *Así cayó Madrid* (Madrid, 1968; repr. 1977)
  The Last Days of Madrid (London, 1939)
Castro Delgado, E. *Hombres made in Moscú* (Mexico, 1960)
Claudín, Fernando. *The Communist Movement* (Harmondsworth, 1975)
  'Dos concepciones de la vía española al socialismo', *Horizonte España 1966* (2 vols.), *Cuadernos de Ruedo Ibérico* (Paris, 1966)
  Santiago Carrillo: crónica de un Secretario General (Barcelona, 1983)
Conze, E. *Spain Today: Revolution and Counter-Revolution* (London, 1936)

Cordero, Manuel. *Los socialistas y la revolución* (Madrid, 1932)

Cordón, Antonio. *Trayectoria* (Paris, 1971)

Cuevas, Col. *Recuerdos de la guerra de España* (Montauban, 1940)

Díaz, José. *Tres años de lucha* (3 vols.) (Toulouse, 1947, edn used, Barcelona, 1978)

Domínguez, E. *Los vencedores de Negrín* (Mexico, 1940; repr. 1976)

Ferrándiz Alborz, F. *La Bestia contra España* (n.p. [Montevideo], 1951)

Fischer, Louis. *Men and Politics* (London, 1941)

García, Regina. *Yo he sido marxista* (Madrid, 1946)

García Pradas, J. *Como terminó la guerra de España* (Buenos Aires, 1940)
    ¡Teníamos que perder! (Madrid, 1974)

González, V. ('El Campesino'). *Comunista en España y antistalinista en la U.R.S.S.* (Mexico, 1952)
    La vie et la mort en U.R.S.S. 1939–1949 (Paris, 1950)

González Peña, R. *Un hombre en la revolución. (Con trabajos de Indalecio Prieto y otros)* (Madrid, 1935)

Gorkín, Julián. *Caníbales políticos. Hitler y Stalin en España* (Mexico, 1941)
    España, primer ensayo de democracia popular (Buenos Aires, 1961)
    El proceso de Moscú en Barcelona. El sacrificio de Andrés Nin (Barcelona, 1974)
    El revolucionario profesional. Testimonio de un hombre de acción (Barcelona, 1975)

Guérin, Daniel. *Front populaire: révolution manquée, témoignage militant* (Paris, 1970)

Hernández, Jesús. *El partido comunista antes, durante y después de la crisis del gobierno de Largo Caballero* (Valencia, 1937)
    Yo fui un ministro de Stalin (Mexico, 1953)

Hernández Zancajo, C. *Octubre–segunda etapa* (n.p., n.d. [Madrid, 1935?])
    Tercera etapa de octubre (Valencia, 1937)

Hidalgo de Cisneros, I. *La república y la guerra de España. Memorias* (vol. 2) (Paris, 1964)

Huerta, A. *Europa en la cruz gamada* (Mexico, 1942)

Ibárruri, Dolores, *et. al. Guerra y revolución en España 1936–1939* (4 vols.) (Moscow, 1966–77)
    El único camino (Paris, 1962)

Iglesias, Ignacio. *La fase final de la guerra civil: de la caída de Barcelona al derrumbamiento de Madrid* (Barcelona, 1977)

Izcaray, Jesús. *La guerra que yo vivía: crónicas de los frentes españoles 1936–9* (Madrid, 1978)

Izcaray, Jesús, *et al. El socialismo español después de octubre* (Madrid, 1935)

Jellinek, Frank. *The Civil War in Spain* (London, 1938)

Kaminski, H. E. *Ceux de Barcelone* (Paris, 1937)

Koestler, Arthur. *Spanish Testament* (London, 1937)

Koltsov, Mikhail. *Diario de la guerra española* (Paris, 1963, Madrid, 1978)

Largo Caballero, F. *Carta a mis hijos* (Madrid, 1978)
    Carta a un obrero (Perpignan, 1963)
    Del capitalismo al socialismo. Proyecto de gobierno para España (Mexico, 1946)

Escritos de la República (ed. S. Juliá) (Madrid, 1985)
Francisco Largo Caballero, 1869–1946. Artículos de F. Largo Caballero y J. Martínez Amutio (Madrid, 1978)
Mis recuerdos. Cartas a un amigo (Mexico, 1954)
¿Qué se puede hacer? Cartas a varios amigos donde se examinan las posibilidades de los españoles en la emigración (Paris, 1940)
Líster, Enrique. *Así destruyó Carrillo el PCE* (Barcelona, 1983)
Memorias de un luchador (Madrid, 1977)
Llopis, Rodolfo. *Emigración, exilio y perspectivas del mañana* (Toulouse, n.d.)
Etapas del Partido Socialista Obrero Español (Toulouse, 1962)
Llopis, R. et. al. *Etapas del socialismo español. 1879–1936* (Valencia, 1938)
McGovern, John. *Terror in Spain* (London, 1937?)
Maisky, Ivan. *Spanish Notebooks* (London, 1966)
Mario de Coca, G. *Anti-Caballero: una crítica marxista de la bolchevización del Partido Socialista Obrero Español* (Madrid, 1936)
Martínez Amutio, J. *Chantaje a un pueblo* (Madrid, 1974)
'Contribución a la historia del PSOE', *Tiempo de Historia*, no. 9, August 1975
Matthews, Herbert L. *Half of Spain Died* (New York, 1973)
The Yoke and the Arrows (New York, 1961)
Maurín, Joaquín. *Hacia la segunda revolución: el fracaso de la República y la insurrección de octubre* (Barcelona, 1935)
Los hombres de la dictadura (Madrid, 1930)
La revolución española (Madrid, 1932)
Mera, Cipriano. *Guerra, exilio y cárcel de un anarcosindicalista* (Paris, 1976)
Morato, J. J. *El Partido Socialista Obrero* (Madrid, 1918)
Morón, Gabriel. *Ante la crisis del PSOE* (Mexico, 1946)
El Partido Socialista ante la realidad política de España (Madrid, 1929)
Política de ayer y política de mañana (Mexico, 1942)
La ruta del socialismo en España. Ensayo de crítica y táctica revolucionaria (Madrid, 1932)
Morrow, Felix (pseud. Joaquín Maurín). *The Civil War in Spain* (London, 1938)
Revolution and Counter-Revolution in Spain (New York, 1938)
Munis, Grandizo. *Jalones de derrota, promesa de victoria* (Mexico, 1948)
Muñoz, Máximo. *Dos conductas: Indalecio Prieto y yo* (Mexico, 1952)
Murillo Carrasco, M. *Partido Socialista Obrero Español (Sector Histórico)* (Bilbao, 1977)
Negrín, Juan. *Epistolario Prieto y Negrín* (Paris, 1939)
Nelken, Margarita. *Por qué hicimos la revolución* (Barcelona, 1936)
Nin, Andrés. *Los problemas de la revolución española* (Paris, 1971)
Orwell, George. *Homage to Catalonia* (London, 1938)
Pamies, Teresa. *Quan èrem capitans* (Barcelona, 1974)
Peirats, José. *Los anarquistas en la crisis política española* (Buenos Aires, 1964; repr. Madrid, 1976)
La CNT en la revolución española (3 vols.) (Paris, 1971)

Peydro, M. *Hombres. Francisco Largo Caballero* (Casablanca, 1945)
    La obra de la República Española. Al servicio de la verdad (Casablanca, 1945)
Pons Prades, E. *Los que sí hicimos la guerra* (Barcelona, 1973)
    Un soldado de la República (Madrid, 1974)
Prieto, Indalecio. *Cartas a un escultor* (Buenos Aires, 1961)
    Confesiones y rectificaciones (Mexico, 1942)
    Convulsiones de España. Pequeños detalles de grandes sucesos (3 vols.) (Mexico, 1967–9)
    Del momento. Posiciones socialistas (Madrid, 1935)
    Entresijos de la guerra de España. Colección de artículos periodísticos sobre intrigas de nazis, fascistas y comunistas (Buenos Aires, 1954)
    Epistolario Prieto y Negrín (Paris, 1939)
    Esbozo de un programa de socialización en España (Mexico, 1946)
    Trayectoria de una actitud (Mexico, 1947)
    Yo y Moscú (Prologue, commentary and notes by Mauricio Carlavilla) (Madrid, 1955)
Prieto. *Prieto, el burgués aprovechado* (Madrid, 1950?)
Ramos Oliveira, A. *Historia de España* (3 vols.) (Mexico D.F., n.d.)
    Politics, economics and men of modern Spain, 1808–1946 (London, 1946)
    La revolución española de octubre (Madrid, 1935)
Ranchal, Miguel. *Ramón González Peña* (Villanueva de Córdoba, 1935)
Rangil Alonso, F. *El ensayo socialista en la República española* (Buenos Aires, 1934)
Rexach, A. *Lo que yo sé de la guerra civil española* (Havana, 1939)
Rivas Xerif, C. de. *Retrato de un desconocido: Vida de Manuel Azaña* (Mexico, 1961)
Rojas, Carlos. *Por qué perdimos la guerra: Antología de testimonios de los vencidos en la contienda civil* (Barcelona, 1970)
Rojo, General. *Así fue la defensa de Madrid* (Mexico, 1967)
Romero Solano, L. *Vísperas de la guerra de España* (Mexico, 1947)
Romilly, Esmond. *Boadilla* (London, 1937)
Rosado, Antonio. *Tierra y libertad. Memorias de un campesino anarcosindicalista andaluz* (Barcelona, 1979)
Rosal, Amaro del. *Historia de la UGT de España 1901–1939* (2 vols.) (Barcelona, 1977)
    1934. El movimiento revolucionario de Octubre (Madrid, 1984)
    El oro del Banco de España y la historia de 'El Vita' (Barcelona, 1977)
Saborit, Andrés. *Asturias y sus hombres* (Toulouse, 1964)
    Julián Besteiro (Buenos Aires, 1967)
    El pensamiento político de Julián Besteiro (Madrid, 1974)
Salazar, Victor. *El presidiario número 317. Ramón González Peña* (prologue by B. Tomás and epilogue by R. Lamoneda) (Madrid, 1936)
Sánchez del Arco, M. *El sur de España en la reconquista de Madrid* (Seville, 1937)
Santiago, Enrique de. *Largo Caballero y La República futura* (Mexico, 1956)
    La Unión General de Trabajadores ante la revolución (Madrid, 1932)

Sanz, Ricardo. *Los que fuimos a Madrid: Columna Durruti 26 División* (Toulouse, 1969)
  El sindicalismo español antes de la guerra (Barcelona, 1975)
  El sindicalismo y la política. Los 'solidarios' y 'nosotros' (Toulouse, 1966)
Serrano Poncela, S. *El Partido Socialista y la conquista del poder* (Barcelona, 1935)
Suárez, Andrés (pseud. Ignacio Iglesias). *El proceso contra el POUM* (Paris, 1974)
Suero Sánchez, L. *Memorias de un campesino andaluz* (Madrid, 1982)
Tagüeña, Manuel. *Testimonio de dos guerras* (Mexico, 1973)
Togliatti, Palmiro. *Escritos sobre la guerra de España* (Barcelona, 1980)
Toryho, Jacinto. *La traición de Señor Azaña* (New York, 1939)
Vidarte, J. S. *El bienio negro y la insurrección de Asturias* (Barcelona, 1978)
  Todos fuimos culpables (2 vols.) (Barcelona, 1978)
Voces. Voces socialistas. Manuel Albar, Luis Araquistain, Trifón Gómez, Indalecio Prieto, Wenceslao Carrillo (Mexico, 1946)
Zugazagoitia, Julián. *Guerra y vicisitudes de los españoles* (Buenos Aires, 1940; repr. Barcelona, 1977)

Secondary Sources

Articles, Monographs and General Works

Abella, R. *La vida cotidiana durante la guerra civil – La España Republicana* (Barcelona, 1975)
Aguado, Emiliano. *La República: El último disfraz de la Restauración* (Madrid, 1972)
Alba, Victor. *La alianza obrera* (Madrid, 1978)
  Dos revolucionarios, Joaquín Maurín y Andreu Nin (Madrid, 1975)
  La historia del POUM (Barcelona, 1974)
  El marxismo en España 1919–1939 (Mexico, 1973)
  Los sepultureros de la República (Barcelona, 1977)
Alexander, M. S. & Graham, H. *The French and Spanish Popular Fronts: Comparative Perspectives* (Cambridge, 1988)
Alpert, M. *El ejército republicano en la guerra civil* (Barcelona, 1978)
  'La diplomacia inglesa y el fin de la guerra civil española', *Revista de Política Internacional* (March–April 1975, Madrid)
Andrés Gallego, José. *El socialismo durante la Dictadura (1923–1930)* (Madrid, 1977)
Arbeloa, V. M. *Historia de la Unión General de Trabajadores* (Bilbao, 1975)
  Orígenes del Partido Socialista Obrero Español (1) (1873–1880) (Vizcaya, 1972)
Arenillas de Chaves, I. *El proceso de Besteiro* (Madrid, 1976)
Aróstegui, J. 'La República en guerra y el problema del poder', *Studia Histórica*, vol. 3, no. 4, 1985
Aróstegui, J. & Martínez, J. A. *La Junta de Defensa de Madrid* (Madrid, 1984)
Aviv, A. & I. 'Ideology and Political Patronage: Workers and Working

Class Movements in Republican Madrid, 1931–4', *European Studies Review*, vol. 2, 1981

'The Madrid Working Class, the Spanish Socialist Party and the Collapse of the Second Republic (1934–1936)', *Journal of Contemporary History*, vol. 16, 1981

Balcells, A. *Crisis económica y agitación social en Cataluña (1930–1936)* (Madrid, 1971)

'El socialismo catalán en la Segunda República', *Trabajo industrial y organización obrera en la Cataluña contemporánea (1900–36)* (Barcelona, 1974)

Ballestero, E. *La política agraria del socialismo español* (Madrid, 1979)

Bar Cendon, A. 'La CNT frente a la República', *Estudios sobre la II República* (Madrid, 1975)

Bayerlein, B. 'El significado internacional de Octubre de 1934 en Asturias. La Comuna asturiana y el Komintern', in G. Jackson *et al.*, *Octubre 1934. Cincuenta años para la reflexión* (Madrid, 1985)

Bécarud, J. *La segunda república española* (Madrid, 1967)

Bernecker, W. *Colectividades y revolución social: el anarquismo en la guerra civil española 1936–1939* (Barcelona, 1982)

Bizcarrondo, Marta. *Araquistain y la crisis socialista de la II República/Leviatán (1934–1936)* (Madrid, 1975)

'De las Alianzas Obreras al Frente Popular', *Estudios de Historia Social,* nos. 16–17, January–June 1981

'La crisis socialista en la Segunda República', *Revista del Instituto de Ciencias Sociales* (Barcelona), no. 21, 1973

'Democracia y revolución en la estrategia socialista de la Segunda República' in *Estudios de Historia Social*, nos. 16–17, 1981

'Julián Besteiro: socialismo y democracia', *Revista del Occidente* (Madrid), no. 94, January 1971

Bizcarrondo, Marta (ed.) *Octubre del 34: reflexiones sobre una revolución* (Madrid, 1977)

Blas Guerrero, A. 'La radicalización de Francisco Largo Caballero, 1933–1934', *Sistema* (Madrid), no. 8, January 1975

El socialismo radical en la II República (Madrid, 1978)

Bolloten, Burnett. *The Spanish Revolution. The Left and the Struggle for Power during the Civil War* (Chapel Hill, 1979)

La guerra civil española: revolución y contrarrevolución (Madrid, 1989)

Bonamusa, F. *Andreu Nin y el movimiento comunista en España* (Barcelona, 1977)

Bosch Sánchez, A. *Ugetistas y libertarios: guerra civil y revolución en el país valenciano 1936–1939* (Valencia, 1983)

Brademas, John. *Anarco-sindicalismo y revolución en España (1930–1937)* (Barcelona, 1974)

Brenan, Gerald. *Personal Record 1920–1972* (London, 1974)

The Spanish Labyrinth (Cambridge, 1943; 2nd edn 1950)

Brome, V. *The International Brigades. Spain 1936–1939* (London, 1965)

Broué, P. *La révolution espagnole* (Paris, 1973)
Broué, P. & Témime, E. *The Revolution and the Civil War in Spain* (trans. from French) (London, 1972)
Calero, A. M. *Historia del movimiento obrero en Granada 1909–23* (Madrid, 1973)
  Movimientos sociales en Andalucía 1820–1936 (Madrid, 1976)
Carr, R. *The Civil War in Spain* (London, 1986)
  Spain 1808–1975 (Oxford, 1982)
Carrión, P. *Los latifundios en España* (Madrid, 1932)
Casanova, J. *Anarquismo y revolución en la sociedad rural aragonesa 1936–1938* (Madrid, 1985)
Castells, Andreu. *Las brigadas internacionales en España* (Barcelona, 1974)
Castillo, S. *et al. Historia del socialismo en Aragón PSOE–UGT (1879–1936)* (Zaragoza, 1979)
Cattell, D. T. *Communism and the Spanish Civil War* (Berkeley, 1955)
  Soviet Diplomacy and the Spanish Civil War (Berkeley, 1957)
Chiponte-Martínez, E. *Alicante 1936–39* (Madrid, 1974)
Chomsky, Noam. *American Power and the New Mandarins* (London, 1969)
Cierva, R. de la. *Bibliografía general sobre la guerra de España (1936–1939) y sus antecedentes históricos* (Madrid, 1968)
  Los documentos de la primavera trágica. Análisis documental de los antecedentes inmediatos del 18 de julio de 1936 (Madrid, 1967)
  Historia de la guerra civil española (vol. 1) (Madrid, 1969)
  La historia perdida del socialismo español (Madrid, 1972)
Comín Colomer, E. *El comisariado político en la guerra española* (Madrid, 1973)
  Historia del Partido Comunista de España (3 vols.) (Madrid, 1965)
Contreras, Manuel. 'El P.S. La trayectoria de un conflicto interno', *Estudios sobre la II República Española* (Madrid, 1974)
  El PSOE en la II República: Organización e ideología (Madrid, 1981)
Cruells, M. *Mayo sangriento: Barcelona, 1937* (Barcelona, 1970)
Díaz, C. *Besteiro, el socialismo en libertad* (Madrid, 1976)
Díaz, E. 'Fernando de los Ríos: socialismo humanista y socialismo marxista', *Sistema* (Madrid), no. 10, July 1975
Elorza, A. *El socialismo utópico español* (Madrid, 1970)
  La utopía anarquista bajo la segunda república española (Madrid, 1973)
Espadas Burgos, M. 'Sobre la figura política de Julián Besteiro', *Hispania*, 31, no. 119, 1971
Estruch, Joan. *Historia del PCE* (2 vols.) (Barcelona, 1978) (1, 1920–39)
Fagen, P. W. *Exiles and Citizens: Spanish Republicans in Mexico* (Austin, Texas, 1973)
Fernández Castro, J. *Alejandro Otero: el médico y el político* (Madrid, 1981)
Forner Muñoz, S. *Industrialización y movimiento obrero. Alicante 1923–1936* (Valencia, 1982)
Fraser, R. *Blood of Spain* (London, 1979)
  'Reconsidering the Spanish Civil War', *New Left Review*, no. 129, September–October 1981

Fusi, J. P. 'El movimiento obrero en España 1876–1914', *Revista del Occidente*, no. 131, February 1974
'El movimiento socialista en España 1879–1939', *Actualidad Económica*, no. 865, 1974
Política obrera en el país vasco 1880–1923 (Madrid, 1975)
García Durán, J. *La guerra civil española: Fuentes* (Barcelona, 1985)
García Venero, M. *Historia de las Internacionales en España* (3 vols.) (Madrid, 1956–7)
Garrido, González L. *Colectividades agrarias en Andalucía: Jaén (1931–1939)* (Madrid, 1979)
Geary, D. *European Labour Protest 1848–1939* (London, 1981)
Germán, Luis G. *El socialismo en Aragón, 1930–1936* (Zaragoza, 1977–8)
Gibson, I. *The Assassination of Federico García Lorca and the Nationalist Repression in Granada* (New York, 1983)
Federico García Lorca. A Life (London, 1989)
Paracuellos: cómo fue (Barcelona, 1983)
Gómez Casas, J. *Historia del anarcosindicalismo español* (Madrid, 1969)
Historia de la FAI (Madrid, 1977)
Gómez Llorente, L. *Aproximación a la historia del socialismo español (hasta 1921)* (Madrid, 1972)
Graham, H. & Preston, P. *The Popular Front in Europe* (London, 1987)
Greene, N. *Crisis and Decline: The French Socialist Party in the Popular Front Era* (Ithaca, 1969)
Hermet, G. *The Communists in Spain* (London, 1974)
Jackson, G. *Costa, Azaña, el Frente Popular y otros ensayos* (Madrid, 1976)
The Spanish Republic and the Civil War 1931–1939 (Princeton, 1965)
Jackson, G. et al. *Octubre 1934. Cincuenta años para la reflexión* (Madrid, 1985)
Juliá y Díaz, Santos. 'Corporativistas obreros y reformadores políticos: crisis y escisión del PSOE en la II República', *Studia Histórica*, no. 1 (4), 1983
'De la división orgánica al gobierno de unidad nacional' and 'Partido contra sindicato: una interpretación de la crisis de mayo de 1937', *Anales de Historia*, vol. 2 (Madrid, 1987)
'Indalecio Prieto: Un líder político entre dirigentes sindicales', *MOPU* (Revista del Ministerio de Obras Públicas y Urbanismo), no. 305, December 1983
La Izquierda del PSOE (1935–1936) (Madrid, 1977)
Madrid 1931–1934. De la fiesta popular a la lucha de clases (Madrid, 1984)
'Manuel Azaña: la razón, la palabra y el poder' in *Azaña* (eds.) V. Alberto Serrano & J. M. San Luciano (Madrid, 1980)
Orígenes del Frente Popular en España: 1934–1936 (Madrid, 1979)
'The origins and nature of the Spanish Popular Front' in *The French and Spanish Popular Fronts: Comparative Perspectives* (eds.) M. Alexander & H. Graham
'Sobre la formación del Frente Popular en España', *Sistema*, July 1986
Kaplan, T. *Anarchists of Andalusia 1868–1903* (Princeton, 1977)

Lacomba, J. A. *La crisis española de 1917* (Madrid, 1970)
Lamberet, R. *Mouvements ouvriers et socialistes (chronologie et bibliographie: Espagne (1750–1936)* (Paris, 1953)
Lamo de Espinosa, E. *Filosofía y política en Julián Besteiro* (Madrid, 1973)
Lefranc, G. *Histoire du front populaire 1934–1938* (2nd edn, Paris, 1974)
    Le mouvement sindical de la libération aux événements de mai–juin 1968 (Paris, 1969)
Lorenzo, C. M. *Los anarquistas españoles y el poder* (Paris, 1972)
Lozano, Jesús. *La Segunda República: imágenes, cronología y documentos* (Barcelona, 1973)
Macarro Vera, J. M. 'Causas de la radicalización socialista en la Segunda República', *Revista de Historia Contemporánea* (Seville), no. 1, December 1982
    La utopia revolucionaria. Sevilla en la Segunda República (Seville, 1985)
Madariaga, S. de. *Spain: A Modern History* (London, 1961)
Malefakis, E. E. *Agrarian Reform and Peasant Revolution in Spain: Origins of the Civil War* (New Haven, 1970)
Marichal, Juan. 'Ciencia y gobierno: La significación histórica de Juan Negrín (1892–1956)' in *Estudios sobre la II república española* (ed.) M. Ramírez (Madrid, 1975)
Martínez Alier, J. *Labourers and Landowners in Southern Spain* (London, 1971)
Martínez Bande, J. M. *Los cien últimos días de la República* (Barcelona, 1972)
Martínez Cuadrado, M. *Elecciones y partidos políticos en España 1868–1931* (2 vols.) (Madrid, 1969)
Martínez de Sas Mª T. *El socialismo y la España oficial. Pablo Iglesias, diputado a Cortes* (Madrid, 1975)
Masip, A. *Apuntes para un estudio de la guerra civil en Asturias* (Madrid, 1973)
Maurice, J. *La Reforma agraria en España en el siglo XX (1900–1936)* (Madrid, 1975)
Meaker, G. *The Revolutionary Left in Spain 1914–1923* (Stanford, 1974)
Miguez, A. *El pensamiento filosófico de Julián Besteiro* (Madrid, 1971)
Moore, B. Jr. *Social Origins of Dictatorship and Democracy* (London, 1967)
Moreno Gómez, Francisco. *La República y la guerra civil en Córdoba (Córdoba, 1983)*
    La guerra civil en Córdoba (1936–1939) (Madrid, 1985)
Morodo, R. *Introducción al pensamiento político de Luis Araquistain* (Madrid, 1972)
Mosse, B. *The Origins of the French Labour Movement* (Berkeley, 1976)
Nadal, Antonio. *La guerra civil en Málaga* (Málaga, 1984)
Nash, Mary. 'La problemática de la mujer y el movimiento obrero en España', *Teoría y práctica del movimiento obrero en España* (ed.) A. Balcells (Valencia, 1977)
    Mujer y movimiento obrero en España 1931–39 (Barcelona, 1981)
Núñez de Arenas, M. & Tuñón de Lara, M. *Historia del movimiento obrero español* (Barcelona, 1970)
Pagès, P. *Andreu Nin: su evolución política 1911–1937* (Bilbao, 1975)

El movimiento trotskista en España 1930–1935 (Barcelona, 1977)

Pastor Ugena, A. *La Agrupación Socialista Madrileña durante la Segunda República* (2 vols.) (Madrid, 1985)

Payne, S. G. *Falange: A History of Spanish Fascism* (Stanford, 1961)
Politics and the Military in Modern Spain (Stanford, 1967)
The Spanish Revolution (London, 1970)

Pérez Yruela, M. *La conflictividad campesina en la provincia de Córdoba 1931–1936* (Madrid, 1979)

Preston, Paul. 'Alfonsist Monarchism and the Coming of the Spanish Civil War', *Journal of Contemporary History*, 7, nos. 3–4, 1972
The Coming of the Spanish Civil War (London, 1978)
'The "Moderate" Right and the Undermining of the Second Spanish Republic, 1931–1933', *European Studies Review*, 3, no. 4, 1973
'The Origins of the Socialist Schism in Spain 1917–31', *Journal of Contemporary History*, 12, no. 1, 1977
'Spain's October Revolution and the Rightist Grasp for Power', *Journal of Contemporary History*, 10, no. 4, 1975
'The Struggle Against Fascism in Spain: Leviatán and the Contradictions of the Socialist Left, 1934–6', *European Studies Review*, 9, 1979

Preston, Paul (ed.) *Leviatán (Antología)* (Madrid, 1976)
Revolution and War in Spain 1931–1939 (London, 1984)

Prost, A. *La CGT à l'époque du front populaire* (Paris, 1964)

Puzzo, Dante A. *Spain and the Great Powers, 1936–1941* (New York, 1962)

Rama, C. *La crisis española del siglo XX* (Mexico, 1960)

Ramírez, M. *Los grupos de presión en la segunda república española* (Madrid, 1969)
Las reformas sociales de la segunda república (Madrid, 1977)

Ramírez, M. (ed.) *Estudios sobre la segunda república española* (Madrid, 1975)

Ramos, V. *La guerra civil. Provincia de Alicante* (3 vols.) (Madrid, 1974)

Reynaud, J. D. *Les syndicats en France* (Paris, 1953)

Richards, V. *Lessons of the Spanish Revolution 1936–1939* (London, 1953, revised edn 1972)

Robinson, R. A. H. *The Origins of Franco's Spain: The Right, The Republic and Revolution, 1931–1936* (Newton Abbot, 1970)

Romero, L. *Desastre en Cartagena* (Barcelona, 1971)
El final de la guerra (Barcelona, 1976)
Tres días de julio: 18, 19 y 20 de 1936 (Barcelona, 1967)

Romero Maura, J. 'El debate historiográfico acerca de la segunda república', *Revista Internacional de Sociología*, Madrid, nos. 3–4, July–December, 1972
La Rosa del Fuego. El obrerismo barcelonés de 1899 a 1909 (Barcelona, 1975)

Ruiz, D. *El movimiento obrero en Asturias* (Oviedo, 1968)

Rupiérez, María. 'Prieto entre la República y el socialismo', *Tiempo de Historia*, no. 13, December 1975

Saiz Valdivielso, A. C. *Indalecio Prieto. Crónica de un corazón* (Barcelona, 1984)

Salas Larrazábal, R. *Historia del ejército popular de la república* (4 vols.)
(Madrid, 1973)

Sanz, J. *El movimiento obrero en el país valenciano (1939–1976)* (Valencia, 1976)

Sedwick, F. *The Tragedy of Manuel Azaña and the Fate of the Spanish Republic*
(Ohio, 1963)

Sevilla Andrés, D. *Historia política de la zona roja* (Madrid, 1963)

Shubert, Adrian. *Hacia la revolución. Orígenes sociales del movimiento obrero en
Asturias 1860–1934* (Barcelona, 1984)

'A reinterpretation of the Spanish Popular Front: the case of Asturias' in
The French and Spanish Popular Fronts: Comparative Perspectives (eds.) M.
Alexander & H. Graham

Smyth, D. 'The Politics of Asylum. Juan Negrín in 1940', *Diplomacy and
Intelligence during the Second World War* (ed.) R. Langhorne (Cambridge,
1985)

Southworth, H. R. *El mito de la cruzada de Franco* (Paris, 1963, Madrid, 1986)

Stearns, P. N. *Revolutionary Syndicalism and French Labour* (New Brunswick,
1971)

Stein, L. *Beyond Death and Exile* (Cambridge, Massachusetts, 1979)

Sueco Roca, M. T. *Militares Republicanos de la guerra de España* (Barcelona,
1981)

Taibo, F. I. *Historia general de Asturias* (Gijón, 1978) (vols. VII, VIII)

'Prieto contrabandista de armas', *Historia 16*, no. 18, October 1977

Tamames, R. *La República, la era de Franco* (Madrid, 1973)

Thomas, Hugh. *The Spanish Civil War* (Harmondsworth, 1977)

Tiersky, R. *French Communism 1920–1972* (New York, 1974)

Torres, F. (ed.) *Teoría y práctica del movimiento obrero en España (1900–1936)*
(Valencia, 1977)

Tuñón de Lara, M. 'La crisis del estado: dictadura, república, guerra',
Historia de España, vol. IX (Barcelona, 1981)

La España del siglo XX (2nd edn, Paris, 1973)

*Historia y realidad del poder (El poder y las élites en el primer tercio de la España del
siglo XX* (Madrid, 1971)

*Luchas obreras y campesinas en la Andalucía del siglo XX. Jaén 1917–20, Sevilla
1930–32* (Madrid, 1978)

Metodología de la historia social de España (Madrid, 1973)

El movimiento obrero en la historia de España (with M. Núñez de Arenas)
(Madrid, 1972)

La Segunda República (2 vols.), (Madrid, 1976)

'El significado político del Frente Popular', *Estudios de Historia Social*, nos.
16–17, 1981

'Sobre la historia del pensamiento socialista entre 1900 y 1931', *Teoría y
práctica del movimiento obrero en España 1900–1936* (ed.) A. Balcells
(Valencia, 1977)

'El socialismo español en la guerra civil', *Anales de Historia* (1) (Madrid,
1986)

Tusell, J. *Las elecciones del Frente Popular* (2 vols.) (Madrid, 1971)

Varela, J. 'Reacción y revolución frente a la reforma', *Revista Internacional de Sociología* (Madrid), nos. 3–4, July–December 1972
Vila Izquierdo, J. *Extremadura: La Guerra Civil* (Badajoz, 1983)
Villena Villalain, F. *Las estructuras sindicales de la guerra civil española y la Comunidad de Europa* (Madrid, 1963)
Viñas, A. *La Alemania Nazi y el 18 de julio* (Madrid, 1974)
 El oro de Moscú. Alfa y omega de un mito franquista (Barcelona, 1979)
Viñas, M. 'Franquismo y revolución burguesa', *Horizonte español, 1972* (3 vols.) (Paris, 1972)
Viñas, R. *La formación de las Juventudes Socialistas Unificadas (1934–1936)* (Madrid, 1978)
Wingeate Pike, D. *Les français et la guerre d'Espagne 1936–1939* (Paris, 1975)
 ¡Vae Victis! Los republicanos españoles refugiados en Francia 1939–1944 (Paris, 1969)
Yagüe, M. E. *Santiago Carrillo* (Madrid, 1977)
Zagón Bayo, J. *El consejo revolucionario de Aragón (textos)* (Barcelona, 1979)
Zapatero, V. *Fernando de los Ríos: los problemas del socialismo democrático* (Madrid, 1974)
Zaragoza, C. *Ejército Popular y militares de la República 1936–39* (Barcelona, 1983)

Index

Adame, Manuel, 179
Adelante, 91
  socialist left loses control of, 120, 153,
    167, 174, 179, 186, 192
Agrupación Socialista Madrileña (ASM),
    152
  as *caballerista* stronghold, 7–9, 23, 35, 38,
    40, 48, 53, 59, 76, 129
  attacks on reformist leadership, 39
  and Casado coup, 234, 239–40
Aguirre, José María, 59, 67, 74
Albacete, 78, 113, 162, 200, 208, 216, 235,
    241
  socialist dissidence in JSU, 223–30
Albar, Manuel, 37, 132, 162
Alcalá Zamora, Niceto, 27
Alcira (Valencia Province), 39–40
Alianza Juvenil Nacional, 70, 228
Alianza Obrera (AA.OO.) (*see* Workers'
    Alliance)
Alicante, 78–80, 113, 179, 191, 208, 235
  and socialist dissidence in JSU, 223, 230
  and Casado coup, 238–41
Almagro, Aurelio, 128
Almería, 39, 119, 121, 189
  and Casado coup, 239–40
Alvarez del Vayo, Julio, 62–4, 90, 139, 141,
    157, 231, 236
Alvarez, Segismundo, 71–2
anarchists (*see also* CNT), 2, 9, 25, 64, 78,
    102, 141, 146, 233, 235
  and 'May Days' (1937), 95–6
  relations with left socialists, 44–5, 86–7,
    196
  relations with UGT, 185–8, 202, 205
Andalucía, 200
  land system, 205
Anguiano, Daniel, 177, 190
Antón, Francisco, 226
appeasement, 138, 142, 150, 234
Aragón, 44, 64, 87, 136, 138, 206
Aranda Mata, Col. Antonio, 134
Araquistain, Luis, 47, 62–3, 67, 91, 128,
    130–3, 156, 170

analysis of post-coup conjuncture, 57–8,
    107
  and Casado coup, 232, 234
Artes Blancas, 83, 124, 146, 175, 191
Artes Gráficas, 37
Asensio, General, José, 63, 87, 90, 92, 94
Asturias, 134, 173, 178
  and CNT, 86
  October 1934 rising, 17, 19–20, 44, 100,
    178
  and Popular Front strategy, 26
Austria, 137
Ayguadé, Jaime, 139
Azaña, Manuel, 34–5, 55, 60–1, 91–2, 94,
    96–7, 100, 128–9, 138, 141, 152, 155,
    180, 231
Azorín, Francisco, 112

Badajoz, 88, 122, 145, 204, 208
'El Baluarte', 190, 216
Baraibar, Carlos de, 47, 90, 92, 130, 170,
    173, 208
Barcelona, 64, 87, 130, 138–9, 144, 154–5,
    191, 210, 233
  'May Days' (1937), 95–6, 181, 187
Besteiro, Julián, 151–5
  accused of capitulation, 155
  opposes left within UGT, 168
  and Casado coup, 232
Bilbao, Cresenciano, 128, 130, 156
Blanco, Eduardo, 128
Blanco, Segundo, 140
Bloc Obrer i Camperol (BOC), 43
Blum, Léon, 62, 137, 142
Bolloten, Burnett, 4–5
Botana, Enrique, 111
Bravo, Adolfo, 207
Britain
  isolationism of, 60, 88, 95, 131–2, 138,
    142, 150, 215
Bueno, Javier, 241
Bugeda, Jerónimo, 37, 91, 110, 112, 123,
    156, 158
  offends A. de Gracia, 116

Bugeda, Jerónimo – *cont.*
  removed from PSOE executive
    (September 1938), 154
Bullejos, José, 179, 208

Cabello, Remigio, 37
caciques, 83, 203, 205
Campos Villagrán, Juan, 128
Cantal, Martín, 116, 230, 239
Cardona Rosell, Mariano, 86
Carretero, Adolfo, 111
Carrillo, Santiago, 18, 31, 32–3, 69–74, 116,
    224–5, 230–1
Carrillo, Wenceslao, 37, 59, 128, 193
  resigns from PSOE executive (December
    1935), 23
  and dispute in UGT, 194, 214–15
  and anti-unitarism, 190, 210, 214–15
  and Casado coup, 236, 239
  elected to PSOE national executive
    (March 1939), 242
Cartagena, 64
  rising, 4 March 1939, 232
Casado, Col. Segismundo, 146
  coup, 5 March, 1939, 162, 224, 231–44
Casares Quiroga, Santiago, 36, 55
Castellón, 113, 154, 189
Castro Molina, Manuel, 128
Cataluña, 8, 11, 43, 96, 146, 153
  and intra-UGT struggle, 168, 210, 212,
    216–17
  and PSUC, 196, 210
  falls to rebels, 231, 234, 237
Catholic Youth, 70
Caz, Eliseo del, 111
Cerezo, Enrique, 128, 156
Citrine, Walter, 194, 215
Ciudad Real, 81, 145, 192, 200, 208, 235
  and socialist dissidence in JSU, 223, 230
  and Casado coup, 239–40
Claridad, 23, 38, 40, 49, 53, 77, 178
  left socialists lose control of, 167, 170–1,
    173–4, 192
  and Casado coup, 241
Claudín, Fernando, 224, 240
Codovila, Vittorio, 90
collectivisation, 87–9, 199–208
Comintern, 4, 62, 94
  and aid for Republic, 60, 72, 131
  and Popular Front, 8, 42, 101
  and unity with PSOE, 90, 125, 129
  and Western democracies, 141
  and Casado coup, 237–8
Communist Youth International, 70
Companys, Luis, 96
Confederación Española de Derechas
    Autónomas (CEDA), 203

ministers enter cabinet, October 1934, 17,
    70
Confederación General de Trabajo Unitario
    (CGTU), 21, 30, 32, 47, 79, 214
Confederación Nacional del Trabajo (CNT)
    (*see also* anarchists), 10, 11, 25
  ascendancy of políticos, 141, 188–9, 196
  relations with left socialists, 42, 45, 74, 82,
    84–5, 101
  relations with Largo government, 61, 74,
    101
  and 'May Days' (1937), 95–6
  and May 1937 cabinet crisis, 97–8
  relations with UGT, 45–9, 74, 78, 86–94,
    102, 140–1, 172, 181–6
  pact with UGT (July 1937), 181–2, 186–
    7 (March 1938), 140, 187–9
  against compromise peace, 138
  and Prieto, 139
conscription, 189
Consorcio Levantino Unificado de la
    Exportación Agrícola (CLUEA), 203
Cordero, Manuel, 25, 132, 162, 184, 194
Córdoba, 44, 78, 121–2, 145, 191, 200, 208,
    240
Cordón, Antonio, 156
(*La*) *Correspondencia de Valencia*, 167, 174–5,
    192, 210
Cruz Salido, Francisco, 37, 155, 158, 162
Cuesta, Luis, 116
Cullera (Valencia), 186, 206

Daladier, Edouard, 142
Diario Oficial, 231
Díaz, José, 19, 22, 27
Díaz Alor, José, 54, 66, 99, 168, 194
Díaz Castro, Emiliano, 128, 156
Domínguez, Edmundo, 161, 187, 189, 241
Douglas, General, 134

Ecija (Seville), 39, 82, 200
Escandell, Isidro, 128
Escribano, Antonio, 239
Espectáculos Públicos, 198
Esquerra, 11, 57, 95
Estruch, Joan, 237–8
Extremadura, 97, 191, 207

Fabra Ribas, Antonio, 37
fascism, 8, 44, 47, 70, 79, 132, 177, 178, 228
Federación Anarquista Ibérica (FAI), 86,
    188
Federación Gráfica, 179
Federación de Juventudes Socialistas (FJS),
    48–9, 71, 101
  reaction to Asturian rising (October
    1934), 18

unity with UJC, 27–32, 41, 44
incorporated by PCE, 4, 8, 18, 19, 22, 41, 44
FJS leaders and PCE, 64–6
within JSU, 72, 112
resurgence, 201, 239
Federación Nacional de Trabajadores de la Tierra (FNTT), 29, 54, 153
pre-war radicalisation, 3, 7, 45, 48
and agrarian collectivisation during war, 89, 118, 122
socialist left's power base in UGT, 3, 7, 171, 198–202, 209
opposes PCE, 91, 93, 118, 122, 200–10, 233–4
Federación Provincial Campesina, 91, 202–3
Fernández, Adrián, 111
Fernández, Amador, 180
Fernández Ballesteros, Alberto, 128
Fominaya, Teodoro, 111
France, 232, 234
fails to aid Republic, 60, 88, 95, 131–2, 138, 142, 150
Francisco, Enrique de, 37, 59, 126, 128, 130
resigns from PSOE executive (December 1935), 23, 59
advocates breaking up JSU, 223
and Casado coup, 239
Franco, General Francisco, 10, 136, 138, 151, 234–6, 238, 240
dictatorship of, 4–6
Frente Rojo, 91

Galarza, Angel, 62–4, 92, 98–9, 128, 130, 156
Gallego, Ignacio, 71
Ganga Tremiño, Ginés, 128, 131, 156
García, Claudina, 189, 241
García García, 156
García Muñoz, Salvador, 128, 156
García Oliver, Juan, 140
García Pradas, José, 189
Generalitat, 11, 95–6
Génova, Antonio, 168, 170, 177, 189
Giral, José, 55–6, 58, 91, 96, 139, 141
Gómez, Sócrates, 239
Gómez, Trifón, 154, 158, 242, 243
Gómez Egido, 242
Gómez Osorio, José, 229, 240, 242, 243
González Peña, Ramón,
elected PSOE president (June 1936), 37
as anti-*Caballerista*, 39, 82, 120, 128, 144, 176, 178, 200, 211, 213, 236, 241
and PSOE national committee (July 1937), 113
and unity with PCE, 116–17

as PSOE president, 116, 120, 211
as justice minister under Negrín, 139–40
as UGT president, 140, 189, 213
and UGT executive, 167, 169, 177, 180, 181, 187, 189, 191, 193, 194, 196, 198–9, 208, 215–16, 241
verdict on Prieto, 143
Gómez Sáez, Paulino, 139–40, 158, 236
Gorkín, Julián, 137
Gracia, Anastasio de, 67, 97, 107, 128, 154, 156, 242
and PSOE national committee (July 1937), 114–17
resignation from UGT presidency, 168
Grupos de la Oposición Sindical Revolucionaria (GOSR), 79–80, 122
Grupos Sindicales Socialistas (GSS), 79–80
Guerrero, Melchor, 128

Henche, Rafael, 19, 83, 113, 123–4, 146, 175, 201
Hernández, Jesús, 91, 96, 124, 141, 160, 161, 232
Hernández Zancajo, Carlos, 18, 30–1, 54, 66, 72, 82, 99, 113, 128, 130, 156, 168, 170, 179, 180, 190–1, 194
and urban transport federation, 210–12, 216
Hitler, Adolf, 137
Huerta, Antonio, 153–4
Huete, Tomás, 230

Ibárruri, Dolores, 138
Iglesias, Pablo, 61, 243
Institute of Agrarian Reform (IRA), 202–6
International Brigades, 224
International Federation of Trades Unions (IFTU), 193, 194, 199, 209, 215–17
Irujo, Manuel de, 134, 139
Izquierda Comunista, 43
Izquierda Republicana, 55, 57, 91, 93, 97, 203

Jaén, 72, 78, 121, 200–8
unification of socialist and communist parties, 122–3
land system, 205
and socialist dissidence in JSU, 223, 225, 229, 230
and Casado coup, 240
Jiménez de Asúa, Luis, 37, 110, 153, 156
Joint committees (PSOE/PCE), 75–85, 146, 187
Jouhaux, Léon, 191, 194, 208, 212
'Jupiter Sporting Madrileño' (JSM), 30
Jurados Mixtos, 46, 49
Juventudes de Acción Popular (JAP), 70

Juventud Socialista Madrileña (JSM), 30
Juventudes Socialistas Unificadas (JSU),
42, 129
terms of unity pact, 30, 73
tensions with PSOE, 31–3, 71–3, 223–31
national conference, January 1937, 69–74
and communist predominance in, 69, 71–
4, 84, 114–17, 129, 224–6
and civil war as one of 'national
liberation', 70
depoliticisation of, 71, 226
and collectivisation, 72
'stalinisation' of, 74, 223
left attempts to mobilise, 112–16, 226,
229
'work brigades', 206
PCE 'massification', 212, 228
and Republican army, 230
withdrawal of socialist youth, 235, 240

Labrador, Orencio, 239
Lacomba, José, 230
Lamoneda, Ramón, 19, 25, 37–41, 53–4,
58, 67, 75–7, 80–5, 94, 102, 126, 128,
135, 142, 144, 151–7
and allegiance to Prieto, 77, 107, 157
attempts to boost party morale, 151–6
control of PSOE executive, 157, 195, 243
and PCE membership, 157
and PSOE left, 107–25, 126, 128
inertia in respect of JSU, 226
political line, 107–9, 112, 200, 243
relations with rank and file, 107–8, 110,
226, 243, 246–7
and UGT, 172, 174, 200, 212
and 'unity of action', 146–9, 196
and Casado coup, 232–3, 243
Largo Caballero, Francisco, 16, 19, 23, 24,
35, 36–7, 41–50, 53–68, 69, 72, 74, 76–
7, 111, 113, 121, 123–4, 134, 152–3
and *Caballeristas*, 17, 20–1, 35–7, 41–50,
59, 62, 76, 78–80, 100, 110, 111–16,
119–21, 124, 126–36, 145, 147, 154,
156, 167–97, 224, 239
and revolutionary rhetoric, 18, 45, 48, 57,
88, 89, 95, 100, 101, 178, 185–7, 196,
199
absorptionist tendencies, 42–7
ideological incoherence, 100 (*see also* 'and
revolutionary rhetoric' above), 102,
130, 169, 185, 187
and Popular Front elections (February
1936), 25–7
and presidency of PSOE, 23
and youth unification, 22, 32–3, 69, 101
appointed prime minister, 56, 58, 77
in government, 62–8

growing isolation of, 67, 74
and government crisis, 90, 92, 94–103
departure from government, 81, 98, 100
ouster from parliamentary party
leadership, 126–31
relations with CNT, 87, 96, 98, 185
relations with PCE, 21, 68–85, 190, 196
Teatro Pardiñas speech, October 1937, 183
and UGT, 167–97, 199, 209
withdrawal from public life, 130–1
and 'workerism', 184, 214
and collectivisation, 185, 199–200
and nationalisation, 185
Levante, 11, 39, 75, 113, 152, 154, 192
and CNT, 86–7
Llaneza, Antonio, 83
Llano, Virgilio, 198
Llopis, Rodolfo, 59, 126–8, 131, 152, 156,
176, 191, 193, 242
Lois, Manuel, 53, 54, 168
Lombardía, César, 177, 187, 190, 191
López, Juan, 86
López Quero, José, 201, 242

Madrid, 11, 17–18, 35, 39, 48–9, 55, 61, 75,
78, 79, 80, 83, 136, 146
PCE defence of, 65
PSOE–PCE rivalry in, 123
and Casado coup, 232, 238, 240
Martínez Amutio, Justo, 39, 110, 113, 209
Martínez Barrio, Diego, 55, 231
Martínez Gil, Lucio, 154–5, 226
Maurín, Joaquín, 43
Meabe, Tomás, 112–13, 231
Medrano, Trifón, 71, 116
Melchor, Federico, 31
Méndez Aspe, Francisco, 139
Mendieta, Isidro, 170
Menoyo, Francisco, 225, 229
Mije, Antonio, 223–4
Milla, Rafael, 238
Mola, General Emilio, 55
Molina Conejero, Manuel, 120, 126, 237
Montiel, Francisco, 127
Morón, Gabriel, 63, 107, 118, 135, 159, 224
Moscow, 5
show trials, 74
(La) Motorizada, 30
Munich agreement (30 September 1938), 9,
234
Muñoz, Mariano, 54, 168, 179
Murcia, 63, 79, 113, 162, 191, 235, 241
socialist dissidence in JSU, 223, 226–7,
230

National Defence Council (Casado), 232,
234, 242

Nationalists, 10, 60, 97, 112, 154
Nazi Party, 6
Negrín, Juan, 59, 67, 89, 93–4, 97, 107–8,
    111, 115, 128–9, 131, 133, 136, 140–4,
    151, 154, 156, 157, 189
  relations with Largo, 94, 97, 193
  relations with PCE, 231
  called upon to form government, 100, 110
  relations with Prieto, 137–44, 141–2, 145,
    154
  stresses international dimension of war,
    137, 150
  prioritises military resistance, 139–41, 150
  'Thirteen Points', 142, 145, 229
  and compromise peace, 151, 154, 235
  and Casado coup, 231–2, 235–6
  departure from Spain, 238
Nelken, Margarita, 127
Nin, Andreu, 140
non-intervention, 6, 10, 60, 62, 92, 131, 142,
    215
(Las) Noticias, 167, 173, 211
Nuestra Bandera, 240
Nuestra Lucha, 228

Octubre Segunda Etapa, 18, 72
Organización Interprovincial Socialista,
    145–6
Otero, Alejandro, 94, 153–4, 158, 162
Oviedo, 134

Pablo, Nicolás de, 207
Partido Autonomista (Derecha Regional),
    203
Partido Comunista de España (PCE),
  relations with PSOE, 1, 4–10, 27, 33, 42–
    3, 60, 62, 64, 75–85, 91, 95, 97, 101,
    109, 115–20, 122–3, 125, 131–5, 138,
    141, 146, 150, 152, 156, 167–9, 207,
    223–4
  and Asturian rising, 19
  and Workers' Alliance, 43
  organisation and discipline, 6, 60, 65, 74,
    80, 214, 229
  incorporates FJS, 18–19, 41, 42, 64, 82
  and middle-class support, 65, 138, 197,
    233, 234
  and domination of JSU, 69–73, 80, 82,
    114–15, 223–31
  and peasantry, 72, 202–6
  and Popular Front, 9, 70–1, 82, 84, 90,
    101, 119, 138, 141, 196–7, 202, 204,
    207, 217, 233, 240
  and 'stalinism', 83, 146
  and 'entryism', 206
  and caciques, 83, 203–7
  and Catholics, 212
  fear of compromise peace, 138, 231, 234

  and sectarianism, 146, 203
  and Republican army, 156, 232
  and ouster of socialist left in UGT, 167–8,
    173, 177, 186, 189, 190, 196
  and confrontation with resurgent socialist
    left, 198–218
  and collectivisation, 205, 207–8
  and Casado coup, 231–40, 243
Partido Obrero de Unificación Marxista
    (POUM), 25, 74, 95–6, 137, 140
Partido Sindicalista, 25, 236
Partido Socialista Obrero Español (PSOE),
  divisions in, 1–7, 15–85, 87, 90–1, 93–
    103, 110, 120–1, 124–49, 167–97, 198–
    218, 223–4
  and Asturian rising, 17
  and 'bolshevisation' of (*see also* Largo
    Caballero, Francisco), 4, 18, 45, 66, 72,
    100–1, 152, 168–9
  and relations with PCE, 4–10, 27, 31–3,
    42, 60, 75–85, 109, 115–19, 121–3,
    131–5, 145, 150, 152, 183, 190, 196,
    223–4
  and Popular Front elections, 24–7
  and 'Popular Frontism', 31–2, 42, 47, 69,
    84, 119–20, 145, 147, 228–9
  executive committee elections (June
    1936, 37–9
  organisational dislocation, 40, 80, 82,
    110, 114
  analysis of war, 55–7, 77
  loss of socialist youth, 64, 68, 69–70, 73–
    4, 112–15
  and JSU, 69–74, 112–15, 223–31
  and anti-fascism, 70, 120
  and Catholic Youth, 70
  analysis of the state, 109, 117
  national committee meeting (July 1937),
    112–25
  reformist conquest of hierarchy, 128–9
  loss of authority, 131, 145, 152, 155
  political crisis of April 1938, 136–49
  grass-roots hostility to PCE, 145–8, 169,
    202, 218, 224, 231, 235, 243
  'atomisation' of socialist movement, 149–
    63, 233
  and compromise peace, 150–1, 154–5
  and PSUC, 153
  and organisational rivalry in socialist
    movement, 3, 6, 15, 183–6, 196, 202
Partido Socialista Unificado de Cataluña
    (PSUC), 9, 11, 95, 115, 129, 138, 153,
    168
  relations with UGT, 198, 210
Partido Socialista Unificado de Jaén, 206
Partido Valencianista d'Esquerra (PVE),
    203

peasantry, 71–2, 202–5
Pedrero, Angel, 239
Peiró, Juan, 86
Pérez, Antonio, 176, 189, 236, 241
Pérez, Leoncio, 30
Peris, Alejandro, 128
Pestaña, Angel, 25
Piñuela, Fernando, 160–2, 227, 242;
  'Piñuela affair' (November 1938),
  160–2
Popular Front, 7–11, 70, 84–5, 119–20, 138,
  141, 145
  elections (February 1936), 24–6
  and Comintern, 8, 70, 141
  and PCE, 9, 70–1, 89–90, 141
  contradictions of, 65, 70, 119, 147, 233,
  244
  and fascism, 8, 79
  threatened by compromise peace, 138
Pradal, Gabriel, 128
Prat, José, 128, 156, 158, 176, 224
Pretel, Antonio, 63
Pretel, Felipe, 54, 66, 99, 168, 170, 177, 179,
  189, 190
Prieto, Horacio, 86, 140–1
Prieto, Indalecio, 16, 21–4, 39, 42, 50, 56,
  60–1, 67–8, 76–8, 81–2, 91, 93–4, 96,
  99, 107, 110–11, 127–9, 132–49, 152–
  6, 200
  struggle with party left, 28–9, 35–6, 49–
  50, 76, 78, 82, 147, 172
  refuses premiership (May 1936), 35–6,
  100
  wartime inconsistencies, 60–1, 68, 77,
  133–4, 143
  resignation from cabinet (April 1938), 81,
  134, 136–7, 142–4, 188
  and PCE, 132, 134–5, 138, 144, 148
  and defeatism, 138–9, 148
  relations with Negrín, 137–44, 154, 156
  and anti-communism, 144–8
  and compromise peace, 151
  and UGT, 172, 213
Primo de Rivera, General Miguel, 2, 3, 15
Puente, Enrique, 30
Pulgarín, Antonio, 207

Quintana, Antonio, 111

Ramos Oliveira, Antonio, 234
Ranchal, Miguel, 122, 200
Reichmann, Charles, 89
Renovación, 31
republicanism, 2, 7, 55, 84, 158
Riego, Elias, 190
Ríos Urrutia, Fernando de los, 111, 113, 153
Rodríguez, Alfonso, 116, 230, 239

Rodríguez Vega, José, 170, 176, 189, 241
Romero Solano, Luis, 128
Rosal, Amaro del, 18, 33, 54, 66, 82, 99,
  168, 170–1, 173, 176–7, 187, 189, 190,
  212
Rosenberg, Marcel, 79, 90, 132–3, 135
Rubiera, Carlos, 123, 128, 156, 201, 239,
  242
Rubio, Pedro, 207

Saborit, Andrés, 152, 154, 242
San Andrés, Miguel, 236
San Juan, Carlos de, 193
Sánchez, Pascual, 230
Sánchez Hernández, 227
Sánchez Requena, J., 236
Sánchez Román, Felipe, 83
Schevenels, Walter, 193–4
Serrano Poncela, Segundo, 30–1
Servicio de Investigación Militar (SIM), 83,
  135, 239
Sindicato Minero Asturiano (SMA)
  expulsion from UGT, 177
(El) Socialista, 23, 38, 53, 75–6, 121, 129,
  132, 139, 153, 159, 169, 174, 179, 226,
  242
Soler, José María, 201
Solidaridad Obrera, 49
Sosa Hormigo, José, 128
Soviet Union
  Republic's reliance on its aid, 6, 8, 62,
  125, 132–5, 148
  and Popular Front, 9, 74
  conditions of aid, 62, 125, 148
  foreign policy, 74, 237
  and gold reserves, 133
Spartacus, 179, 181
Stalin, Joseph, 90, 125

Tabaqueros, 191
Tercera Etapa de Octubre, 72, 113
Third International, 132
Tillett, Ben, 89
Timón, 186
Tizón, Juan, 111
Togliatti, Palmiro, 237–8, 240
Tomás, Belarmino, 156
Tomás, Pascual, 23, 37, 54, 99, 128, 168–70,
  179, 194, 214–15, 242

Unión de Juventudes Comunistas (UJC),
  22
  unity agreement with FJS, 27, 29–31, 66
Unión General de Trabajadores (UGT), 1–
  4, 7, 16, 21, 34, 39, 46–7, 53–4, 56, 59,
  64, 75–6, 78, 99–101, 112, 114, 122,
  124, 128–9, 136

and CGTU, 21, 32–3
and divisions in PSOE, 75–6, 101, 112,
129, 136, 140–1, 167–97, 201
militancy of rank and file, 48–9, 184, 199,
202, 217–18
rivalry with CNT, 48, 74, 86–94, 102,
182, 185–6, 206–7
industrial federations, 79, 89, 125, 127,
169, 174–5, 180, 191–2, 194–5
and PCE, 4, 168, 173, 177, 186, 189, 190,
198–218
national committee censures Largo
executive (May 1937), 169–70
battle for control of, 129, 136, 167–97,
198–218
unitarist tendency, 172–218
Largo executive expels industrial
federations, 175–7
pacts with CNT (July 1937, March
1938), 140, 181–2, 186–9
'syndical pretensions' of leadership,
181–3
factory committees, 185
political demobilisation, 187–9
urban transport federation, 210–18
and Soviet trade unions, 215–16
Unión Iberoamericana, 144
Unión Republicana, 57, 93, 97
Urales, Federico, 89

Ureña, Ezequiel, 189, 230
Uribe, Vicente, 27, 89, 91, 93, 96, 199, 201,
207, 231, 236

Val, Eduardo, 236
Valencia, 11, 40, 69, 75, 77, 78, 80–1, 90,
91, 112, 113, 121, 126, 146, 186, 191,
202, 203
land system, 205
socialist dissidence in JSU, 223, 230, 235
Casado coup, 239–40
Vázquez, Mariano R., 172
Vázquez, Narciso, 112
Verdad, 91, 240
Vestido y Tocado, 191
(La) Victoria, 192
Vidarte, Juan-Simeón, 20, 26, 38, 91, 126,
133, 134, 143, 146, 158
Vidiella, Rafael, 111
Villalta, Miguel, 128

Workers' Alliance, 43, 44, 87, 88, 102, 201

Zabalza, Ricardo, 54, 99, 128, 153–4, 156,
168, 171, 179, 190, 191, 194, 233, 241,
242
FNTT general secretary, 199–208
Zugazagoitia, Julián, 61, 110, 120, 123, 126,
139, 140, 143, 174, 181, 192